Administrative Relationships /

A CASEBOOK

Administrative Relationships/

A CASEBOOK

JACK A. CULBERTSON

Executive Director of UCEA
Associate Professor of Education
University of Oregon

PAUL B. JACOBSON

Dean, School of Education
University of Oregon

THEODORE L. RELLER

Professor of Education
University of California
Berkeley, California

Englewood Cliffs, N. J.
PRENTICE-HALL, INC.

PRENTICE-HALL EDUCATION SERIES
Dan Cooper, Editor

©, 1960, by Prentice-Hall, Inc.
ENGLEWOOD CLIFFS, N. J.

Current printing (last digit):
12 11 10 9 8 7 6 5 4 3

LIBRARY OF CONGRESS
CATALOG CARD NO.: 60–8214

PRINTED IN THE UNITED STATES OF AMERICA
00845C

Preface

While this book is a product of individuals, it is also a product of the times in that it capitalizes on some of the new ideas that have been flowing into the stream of administrative thought during the 1950's. In line with the recent interest in case-method instruction, the book contains 17 cases on school administration. The inclusion of a variety of inter-disciplinary materials also fits in with the increasing professional interest in a broader training program for administrators. The concepts presented in Part III relate to the current search for a more adequate theory of administration. That the book focuses on "administrative behavior" is another indication that it has been influenced by some of the newer developments in the study of administration.

Like multipurpose rooms in modern school buildings, the book can serve a variety of functions. For those interested in teaching with a strong emphasis on the case method, the cases in Part II can serve as the main content for the course. Case analyses and discussions typically motivate students very early to turn to and to grapple with underlying theoretical issues. The concepts and bibliographical resources in Part III have been included as aids in the exploration of such issues.

Both the cases in Part II and the concepts in Part III can supplement most courses in school administration, and they would be particularly appropriate for core or block programs. Chart I in the chapter "Preparation of Cases" indicates the relationship of the various cases to different aspects of administration.

Those who are teaching courses on administrative theory, or courses which focus on leadership and administrative process, will also find the book useful as a text. It should be especially appropriate in such courses when faculty members from different disciplines are involved.

The cases contain data pertinent to such disciplines as psychology, sociology, political science, economics, and educational administration. As is demonstrated in the chapter "Case Analysis," case data can be analyzed from various social science perspectives. Of equal importance is the fact that cases can be a highly effective facilitator of communication among academic specialists and school administrators with markedly different backgrounds. It is hoped that the annotated bibliography of inter-disciplinary sources in Part III will be useful to those who are engaged in inter-disciplinary approaches to research and teaching.

The authors would like to express special appreciation to the following persons who have participated in the preparation of cases for the book:

Howard S. Bretsch, University of Michigan; Mrs. Mary Virginia Culbertson, Columbus, Ohio; Howard Eckel, University of Kentucky; Donald Emberlin, Principal, Wichita School, Milwaukie, Oregon; Wayne Foster, Superintendent of Schools, Hood River, Oregon; Arnold Hagan, Pacific Lutheran College; Clarence Hines, University of Oregon; Ben M. Harris, University of Texas; Erwin Juilfs, Principal, Jefferson Junior High School, Eugene, Oregon; Anne Moses, American School, Bad Kreuznach, Alzeyer Strasse, Germany; Francis B. Nickerson, State System of Higher Education, Eugene, Oregon; F. Robert Paulsen, University of Utah; William Ranniger, Elementary School Principal, Yakima, Washington; Miles C. Romney, University of Oregon; Dave Staley, Principal, Grants Pass Junior High School, Grants Pass, Oregon; Roy Tozier, Los Angeles State College; Ralph Tyson, Collegeboro Teachers College; Raymond Wochner, Arizona State University.

We are indebted to our colleagues who have participated in the University of Oregon inter-disciplinary seminars on administrative behavior during the past eight years. For stimulating our thinking about case preparation, case analysis, and case teaching, we express appreciation to: Richard Colvard, Department of Sociology, The University of Texas; Robert Dubin, Department of Sociology, University of Oregon; Phillip Foss, Department of Political Science, San Francisco State College; Keith Goldhammer, School of Education, University of Oregon; Carl Hintz, University of Oregon Library; Lucian Marquis, Department of Political Science, University of Oregon; Lester Seligman, Department of Political Science, University of Oregon; Frank Sherwood, Department of Political Science, University of Southern California; Norman Sundberg, Department of

Psychology, University of Oregon; Egbert Wengert, Department of Political Science, University of Oregon; and C. F. Ziebarth, School of Business Administration, University of Oregon.

Several persons have read one or two chapters of textual material and have provided constructive suggestions. Special acknowledgement is given to Paul Allen, Assistant Secretary, A.A.C.T.E., Washington, D.C.; Howard Eckel, University of Kentucky; Dan Griffiths, Teachers College, Columbia University; Richard Houseman, San Diego State College; Robert Howsam, University of California; Ray Lowe, University of Oregon; Stewart North, University of Wisconsin; Donald Tope, University of Oregon; and Don Willower, Pennsylvania State University.

We are indebted to Viola Volkens, who typed the manuscript in its entirety. Her careful and thorough work is especially appreciated and has significantly contributed to the production of the book. Finally, we express appreciation to Mary Virginia Culbertson, who made editorial suggestions concerning various parts of the book.

J. A. C.
P. B. J.
T. L. R.

The Case Method in Teaching

In January, 1952, the School of Education faculty at the University of Oregon, a group of successful administrators from the State of Oregon, and selected social scientists from the University of Oregon held a three-day conference at a resort on the Pacific Ocean, to consider preparation programs for school administrators. One assumption which underlay the conference was that social scientists had important contributions to make in the education of administrators. One important purpose of the conference was to determine ways by which social scientists could contribute more effectively to the preparation of school administrators.

Inter-Disciplinary Seminars

The conferees decided that there was a need for inter-disciplinary seminars in which faculty persons from different disciplines would be brought together to focus their special knowledges on the problems of school administration. It was thought that a group of persons was necessary because no one individual possessed sufficient background to provide adequate information.

There was some precedence for this idea in that one exploratory, inter-disciplinary seminar, called "The Scope and Sequence of the Social Sciences," had already been offered the preceding year with some success. In this seminar were included an anthropologist, a political scientist, a sociologist, an economist, and an educator. These persons soon found that their basic difficulty was understanding the professional jargon in each of their respective disciplines. Since that time, the seminar has continued over a period of eight years with considerable success.

Throughout the deliberations at the Pacific Ocean resort, one of the important problems in the eyes of the conferees was the need to help administrators develop insights about dealing with persons systematically and sympathetically. Out of these discussions a group of persons in Business Administration, Economics, Psychology, Sociology, Political Science, Anthropology, and Education discussed and finally organized another seminar which was held for the first time in the summer of 1952. It has been held annually since that time. Because of the experience with the former seminar, it was much less difficult to communicate with persons in the other disciplines, since each was better able to understand his colleagues. The case method of instruction was used in this seminar, which was entitled "The Nature and Problems of Administrative Behavior." Since that time, the seminar has dealt very largely with human relations in administration, but has differed considerably from the usual courses in personnel administration in that it has dealt much more largely with decision-making and problems of human relations than with recruitment, promotion, in-service training, and separation of personnel. It has also been concerned with the problems of effecting change in an organization and of communicating within organization.

During the first year, the faculty used cases from the areas of business and public administration. In addition, the faculty wrote cases for the seminar. The cases that are printed in this book are very largely the outgrowth of the seminar, through writings of either persons who have been enrolled in the seminar, or seminar faculty members, or persons who have become interested in the project. These cases were selected from a larger group and are illustrative rather than exhaustive. It is thought that in due season many more case materials should be developed for programs in school administration.

Development of the Case Method

A study of the history of the case method of teaching shows that it has stood the test of time. First originated by Langdell in the Harvard Law School about 1870, it was very intensively and adversely criticized by exponents of traditional methods of teaching. By 1915, however, it had proven itself to the extent that most of the well-known law schools in the country were using the case method.

As a result of the experiences in the Harvard Law School, the case method spread to the Harvard Medical School, where its value was quickly recognized, so that it expanded readily. Today it is, of course, widely accepted as a standard part of medical training programs. About 1919, Dean Wallace Donham began to apply the method at the Harvard School of Business. The effectiveness of the case method of teaching in that school after a 30-year test was attested by former President Conant in his annual report of 1950–1951, in which he indicated that it had been the key to the success of the Harvard Graduate School of Business Administration.

By the mid-1940's Dean Donham was strongly convinced that the case method could help develop responsible attitudes and, therefore, that the approach could contribute to general education. Consequently, he introduced the method as a systematic way of teaching human relations to undergraduates at Harvard College. Although he had some reservations about whether the method would generate widespread participation among undergraduates, they were quickly dispelled when 34 out of a class of 37 took part in discussing the very first assigned case. Instructors in other universities have used the method in various courses for both graduates and undergraduates.

The method began to be used in the teaching of public administration in the 1930's with the formation of a special committee on research materials. This committee prepared a three-volume publication of 120 cases. Subsequently, the Committee on Public Administration was formed to develop cases for instructional purposes. This led to the well-known collection of cases in the book *Public Administration and Policy Development—A Case Book* edited by Harold Stein. Additional cases have since been developed through the Inter-University Case Program, and the expanding use of the case method for training public administrators is clearly evident. In 1957 the Ford Foundation made a grant of $325,000 to the Inter-University Case Program for continued case development. The record of the method in public administration speaks for itself. There is also considerable testimony of the value of the method in other fields, such as public health, guidance, and social work.

In the 1940's, the case method began to be applied in programs for educating school administrators. In 1955 Cyril Sargent and Eugene Belisle produced the first collection of cases in education administration in a book entitled *Educational Administration: Cases and Concepts*. The next year Daniel Griffiths presented some additional cases in his book *Human Relations in School Administration*. More recently, the method has been used systematically for educating school administrators in a number of colleges and universities. There is also some evidence that the method has a place in in-service programs for administrators.

Although the use of the case method in educational administration is relatively new as compared to its use in other fields, its over-all record during the last century makes an impressive chapter in modern educational history. It has worked in many places with many persons in many subjects for many years. Undoubtedly this is an important factor in the increased interest in the method among those who are educating school administrators.

Even though the method has been used with ever-expanding success, one should not view it as an educational panacea. Other methods are undoubtedly more appropriate for achieving certain purposes in the education of school administrators, and specific limitations of case-method teaching are developed more fully in other portions of the book. Success in the method, as in all instructional methods, is, of course, highly dependent upon the enthusiasm, sensitivity, and creativity of the teacher.

Contents

Part I: METHOD

Part II: CASES

Part III: CONCEPTS

Administrative Relationships /

A CASEBOOK

Method

The Valley City
Consolidation Issue

In the following case study, a school superintendent, a local school board, the people of the community, and the people of surrounding rural communities were involved in a wrangle which probably never should have happened. The study is written to show how it came to happen, what the issues appeared to be, the alignment of power factors for and against proposed solutions to problems, and the administrative behavior of the superintendent as he tried to find workable answers to school reorganization.

Real names are not used in this case, but the characters are all real people contending in a real-life drama staged on a very real setting in a small western town. In retrospect, it would appear that none of the parties could deny that some errors of judgment were made, that hasty words were spoken, and that personalities were treated with something less than the respect which may have been their due. It should also be said that, at the time the events occurred, these persons acted in the belief that they had just cause to speak and act as they did. By hindsight, however, it does appear that other courses of action would have been more reasonable, more conciliatory, more harmonious, and more effective in resolving Valley City's problems. Would it have been desirable to prevent the repercussions that followed the violent emotional outbursts recounted in this study? If so, how might the repercussions have been avoided?

Valley City

Valley City is one of the oldest towns in its state, having been settled and named about 1850. Very early the settlement became a trading center by virtue of its location upon the Valley River, on

1

which early pioneers traveled to trade for goods brought in by boat and wagon train. There was never a great prosperity boom, but a steady growth based upon trade and agriculture. There was some logging and lumbering, although such business flourished mostly in more accessible places.

The old families of Valley City grew in wealth and in position. Typically they lived placid, unchallenged lives. The very seclusion of the spot prevented any great number of new settlers from rushing in to take advantage of this "little Eden." It was a secure place. Those who did find it, and who sought to stay, were somehow relegated to outlying farms or to the less desirable jobs about the community. From there they had to work their way slowly into a place of respectability and acceptance in the neighborhood.

Inevitably, there developed a kind of a rivalry between those on the "pretty" side of Hazelwood Creek and those on the "low" side of that stream. Any issue which came up for decision gave rise to an opportunity for taking sides along this rift and thus keeping it alive. However, there was never any real contest, because the well-established natives retained the effective means of control.

Valley City remained a small town right up to World War II. It had become the overt policy of the Chamber of Commerce and of the influential people who lived there to keep it that way. The "lunch pail" type of people was not wanted, and no effort had been made to lure industry into the area. As of the 1940 census, there were about 5,000 residents.

School superintendents in Valley City had had stable administrations. Between 1920 and 1940, three superintendents had held office and had discharged their responsibilities without major upheavals. Valley City's grade-school enrollment had also shown considerable stability. During the period from 1912–1913 until 1940–1941 elementary enrollment remained close to 900. (See Figure 1.) High school enrollment was a different story, however, and the story contained the seeds of discord that was later to blossom into a major district organization controversy.

One of the most striking facts was that roughly one-third of the secondary school pupils accommodated was not from Valley City at all, but was from more than ten elementary districts in the neighboring rural areas which were too small to support high schools of their own. (See Figure 2.) These pupils had been coming to Valley City on a "tuition basis" in line with the state law requiring home districts to pay tuition costs when their students attended neighboring high school districts. This tuition charge had also been set by state law so that it might not include costs for capital outlay but only such current school expenditures as were required. By this arrangement Valley City found itself providing the cost of housing the pupils who were transported from two to fifteen miles from the rural districts.

From the beginning, Valley City had encouraged rural pupils to come into its high school. This tended to increase enrollment, add to finances (since they had a building anyway), make possible a more extensive curriculum, and, perhaps even more important in the eyes of some, provide a bigger athletic program. In time the rural people began to look upon this arrangement as sort of a "vested intrest" on the part of the townspeople. It became a problem which politically astute citizens did not discuss in public. Nevertheless, the school superintendent found the whole problem so vexing in 1934–1935 that he conducted a study of the matter with an eye toward consolidation of the whole area.[1] Nothing was accomplished before he moved to his new position with the government in 1937. From there the matter lay dormant until after World War II, when Mr. Galloway took notice of it again.

Galloway's Administration

Mr. Galloway came to Valley City in the fall of 1939, two years before Pearl Harbor. He remained in office until July 1948, when at a special meeting of the school board his contract, which had another year to run, was terminated. A cash settlement was made and Mr. Galloway moved to another city. It shall be our endeavor in this section to set forth briefly a summary of the climactic events which led up to his dismissal, with special attention to those which shed light on the character of the community and those which lend perspective to the consolidation issue.

It is conceded, by those who know him, that Mr. Galloway is a

[1] *Consolidation* in Valley City's state meant unifying the elementary schools in Valley City and the outlying districts with the high schools under one administration. *Unionization* is a method whereby several independent elementary districts form a district for high school purposes only. In this arrangement the elementary school districts are left undisturbed.

"good schoolman." Well trained in school administration, he had enjoyed successful experience before coming to Valley City. However, his personal character was of such a nature that he insisted upon being given the necessary authority to deal with his problems and upon being allowed what he thought to be the ordinary prerogatives of his office. Those who knew him on the job in Valley City seemed to think that this was his fatal sin—if a sin it was. Some believed that this trait affected the way he handled the consolidation issue.

Valley City, the "little Eden," smug, conservative, quiet, sedate, removed from the world of hustle and bustle, surely did not know what lay ahead in the year 1939, although faint rumblings were discernible to ears not yet willing to understand what their import might be. During that year, for instance, the United States Government established the Federal Research Center at Valley City on an old college site, bringing into the community government money and government personnel numbering some 200 families. These people sought houses, food, shelter, clothing, and entertainment. By and by, friends came to visit them, and some of them were so struck by the quiet dignity of the place that they stayed to enjoy its way of life.

The war hysteria grew into a steady clamor through 1940. Plywood and lumber products were needed in greatly expanded amounts because of the war effort. Mills moved into Valley City and the surrounding area. They brought with them money and a type of worker that Valley City traditionally had not wanted.

Pearl Harbor came. The United States Government began to build Camp Williams on a tract not far from Valley City. The training cadre brought their families, and many divisions received their training at Camp Williams before being sent to Europe or the Pacific. To provide for increased transportation demands, the state rerouted the main trunk highway and improved it to resemble a parkway skirting the southern edge of the city. Along this new trade artery businesses of every description sprang into being. It came to be known as "The Bright Mile." Modern motels, large supermarkets, filling stations, and every kind of business enterprise made its appearance. Land skyrocketed in value and people clamored for more at any price.

The town of 5,000 in 1940 had grown to double that in 1950. It is hardly necessary to explain what this sudden growth did to every aspect of community organization—churches, schools, parks, sanitary services, planning, and city government. What had been an orderly little community had become a beehive of activity and of conflict. Some folks were more than confused: they were deeply disturbed about the crass turn of events.

Inevitably there were divisions and some misunderstanding between the old and the new citizens. The new folks were anxious to succeed, unashamed to carry dinner buckets, unimpressed with pedigrees, and generally determined to make a go of it in their new homes. These new people began to edge their way into elected positions, into organizations, and into positions of power in the community. Traditional leadership had never been seriously challenged before. Desired positions had been reserved for a few of the community's favored ones, who now found it difficult to see their preserve transgressed upon. Thus, there came into being some bitter jealousies, not always expressed, but incipient and ever poised to divide the city on issues.

All these changes in community population could not help but affect the school. Figure 1 shows the results graphically. The elemen-

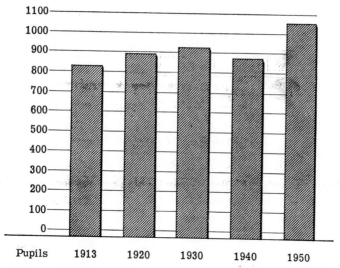

Figure 1. Enrollments in Valley City's Elementary Schools. (*Data were obtained, except for 1913, by taking an average of three years including the year preceding and the year following the dates given.*)

tary population had remained quite stable through 1940. Organization of the junior high school prior to 1932 certainly had an effect upon the size of the elementary enrollment by drawing off the seventh and the eighth grades. This move, while solving the problem of additional elementary building space, created an illusion of adequacy which was false. Mr. Galloway understood this but found himself simply "laughed down" by the school board and the general populace; they simply could not believe that the Valley City grade schools were ready to make any spectacular growth.

However, there was a more serious problem, illustrated graphically in Figure 2. The secondary grades had shown a steady growth

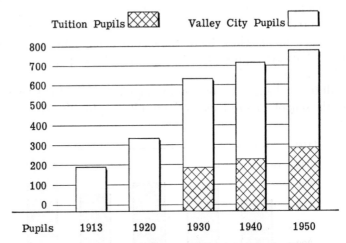

Figure 2. Enrollments in Valley City's High School. (*Data were obtained by the method used in Figure 1. Tuition pupils were accepted in Valley City High School before 1930 but complete records are not available.*)

right up through 1940. Both the junior high and the senior high buildings were filled to capacity. Before 1950, teachers and principals were running out of suggestions for adding space to accommodate the extra classes which they knew would have to be housed each successive year. The school day had been extended and some classes even met during the noon hour. All but the attic had been converted to classroom space, and the fire chief balked at all suggestions for making use of that.

There were several reasons for enrollment increases. Undoubtedly parents had begun to see that, in times as tough as the mid-1930's, every boy and girl would need all the preparation available in order to secure the best possible livelihood. Later, in 1947, the so-called "18-year-old" law may have had some effect in requiring certain pupils to attend school where they might otherwise have stayed at home to work on the farm. But there was a third reason for Valley City's overcrowded situation in the high school, a reason which hardly anyone dared mention aloud. The reason is clear from an examination of Figure 2. If the tuition pupils were to be removed, Valley City's building problem would vanish.

Mr. Galloway knew instinctively that the problem was too big for him to handle by himself. Therefore, during the second year of his tenure, he secured school board permission to engage the services of Dr. Windom, a school consultant from the neighboring university, who had achieved considerable reputation in advising school districts on their knottiest problems.

Dr. Windom set to work at once assembling the necessary materials. At least two preliminary reports were completed and turned in to the school board for study before the final report was at length completed on January 8, 1948. A special meeting of the board to consider this report was reported in the *Valley City Herald* under the headline: "School Board Warned Congestion Will Be Intolerable in Five Years." Significantly, this news article made no mention of the tuition-pupil problem, although this was one of the prominent issues developed in the report. It was known to be a "hot issue" with the country folks and one to be avoided whenever possible. It is also important to notice that the report had made prominent mention of consolidation as being the preferred method for solving Valley City's school-housing problem and the tuition-pupil situation. This was not mentioned in the news report either. Possibly the editor kept silent in consideration of the known bias against consolidation prevailing among the rural people.

During the period while these reports were being prepared and studied, at least two attempts were made by Mr. Galloway to secure consolidation. Both attempts failed. Dr. Windom had been called upon to speak to various groups in the outside districts and did so, strongly supporting and urging consolidation. One may judge the

character of the reception from the report of one informant as he remembers those talks: "The more he talked, the madder they got."

During this time there was also an attempt to secure Valley City's
consent to unionization. At the time, the newspaper opposed unionization. Besides the newspaper, other organizations took an active
part and a decisive role in the efforts to reach a solution to the problem. Representing the rural areas, the Grange took a most active
part. This organization had had a long history of championing the
union high school movement in this state. It was no surprise to find
it strongly opposed to consolidation and very much partisan toward
the union high idea. Valley City itself was most strongly represented
by the Chamber of Commerce. It took a strong stand against consolidation as a means of keeping peace among the rural folks, who
represented some of their most valued customers. The proposition
failed by a large margin.

Thus, Mr. Galloway had seen the problem and had attacked it
as best he knew. In the end, every measure he tried failed. The rural
people would not have consolidation and the city folks voted down
unionization. At this point, Mr. Galloway began to lose favor with
the school board. His handling of the consolidation issue certainly
must have contributed to his downfall. The *Valley City Herald*, in
reporting a special school board meeting held the night before, reported in its July 14, 1948 issue that Mr. Galloway's contract, with
still a year to run, had been terminated. The school board somehow
felt that his continued presence would be so deleterious to the welfare of the district that it would be worth a year's salary to get rid
of him.

Superintendent T. R. Benson: The Honeymoon Period

The July 20, 1948 issue of the *Valley City Herald* carried a prominently displayed news story about a special meeting of the school
board. In less than a week from the date on which Mr. Galloway's
contract had been terminated, the board had found time to secure
applications, evaluate them, and decide upon the man to succeed
him. Mr. Benson, the successor, was described in most glowing terms.
Prominent place was given to a letter written by the Mayor of his
home town to the Mayor of Valley City saying in part: "—Mr. Benson

has never failed to give his utmost co-operation to his teachers and his board."

Mr. Benson secured his education in a midwestern state and moved from there to the Midland Empire, where he taught and administered schools for some 25 years prior to receiving the invitation to come to Valley City. He had a reputation for successful work and for being a fine administrator. In his last position, he had successfully managed the planning and building of a very fine and modern high school building. A prominent place was given to a description of it in an issue of *The American School Board Journal*. Mr. Benson was, and rightfully, very proud of his accomplishments.

Mr. Benson came to Valley City under the most glowing representations. From this point of view he had the finest possible introduction to his new job. Amply attesting to this are the news headlines he made during the first six months of his stay in Valley City. During this time he was invited to speak to every club and organization in the city; glowing newspaper notices followed each appearance.

From a long-term point of view, Mr. Benson had some personality difficulties that plagued him. One of these was his rather poor speaking voice. His talks were strong on content, but failed in many instances to hit the mark because of an unpleasant voice quality. Nor was Mr. Benson what one would call a handsome man. Some people would say that his visage was rather rough hewn, or forbidding, although people who knew him well did not feel that way. He had a penchant for striking directly at a point of crucial importance without first smoothing the way or providing some sort of a cushion for the blow. Some were quickly irritated when he demanded efficiency in no uncertain terms. Some were displeased when he began to introduce more systematic business methods into school affairs. Teachers were no longer able to buy when and where they pleased without first securing proper authorization from the superintendent's office. They took this to mean that Mr. Benson did not trust them. Merchants were informed that from now on no bills would be allowed without an accompanying requisition signed by the school superintendent. This news was interpreted by merchants as an unfavorable reflection upon their honesty in school district dealings. Not all persons were disturbed by the changes. There were many who considered business practices in Valley City out of date, and to them changes were accepted as improvements.

Among Mr. Benson's admirable qualities was his ability to evaluate a situation and to make up his mind about how to proceed in handling it. He did not wait long to provide an illustration of his shrewd timing. The December 7, 1948 issue of the *Valley City Herald* carried this streamer headline blazing across the top of the first page: "Overwhelming Approval Given to School Bond." "Ted," as he was already familiarly known, had in four short months accomplished what the board and its former superintendent had not been able to do in years. During these hectic months, hardly a week went by that his name was not in the headlines. "Ted" had been able to capitalize to some extent upon the groundwork of his predecessors and upon the inordinately splendid reception accorded him by the press and the community at large. He was at that moment, without a doubt, the most talked about man in Valley City. It seemed that he had but to make his slightest wish known and men sprang to effect its accomplishment.

Although the honeymoon was still warm, the newly formed and exciting relationship began to dim somewhat as each party to the contract dug into the real work of making the whole project a success. "Ted," for his part, became immersed in the interminable business of seeing architects, making change orders, taking inspection trips, and such. There was little occasion for his name to be in the paper any more. He suddenly became too busy. Teachers found it hard to see him about their problems. Parents, calling at the office, found themselves cooling their heels on the outer bench, while mysterious figures strode in and out on the authority of a whispered conference with the secretary—and to the accompaniment of stale whiffs of cigar smoke.

The people, on their part, began to reflect soberly upon the part of their bargain which a $650,000 bond issue might represent when translated into tax receipts. Some were really disturbed about this matter, especially the older folks whose children had long since gone through school but whose pensions were hardly sufficient to keep body and soul together. They had very little power in the community, but they could and did talk, planting seeds of doubt wherever and whenever they could. Some doubtless fell on fertile ground. Some of the businessmen also felt that these dollars would eventually have to come out of their own pockets—which was not an altogether reassuring thought.

A more insidious type of dissatisfaction and latent opposition was in the community as a result of Mr. Galloway's summary dismissal. Mr. Galloway was not without staunch supporters in the community and among the staff members of the school system. Among these there was a strong feeling of injustice done to a man who in no wise deserved such treatment. Some of these vowed openly that they would wreak vengeance upon anyone who was even remotely connected with the affair. Mr. Benson, although he had manifestly nothing whatever to do with Mr. Galloway's dismissal, was looked upon as a usurper. In the staff itself there were those who openly challenged the authority of the new man. These needed but little encouragement and support from the outside and from other dissident groups to become a nucleus for sabotage and criticism of Mr. Benson's program.

"Ted" did nothing about this the first year, since contracts were issued before he arrived. But in the second year, he began to weed out the most blatant and vocal of the rebels. As might be expected, he reached only a few of the most daring, leaving the bulk of his opposition still on the staff. When these saw what happened to a few of their number, they simply went "underground" and continued to throw rocks into the works. Since this group was not large enough by itself to attract much attention or to swing much political weight, it simply bided its time to await reinforcements from other quarters in the community. As already pointed out, this was not an altogether hopeless strategy, since there was already a basic history of division in the town upon which to build a further rift.

It is also reported from sources which the writer considers credible enough to warrant repeating here that the school board itself selected Mr. Benson on a three-to-two split vote. The two members voting against Mr. Benson are said to have represented a rather strong local group which desired the selection of a man already well known in the locality. Being outvoted, they were content to go along with the selection determined by the majority. However, there remained a potential source of misunderstanding and insurgence in this group, since they could never be really satisfied with the official choice.

The honeymoon had been short, but Benson had exploited it to the fullest. The seeds of discontent had really been there from the very beginning. The people, the staff, and the school board had not changed enough to account for any basic change in the community. The hostility which began to appear manifested deeper roots of rebellion than the sometimes rather trivial irritations which brought them into view.

Beginning in 1949, there was a period of relative quiet reaching into the middle of 1950. This was a time spent in reorganization of staff and in building the three grade schools authorized on December 7, 1948. The period was not without its difficulties. The building schedule caused particular problems because of the materials shortages then prevalent. Another difficulty, quite unforeseen, developed at the South End site, where the building was completed on schedule but arrangements could not be made to provide sanitary facilities. The sanitary authorities would not allow construction of a septic tank, and the city was in no mood to build a trunk line from Main Avenue out to the site—a matter of some 1,000 feet. Part of the difficulty revolved about the fact that the South End school was lower than the Main Avenue sewer and would, therefore, require a pumping station to lift the sewage to the Main Avenue trunk.

Another difficulty also developed relative to the South End site, having to do with the construction of a paved street from Main Avenue to the school. It had been supposed that the United States Research Center, which owned the adjacent property on one side, would co-operate in this bit of improvement. As it turned out, the United States Government had no intention of spending any more money improving that particular roadway. After some unpleasantness, the school district was obliged to undertake grading and pavement at a considerable extra cost to the school district.

Meanwhile, South End School was completed, but was unoccupied through the school year 1949–1950. This was not a very pleasant circumstance, since the overcrowded conditions it had been designed to remedy developed even more rapidly than had been predicted. This involved the school district in the matter of transporting pupils to other schools and making such other temporary adjustments as were deemed necessary.

Altogether, this episode did not bring friends into the fold, although most people recognized that the difficulties encountered were of such a nature that they could not well have been avoided. In any event, Mr. Benson had "built a fire" under the school board to such a degree that "double shifting" was no longer necessary. He was

still regarded by many as occupying a strong position with the
school board and in the community.

Also, during this period, there developed some personnel problems that needed attention. Mr. Benson felt that he needed loyal
support from his whole staff, but most particularly from his principals. The most sensitive spots seemed to be in the senior and junior
high schools. Mr. Ott at Senior High had found it quite difficult to
see eye to eye with Mr. Benson, and, therefore, he resigned at the
end of the 1948–1949 school year.

Mr. Meyer at Junior High also appeared to have problems. Mr.
Benson felt that he was essentially a capable man but somewhat weak
on organization and discipline. Since the superintendent's office was
located in the senior high building, Mr. Benson thought he might be
able to support Meyer somewhat if he were moved to that school.
This was done and a Mr. Williams was secured to take over at Junior
High.

The Honeymoon Ends

School opened in the fall of 1950 with an impressive show of
concord. Mr. Benson, having a favorable majority on the school
board, had been able to achieve all the objectives he had set out to
attain. On the first day of "In-Service Training," he spoke to the assembled teachers in glowing terms about the future of Valley City
schools. The school board chairman and the mayor were also present
and spoke with great confidence about the future. Pictures were
taken, news stories were written, greetings were exchanged, new
teachers were introduced, and most every teacher felt a challenge
to do his or her best in the year to come.

Mr. Benson was "riding high in the saddle," having obtained the
support of an additional board member in the summer election. (See
Figure 3.) He had completed the several pressing projects requiring
his attention and was now ready to tangle with another problem:
the matter of finding an answer to the tuition-student problem. This
issue had remained inactive since Mr. Galloway left in July of 1948.
The sheer fact of numbers made further avoidance of the issue impossible.

In order to come to grips with this problem, Mr. Benson obtained the consent of the school board to make studies and recom-

SCHOOL YEAR	SCHOOL BOARD MEMBERSHIP				
	Chairman	4th Year	3rd Year	2nd Year	1st Year
1947-48	Perry	Miller	Holy	Benny	Nestor
1948-49	Miller	Wise	Benny	Nestor	Perry
1949-50	Wise	Benny	Nestor	Perry	Wherry
1950-51	Benny	Nestor*	Perry	Wherry*	Wise
1951-52	Nestor*	Perry	Wherry*	Wise	Links*
1952-53	Perry	Wherry	Wise	Links	Raves
1953-54	Wherry	Wise	Links	Raves	Emory
1954-55	Wise	Links	Raves	Emory	Whittles

LEGEND: Smith: Pro-Benson member.
Smith: Neutral member.
Smith: Anti-Benson member.
(*) Members favoring unionization while it was an issue.

Figure 3. School Board Membership for the Valley City School District from 1947–1948 through 1954–1955.

mendations for their consideration. To this end he designated Mr. Arthur, his second in command, to dig out and arrange the facts in usable form. Mr. Golden, business manager and clerk of the board, became a useful helper in this matter. Arthur and Golden did their work with dispatch and were ready to report to the board in November. Essentially, these were their findings:

(1) Roughly 40 per cent of the pupils in Valley City High School came from the "feeder districts" and 60 per cent from Valley City.

(2) Roughly 33 per cent of the taxable valuation was in the "feeder districts" and 67 per cent in Valley City.

(3) The combined rural and city high school population would grow from 841 in 1950 to 1153 in 1955.

(4) There was in sight no possible means of housing this many pupils in the present physical plant.

(5) There were three alternative solutions open to the school board:
A. *Status Quo:* This plan would leave the organization as at present with Valley City accepting the rural pupils on a tuition basis. The necessary building requirements would be provided by bonding Valley City to the full legal limit and by planning the buildings on a "unit basis."

B. *Unionization:* Valley City could unite with the rural districts in the formation of a union high school for all the children at one location; or, the rural districts could proceed to form their own union high school oustide of Valley City. The latter choice would leave Valley City with sufficient space to provide for their own pupils through 1960.

C. *Consolidation:* The rural districts could unite with Valley City to provide a unified educational system for their children from grade one through grade twelve. This would not necessarily mean the discontinuance of any local elementary schools, but would mean their administration and supervision from one central office in Valley City. This would mean that all the smaller districts would have access to the special services and materials available to Valley City schools.

The report was accepted by the school board for consideration. After some study, it was suggested that a meeting of all the board presidents and clerks representing the "feeder districts" should be arranged, at which time this matter could be explained to them and their co-operation solicited. It was understood that the board and the administration would voice no preference for a given plan. Rather an informal meeting for giving and seeking information was proposed.

The meeting was arranged and a good representation was present. Mr. Benson, Mr. Arthur, and Mr. Golden explained as best they could the situation as it existed. The report apparently was accepted as substantially correct by the rural representatives. As to suggestions, there were none, at least not from the floor, although it is reported that during an intermission a few of the rural folks met in the hall and formed a loosely organized committee to look into the possibility of unionization outside of Valley City. This was not brought out in the meeting itself. There, after some discussion, it was proposed that a committee be formed to study the whole problem and to write up a brief which could be distributed to all the voters throughout the various districts. The plan called for meetings to be held in each district, as called by the local school board chairmen. If requested, someone would be sent out from Valley City to answer questions.

The immediate impact of the decision upon the community was one of consternation and of confusion, then of anger and rebellion.

There were some meetings called in rural Grange halls, to which Mr. Arthur, Mr. Golden, and Mr. Henry, a grade school principal, went as explainers and as representatives of Valley City school district. They were generally treated with respect, but there was a distinct undertone of hurt feelings and impatience with Valley City for letting the rural folks down and for "shoving them around." Some of the district chairmen refused to call meetings. The plan as conceived by Mr. Benson was obviously being bogged down by both active and passive resistance of the country people.

Mr. Benson did not go out on these explanation trips himself. It is not known why he avoided this opportunity to speak to the rural folks. Mr. Henry, in reviewing this period, noted that he repeatedly urged Mr. Benson to visit the rural districts, that the people wanted to see the "boss." Henry believed strongly that a personal appearance by Benson would have worked wonders in developing good will. He could also have gauged more accurately the temper with which the farm folks viewed the problem and, in turn, could have adjusted his own tactics.

Strongly influencing the situation was another individual—in this case, Mr. Golden, the business manager and clerk of the district. Mr. Benson was in the habit of trusting him with a good deal of the administrative chores. The impression made by this individual, particularly among the farm people, brought on rather severe repercussions. Mr. Golden, while intelligent, capable, and well versed in the problems involved, assumed such a cocky and self-righteous attitude that many could not stomach him. His explanation periods left a trail of angry, unfriendly people.

A number of special meetings were called by the so-called Rural Unionization Committee. These meetings gave the farmers an opportunity to air the problems and feelings they had on the issue. Many of them had graduated from Valley City High School and had been satisfied with its program. They hated to see the time come when their children would have to go to another high school. Still others, hotheads such as one finds in any group of this kind, aired trivial difficulties for which they held the Valley City school system accountable. It was asserted, for example, that rural boys were discriminated against in the athletic program, or that they did not have an equal chance in earning scholastic honors when pitted against the city youngsters. The teachers were accused of favoring the city kids, who, it was charged, knew better how to conduct themselves to receive favors from the teachers.

Gradually, with the opening of the year 1951, tempers flared and the various elements of the communities involved began to take sides. Up to this point, the newspaper had been quite neutral, the school board had taken no sides on the matter, and the administration had expressed no strong preferences in public, although it was generally known that the school profession throughout the state favored consolidation over unionization. The Grange, again, played its part among the rural folks by throwing its support in favor of the union high school.

The "feeder districts" began to make definite plans to unionize outside of Valley City at a site called Sage Flat about four miles south on the main highway. The first public notice of this movement was given through an editorial in the *Valley City Herald* dated January 10, 1951, and entitled *Maybe They're Not Bluffing*. This editorial brought out the fact that the Valley City School Board, not knowing which way to turn, had adopted what it called the *status quo* policy. That is, for the moment, Valley City was not prepared to do anything. But the main import of the editorial brought to light the development that the rural "feeder districts" were in dead earnest about forming their own union high district outside of Valley City. This was not a wholesome thought any way you looked at it, according to the editor. Surely there must be some other way that would insure the harmonious formation of a single high school located in Valley City. That is where it had always been! Valley City did not want, nor could it afford, to alienate its best customers.

A look at Figure 3 will show that the school board was split upon the issue of unionization. Two members were for it and the other three were neutral, as of early 1951. This division did not exist from the beginning, but grew into being as different organizations and individuals began to apply power to the settlement of the issue. It may be safely asserted that some of the Valley City School Board members were annoyed by the type of "irresponsible" declarations which were being made by the representatives of the rural people. Also, they were influenced by Mr. Benson's attitude toward the issue of consolidation. His viewpoint was expressed in a talk reported in the *Valley City Herald* for March 20, 1951: "I feel that the board should not ask the people to vote on any educational issue that we as educators could not support." As the lines of conflict became clearer, there was a tendency for the three *status quo* board members to rely more and more upon personal loyalty to Mr. Benson and less and less upon rational arguments for or against the proposition.

This type of reaction came out quite clearly in an incident reported in the *Herald* of March 14 and March 17. On the first date it was prominently—and hopefully—reported that the Chamber of Commerce Educational Committee had made arrangements to meet with the school board and to discuss the problems of authorizing an election at which the people of Valley City would vote on the question of joining the "feeder districts" in a union high school. On the latter date it was reported, also very prominently, that "Board Absenteeism Blocks Action on School Question." The two pro-unionization members had been present while the other three were not to be found. One member was reported as being ordered to California to recover from a severe cold; another had been ordered by his physician not to attend any meetings for a whole month; and the third had replied, when queried, that he would not attend any meetings at which any board member was absent. On March 19, the editor wrote a blistering editorial in criticism of the board's obstructive behavior, saying in part: "By this time it is apparent that some members of the Valley City school board are giving the run-around to a large number of the Valley City school district and 'feeder district' residents by dodging action on a request for a union high school district election." But, the Valley City School Board remained adamant in its stand, refusing to alter its position regardless of pressure.

The Chamber of Commerce became intensely interested in the issue when it became apparent that there was a serious threat of a high school being built outside Valley City. This was a threat to its constituency from several directions. First, there was the economic aspect. This was expressed in an editorial written for the March 6 issue of the *Herald:* ". . . From a purely educational standpoint consolidation may be the best solution . . . (but) . . . the most effective high school in the world here would be valueless to the people of Valley City if it must be purchased at the cost of enmity among even a portion of the residents of the present 'feeder districts.'" Putting it bluntly, there was a fear of losing good customers. Second, the Chamber of Commerce had been involved in support of what was known as The Veterans' Stadium Association, an organization conceived to build a municipal stadium from contributions and memberships as a memorial to the war dead. Some overenthusiastic Junior Chamber boosters had carried the ball in the early stages of the promotion, while the going was relatively easy, but the Senior Chamber found itself with the ball when the going got tough. Some of their members had given considerable sums to this project, now only partly finished, and it was hoped that it would become the home of the Valley City high school athletic teams eventually. Moreover, the stadium was located on a large site owned by the school district—in fact, a site purchased by the school district with the ultimate objective of building a high school there. In the course of time, the Veterans' Stadium became sort of a "white elephant" which the Chamber of Commerce and the Stadium Committee very much desired to get off their hands. Obviously, building a high school for the rural pupils at a point four miles south of town would not contribute to this end. Such an eventuality would delay for ten years the date when Valley City could build its own high school on the Stadium site and thus, perhaps, be cajoled into taking over this financial liability. Third, there was the matter of civic pride. A larger high school with better athletic teams and more complete facilities as compared with neighboring teams was something to be desired in and of itself.

It was for the above reasons, mostly covert rather than expressed, that the Chamber of Commerce charged its Educational Committee under the leadership of Mr. Vincent to negotiate a settlement between the Valley City School Board and representatives of the rural districts. This relationship at first began in a very unbiased, conciliatory manner, without a show of taking sides. As discussions and countermoves developed, the Educational Committee became strongly pro-unionization, and its members fought some acrimonious verbal battles with those school board members aligned with Mr. Benson. The experience previously mentioned about the school board's promising to meet for discussion and then not showing up was typical of the sort of thing which kept tempers at a high level. Such behavior also convinced the Educational Committee of the need for exercising some "missionary zeal" in dealing with the problem, which it most certainly did.

To make a long story short, the Chamber of Commerce became one of the chief protagonists of unionization by way of campaigning for a pro-unionization school board candidate in the 1951 election.

As can be seen from Figure 3, its efforts were well directed, and they were rewarded with the election of Mr. Links, who broke the deadlock on unionization. Unfortunately, events in the rural community had already progressed so far that Valley City could do very little except wait.

The Parent-Teachers' organization came into the picture in that Mr. Benson considered it a "personal propaganda voice," which should serve the purposes of the administration. This was well illustrated when the P.T.A. was used to promote a meeting at the high school on March 12, 1951, at which prominent speakers discussed a recently completed state study of the problem of unifying school districts. Without prior arrangement with the school board, Mr. Benson sent out letters through the grade schools inviting parents to this meeting. There might have been no objection to this except for the fact that he used the opportunity to belabor the administration's viewpoint on the unionization issue. The newspaper editor took a particularly dim view of this maneuver in an editorial of the March 9 issue entitled: "This is Our Letter." The editor said in part: "The propriety of the Valley City school administration's circulation of anti-union high school propaganda without sanction of the school board has been questioned by many, including, we understand, some board members, on the ground that the board, rather than its employees, should determine the school system's policies as they pertain to political matters. . . . Furthermore, it is tinged, in the case of Valley City, with economic aspects by reason of the dependency of Valley City's economic welfare upon good will of the rural residents."

Some 300 citizens attended the meeting. One of the state senators particularly interested in education was present and was particularly effective in presenting the idea that the school board was correct in refusing to take any action involving the school district until the legislature had made some decision upon the special study of district reorganization which had been completed. A show of hands, at the end of the meeting, showed overwhelming support for this position. This was taken by the school board and the administration to be a mandate from the people for the *status quo* policy. The P.T.A. did not prove itself an altogether helpful organization for Mr. Benson, however, because the Chamber of Commerce was able to bring Mrs. Ford, President of the Valley City P.T.A. Council, into the fold in

favor of unionization. She made some declarations which undoubtedly had their effect in the community.

Mr. Meyer, the principal moved from Junior to Senior High, also
was to play an important role in the consolidation issue. As matters
developed, his relationship to Mr. Benson did not improve, but constantly deteriorated to a point where he was open to suggestions
for another position. Such an opportunity arose three months after
his move when the County Superintendent passed away. Mr. Meyer
was released to accept the position.

As county superintendent, Mr. Meyer was in a position to advise
the rural districts in their drive for a union high school outside Valley
City. This he did most effectively, and with apparent delight. There
could be no doubt about the stand he was taking upon the issue, even
though in the Valley City school system he had frequently expressed
himself in favor of consolidation. Mr. Meyer was well versed in the
law and knew that consolidation, or even a continuance of the
status quo, would in effect reduce his domain. Unionization, as a
policy, would permit his office to exercise more control over the
schools in the area.

"Billy" Duke, local editor, had been among those most enthusiastic
in welcoming Mr. Benson to Valley City. Newspaper references to
Mr. Benson and the educational system for the period from July,
1948 to December 6, 1948 provides proof enough that the newspaper
certainly co-operated with Mr. Benson to the fullest. An examination of the headlines and important observations made by this same
newspaper from January 1, 1951 to March 20, 1951 suggests that the
policy of the press over against Mr. Benson and his work had changed
very drastically. The editorials became quite strongly "anti-Benson"
and very critical of the school board for their stand on the matter of
unionization. This bias is not difficult to understand, since Mr. Duke
was one of the prime movers in the Chamber of Commerce.

"Billy" Duke had a habit of reporting an event from secondhand
information, which annoyed Benson no end. Very possibly some of
the errors in reporting resulted from this technique rather than from
intentional bias. A small-town editor cannot be everywhere and must
perforce depend to some extent upon informers who are willing to
bring him information. This was trying to Mr. Benson, because, as he
complained bitterly, he could never tell when the press was represented in a group. Thus, he faced the problem of making all his ut-

terances "on the record." Mr. Duke prefers his version that the administration held all the important meetings in secret or made no decisions when the press was openly represented.

The Valley City Teachers' Association was expected by Mr. Benson to mirror his viewpoint on any important issue. The president of the organization, a relative newcomer to the situation, was asked by Mr. Benson to call a special meeting for the sole purpose of getting a vote of support on the administration's policy of *status quo*. Considerable argument over the matter failed to produce any agreement, although there were many who supported the administration. The net result was that the teachers refused to take a stand either for or against.

Interestingly, the teachers had every reason to believe that they were meeting in closed session. They were surprised, and much chagrined, when the next issue of the *Herald* carried a prominent front-page story airing all their "private linen." Again, there were significant omissions and slight changes of emphasis which put the teachers in a rather unfavorable position with respect to the whole matter. The real effect of this incident was to silence that organization for the duration of hostilities.

Through all this confusion, bickering, and bitterness, it is of interest to see how the "boss," Mr. Benson, stood up. It is no secret that he was a man of resolute determination. Mr. Benson was not afraid to take a stand and to hold to it against every difficulty. Many people admired him for this quality, but more resented him when they became convinced that he stood in the way of an amicable solution. During this period Mr. Benson became more and more distrustful of his subordinates. He revealed his distrust by making what he thought to be discreet inquiries among staff members relative to "shadowy" activities which other staff members were supposed to have carried on. Such inquiries made news along the grapevine and contributed not a little to the growing unrest among staff members.

It was also observed that Benson took delight in trying to belittle or degrade his opponents. For example, he made frequent reference to the "First Street Gang," which to him consisted of some of the older and better-established businessmen who were also pillars in the Chamber of Commerce. "Billy" Duke was held up to ridicule as a stool pigeon and a spy. Mr. O'Donnell, Secretary of the Chamber of Commerce, was given the treatment by Benson when he implied that O'Donnell encouraged unionization because his church wanted the high school building to use for a parochial school. There were special epithets for Mr. Vincent and Mr. Wherry, the latter being a board member who was particularly troublesome to Mr. Benson. Mr. Benson was not the only one who indulged in name-calling and vindictiveness. A good deal of the language and many of the stories that were current at the time could not properly be repeated here.

Victory

On May 23, 1951, a petition was filed asking that a special election be called to form a union high school with Sage Flat as the parent district. June 16 was chosen as the date for this election. The ballots cast were 238 for and 137 against.

The Valley City School Board was now faced with an accomplished fact of a union high school organized independently of Valley City. Further negotiations had to await the election and organization of a new school board for the new district and the legal validation of this procedure by the courts. Then, Valley City might examine the wishes of the new organization.

An election was held on September 25, at which a board of education was selected. They at once organized, selected a chairman, and appointed Mr. Meyer, the county superintendent, as the clerk. On November 19 the Attorney General held that the election had been legal and that the new district was regularly constituted.

Finally, on March 10, 1952, after discovering that the matter of organizing a new school from scratch had its drawbacks after all, the new union high district filed a petition asking for an election to include Valley City and certain other districts from an adjacent county. The election was held on May 27, 1952. The proposition carried by a narrow margin, 274 to 251. Beginning on July 1, 1952, the high school was under the direction of the new union high school board.

Essentially, this completes the narrative, except that there were some interesting complications arising from the necessity of the new union high school district for renting the building, books, and all equipment from the Valley City school district for one year while plans were drawn up and a new building completed to receive the newly formed institution. This would constitute another case study in administrative behavior!

Finale

Because this case deals with administrative behavior, it may be appropriate to look at some of the events following the close of the story. Certainly these events did not take place in an atmosphere favorable to Mr. Benson, and nothing was done to add to his pleasure as he continued to administer the Valley City schools. Whatever projects he suggested were largely ignored or so "hamstrung" that no good could come out of them.

It was at the beginning of this period, on March 15, 1952, that the deadline for notification of teachers had come. (In this state, all teachers not otherwise notified on or before this date are automatically rehired.) Mr. Benson was in conference with the board chairman and the clerk relative to the issuance of teachers' contracts. Among the contracts coming up for board action was Mr. Benson's own. He judged that two of the members were against him and two were for him, with one on the fence. During the meeting, by some slip on the part of the clerk, the record did not show for what period of time Mr. Benson's contract should run, although it is claimed by some board members that they only grudgingly approved a one-year contract. Whatever did happen, we know that at the next meeting of the board a three-year contract for Mr. Benson was presented, signed by the board chairman and the clerk. Mr. Benson, in recounting this occasion, tells how his archenemy, Mr. Wherry, turned every color of the rainbow when he saw this document. But there was not much to say, since the document appeared to be in every respect legal.

Now began a war of attrition that made life miserable for everyone connected with Valley City schools. The school board sought out every means by which to make Mr. Benson's position difficult. One of the favorite devices was to encourage teachers and principals in their opposition to his policies. The junior high principal, Mr. Williams, had crossed swords with the superintendent on many issues and was, with proper encouragement, beginning to be nothing short of obnoxious. Mr. Benson recommended his release, but the board re-employed him at a better salary. Several elementary schools needed new principals during this time. Mr. Benson would make his recommendations, only to find that the board sought out and employed men whom they felt would oppose or even discredit the administration. Generally, principals' salaries were increased while Mr. Benson's salary was not. So the war went on.

It is not necessary to repeat here the multitude of other annoyances which have been heaped upon Mr. Benson's back during the past two years. At the time of this writing, his contract has one more year to run, and he is determined to stick it out. He frankly admits that he is through, not just through at Valley City, but through as an administrator. It is not difficult to see why when you meet the man. His spirit has been entirely crushed; speak about him in the community, and you will know that his reputation has been thoroughly discredited.

Mr. Benson, in his last interview with the writer relative to this case study, reflected upon his plight with this remark: "Just at the very moment when I should be most valuable to the school profession, I am literally forced to retire from it." This is not a pleasant fact, nor is it an altogether unfamiliar turn of events.

Several who have been kind enough to assist by contributing information for this narrative have said that Mr. Benson, if he had "played his cards right," could have had the people of Valley City "eating out of his hand." They say he could have been the hero of this story. Instead of being out of a job, he could have been superintendent of both the elementary district and the union high district.

CHAPTER ONE

Case Analysis

Concepts are mind-stretching; they enlarge the horizon of one's mental grasp.

KIRTLEY MATHER

If there are nine and twenty ways of making tribal lays, as Kipling maintained, then there must be an even greater number of ways for analyzing a case. The potential number would be equivalent to the range of different perspectives or frameworks for viewing human situations. The way a person views a case depends largely upon his experience, including his formal education. In regard to the latter, some college courses are judged to be more appropriate for developing adequate perspectives in potential administrators than are others. Among the courses sometimes recommended for improving administrators' understanding, particularly as it relates to human situations and events, are those in the social sciences and the humanities. Such courses are judged to help one view administrative situations more comprehensively, systematically, explicitly, and rationally.

This chapter contains examples of how persons from different social science disciplines analyze a case. The four examples included were written by representatives of the disciplines of education, political science, psychology, and sociology. The perspectives presented are systematic in approach; however, they do not aim to be comprehensive in the sense that all of the relevant concepts in the various disciplines are used, or that all the facts of the case are included in the analysis.

The case chosen for analysis is the "Valley City Consolidation Issue." Since the case is broad in scope, it contains data that pertain to the four social science disciplines represented, although not in equal amounts. The different analyses of the case may be considered as brief illustrations of how social science concepts can be used to make sense out of human situations. However, the presentations can also serve a more fundamental function. A careful assessment of the different analyses will undoubtedly raise a number of questions related to the adequate description and explanation of the "reality" to which the term "administrative processes" refers.

Benson's Administration: A Study in Conflict[1]

The rise and fall of Superintendent Benson in Valley City is a chronicle that has unpleasant, if not tragic, overtones. It is the story of a school superintendent who, according to the case writer, had only to make his wishes known during his first months in Valley City in order to have them take effect, but who, after four years of tenure, stated that he was being literally forced to retire from his profession. What is the essential meaning of the change in community reaction from the unusually warm initial reception accorded Benson to the unusually negative, if not hostile, final treatment?

In interpreting the case, the concepts of the decision-making framework set forth in Chapter 8 will be used as tools for analysis. Underlying this framework is the assumption that the administrator participates in three different levels or units of decisions: he makes choices as an individual; he plays a role in decisions made by small groups; and he influences choice formally and informally at the organizational level. The concepts elaborated in Chapter 8 are designed to illuminate administrative behavior in all these units, and they may be briefly summarized before proceeding to the analysis.

Three channels of personality through which the administrator may express himself are highly significant in individual, group, or organizational decisions: *cognition, feeling,* and *volition. Cognition* relates to the perception, definition, analysis, and comprehension of choice situations; *feelings* relate to the emotional behavior that results when the attainment of one's goals or values is positively or negatively affected; *volition* relates to how the administrator shapes or does not shape decisions at key *choice points.*

The communication systems that surround or have surrounded

[1] Prepared by Jack Culbertson, School of Education, University of Oregon.

the administrator continually provide him with actual or potential premises for decisions. Communication content can be classified into three decision-making premises: *facts, values,* and *unsubstantiated information.* The dynamics of choice processes involves an interaction between the elements of personality and the various decision-making premises. In decisions related to change and to morale problems, *conflict* is the inevitable result. Thus, in such choice situations decision-making is essentially the *resolution of conflict.*

The decision-making concepts suggest numerous questions that can be used for case analysis. In the present discussion of Benson's administrative behavior, only three questions will be posed. What was the nature of the conflicts that Benson faced? How did he handle the conflicts? Why did he handle the conflicts as he did?

The nature of the conflict. Not only was Benson faced with conflict in his own organization, but also basic to the reorganization decision was inter-organization conflict. Conflict between organizations in Valley City and in the outlying districts was illustrated, for example, by the Chamber of Commerce and the Grange. Grange members valued "home rule" and wanted to maintain control of their schools. On the other hand, members of the Chamber of Commerce within Valley City valued the continuing and increasing high school enrollment, because it meant more trade and more profits. Therefore, when they concluded that the outlying districts might solve their problems independently, their economic values swayed them to favor unionization. On the other hand, the school organization represented by Benson favored consolidation, and he apparently worked behind the scenes to achieve this goal, although publicly he announced a *status quo* policy. Benson purportedly believed that consolidation was desirable because he thought it best from an educational viewpoint. The view held by Benson was further reinforced by the fact that various state and national groups within the educational profession had openly committed themselves to consolidation as the best *educational* solution to reorganization problems.

Conflict at the face-to-face level is clearly reflected at the group decision-making level by the Valley City School Board. During the two-year period, when reorganization was a crucial issue, the members were split two to three in 1950–1951 and 3 to 2 in 1951–1952 in favor of unionization. Members of the teachers' organization or the

PTA could not even agree with Benson or among themselves on the issue. The open conflict indicates that Benson as an influencer of school policy found himself in a difficult position.

While the case does not adequately report Benson's ideas and feelings, certain inferences can be made indirectly about his own conflicts. Certainly such differing expectations as those of the Chamber of Commerce, the Grange, and his own profession must have added to his personal conflict. To what extent his belief in consolidation was determined by the expectations of professional colleagues and to what extent it stemmed from independently held personal values is not clear. One can speculate that he was motivated more by personal than by professional considerations, because his decision-making behavior was undoubtedly different from what one would expect of a typical superintendent. It is also worth noting that unionization as a policy would have diminished the size of his administrative organization, while consolidation would have markedly increased it.

Certainly the differing expectations of the school board members must have affected the conflict for Benson. His own conflict was perhaps further intensified because of personal values that he was seeking to achieve. His very unusual tactics to retain his position, which are described at the end of the case, for example, suggest that the preservation of his status was extremely important to him. This conclusion is further warranted by his reaction of deep disappointment about his future as an educator.

In a related fashion Benson valued successful performance. According to the case writer, he came to Valley City rightfully "proud of his accomplishments." His success continued immediately in that he "in four short months accomplished what the board and his former superintendent had not been able to do in years." In summary, then, the many conflicting personal, educational, and economic values about reorganization undoubtedly intensified the individual conflict that Benson experienced and that in some way he had to resolve.

Benson's behavior in the face of conflict. In the handling of the conflict, various facts suggest that Benson's behavior intensified rather than allayed the feelings of those involved with the reorganization issue. This was illustrated in Benson's first move to handle the conflict when the meeting was held with the various board presidents and clerks in the outlying districts so that the "matter could be explained to them and their co-operation solicited." In the words of the case writer, the immediate impact upon the community was one of "consternation and confusion, then of anger and rebellion." Feelings among members of the outlying district were so strongly aroused that, instead of gaining co-operation, Benson succeeded in widening the rift. Since they thought that Valley City was "shoving them around," the outlying districts began to work for unionization within their own community. Thus, Benson's early moves led to results that were in opposition to his desired goals.

At first, when the "feeder districts" showed real signs that they were going to unionize, the Chamber of Commerce members in Valley City became concerned, and their education committee made arrangements to meet with the school board to discuss the possibility of authorizing an election, so that the people in Valley City could determine whether or not they wanted to join with the outlying districts to form a union high school. For various reasons the three board members who were loyal to Benson did not attend the meeting. Since these board members, according to the case writer, showed great personal loyalty to Benson, he must have influenced their failure to attend. Significantly, he made no further efforts to get the two groups together to work out a compromise. With the lack of support for consolidation, he announced a *status quo* policy, openly favoring neither unionization nor consolidation. Thus, the local newspaper editor, a member of the Chamber of Commerce, wrote an editorial criticizing the board's "obstructive behavior." The Chamber of Commerce then adopted a pro-unionization stand, which again was in opposition to what Benson wished to achieve. Feelings were further heightened in later stages of the conflict when Benson and those with whom he disagreed began calling each other uncomplimentary and disparaging names. In such an atmosphere, reason retreated and emotions reigned. Other illustrations in the case further warrant the conclusion that Benson's tactics generally aroused negative feelings, as, for example, his seeking support from the teachers' organization, with the result that "dirty linen" was washed in public.

The manner in which Benson handled the conflict suggests a touch of irony. He chose various courses of action at key choice points in order to direct the decision toward consolidation; these various actions consistently worked against the attainment of Benson's personal and professional goals. His actions were undoubtedly reasonable ones from his own point of view; however, they promoted destructive conflict and fanned feelings to such a glow that reason could not prevail. Why, then, did Benson choose actions that had such opposite effects from the ones that he desired?

Why did Benson stir such emotional reactions? In seeking to explain why Benson chose the actions that he did, the personality concepts of *cognition, feeling,* and *volition* are of use. It can be hypothesized, for example, that Benson did not *cognize* the issues related to reorganization accurately or comprehensively, with the result that there were many unanticipated consequences. More specifically, he was limited in his ability to perceive and to understand the human factors in the decision-making process. Seemingly he tended to view persons more as things and minimized the emotional springs of behavior. Thus, his decisions were made with a strong focus on his goals and with only incidental understanding of how the persons involved would react. The case clearly suggests that Benson was more competent in assessing technical situations than he was in assessing human situations.

Benson's greater facility in dealing with technical problems helps to explain why the community reacted to him so differently in the early and in the later stages of his tenure. In the beginning he was dealing with the technical problem of school building construction. In handling such a situation, he could strike "directly at a point" and could make decisions about such things as change orders and building inspections with little probability of ruffling the personal feelings of colleagues. Consequently, he completed the task rapidly and efficiently, which undoubtedly helped to create the very cordial initial reception. When Benson faced the reorganization issue, however, he was confronted with a problem that was steeped in human emotion. Although he exercised *volition* at various choice points, his individual decisions were not enough. Seemingly he could not set up arrangements whereby the citizens of Valley City and the outlying communities could somehow compromise the conflict. He refused to change his course of action as he inflexibly pursued a *status quo* policy. He did not and perhaps could not reassess the situation and adapt accordingly, even though it continually worsened. Consequently, more and more persons were alienated from his point of view, and negative feelings were continually generated. Conditions degenerated into the "war of attrition" that occurred during his final days in Valley City.

One can also speculate about Benson's *feelings*. Certain facts suggest that he did not feel warmly toward his colleagues. Note, for example, his "discreet" inquiries about personnel, which because of "grapevine" communication turned out to be indiscreet. The case writer suggests that such behavior on the part of Benson stemmed from feelings of suspicion and distrust.

Apparently Benson did admire the intelligence and efficiency of the district's business manager Golden. However, when he sent Golden to speak to citizens of the outlying districts about reorganization, it was agreed that Golden knew his facts but that the attitudes he displayed left a "trail of angry, unfriendly people." This is another example of Benson's inadequate human understanding and his difficulty in making accurate judgments about the effects of human interaction.

Benson apparently *felt* strongly about the threat to his personal status and professional goals. Such emotional involvement undoubtedly interfered with his capacity to assess and reassess the conflicts that he faced. Greater detachment about the outcome of the reorganization issue might have helped create better conditions to work out some compromise and to save his own position. However, Benson's efforts did not make for a proper blend of intellect and feeling in the total choice process, and this was his undoing.

In summary, then, Benson's perception and comprehension of human motivation and human interaction and his strong emotional involvement were such that they provided him an inadequate basis for choice. It can be said in his favor that he was not "afraid to take a stand," and he showed "resolute determination" in the face of Valley City's conflicts. However, his strong *status quo* stand was made with weak community support. He inflexibly held to his position and went down with the ship in a sea of emotion. Leadership then emerged from the citizens of Valley City and the outlying districts, and a compromise to the reorganization conflict was effected. The solution was not the perfect one, but it was apparently less damaging to Valley City than was the manner in which Benson resolved his own conflicts. Therein lies what was referred to earlier as the tragic overtones of the case.

A FRAMEWORK FOR THE ANALYSIS OF ADMINISTRATIVE CASES FROM THE PERSPECTIVE OF POLITICAL SCIENCE[2]

Even at the risk of invading the overpopulated preserve of Mr. Arbuthnot, the cliché expert, it is worth reaffirming that life is a seamless web. Thus, to view an event, such as the case at hand, from the perspective of political science is, in a sense, to do violence to the character of social phenomena. The concepts of political science applied to the Valley City School Consolidation Issue are analytical devices; they represent only one of many ways of slicing the apple of life, and the incision at best is not a very neat one.

What kinds of questions does a political scientist raise as he looks at an administrative case? He will first of all ask himself whether the case is political. In the ordinary usage of the term, this means: do the events described in the case happen around the decision-making centers of government? In a broader sense, politics means the making of policy and the distribution of power at every social level. In fact, the extension of politics into every nook and cranny of modern life, and the character of life and leadership in organizations, guarantee the political character of the majority of case studies dealing with administration.

The following concepts are suggested as a framework for analysis. There is nothing final or exhaustive about it; its appeal lies solely in attempting to bring some order into that great buzzing and bumbling confusion that is life.

Political events may be analyzed by encompassing them within the framework of *institutions, ideology, power,* and *decision-making*.[3] The analogy breaks down, however, as will be seen, since these concepts are closely interrelated. Thus, the institutions of Valley City are imbued with ideologies; the pattern of decision-making within the Valley City School Board is contingent upon specific constellations of power.

The first task is to identify the *institutions* that are relevant to an understanding of the case at hand. Institutions may be defined as

---

[2] Prepared by Lucian Marquis, Department of Political Science, University of Oregon.

[3] I am indebted for my model to the work of Macridis (7).

patterns prescribing specific rules of behavior. Political institutions that are associated "with the identity of a group, with group life as a whole, have special coercive, symbolic and ceremonial aspects. There is inevitably a sacred aura surrounding some aspects of government." (17, p. 9)

Political institutions are concerned with the attainment of community goals; they seek, at the same time, to legitimize authority and to enforce it.

The following institutions that are directly relevant to politics in Valley City are:

1. *The governmental institutions of Valley City:* We have relatively little information on these. Only the mayor's office seems to have a tangential bearing on the case.

2. *The educational institutions of Valley City:*
   A. The School Board
   B. The Office of the Superintendent
   C. The Schools

These institutions stand at the center of the case. The political scientist might be interested in the physical setting, that is, the relationship of these institutions to one another. For example, is the Office of the Superintendent located in the same building as the high school? If it is, what bearing does this have upon the decision-making process?

The ambiguities as to policy formulation as between (A) and (B) are central to an understanding of the case. The network of relations as between the educational institutions and other political institutions must be understood.

The extent to which individuals (Billy Duke of the *Valley City Herald*) and associations (The Grange, Chamber of Commerce, and so forth) were able to gain access to policy-making in the educational institutions of Valley City is relevant.

3. *Competing educational institutions:* The roles of the various outlying school districts are of particular importance here. Most of these districts apparently wanted to maintain their identity, and this in turn is connected with questions of ideology and power.

4. *The electoral process as an institutionalization of decision-making.*

5. *The courts as institutions for legitimizing community decisions.*

6. *The Federal Government and its role in refusing to act on the construction of a paved street.*

All these are institutions that must be understood, separately and in their interrelations, in order to make political sense out of the case.

At the same time, the role of the "nonpolitical" institutions involved must be assessed: Which of the following institutions played the most important role in the controversy: Chamber of Commerce, Grange, State University through its consultant, the P.T.A., the Rural Unionization Committee, the Valley City Teacher's Association?

A second concept that may prove useful in examining the case is that of *ideology*. By "political ideology" is meant the patterns of thought and belief related to the state and to government that constitute the source of consent, the mechanism for control, and the mainspring for political action.

In the Valley City case, Hazelwood Creek becomes the symbol of ideological, economic, and political divisions within the town. The pioneer spirit of the original inhabitants of Valley City has become the dominant ideology which must be accepted by the newcomers, who can only gradually be absorbed. This, again, is symbolized by a gradual movement from the rural areas into town. The ideology of the pioneer remains a powerful device in insuring maintenance of economic and political *status quo*. The conflict arises only as the town becomes swamped with new inhabitants who do not share the original ideological position and who in turn make claims on behalf of their beliefs as to the function of government and education. It seems that a clue to the seemingly inexplicable animosity toward Benson can be found in this sentence, "Thus, there came into being some bitter jealousies, not always expressed, but incipient and ever poised to divide the city on issues."

It might be suggested that the issues were never clearly spelled out because the ideology of the pioneer spirit is so deeply imbedded in the American system of beliefs. Benson, an "outsider," was either incapable of challenging or did not feel free to challenge these beliefs. Even the movement for unionization of the outlying districts was expressed in the rhetoric of pioneer self-sufficiency and independence. In fact, both Valley City and the outlying districts were forced by hard necessity to "unionize," while paying continuous lip service to an anachronistic ideology. Benson, motivated by a desire for organizational reforms which involved the bureaucratization of the educational institutions, was incapable of clarifying his ideological position and thus was frustrated as an administrator. In effect, Benson was the victim of ideologically rooted value conflicts, trapped as he was between his professional goal of establishing administrative standards and the community leaders' goal of maintaining a flexible, *laissez-faire,* pioneer attitude.

A third instrument for analysis is the concept of *power.* By "political power" is meant social power focused on the decision-making centers of government. Power becomes authority as it becomes legitimized and institutionalized. Without consensus, there is no authority.

In this particular case, we should be interested in the power positions of individuals and institutions as related to class, status, and occupation.

We are told that agriculture, retail trade, and a small amount of lumbering formed the base of Valley City's economy. This economic organization is reflected in the alignment of the two major political pressure groups, the Chamber of Commerce on the one hand and the Grange on the other. It also helps to explain why a final compromise was inevitable, why consolidation became unionization. The farm groups in the outlying districts were as much dependent upon the retail outlets in Valley City as these were dependent on the farmer.

Undoubtedly, the ambiguous position of Benson is inherent in the institutional ambiguities between school board and superintendent. The school board possesses authority because it holds power legitimately; the superintendent has authority because of his professional status. However, in a conflict between these two, the outcome is not clearly determined. Benson, by appealing to the relevant publics in the community, might have secured the consensus necessary to support his authority. However, he seemed singularly unskillful in securing such consensus. This raises, of course, the thorny question as to whether the expert merely executes policy or whether he in turn shapes policy. (3)

In asking questions about power, the political scientist would want to know where power is located, what groups seek access to the locus of power, and through what instruments power is secured.

A final dimension for the analysis of a case is *decision-making*, which David Easton has called the "authoritative allocation of values." (1, p. 135) This process is fundamental to politics, since politics is the making of policy. The first question relevant to decision-making that might be asked in considering a case is: what was the critical decision in the case? In the case at hand, it seems that the critical decision was not made in Valley City at all, but in the outlying districts, where the people chose to form a union high school. This may also help to explain the frustration and failure of Benson, since the decision-making action, which could have been his, was taken out of his hands. It also reveals the area in which the case is least informative, since we know almost nothing about the composition of the decision-makers, their ideology, or the institutions and processes of decision-making in the outlying districts.

This, in turn, directs attention to the kinds of questions that a political scientist would address to this case, namely:

1. Who makes the decisions?
2. What is the background of particular decision-makers; what is their political ideology?
3. How are decision-makers selected?
4. What is the composition of particular decision-making groups?
5. What is the nature of the deliberative process?
6. How is the decision-making action legitimized?

Since decision-making is a choice between alternatives, the political scientist can never lose sight of the question of the values that are involved in a particular decision. In this case, a fundamental choice between values was spelled out by the *Valley City Herald* when it wrote: "From a purely educational standpoint consolidation may be the best solution . . . (but) . . . the most effective high school in the world here would be valueless to the people of Valley City if it must be purchased at the cost of enmity among even a portion of the residents of the present 'feeder districts.'"

It needs to be re-emphasized that the above framework is meant to be analytical, but that it does not seek to detract from what is perhaps the most valuable aspect of the case study: to provide a vicarious administrative experience. The student should be able to get "inside" the case by empathizing with the protagonists, by raising such questions as: What would I have done had I been in Benson's position? What were some other alternatives that might have been tried? How might the administrator have obtained initial acceptance for these alternatives?

Since the case is a dramatic incident, it makes a very special demand upon the social scientist. As Robert Redfield (9, p. 188) has noted:

> In spite of the great advances in formal method in social science, much of the understanding of persisting and general relationships depends upon a grasp that is intuitive and that is independent of or not fully dependent on some formal method. In advancing social science, we invent and practice techniques, and we also cultivate a humanistic art.

TOWARD AN UNDERSTANDING OF PERSONS IN ADMINISTRATIVE SITUATIONS[4]

All administration must ultimately be transmitted through a human chain, any link of which may be weak. Sound administrative plans often fail because people are not seen as individuals with special needs and expectations of their own.

When we start out to understand persons in situations, we realize that what is directly given to us is only one thing—a stream of observations and impressions. From this stream, patterns stand out as we bring into play our particular interests, purposes, and prejudices. In order to make manageable the "big buzzing confusion" of behavior around and experience within, we use concepts for sorting out and interpreting whatever happens in our world. Mostly we are unaware of our conceptual scheme, and often it harbors conflicting and untrue elements.

The scientific tests of any conceptual framework, including administrative models, are reliability, comprehensiveness, consistency, stimulation of research, and congruence with reality. At the present time there are various models for describing administration. (2) All

[4] Prepared by Norman Sundberg, Department of Psychology, University of Oregon.

of them are limited in scope and none of them has the firm support of empirical evidence. Apparently, the best strategy for understanding administrative processes is to use a multi-theoretical approach and to test various theories through research and administrative practice.

Psychological Concepts

Among the many personality concepts developed by clinical and social psychologists, three that are prominent in current psychological thinking will guide the following discussion: role (10), motivation (6), and interpersonal processes (4, 11). A brief elucidation of the three concepts will first be given. Then the concepts will be applied to the case, "The Valley City Consolidation Issue."

Role. Sarbin (10) points out that many generalizations of social scientists center around the concept of *role*. This concept relates to *what* a person is doing and can be defined in terms of a person's characteristic kind of contribution to a group, or in terms of the behavior that is characteristic and expected of the occupant of the defined position in a group. In a school system, for example, such positions as principal, teacher, and janitor are designated. Each of these positions is defined by a set of *role expectations* (obligations or responsibilities) that people have about them. Also, the behavior of a person relevant to a given position can be called *role behavior*. In analyzing cases, it is useful to ask what the expectations of the leading characters are regarding the roles they are supposed to play. The next point, then, is to find the discrepancies among the expectations of different people and the discrepancies between role expectations and role behavior.

Motivation. The concept of *motivation* relates to the question of *why* persons behave as they do. In this regard the concept of *need* is frequently used to refer to the strength and direction of the goal-oriented aspects of behavior. A person who always takes the back seat in meetings and who seldom does things on his own may be said to have a high dependency need, for instance. A system that may be very useful in analysis of social situations is the interpersonal need system developed by Schultz (11). He postulates and presents some evidence for three primary interpersonal needs: the need of an individual to be included in or excluded from a group, the need of an individual to control or avoid control, and the need of an individual for affection.

Interpersonal processes. The concept of *interpersonal processes* ties together the concepts of *motivation* and role. It refers to *how* persons behave, and encompasses the behavior and experience of a person in an interpersonal situation. An interpersonal situation is one in which two or more persons take account of each other for some purpose or decision. (11) Two aspects of interpersonal processes can be viewed: interpersonal perception, which is related to role expectations, and interpersonal interaction, which is related to role behavior.

The individual's typical modes of interaction in interpersonal situations are very important aspects of case analysis. Part of our vocabulary for describing these modes of interaction comes from the familiar *adjustment mechanisms* that the individual uses in coping with the ego-threats of the world. Common mechanisms are *projection*, the imputing of one's own intentions or attitudes to others; *compensation*, the attempt to make up for inadequacies in one's sphere by overemphasis on another; *rationalization*, the giving of spurious reasons for one's behavior; and *displacement*, the shifting of emotions and reaction from the original source of irritation to another less threatening person. As Leary (4) has noted, an important aspect of interaction is that persons develop characteristic ways of eliciting behavior from others. The dependent child elicits nurturant behavior from the teacher. People behave in such a way as to set up the kind of interpersonal relationships that suit their personal needs. Thus, the concept of motivation can be seen to be partially interdependent with the interpersonal processes.

Application of the Concepts

In analyzing the case, "The Valley City Consolidation Issue," the focus will be on Superintendent Benson. Although the analysis centers on the school superintendent partly because he is the most clearly portrayed person in the case, one should in case analyses avoid blaming any one individual for the course of events. When things go wrong, the simplest procedure is to point to the individual who is closest to the scene of the accident. Actually, Benson came to a situation that was already fraught with conflict, and he may well have had no trouble at all with it had it not been for the rural-urban split and other group differences. Be that as it may, let us try to observe how Benson played his part as the drama unfolded.

First it is well to note that we are dealing only with an image of the man and not the actual man. The image is one that is distorted by the author's limited perspective and his biases. The only data we have, as readers, are in the case itself. To what extent these data are opinions and to what extent they are facts is a good question to keep in mind while reading a case. Generally, the view we have of Mr. Benson is from the outside and is in terms of descriptive adjectives rather than reported actions or statements. In discussing Benson the man, the author presents a view of him in the following terms: "Poor speaking voice," "unpleasant voice quality," "not a handsome man," "visage was rather rough hewn," "talks were strong on content," "He had a penchant for striking directly at a point . . . without first smoothing the way." The presence of this series of generally negative terms suggests a negative reaction on the part of the author toward Benson as a person. We wonder if there are other more favorable views, but we are given very little opportunity to see the man from other viewpoints.

Various questions related to role can be raised concerning Superintendent Benson. For example, what were Benson's expectations of the role of the superintendent, and what were the discrepancies between his role behavior and the expectations of others? Was there consensus over what the superintendent was expected to do? First, it is likely that Benson did not clearly understand what the various conflicting groups expected of him. He also seemed, at least in the case writer's view, to be unappreciative of certain aspects of his job; he was strong on some of the structuring aspects of administration and very weak in taking personal considerations into account. We can hypothesize that Mr. Benson viewed his role as an administrator as one in which the school was perceived as a kind of business to run. One of his highest values appears to be efficiency. Another factor related either to his perception of the superintendency role or to his personal needs for recognition is revealed in his willingness and interest in getting much newspaper publicity when he first arrived in town. The writer evidently interprets this immediate use of publicity as "shrewd timing" and speaks of Benson's ability to make up his mind and select the right moment for attack, but in later events this ability seems questionable. In general, we see a man who is comprehending only part of the role of the superintendency. He views himself as an educational expert who is hired to run a school system; he fails to comprehend such human relations aspects of the superintendency as how to get dissident community groups to work together and how to serve teachers' needs for two-way communication. In a nutshell, perhaps we could say that Benson construed his role as that of problem-solving *about* the community rather than problem-solving *with* the community.

With regard to the concept of motivation, several questions can be posed. What is Benson striving to accomplish? What kinds of situations does he approach and avoid? What kinds of situations are satisfying to him? What are his values, interests, needs? Benson's typical interpersonal relationships suggest a strong need for structure and order. Perhaps we also see a strong need for distance between himself and others in that the author emphasizes Benson's negative physical qualities; such qualities and characteristics are often overlooked if the individual is likeable as a person. Because of the limited amount of information about Benson as a person, we cannot infer much about his private motives. One can guess with a high degree of probability from his socioeconomic status and position alone that he is highly motivated to achieve, to better his situation, and to earn more money. We would guess that he is the sort of person who does not like to "have the boat rocked." An important question about Benson's goal-oriented behavior that the reader might like to speculate about is what personal needs were being satisfied in his avoidance of interpersonal situations, such as speaking to the rural groups.

In analyzing interpersonal processes, such questions as the following arise: Who are the others with whom the administrator habitually interacts? How does he typically structure interpersonal relationships with others? Does he tend to see subordinates typically as inferior or about equal to himself? What are his typical interpersonal adjustment mechanisms? Benson attempted to set up interpersonal relationships in terms of hierarchical dominance rather than in terms of a high degree of communication and influence up and down the system. He used participation very little in attempting to solve problems. This action was undoubtedly related to his authoritarian and efficiency-oriented perception of the superintendency role. We find that he "demanded efficiency in no uncertain terms," and he "informed" merchants that requisitions signed by the school superintendent were required. We learn that after Benson's actions, both the teachers and the merchants began to feel that he did not trust them.

Another aspect of his interpersonal behavior pattern is that he set up the atmosphere of "busyness" about his office. "Teachers found it hard to see him about their problems. Parents calling at the office found themselves cooling their heels on the outer bench, while mysterious figures strode in and out on the authority of a whispered conference with the secretary." Later on we find that he does not go out to meet the people in the rural area to discuss consolidation, even though the people wanted to see the "boss." We see, then, a man who wants loyal support and obedience from people without allowing the governed to have much voice in their government. We can hypothesize that Mr. Benson's personality, though it might work out in the other kinds of situations, did not fit the expectations and desires of the school people and community in which he was attempting to operate. This personality is particularly unsuited for the task of establishing communications between warring groups.

Before long, open opposition developed in response to Benson's interpersonal tactics. He elicited from people tension, anger, and a feeling that they were being shoved around. As this opposition developed, it certainly must have been transmitted to Mr. Benson in many ways. Now the question comes, how did he react? What was his secondary tactic after the first general tactic in interpersonal relationships failed? Apparently the break between Mr. Benson and those from whom he had expected loyal support became wider and wider. The writer reports, "During this period Mr. Benson became more and more distrustful of his subordinates. He revealed his distrust by making what he thought to be discreet inquiries among staff members relative to 'shadowy' activities which other staff members were supposed to have carried on. Such inquiries made news along the grapevine and contributed not a little to the growing unrest among the staff members."

We are also told that he belittled and degraded his opponents and had special epithets for some of the community leaders and the "First Street Gang." Thus, Mr. Benson, instead of finding out more about opposing views by taking a more or less detached view and by studying attitudes toward the problem, began to construe the situation in very personal terms. We suspect, if the writer's report is correct, that Benson is making use of the mechanism of projection in attributing to others his own motivation. He tended to encourage in others the kind of behavior he expected. We find him expecting gangs in opposition, and this is what developed.

At the end we find his spirit crushed and his reputation discredited. In one of the few quotes in the paper, the writer states Mr. Benson's reflections: "Just at the very moment when I should be most valuable to the school profession, I am literally forced to retire from it." This statement suggests that his last adjustment mechanism was giving up. The three phases he has passed through in his sequential adjustment tactics were as follows: (1) imposition of authority, (2) a contest of power, and (3) rejection and withdrawal from the field.

THE PROFESSION AND THE PERSON:
A SOCIOLOGICAL APPROACH[5]

Sociology takes its basic orientation from the fact that man is always a member of groups. Whatever the society, whatever their personal make-up, men must in some ways act with others. In studying specific situations, looking for general processes, the sociologist tends to look for the influence of other persons and groups. They may be physically present or not. Men act in terms of their *definitions* of situations, and "if men define situations as real, they are real in their consequences." (15, p. 572)[6]

One way to try to understand and to learn from the case is to determine how the various events and decisions looked from the standpoints of relevant persons and groups involved. Here we shall seek some of Benson's main expectations of himself, including those that he imputed to groups whose opinion of him was particularly valued. The very difficulty of taking this approach to case materials without imputing one's own or merely plausible "motivations" points up an interesting general problem in the relationship between a

[5] Prepared by Richard Colvard, Department of Sociology, The University of Texas.
[6] Also see Chapter 11 in Merton (8) and the work of Volkart (16).

superintendent and various groups affecting decision-making. The present discussion is oriented around the two concepts of "profession" and "personification."

The concept of profession. In Valley City the "will of the community" prevailed. In a sense we should not ignore, this is in accordance with democratic procedures. Why, then, is it so natural for the American schoolman reading the case to think that Benson bungled, or to feel, with the author, that, "if Benson had played his cards right" . . . (he) . . . "could have been the hero of this story"? At least one fundamental clue to this question stands out. It is, at the same time, a clue to the status-quo policy in which Benson and the board lost the initiative on the overcrowding issue. What can be a basic dilemma for superintendents is revealed in Benson's key statement, "I feel that the board should not ask the people to vote on any educational issue that we as educators could not support." The education profession as Benson perceives it is a group not immediately visible but which has a crucial influence on events. The profession is a reference group (13) used for intellectual and moral support by Benson, who takes a stand here not merely as Valley City's superintendent, but as a professional educator.

Clearly there are conflicting expectations and sources of authority confronting Benson. As many writers on educational administration are aware, the role expectations of the superintendent as both leader and expert are in some basic ways functionally and morally incompatible. Legally, he is an expert administrator employed to act as the board's agent. In practice, particularly because he *is* an expert, the board is often a prisoner of his knowledge. He may be asked to lead, come to feel that he has to lead to get things done, or personally want to lead. Through professional training and experience he may have come to define the "good superintendent" —the one who earns respect (and recommendations) from other schoolmen and rewards from school boards—as one who leads his board and perhaps his whole community.

In the case at hand, Benson is pulled in conflicting directions not only between the pressure to make policy fit community wishes and to make it fit professional expectations, but also between conflicts in the professional expectations themselves. There is a basic ambivalence within the profession on the role of the superintendent. According to Lieberman (5, p. 81).

The policy of treating the local community as the source of intellectual authority on controversial issues may, in the short run, make it easier for teachers and administrators to "get along" in the community. But the long-range effects have been to undermine education as a profession. The continued delegation of professional decisions to lay bodies, not only without protest, but even with the enthusiastic approval of educators, has created the impression among laymen that they ought to make decisions which in reality should be made by educators if the latter are a professional group.

Though many educators would quarrel with the idea that the professional should set policy, it has considerable support in practice and appears to enter into Benson's advocacy of the *status quo*. He recognizes that the overcrowding issue is a political as well as a strictly educational one. But in this policy he seems almost to wish that this did not have to be so, or to think that, perhaps after the redistricting study, a solution in line with good educational practice will be possible without shoving it down the community's throat, so to speak, or staking his job on the issue. Benson fights a weak delaying action here as expert.

In Benson's, as in the typical American situation, the leadership function seems to be formally delegated to the board but is actually held in an unstable balance between it and the superintendent.[7] To meet his responsibilities as he sees them, the successful superintendent ordinarily acquires more power than he is granted in the formal organization of school and community.

One way by which superintendents do this is to stress their qualifications as experts both to themselves and, actively, to their publics. They seek to gain power *throughout* the community as an accepted educational authority. Done more effectively than Benson did in his passive *status quo* policy, this would probably have meant earlier and longer-range planning, and an attempt to educate the board and community. Such an approach focuses on issues and may lead to constructive rather than destructive conflict within the school, the community, and the superintendent himself. It also has some of the trappings and some of the substance of democratic procedure. Nonetheless, it is an informal way around rather than a permanent solution to the various leader-expert conflicts in the

[7] For suggestive analyses of the reciprocal relationships between leader and led, see the works by Selznick (12) and Wolff (18).

American system where political leadership is the responsibility of the board and, ultimately, the community.

The concept of personification. An alternative way of handling the conflict in which Benson is placed, and one used by many superintendents, is to commit themselves to the belief that direct political behavior in the community is legitimate and/or necessary to get their vital work done. This approach involves building a personal power base, not just in the board, but in the wider community. The superintendent does not mask his ability as an expert, but he does not stress it either. He realizes that it may be a handicap in his relations with farmer and labor groups and also with other professionals, for example, lawyers, who may rank with him in depth and quality of professional training and also know something of the internal conflicts in education.

The superintendent taking this tack seems to recognize that people act in terms of their definitions of him as superintendent and, more generally, as human being, not in terms of what he thinks of himself as expert. This has support in sociological and interpersonal theory. (14) We never get to know one another completely. Even in the closest of social relations, we act toward unique personifications of other persons or groups—personal images to which attitudes are attached. These have been built up in face-to-face interaction or, less directly, for example, through gossip or reading, as many Valley City voters undoubtedly read about Benson in Billy Duke's newspapers. The superintendent seeking power this way sees and accepts the functional character of personal public relations. He presents himself to politically relevant groups as a man who knows his job but also knows the score locally. He stays familiar with and respects the often divergent local expectations and seeks, as much as possible, to work in terms of them. Benson, by evasive and impersonal tactics, was re-personified as a man who didn't understand Valley City folks.

The personal-power approach does not require an outgoing personality or a secretary who runs off reams of material for public consumption. The superintendent must have enough sensitivity to know how he can honestly earn personal respect where it counts. Some community groups he may pray with; some he may play with. Some groups he may formally talk to; others he may informally listen to —in order to experience and know what the expectations and images of various groups actually are. This approach, which Benson felt drawn to but was personally and professionally repelled from, can be a way of getting the work of the superintendent done. Again, however, it does not permanently set up a way of answering the question of where the superintendent's responsibility lies when latent lines of conflict come actively across one another. And it has practical disadvantages, including psychological hazards, which Benson may have sensed.

Building a personal-power base may involve the development of friendships and personal or administrative commitments that will be strongly binding on the superintendent as human being, strongly limiting what he can and is willing to do across the wide arc of his objectives and responsibilities. If he stays in a community a long time and does not maintain partial detachment from it, when a strong conflict arises it may be impossible for him to meet his friends' expectations and his contractual and professional obligations and still maintain his health, integrity, and even his sanity. Personal community ties may especially conflict with the more universalistic but nonetheless strongly internalized values and standards of success in the profession. Some unanticipated effects of professional commitments can be seen in a further examination of the case at hand.

Benson's professional orientation went deeper, apparently, than his using the profession as a source of intellectual authority, as in the above key quotation, "we as educators." His conflicts seem to go deeper than those between and within roles. Unlike a foreman, who also has conflicting role expectations, the professional's reputation for competency among a set of colleagues and opinion leaders can easily be the core of his very personification of himself. Supporting indications he gets from, or imputes to, professional colleagues in his own orbit can be more important to him (and to his psychological balance) than those from laymen, subordinates, employers, or even his own family.

Though we need more information on Benson's personification of himself, there are some clear indications that it was approval and esteem within the profession that Benson used as a basic moral support and sought as a primary psychological reward. His pride in the *American School Board Journal* article on his previous building program bears this out. So does his otherwise difficult-to-understand *status quo* policy, although this stand and the way it was handled indicated that, paradoxically, Benson was both too much and too little a professional. As expert, he could have taken a strong stand for consolidation, trying to keep attention focused on its curricular and administrative advantages to all groups in the long run. In this way he might have kept the initiative and kept the arguments on educational objectives as much as possible. Then, particularly if he had also stressed that it was up to the board to decide, even defeat on consolidation could have come with honor at home and in the profession. To return to the specific point, however, perhaps the best illustration of Benson's professional commitment comes when Benson says, "Just at the very moment when I should be most valuable to the school profession, I am literally forced to retire from it."

The above indications plus the author's statement that (Benson) . . . "frankly admits that he is through, not just through at Valley City, but through as an administrator," show the not unusual but overbalanced depth of Benson's professional commitment. They also provide an answer to the original question of the specific sense in which Benson failed. It is as a professional administrator that Benson failed, but for him this was failure as a human being. This was true on the overcrowding issue and was accelerated in later actions. Benson is acutely aware of the failure, but still is uncomprehending. Like personifications of others, our personifications of ourselves are held, as it were, in social suspension, dependent on validating indications from others. Benson's troubles on the *status quo* policy undercut his image of himself as a competent administrator. As this bulwark of his self-esteem became increasingly eroded with the election of the new board, the vote for unionization, and the question of his retention, Benson changed from a brusque but by no means completely incompetent administrator to a pathetic schemer in relative social isolation. At the end of the case, he was literally not the same man who came to Valley City.

To summarize, then, the fundamental structural conflicts between community and professional expectations and within professional expectations, exaggerated by the reciprocal nature of leadership and of power, can create deeply personal conflicts for a superintendent. He must live with himself; but, as a social being, he has incorporated expectations of others as a basic part of himself. Events in Valley City left a community with a weaker instructional program than it might have had, lost one member to a vital profession, and destroyed a human being's conception of his own worth.

References

1. Easton, David, *The Political System: An Inquiry Into the State of Political Science.* New York: Alfred A. Knopf, Inc., 1953.
2. Halpin, Andrew W. (ed.), *Administrative Theory in Education.* Chicago: Midwest Administration Center, 1958.
3. Laski, Harold J., "The Limitations of the Expert," *Harper's Magazine,* Vol. CLXII, (December 1930), pp. 101–110.
4. Leary, Timothy, *Interpersonal Diagnosis of Personality.* New York: Ronald Press, 1957.
5. Lieberman, Myron, *Education as a Profession.* Englewood Cliffs, N.J.: Prentice-Hall, Inc., 1956. Copyright 1956 by Prentice-Hall, Inc. Reprinted by permission of the publisher.
6. Lindzey, Gardner (ed.), *Assessment of Human Motives.* New York: Rinehart and Co., 1958.
7. Macridis, Roy C., *The Study of Comparative Government.* New York: Random House, Inc., 1955.
8. Merton, Robert K., *Social Theory and Social Structure.* Glencoe, Ill. The Free Press, 1957, rev. ed.
9. Redfield, Robert, "The Art of Social Science," *The American Journal of Sociology,* LIV (November, 1948), Copyright 1948 by the University of Chicago.
10. Sarbin, Theodore R., "Role Theory," in *Handbook of Social Psychology.* Cambridge: Addison-Wesley Publishing Co., 1954.
11. Schultz, William C., *Firo, A Three-Dimensional Theory of Interpersonal Behavior.* New York: Rinehart and Co., 1958.
12. Selznick, Philip, "An Approach to a Theory of Bureaucracy," *American Sociological Review,* VIII (February, 1943).
13. Shibutani, Tamotsu, "Reference Groups as Perspectives," *American Journal of Sociology,* LX, No. 6 (May, 1955).
14. Sullivan, Harry Stack, *The Interpersonal Theory of Psychiatry* (Helen Swick Perry and Mary Ladd Gawel, eds.). New York: W. W. Norton and Company, Inc., 1953.
15. Thomas, W. I., and Dorothy Swaine Thomas, *The Child in America: Behavior Problems and Programs.* New York: Alfred A. Knopf, Inc., 1928.
16. Volkart, Edmund A. (ed.), *Social Behavior and Personality: Contributions of W. I. Thomas to Theory and Social Research.* New York: Social Science Research Council, 1951.
17. Waldo, Dwight, *The Study of Public Administration.* New York: Random House, Inc., 1955.
18. Wolff, Kurt H. (trans. and ed.), *The Sociology of Georg Simmel.* Glencoe, Ill.: The Free Press, 1950, Part III, "Superordination and Subordination."

CHAPTER TWO

Preparation of Cases

> *The important strategy, and the hard thing to communicate, is that the case should be open-ended in its purposes, tell a story which will be many parables in many hands, yet a story which has coherence and singleness of narrative focus.*
>
> GARCEAU

Case preparation represents both a scientific process and a literary endeavor. Thereupon hinge many of the issues in case development and use. As a literary creation, a case presents content so that it has interest and appeal in a form that is more or less pleasing esthetically. In this sense, a case is like a novelette, full of life and drama arranged in an appropriate plot. However, a case is a work of art only in a very general sense, because the writer as a creator cannot change or take special liberties with his data.

As a scientific endeavor, a case represents a process of careful study and observation, an enterprise of fact-gathering, an activity motivated by a deep concern to capture a truthful picture of selected human events. For the field of school administration, this means the accurate depiction of a school administrator or school administrators grappling with real problems in real situations. In this sense the case-preparer, like any other scholar, seeks to understand and accurately represent the "reality" of his chosen field of study.

To be sure, a case can be more or less scientific, depending upon the amount of care that is exercised in data-gathering and the level of conceptualization that is employed in the process. By the same token, case-writing can be more or less artistic, depending upon the degree of creativity expressed by the person preparing the written report of the case. The point to be made here, however, is that a case

51

that is prepared for effective instructional purposes inevitably represents a blend of procedures that are relatively scientific and of literary expressions that are relatively artistic. It is also worth noting that both art and science have the general goal of giving a truthful representation of life and nature, and in this sense do not oppose one another. However, the scientific and artistic facets of case preparation, while interrelated, will be viewed for present purposes as different phenomena.

Partly because a case represents both science and art, it cannot be neatly defined by a statistic or a formula. Furthermore, there is some danger at this stage in case development of adopting precise case definitions in that the effect might be to place artificial limits on case-preparers. A better procedure would be to set forth some of the issues and to suggest general guide lines for case development. Such a procedure should be of interest to those preparing additional cases on school administration.

In law, cases emerge from everyday practice and may be used directly in the classroom. In medicine, a case may be wheeled in on a cot and then used for instructing an intern. School-administration cases, however, must be developed through careful and systematic efforts that are independent of administrative practice. Thus, there is currently a great need for more cases and a wider variety of school-administration cases.

The growth of a case is like the growth of a human being, in the sense that both go through developmental stages. Three stages in case development can be clearly distinguished: data-collection, case-writing, and instructional use. The third stage, instructional use, is discussed in Chapter 3. The present chapter will deal with the first two stages of case development. Data-collection is the stage that is more closely associated with the scientific side of a case and, therefore, will be viewed within such a perspective.

Scientific Aspects of Case Development

How scientific can research procedures in case-preparation be? Those who are committed to strict experimental design would undoubtedly answer that case research is not highly scientific. However, experimentalists have not advanced very far in studying many of the difficult problems related to school administration, and much faith and optimism are required to believe that they can *presently* design a wide range of studies in which the many complex variables in administrative settings are scientifically controlled. For this reason, as well as for others, an argument needs to be made for case research as *one* scientific approach to the study of administration.

Is case research scientifically sound? Reasons have been presented elsewhere (4) for supporting case research as a scientific activity, and they will be briefly summarized here.

Research considerations. In the early stages of study in almost any field of scientific endeavor, concepts and hypotheses are first derived from the study and observation of individual cases. An excellent illustration of this point is found in the field of psychoanalysis. Freud, for example, continually gathered facts through case studies of individuals to prove or disprove concepts and generalizations that he had formulated. His theories about human behavior, which have produced so much scientific debate and investigation, were developed through the careful examination of case studies. Thus, at the present stage in the study of administrative behavior, the thorough preparation of case studies, with a conscious awareness of the implications and possibilities for formulating and/or for reformulating theory, seems very desirable.

It seems clear that no one scientific method is appropriate for studying all types of administrative problems. The strength of the case method lies in its appropriateness for capturing a more comprehensive and intensive view of complex situations. Few other methods, if any, can provide as much richness of detail about historical and environmental factors impinging upon administrative behavior as can the case method. The careful depiction of the situational variables affecting leadership is clearly needed, since leaders can only be understood in relationship to and in interaction with the social and cultural setting in which they operate. Case studies that view the total administrative setting as a *gestalt* can help to meet this need.

Case studies of administrative behavior seem valuable from the standpoint of the social sciences in general, in that many of the same processes and elements that operate within an administrative organization also operate within the larger society. For example, a school principal occupies a status position in the school organization just the same as he would if he belonged to a service club. There are informal and formal rules that affect life in both of these organizations. A careful study of administrative organizations through cases could throw light on other types of community organization and could have implications for general organizational theory.

Pedagogical considerations. Some persons have maintained that cases, even if they have the potential, should not be scientifically oriented. Usually the arguments of such persons stem from pedagogical considerations. They maintain that successful learning through the case method must have an emotional base, and that a case that is objectively ordered does not encourage students to project themselves wholeheartedly into case discussion. In addition, they object to organizing data around scientific concepts. For example, in Case 17, "Changing the Curriculum at Southside," some of the data are organized around the concept of "informal organization," which is a scientific concept in the sense that it is assumed to be applicable to aspects of life in all organizations. Some persons would argue that the use of such concepts structures the meaning of the data for students and, thereby, places limits upon their personal perceptions and the development of their own concepts.

Persons who argue against scientifically oriented cases for pedagogical reasons generally place more emphasis in case-method instruction on the goal of self-learning than on the goal of scientific generalizations about administration. While self-learning is important in a potential administrator, it is by no means the only instructional goal. Attention also needs to be directed to the learning of general concepts. In the last 30 or 40 years, many social science concepts have been developed that have *general* value to most students in helping them to interpret the facts of experience. Are not cases a very appropriate and economical way to communicate the meaning of general concepts to students? Just because the case-preparer uses careful research procedures and concepts to guide his data-gathering, does it follow that he must structure his data in the written report so tightly that a student's view is limited? Does careful data-gathering necessarily mean that the emotional appeal will be taken out of the case in the written presentation? Rather, is it not reasonable to believe that careful and comprehensive data-gathering offers the writer greater opportunity for scientific understanding and a cogent presentation?

Any field of knowledge that is to advance must continue to

develop new concepts and seek to refine old ones. This can best be done through testing concepts against facts or deriving new concepts from an analysis of facts. Cannot knowledge of administration be expanded through examining the content of a variety of carefully prepared cases? The discussion to follow, which analyzes some of the scientific problems in case development, assumes that this question has an affirmative answer.

Sampling problems in case research. Stein (18) has spoken of the problem of abundance facing case-writers. Another way of viewing this problem is to raise the question of how the case-preparer can select cases that meet scientific criteria of sampling when he is faced with so many alternatives.

What is "representative"? Samples, it has been said, should be representative. What does "representative" mean as related to cases? Does it mean representative of types of school districts, types of communities, sizes of school districts, levels of administration, types of administrative process, areas of administration, or what? Should "representative" be defined as that which occurs frequently, as Stein (19) has suggested? If so, how does one determine frequency of occurrence? Obviously, attaining a representative sample of cases is more complex than attaining a representative sample of persons for a Gallup poll. The matter of random sampling seems to be even less susceptible of immediate and complete solution.

Chart I presents some categories related to sampling with the cases in this book classified accordingly. In addition to serving as a guide for selecting cases for particular courses or for particular purposes, the classification suggests a number of problems related to sampling.

Limitations in the present sample. Although Chart I indicates a variety of cases representing different aspects of administration, it is also clear that some aspects are not represented at all or are represented only by a few cases. There are, for example, no cases representing the state unit of administration. There is only one case that occurred in a district with more than 50,000 population. Since the large majority of the school population attend schools in larger districts, more cases representative of these districts are needed.

It is also worth noting that decisions about case classification can be made more easily and more reliably for some categories than for others. The criteria for the "Size of District" category, for example, are much more objective than are those for the category "General Administrative Process." In the latter category, there is overlapping among the categories, so that all of the cases could be classified into two or more categories. To a lesser extent the same is true for the category "Areas of Administration." In a sense, then, these two general classifications do violence to the cases in that they do not completely reflect their true content.

Normal or abnormal cases? Still another issue needs to be made explicit. Even though cases are representative of such categories as "Size of District" or "Unit of Administration," there is a deeper question about representativeness. More specifically, are the four cases that come from districts of 20,000–50,000 populations in the present collection representative of the usual or normal problems faced by administrators in such districts? What is a normal case? Stein (19) has stated that a normal case is one that strikes most people as neither highly surprising nor shocking. But will not "shocking"

ASPECTS OF ADMINISTRATION REPRESENTED BY THE CASES

CASE* NUMBERS	SIZE OF DISTRICT (Total Population)				UNIT OF ADMINISTRATION				ADMINISTRATIVE RELATIONSHIPS					AREAS OF ADMINISTRATION								GENERAL ADMINISTRATIVE PROCESS			
	2500 or less	2500 - 20,000	20,000 - 50,000	Above 50,000	School (K-6)	School (7-12)	District	County	Supt. Board	Supt. Staff	Supt. Community	Principal-Staff	Principal-Students	School-Community Problems	Staff Personnel Problems	School Building	School Finance	School Organization	School Supervision	Curriculum	Pupil-Personnel Problems	Communicating	Decision-Making	Maintaining Morale	Initiating Change
1.	X						X				X							X							X
2.		X			X										X							X	X		
3.	X						X				X			X										X	
4.		X			X					X						X						X			
5.	X						X				X						X					X			
6.		X			X						X			X								X			
7.		X					X				X								X					X	
8.		X						X			X									X					X
9.		X					X	X			X								X			X			
10.		X			X							X								X					X
11.	X				X						X								X			X			
12.		X					X	X							X							X			
13.		X			X						X				X										X
14.		X					X	X						X											X
15.		X					X	X									X					X			
16.		X			X								X							X					X
17.			X		X						X									X		X	X		

*Numbers refer to the cases as they are listed in the table of contents.

Chart I.

have a different meaning at the time a case occurs as compared with five years later, and how surprising is "highly" surprising? As the case research of the future progresses, the question of the normal or typical will need more careful definition.

So far in case research, it seems clear that the cases tend to typify the unusual more than the usual. This is true of most of the cases in the present collection. A minority of the cases in this book, for example, deal with problems that were handled in a routine way. It is also true that a minority of the cases deal with decisions in which the administrators were highly effective. Undoubtedly there is some significance to the fact that many of the cases deal with situations that were highly charged with emotion.

The limitations in sampling undoubtedly relate to the fact that the unusual is much more likely to be noticed than the usual. Consequently, data are much more likely to accumulate, and, in many cases, such data are more easily gathered. Personnel are not very interested in or concerned about routine problems. They do not remember details about the commonplace, and they are not motivated to talk or write about the routine. Thus, evidence about routine matters is usually scanty. On the other hand, a great deal of information is frequently available about problems that are unusual or that arouse strong emotional feelings. There is much available information, for example, about personnel problems that has been collected by ethics commissions of state and local teachers' organizations throughout the country. Such material makes the headlines of papers and provides potential case-writers with data. It is understandable, then, that unusual situations are more likely to find their way into written cases than are the usual.

In the long run and from a scientific standpoint, it would be desirable to obtain cases that represent routine as well as cases that represent unusual situations. In the meantime, there is value, from an instructional point of view, in using unusual cases. In the first place, students show greater interest in examining and analyzing the unusual than the routine. Second, the unusual frequently involves situations that make much greater demands on the administrator than do routine situations and, therefore, represent problems that potential or actual administrators can carefully examine with profit.

Case perspectives. A "perspective" may be defined as "that which determines what one looks for and what one sees in a potential case." (2, p.2) That persons may see and report quite different things about a case is suggested by the following description by A. Averchenko:

POINT OF VIEW[1]

"Men are comic!" she said, smiling dreamily. Not knowing whether this indicated praise or blame, I answered noncommittally: "Quite true."

"Really, my husband's a regular Othello. Sometimes I'm sorry I married him."

I looked helplessly at her. "Until you explain—" I began.

"Oh, I forgot that you haven't heard. About three weeks ago I was walking home with my husband through the square. I had a large black hat on, which suits me awfully well and my cheeks were quite pink from walking. As we passed under a street light, a pale, dark-haired fellow standing near by glanced at me and suddenly took my husband by his sleeve.

" 'Would you oblige me with a light?' he says. Alexander pulled his arm away, stooped down, and quicker than lightning banged him on the head with a brick. He fell like a log. Awful."

"Why, what on earth made your husband get jealous all of a sudden?"

She shrugged her shoulders. "I told you men are very comic."

Bidding her farewell, I went out, and at the corner came across her husband.

"Hello, old chap," I said. "They tell me you've been breaking people's heads."

He burst out laughing. "So you've been talking to my wife. It was jolly lucky that brick came so pat into my hand. Otherwise, just think; I had about fifteen hundred rubles in my pocket, and my wife was wearing her diamond earrings."

"Do you think he wanted to rob you?"

"A man accosts you in a deserted spot, asks for a light and gets hold of your arm. What more do you want?"

Perplexed, I left him and walked on.

"There's no catching you today," I heard a voice say from behind.

I looked around and saw a friend I hadn't set eyes upon for three weeks.

"Lord!" I exclaimed. "What on earth has happened to you?"

He smiled faintly and asked in turn, "Do you know whether any

[1] Reprinted from THIS WEEK Magazine. Copyright 1947 by the United Newspapers Magazine Corporation.

lunatics have been at large lately? I was attacked by one three weeks ago. I left the hospital only today."

With sudden interest, I asked: "Three weeks ago! Were you sitting in the square?"

"Yes, I was. The most absurd thing. I was sitting in the square dying for a smoke. No matches! After ten minutes or so, a gentleman passes with some old hag. He was smoking. I go up to him, touch him on the sleeve and ask in my most polite manner: 'Can you oblige me with a light?' And what d'you think? The madman stoops down, picks something up, and the next moment I am lying on the ground with a broken head, unconscious. You probably read about it in the newspaper."

I looked at him, and asked earnestly: "Do you really believe you met up with a lunatic?"

"I am sure of it."

An hour afterwards I was eagerly digging in old back numbers of the local paper. At last I found what I was looking for: a short note in the accident column:

UNDER THE INFLUENCE OF DRINK

Yesterday morning the keepers of the square found on a bench a young man whose papers show him to be of good family. He had evidently fallen to the ground while in a state of extreme intoxication, and had broken his head on a nearby brick. The distress of this prodigal's parents is indescribable.

Detached or personal perspective? The above statement demonstrates quite clearly, even if in an exaggerated fashion, the difficulty in making reliable observations and in reporting them accurately. One of the reasons for differences in point of view evident in "Point of View" undoubtedly arose from differences in interests, attitudes, and motivations of those reporting. This statement is further illustrated by the multiple-perspective case in this book entitled "A Coin Has Two Sides," where the administrator's point of view was quite different from that of the teacher's even when both were viewing the same events. It is also evident from the case that their motivations, attitudes, and concerns were quite different.

With some exceptions, cases in the past have been written by persons who were not active participants in the case. This book includes a number of cases that were written by important case participants, namely, the administrators. The cases numbered 3, 4, 5, 6, 7, and 13 fall into the category of autobiographical cases. Undoubt-

edly there is value in examining cases of this kind as a supplement
to cases written by more detached observers. Such cases reflect the
administrator's perceptions and, conceivably, can give even a better
basis for understanding administrative behavior than one written
with a more detached view. In addition, the administrator is at a
key point in the communication system and is likely to have as much
immediate information as, if not more than, other participants in
the case. Since interests and motivations inevitably are reflected in
case reports, a series of autobiographical cases could provide a basis
for developing hypotheses about aspects of the administrator's perceptions. Such hypotheses would, of course, have to be tested through
appropriate scientific procedures.

Broad or focused perspective? Another factor that influences
a case-writer's perspective is the field of study in which he is writing
cases. This point can be illustrated by examining cases in fields other
than school administration. Although case-writers have been somewhat experimental, both in public and business administration, they
nevertheless have been guided generally by different perspectives.
The cases about public administration have had a broader perspective
than those dealing with business administration in the sense that
they have encompassed more historical information and have focused
more upon events outside the organization. This broader perspective
undoubtedly stems at least partially from the fact that administrators
in public organizations are working in a service agency responsible to
the people and are much more dependent upon the people for the
determination of policy than are executives in business organizations.
Thus, business cases are generally shorter and the problems are more
limited in scope than those dealing with public administration. In
general, a broad perspective that is sensitive to historical and environmental factors seems more appropriate for case-writers dealing
with school administration. This conclusion is no doubt related to
the fact that there is greater similarity between public and school
administration than there is between business and school administration. Thus, the following definition of a public administration case
would seem to be one very appropriate model for cases in school
administration (18, p. 480):

> . . . a detailed narrative of the events that constitute a decision
> or group of related decisions by an administrator or administrative
> group, together with some description of the social, economic, legal,

political, personal and other factors that surrounded, or were in a position to affect the administrator or administrative group during the process of arriving at a decision.

Implicit or explicit perspectives? If a case-writer clearly states or can state the concepts that guide his data-gathering procedures, then the perspective is explicit. If he is unaware or only vaguely aware of what causes him to select one type of information instead of another type, then his perspective is implicit. In the beginning of a relatively new area of investigation, the perspectives for case-writing even when explicit are often general in nature. Cunningham (5), for example, made five case studies of school-board deliberations, and his data-gathering was guided by a policy-development perspective. O'Donahue (13) selected a similar approach in studying the actions of a teachers' organization, in that he used a decision-making perspective. After the cases were written, both O'Donahue and Cunningham formulated a number of specific hypotheses about the perspectives they had chosen.

The case studies of Tilden (20) illustrate a different degree of explicitness in the use of theoretical perspectives. Instead of taking a general perspective, he took specific hypotheses formulated by Selznick and used them as guides to data-gathering. As one example, he tested Selznick's generalization that an organization, when threatened by internal or external forces, will adapt to the threat by formally or informally co-opting the opposing persons (15). He carefully gathered data on three cases in order to find evidence concerning the accuracy of Selznick's generalizations.

If a case is to be scientifically oriented, the perspective during the data-gathering process must necessarily be relatively explicit. This gives other researchers an opportunity to evaluate the adequacy and the appropriateness of the persepective and to examine the data in relationship to it. If the case-researcher is concerned only about immediate instructional purposes, he may choose not to reveal the concepts that guided his data-gathering in the written presentation. Or, if he does reveal them, these will be written as commentary that is clearly separated from the narrative, as is exemplified in various cases in the Stein (19) collection.

Types of perspectives. If it is important for scientific purposes that case-preparers make their perspectives explicit, then it is important to define possible types of case perspectives. A number of alternatives can be suggested, and the different types that follow are not mutually exclusive. As a matter of fact, it might be advisable to use a combination of the perspectives in preparing some cases.[2]

One way of handling human events is to reconstruct their temporal sequence. Such an approach would view a case as a chronological series of actions and events, and the perspective might be described as *historical*. To a greater or less extent, such a perspective is frequently used in case preparation. As an example, assume that Superintendent X in District Y, after considerable turmoil in the school system, lost his position. A case-preparer using an *historical* framework would seek out the events that led up to the superintendent's dismissal. Since the case-preparer cannot obtain a complete chronology of events, he needs other bases of selection. One alternative is for the case-preparer to discover those events that are related to and that give meaning to the climax of a case. In the illustration above, for example, the case-preparer would winnow out the series of events that shed light upon Superintendent X's discharge. A careful report of such events, as well as a recording of the attitudes that people held toward them, would be useful to students of administration. In general, most of the relevant events in such a case would occur near the critical action (that is, Superintendent X's discharge). Experience with cases in public administration shows that understanding is not significantly sharpened by extending the chronology in a detailed way into the past and future. However, pertinent facts may be briefly treated in an "Introduction" or "Aftermath" (9). These are usually best written when the case proper is near final form.

Another perspective that has been used frequently in case preparation might be described as a *problem* framework. In this approach, the focus is upon a situation that demands a solution or decision from the administrator. Sometimes the problem situation may involve a dramatic episode, such as the strike in Case Two, "The Rock and Roll Ruckus." Typically, the problem is one in which the administrator is faced with conflicting demands which, in some way, must be resolved. Facts are gathered by the case-preparer to illuminate the choice alternatives.

This type of perspective has been used frequently by those preparing cases in business administration. Often the written reports

---

[2] Some of the perspectives discussed in this chapter have already been developed elsewhere (4).

of cases developed through such a perspective are open-ended in the sense that they stop at the point where the administrator is to take action. This type of ending is illustrated to some extent in Case Four, "The Sword of Damocles," where Superintendent Kennedy is faced with a choice about what to include and what not to include in a letter of recommendation. In using such a case, the purpose typically pursued by an instructor is to get students to project themselves into the case situation and to take responsibility for making the decision. Such a perspective generally focuses more upon individual than upon group and organizational aspects of choice.

A third kind of perspective is the *thematic* framework. This approach is one that selects a central theme or motif that serves as a guide for data-gathering. It goes without saying that the theme should not express a particular bias. For example, if a potential case deals with efforts to eliminate textbooks from the school system because they allegedly were written by members of communist-front organizations, the motif might be the struggle to censor ideas. In such a case, facts would be gathered from all sides to illuminate the administrative behavior and the events pertinent to the theme. This framework could be used in connection with the *historical* approach as an aid in selecting relevant actions and events. Case One, "The Valley City Consolidation Issue," illustrates case preparation in which the author apparently tried to illuminate the theme of district reorganization.

The *process* framework is another kind of case perspective. This perspective is broad in scope and focuses upon such general administrative processes as communication or decision-making. It has been used most by those preparing cases in the field of public administration. The Stein collection (19), for example, was largely developed within a policy-development or decision-making framework. In contrast to the *problem* perspective, which focuses on the individual aspects of choice, decision-making within a *process* perspective focuses more broadly upon various groups and individuals interacting with one another to reach some conclusion. A case written from such a perspective is one that, instruction-wise, can be used for developing diagnostic skills. Students can be encouraged to analyze and to comprehend the various factors that influence the setting in which administrators function. Specific questions related to the decision-making process have been set forth elsewhere as possible guides for case-preparers (4). The communication process affords another example of a *process* perspective. The data for Case Seventeen, "Changing the Curriculum at Southside," were gathered by focusing on the communication processes in the Southside School.

A final perspective of note is the *causal* framework. Such a framework is one that concentrates on cause-and-effect relationships in administration. Such relationship can be expressed in terms of specific hypotheses, related to such things as the effects of administrative behavior or the causes of organizational change. Selznick (15), for example, has formulated some theory related to change in an organization.

An organization behaves, according to Selznick's theory, to preserve and to defend itself. This behavior is expressed rationally and consciously through its formal process as well as irrationally and unconsciously through its informal and institutional processes. Thus, the theory conceives of an organization essentially as a powerful defensive organism, and a pessimistic view emerges about the potentiality of leaders in effecting planned change. It can be hypothesized that the theory is generally relevant for shedding light on cases in which an organization must defend itself from either internal or external threat, but is less adequate for dealing with cases where leaders effect constructive and guided change. Such an hypothesis could serve as a guide in data-gathering and would be illustrative of a *causal* perspective. By gathering data on a number of cases involving change, it would be possible to test the hypothesis. With enough carefully developed cases, the hypotheses could be proven, revised, or discarded.

The *causal* perspective is highly desirable from a research standpoint in that the discovery, confirmation, or disproof of hypotheses is central to the work of science. The use of such a perspective could provide leads for more controlled studies and could also encourage the development of more systematic administrative theory. The danger of a strong scientific emphasis in data-gathering is that the written report will be too structured. From an instructional standpoint, sharply structured presentations can limit the possible meanings that students can derive from case discussions. Since the nature of science is to delimit and to define, one runs the risk of oversimplifying the complex and interrelated variables that make up the administrative setting. Thus, case development in the future, particularly for instructional purposes, will need to steer a course between the danger of overly prescribed perspectives, on the one hand, and the complete lack of explicit perspectives on the other. Such a policy should provide one basis for advancing knowledge about administration and for encouraging critical and comprehensive thinking about administration by students and teachers of administration.

In summary, then, what one looks for and what one sees in human events are always determined by a perspective, either implicit or explicit. Since the work of science is to make knowledge public, this means that researchers who use scientific procedures in case development will need to clarify the nature of the perspective that they use for gathering data. In presenting the data in written form for discussion, however, a certain open-endedness is desirable. Open-endedness will enable the student to examine the case from perspectives other than that of the case-preparer.

Since case-writing is in its infancy, writers should be cautious about accepting ready-made perspectives. If one of the five perspectives set forth above should fit the purposes of the case-preparer, well and good. If not, another perspective is indicated. Although the perspectives elaborated above can be useful as guide lines in case preparation, they are not designed to limit a case-preparer.[3]

Literary Aspects of Case Development

Although there is some overlapping between data-gathering and case-writing, the operations are different and, for analytical purposes, can be considered separately. It is clearly evident that the competencies involved in data-gathering are different from those involved in case-writing. The quality of the writing is crucial in determining whether or not a vicarious experience is communicated to the case reader.

[3] Specific techniques for gathering data are not considered here. Undoubtedly such techniques are similar to those of other types of research, and the general problem has already been treated widely (11). Imaginative use of the multiple or repeated interview is judged to be the most promising technique for gathering data, according to the experience of case-writers in public administration (6). According to some sources, written autobiographical material by the case participants is superior for communicating the "personal feel" of the administrative situation. For references that deal with the problem of how the researcher can gain rapport in functioning organizations, see Jacobson, et al. (10), Mann and Lippitt (12), Argyris (1), and Hines and Grobman (8).

What type of writing is appropriate for cases? The question may be answered generally by saying that the style of the reporter or journalist is fitting. This means a style that expresses ideas clearly, interestingly, and objectively. Each of these attributes needs further discussion.

Objectivity in case-writing. Objective reporting is important not only to assure an authentic presentation in general, but also to ensure a fair portrayal of the case participants.

Several techniques can be suggested to increase the objectivity of case-writing. One way is to write so that the reader knows the source of the data. For example, one should write: "The principal thought that the superintendent had good relationships with the teachers," and not "The superintendent had good relationships with the teachers." Direct quotations either from documents or from interviews also can be used to increase objectivity.

Another technique is to guard against bias that might cause a more sympathetic treatment of some members of a case than of others. For example, if a writer has unconscious prejudices toward authority figures, this may mean that he will have a greater sympathy for teachers than for administrators. This prejudice could be reflected in a case through his depicting an administrator's actions less favorably than the teachers' behavior. Objectivity will be increased if everyone in the case has his actions and perceptions accurately presented.

Still another technique for making a case more objective is to "clear" the written record with the chief participants in the case. This means that the case is returned to the chief participants and they are asked to make corrections or to offer additional information. If the different participants can agree on the accuracy of the report without making special demands on the writer, this ensures objectivity. On some occasions, minor changes are necessary for clearance. This may take the form of changing names and places or of disguising unimportant information. Sometimes it is necessary to abbreviate or summarize information. If drastic changes are demanded that interfere with the objectivity of the case as a whole, then it is generally best to drop the project. Such unpleasant situations can usually be avoided if the possibility of getting the case cleared is carefully assessed in the beginning.

In general, case-writers in business administration have disguised the situations and participants in cases. One method of disguise, for example, is to multiply all the figures to be included in the case by a constant number, such as 1.4. The general policy of disguising names and places has also guided the collection of cases dealing with school administration, as can be seen in such collections as Griffiths' (7), Sargent and Belisle's (14), as well as the cases in this book. Case-preparers in public administration, on the other hand, have followed the general policy of publishing cases with the actual names of persons and places. Although they have been able to follow this policy with considerable success, it is well to note that a large number of the cases in the Stein collection (19) involve Federal situations in which the participants are more accustomed to interviews, investigations, and published reports than are administrators in local school systems. There is also a danger, when the writer plans to present a case for clearance, that he will be strongly motivated to include what he thinks will satisfy the participants and thereby interfere with the objectivity of the report in general.

Another problem in achieving objectivity relates to the emotional tone of the language used. In general, the case-writer needs to steer a course between using language that makes for dull reporting and using language that incites strong emotions. For example, adjectives should be used sparingly and judiciously so as not to arouse predispositions and emotions in the reader. The writer's report will be more adequate if he includes a factual description of what is meant than if he labels a person or a situation with a value-laden adjective. For example, for the case-writer to report that a principal was "poorly prepared professionally" is something different from saying that the principal "had spent one quarter in summer school beyond the bachelor's degree." Such a distinction would not apply to quotations, because the sources would be evident and could be evaluated by the case readers.

Clarity in case-writing. A number of suggestions can be made to enhance the clarity of a case presentation. Some of these suggestions are also related to making a case more objective. As in other kinds of writing, an outline can be useful in the early stages of writing. In this connection, some writers develop a chronology of events. Such a record is especially appropriate if there are several concurrent threads to be presented and if the research is guided by a historical perspective. It has also been suggested that in complex cases a chronology of events may be included in the appendix (9). Such an outline can makes the series of actions clearer to the reader.

Another problem in achieving clarity is one of focus. The aim in writing a case should be to tell the story from a consistent point of view, and this is one advantage of autobiographical accounts, as can be witnessed in Case Four, "The Sword of Damocles." The problem is relatively easy if most of the actions in a case move around a given individual. If many groups and individuals are involved, it is much more difficult to present the whole picture from a given focus. One should definitely avoid jumping from camp to camp without relating the happenings in these camps to a central locale or center of action. In this regard Garceau writes about the cases in public administration: "The ones that are hard to read seem to be ones where the focus was not established in the writer's mind" (6, p. 23).

Perhaps this point can be illustrated by referring to Case One, "The Valley City Consolidation Issue." The case involved various individuals and groups. There were Galloway, Benson, Meyer, Arthur, Golden, and Duke, among others. There were also the Grange, the Chamber of Commerce, the Valley Teachers' Association, the PTA, and the Rural Unionization Committee. How to give narrative focus to a case involving so many participants was no doubt a problem to the case-writer. It is apparent that the chronology of events and the theme of district reorganization were two guides that helped to give order to the case. However, in telling the story, there was frequent shifting from one scene of action to another. In such complex cases, much skill is needed to accomplish what the novelist does when he unfolds a story through the eyes of a single observer. Such difficulty undoubtedly accounts for the fact that there is often a shift of focus in presenting highly complex case materials.

Still another technique for making cases clear is to include not only a record of the events but also the ways in which participants in the case perceived the events. In reading cases, one is frequently left with the feeling that he does not know enough about the participants in the case. In this regard, Garceau (6, p. 7) has written of the cases developed by the Inter-University Case Program: "Perhaps the distinguishing character of these cases lies in the fact that we never learn enough about individual careers, personal frames of reference, aspirations and rationalizations to attribute convincingly any independent role to them." He suggests that more "psycho-biographical" material is needed for picturing clearly both the thoughts and the deeds of administrative experience. Although such data are not always easy to obtain, they add an extra dimension to a case. Examples of psycho-biographical material are found in Case Six, "A Coin Has Two Sides," and in Case Fourteen, "The Case of a Tenacious Superintendent."

Another technique for clarifying as well as for provoking thought is the use of commentary by the case-writer. Such commentary should be clearly separated from the case. The usual practice is to place it at the beginning or at the end of a case. Bauer (3) reports that there is an increasing tendency to include case commentary. The practice is most notable in those cases prepared by the Inter-University Program in public administration (19). The purpose is to point up some basic issues or questions for students to consider. Several cases in this book contain brief commentaries. They are not designed to circumscribe case discussion, however.

Writing to gain the reader's interest. Several leads for making a case more interesting can be suggested. Experience indicates that biographical and psycho-biographical materials not only make for a clearer presentation as noted above, but also add interest to a case. The reader is helped to become more personally involved. He has an opportunity to examine thoughts and feelings and tends to identify himself with or to reject participants in a case. For example, the biographical data about Galloway and Benson in Case One, "The Valley City Consolidation Issue," add interest and meaning to the story. The background of the actors in a case is certainly as important as the background of the situation for providing a basis for understanding administrative behavior. The judicious use of conversation, when it accurately represents interpersonal interaction, can also hold the reader's interest.

Another technique is to unfold the total story so that there is a sense of drama. Although the drama of a case is largely dependent upon its nature, the treatment and organization of the events in the case can make it more or less dramatic. The environment can be presented and the events arranged so that the conflicts and tensions of the situation are made clear. An air of impending decision may be conveyed to the reader so that he is motivated to read and to learn the outcomes of a case. For example, the writer of Case Four,

"The Sword of Damocles," communicates a sense of drama to the reader. "Is the rumor about White really true?" is a question that comes to the reader's mind early in the case. Later on, another question enters the reader's mind, namely, "What will happen to White?" Throughout much of the case, there is an air of impending decision and conflict that creates reader interest. Needless to say, drama in case-writing should not be achieved at the expense of a fair presentation of the facts.

One issue related to reader interest is the length of the case. Cases in business administration have often been brief, sometimes three pages or less. Some of the public administration cases in the Stein collection (19) have been very long. The case, "The Sale of the Tankers," for example, is over 100 pages in length. Experience has caused some persons to question the appropriateness of such long cases. It is more difficult to sustain the interest of the reader in a long case, and it is difficult to explore carefully such a case in discussion. The more recent cases in public administration reflect a trend toward somewhat shorter cases (16). To be sure, length will be largely determined by the nature of the case and the purpose for which it is used.

One technique for creating interest, particularly in the discussion of a case, is to end it at a point where a crucial decision must be made by the administrator. Case Fourteen, "The Case of a Tenacious Superintendent," which ends at a point where Superintendent Ash is faced with a decision to resign or to "fight" the school board, is an example of an abortive case ending. In such a case, the reader is encouraged to project himself into the choice situation and to assume the responsibility for action as if he were Ash.

Although such an open-ended model for case-writing promotes student interest and motivation, it also contains certain disadvantages. For one thing, the reader of such cases is not able to see the situation as a whole. He cannot do a thorough job of diagnosing the effects of administrative behavior, because the effects of such behavior in crucial situations are not reported. In addition, such cases are not appropriate for those who are interested in cases as research in that abortive cases provide an inadequate basis for formulating hypotheses or for generalizing about administrative behavior. For advancing general knowledge about administration, relatively complete reports of cases are needed. Herein lies the main weakness of the abortive case.

❀   ❀   ❀

The idea of using cases for teaching law students originated more than three-fourths of a century ago (17). Since that time, the case method of teaching has grown slowly and steadily. Undoubtedly this approach to instruction will continue to grow and will contribute much to educating administrators in the years ahead.

Myriads of unwritten cases about school administration offer instructional possibilities. An important first step in encouraging case-method teaching is to change a sufficient number of the unwritten cases into written ones. Therein lies a great challenge to students and teachers of school administration.

References

1. Argyris, Chris, "Creating Effective Research Relationships in Organization," *Human Organization*, Vol. 17, Spring, 1958, pp. 34–40.
2. Averchenko, A., "Point of View," *This Week Magazine*, August 16, 1947, p. 2.
3. Bauer, Ronald, *Cases in College Administration*. New York: Teachers College, Columbia University, 1955.
4. Culbertson, Jack, "The Case for Cases in the Study of Administration," *Educational Administration and Supervision*, Vol. 42, No. 7, 1956, pp. 420–427.
5. Cunningham, Luvern, *A Community Develops Educational Policy: A Case Study*. Unpublished doctoral dissertation, University of Oregon, 1958.
6. Garceau, Oliver, "Ten Years of Cases: An Appraisal." Mimeographed, East Boothbay, Maine, March 3, 1955, 38 pp.
7. Griffiths, Daniel, *Human Relations In School Administration*. New York: Appleton-Century-Crofts, Inc., 1956.
8. Hines, Vynce, and Hulda Grobman, "Rapport in Field Research," *Educational Administration and Supervision*, Vol. 42, No. 7, 1956, pp. 403–411.
9. Inter-University Case Program, "Suggestions for Case Writers." Mimeographed, 1953, 6 pp.
10. Jacobson, Eugene, *et al.*, "Research in Functioning Organizations," *Journal of Social Issues*, Vol. 7, No. 3, 1951, pp. 64–71.
11. Kahn, Robert, and Charles Connell, *The Dynamics of Interviewing*. New York: John Wiley and Sons, Inc., 1957.
12. Mann, Floyd, and Ronald Lippitt, "Social Relations Skills in Field Research," *Journal of Social Issues*, Vol. 8, No. 3, 1952, pp. 2–56.

13. O'Donahue, John, *The Green River Teachers' Association: A Case Study of the Decision-Making Process*. Unpublished doctoral dissertation, University of Oregon, 1957.

14. Sargent, Cyril, and Eugene Belisle, *Educational Administration: Cases and Concepts*. Cambridge: Harvard University Press, 1955.

15. Selznick, Philip, "Foundations of the Theory of Organization," *American Sociological Review*, Vol. 13, February, 1948, pp. 25–35.

16. Somers, Herman, "The Case Study Program: Where Do We Go From Here?" *Public Administration Review*, Vol. 25, No. 2, Spring, 1955, pp. 115–120.

17. Sperle, Henryetta, *The Case Method Technique in Professional Training*. New York: Teachers College, Columbia University, 1933.

18. Stein, Harold, "Preparation of Case Studies: The Problem of Abundance," *The American Political Science Review*, Vol. XLV, No. 2, 1951, pp. 479–487.

19. Stein, Harold, *Public Administration and Policy Development: A Case Book*. New York: Harcourt, Brace and Company, Inc., 1952.

20. Tilden, Charles, *Administrative Adaptation to Social Forces*. Unpublished doctoral dissertation, Stanford University, 1952.

CHAPTER THREE

Case-Method Teaching

Rather, the case book asks the teacher to take on the task of building some basic attitudes traditionally associated with a liberal education.

E. S. WENGERT

The old saw that there is nothing new under the sun applies in one sense to case-method teaching. If one recalls, for example, the context in which the story of the Prodigal Son or the Good Samaritan arose, it is evident that the Greatest of all teachers sought to develop understandings about ethical problems through stories that were close to actual experience. The various fables that have deep roots in many cultures also have been used for instructional purposes. Thus, the basic idea of case-method teaching is deeply rooted in educational history.

There are relatively new aspects of the method, however. For one thing, researchers more recently have developed cases that give a more careful and a more accurate picture of real persons, events, and situations. In addition, the last three-quarters of a century has seen a much more systematic and intensive use of the method in colleges and universities. Originating in the Harvard Law School, the method has spread to undergraduate courses and from one subject-matter field to many subject-matter fields (24). In many courses today, cases are the central content. Such developments have led to explicit statements about the assumptions that underlie the method. In addition, instructional techniques have been more carefully refined. In the last three decades especially, the method has had increased use in the fields of school, public, and business administration. At present the method shows continued promise in these fields, and there is an increasing interest in its use.

Why is this true? The purpose of the discussion immediately following is to describe briefly some of the factors associated with the increasing interest in case-method teaching. In treating the problem, the discussion will be limited principally to case-method use in programs for training school administrators. Many of the statements, however, will undoubtedly apply to other administrative fields.

Increasing Interest in Case-Method Teaching

The changing goals of training programs. In the 1950's especially, there has been a conscious swing away from the single and more limited goal of making subject-matter specialists out of potential administrators. At the same time, there has been a swing toward the broader goal of developing educational leaders. The statement (22) by the National Conference of Professors of Educational Administration in 1951 on the improvement of educational leaders was an early landmark in this development. The activities of the Cooperative Project in Educational Administration and, more recently, of the University Council on Educational Administration also reflect this changing emphasis. It is becoming ever clearer that there is a yawning gulf between teaching students *about administration* and teaching them *to administer*. To teach students how our population is distributed among the various socioeconomic classes, for example, and to teach them how to show leadership in providing adequate educational opportunities for the various classes are two distinctly different matters. The following limerick illustrates the point:[1]

> A student of administration with tact
> Learned all the answers he lacked
> But acquiring a job,
> He said with a sob
> How do you fit answers to fact?

The recognition, then, that knowing is not the same as doing forms the basic underpinning for the more inclusive goals of training programs today. A re-examination of goals also means a re-examination of methods. Can methods that are appropriate for imparting information also be appropriate for developing responsible leadership? On the assumption that the answer is negative, various insti-

[1] The limerick is adapted from a statement of Charles Gragg (16, p. 8).

tutions are experimenting with different methods for developing leadership, and among these methods is the case approach. Langdell, its modern-day originator, judged that it would develop leadership skills closely related to "on-the-job" behaviors (22, p. 251). Many believe that its successful record has supported his judgment.

Relating theory to action. The statement that courses in administration are too theoretical is a trite expression in some student circles. What does this statement mean? Perhaps its real meaning is that appropriate methods for relating theory and action, ideas and behavior, have not always been used in educational programs.

Such a conclusion does not indicate that theory should be decried, and even less that it should be eliminated from training programs. Rather, it means that methods must be sought that can better link the abstract to the concrete, so that a more useful and meaningful relationship can be forged between the two. What could be more appropriate for this task than a method that seeks to wed the specific and the general, as case descriptions of real situations become both a springboard and a testing ground for understandings and insights. The case method's unique capacity for uniting theory and action no doubt helps to explain the increasing interest in this approach to learning and teaching.

The case method and modern learning theory. Under what conditions is learning most effective? Although such a question cannot be answered here completely, a few of the important generalizations about learning and their relationship to the case method can be made clear. One principle, for example, is that learning takes place through meaningful experience. The case method meets this criterion to a very high degree, in that it starts with content from experience in the form of cases. Discussing a case—for example, where the issue is whether or not to give tenure to a probationary teacher—starts with a real problem. Group efforts to solve such problems gives the process a high degree of meaning. Such content helps to generate a discussion process that is grounded in experience and, in turn, produces experience. Students who have participated in the case method at the University of Oregon have consistently stated in anonymous questionnaires that the method's main value lies in the fact that the content has maximum meaning.

Two other important concepts associated with modern learning theories are psychological involvement and self-direction of learning.

Wrestling with actual problems makes for intense psychological involvement in that students typically project themselves into the situations studied and frequently identify themselves with persons in the case. In addition, the method places a major responsibility on the student in that he is expected to analyze the problems and contribute to the solution. This promotes the self-direction of student thinking and understanding. Psychological involvement, coupled with the experience content of cases, no doubt accounts for the high degree of student interest and motivation that is almost universally reported by those who have used cases.

Modern research on the learning process indicates that transfer takes place when students perceive similarities between one situation and another. For this reason it can be predicted that the amount of transfer of learning could be much greater in the case method than in many other forms of teaching. In other words, a study of actual experience through cases should develop perceptions that would have meaning in future administrative situations.

The case method and inter-disciplinary approaches. A widely recognized trend in the social sciences today is the rapprochement of the various social science disciplines. This is evidenced, for example, in the team approach to research problems. The co-ordinated, inter-disciplinary approach to teaching, where resource persons with different training backgrounds attack problems in a united way, is another expression of the same trend. Thus, it would seem that in some ways the walls of the different disciplines are being lowered, and at points there is mutual illumination. Such concepts as role, status, perception, communication, and leadership have infiltrated various disciplines and are on the way to becoming core concepts common to the social sciences.

Such concepts, to some extent, provide interconnecting links between and among the disciplines. However, it is a well-known fact that there are still serious problems of inter-disciplinary communication. These arise not only between the social scientists and practitioners of administration, but among social scientists themselves. Since teams of social scientists are taking part in training school administrators in a number of institutions today, the problem is one that deserves consideration. It is at this point that the case method has particular significance. It is significant in that it can serve as an important medium and focus of communication for students and teachers with different backgrounds. It offers itself as a facilitator of communication, as a focus for the meeting of minds, as a medium for the improvement of understanding among persons with different orientations and backgrounds. It does this when there is an obvious need for such a technique. This is, no doubt, another factor associated with the expanding interest in the case method of instruction.

An expanding view of administration. Another significant trend in the training of administrators today is the expanding concept of administration. A new content has been added, and, as Griffiths (17, p. 7) has suggested, this "new content is people." The early and more traditional focus was on the specifics of procedures and law and the more technical aspects of administration. Such a view neglected such subjects as administrative behavior, human relations, and social interaction. This limited view, no doubt, has sometimes tended toward facile answers, loaded questions, and inadequate generalizations about administration.

When human behavior, with its many manifestations and subtle nuances, is conceived as a part of the content of administration, formulating administrative principles becomes much less easy. And yet it seems inevitable that the new content is here to stay. What problem in administration is so technical that it does not in some way impinge upon people? Since a case seeks to capture the administrative situation as a whole and thereby to encompass the content of administration in terms of its broader and more modern meaning, it cannot help but convey human-technical relationships. Perhaps a case is one of the few vehicles that can go a long way toward capturing these relationships. This is another reason why the case method has particular relevance in the training of school administrators today.

In summary, it can be said that various events and forces have thrown a spotlight on the case method of teaching. Its capacity for uniting fact and theory suggests that it is a very appropriate approach to training administrators. This conclusion is further warranted by the technique's grounding in modern learning theory and its relationship to the changing goals of training programs. It also fits in with recent inter-disciplinary trends and the expanded view of administrative content that includes technical and human factors. Finally, the method has stood the test of time and has served as an instructional method in many areas of study.

Course Organization and the Case Method

There are various questions about how cases should fit into programs for educating school administrators. These questions relate to such matters as the size and composition of classes, and the time and place in a program where cases can be used to greatest advantage. In organizing the material for this section, as well as for the remaining sections of the chapter, the aim is to summarize the experiences and ideas that users of cases have had in general. The ideas will be presented as they relate to specific problems faced by those contemplating the use of the method.

At what stage should cases be used? Should students be exposed to cases early, later, or throughout their program of study? Experience suggests that students can profit from the study of cases at both the undergraduate and the graduate level of instruction. However, cases serve a somewhat different function for students who have had administrative experience as contrasted with those who are lacking in experience. Reining (25, pp. 63–64), a teacher of public administration, has this to say about the problem: ". . . I discovered some time ago that, pedagogically speaking, one has really two different problems with those groups. The undergraduate needs to be given a sense of reality. He needs to be given these case materials as a sort of vicarious experience. The graduate student, on the other hand, and particularly the man who has had experience, knows that also he needs even more a frame of reference or a body of organized thinking—a terminology which he can then use to identify and organize his own experience." Experience with case teaching at the University of Oregon gives general support to this statement. For those who have had some administrative experience and have also had advanced general training in social science concepts, the method is an excellent stimulant for further development of conceptual viewpoints and understandings. Cases also serve a valuable function with students who are beginning the study of administration, particularly in providing a feeling for what school administration actually is and in motivating students to pursue specific questions and problems.

How large should classes be? How many students should there be in a class devoted to the case method? It is widely assumed that case-method classes should be relatively small—for example, 25 persons or less. There are others who take exception to this rule. The late Irving Lee (20, p. 4), for example, spoke of his own experience thus: "Size and composition of the group are not significant factors. The numbers may range from 5 to 150." Instructors in the Harvard Graduate School of Business Administration have also utilized cases in classes of 100 students. This suggests, then, that although some instructors believe that small classes are more desirable, cases can be used with larger classes. There are other important factors related to size, such as the amount of experience an instructor has had in the method and the specific goals that he is seeking to achieve. No doubt it would be easier to begin the use of the method in smaller classes. Also, the opportunity for *verbal* participation among students is greater in smaller classes.

What about the composition of classes? Should students in case-method classes be fairly homogeneous in experience and training, or should there be a wide diversity in background? Evidence is not available for a clear-cut answer to this question. It seems desirable in advanced classes for most students to have similar levels of academic training and administrative experience. At the same time, there are advantages in having a few teachers in a class who have had no experience as administrators, because they are able to express the teacher's point of view. In turn, they have the opportunity of hearing ideas from those who are administratively oriented. In addition, teachers in introductory courses who are aspiring to be administrators will profit from examining the points of view of administrators and other school specialists. Such an arrangement can also help a class develop insight about teacher-administrator relationships.

At what points in the curriculum should cases be used? There are various places to include cases in a curriculum, and a number of the alternatives will now be set forth. Those who use the technique should consider the possibilities that follow relative to their own interests, inclinations, values, programs, and the cases available. Some of the suggested alternatives are such that the case method could become a central core of courses and even a major part of an instructional program. In other alternatives, the technique is an incidental and supplementary aspect of administrative training. The latter alternatives are offered because of limitations arising from existing course structures or certification regulations. The discussion will move from the more incidental to the more central uses of the case.[2]

One use of the case is as illustrative material in lectures by the instructor. This is a way of relating generalizations and concepts to something concrete. The use of cases based on experience rather than on careful research has been employed from time immemorial. More carefully documented cases should enable the instructor to do an even more meaningful job of illustrating ideas that he seeks to communicate. Some case users might find this approach more appropriate in classes of undergraduates or in classes where students have had no administrative experience—at least no experience with the topic under consideration.

Many case users would oppose the idea of using cases for illustrative purposes. They would argue that such use is basically opposed to the philosophy of the method, especially as it has been developed and expressed by members of the Graduate School of Business Administration at Harvard University. They would say that it is the student's responsibility to develop his own meanings about ideas related to the case, and that a teacher who tries to impose his own ideas may do more harm than good. Therefore, it is well to note that a minority of case users would use cases for illustrative purposes in lecture material.

Some instructors use the case method only in the sense that they have students study cases to supplement other reading material. For example, if a class were studying school district organization, the students might be asked to read the case called "The Valley City Consolidation Issue." This case would furnish a concrete example of various aspects of district organization. Students can be asked to do a written analysis of the case or it can be used for discussion or illustrative purposes.

Cases can also be assigned to be discussed outside the regular class period in smaller class sections or groups. Reports of conclusions arrived at by the discussion groups may or may not be reported back to the total class membership. This alternative has advantages for very large classes. In a related fashion, cases can be the focus of discussion in large classes by the use of the "buzz-group" technique. In such a procedure, the class is organized into groups of 6 to 10 per-

---

[2] The author is indebted to the work of Ronald Bauer (3) for a number of the suggestions that follow.

sons, and these groups spend part of the class period in discussing certain aspects of the case.

Cases are frequently used as a partial basis for a course. One out of every three or four class meetings, for example, might be devoted to case discussions. Under such an arrangement, a case could be used to introduce a unit of study. Out of the ensuing discussion students could formulate questions that they would pursue further. In this way the case would become a springboard to some other educational activity. Of course, there would be other possibilities, such as utilizing a case at the end of a given unit of study. This alternate might be appropriately used in relation to core or block courses for training administrators. Such use of the case method might also appeal to those who wish to experiment with the method. As teachers become more proficient in the use of the method, it can be utilized in a more extended manner.

A fifth possibility is to use the cases as the central and major course content. Although there would be related reading, class discussions would focus mainly on case analyses. A usual procedure is to take a case for each class meeting and devote an entire period to its discussion. Those who have used the method in this manner strongly emphasize the important cumulative effects that result from the uninterrupted exploration of cases. Few persons, if any, believe that a total program for educating school administrators should be centered entirely around cases. The case method, while versatile, cannot achieve all educational purposes. Besides, there are not now nearly enough cases available for a total training program even if it were desirable.

There are increasing indications that the case approach has distinct values for in-service training. Personnel in school districts, with the assistance of their own or outside consultants, can employ the method. Cases are already being utilized for the in-service training of school personnel by professors in such institutions as the University of Texas, the University of California, and Columbia University. Doubtless this use will increase as closer relationships develop between those teaching administration and those administering. This trend toward closer relationships is already evident through the contacts arising from internships, consultant work, action research, and various types of in-service programs.

There are a considerable number of precedents in other fields for the use of the case method in in-service training programs. The Southern Pacific Railway, for example, has employed a management consultant who spends six months annually training supervisors through the case method (8). To achieve this purpose, the Southern Pacific Company has an especially equipped car for training its supervisors. The car contains a long, oval table and other appropriate fixtures for facilitating case discussion. It travels from one station to another, and therefore can accommodate many different groups of supervisors in in-service programs. There are various other examples where the case method is being applied in industrial and business organizations (2, 27).

The various suggestions above illustrate some ways that cases may be introduced into programs for training administrators. There are no doubt many others. Because of the many uses, the term *case methods* is more accurate than the term *case method*. It should also be clear that various assumptions about learning underlie the various uses of cases. It should be stressed again that those who use cases primarily for lecture material undoubtedly have different educational values and goals than those who use cases for discussion purposes. The authors of this book are committed to the use of cases primarily as instruments for discussion. The unique and essential function of a case is believed to be expressed best through the interaction of class participants. The succeeding ideas are cast within this framework.

Case-Method Purposes

An examination of the written reports on case-method teaching will reveal considerable diversity in purpose. At the same time, there are certain uniformities in purpose statements. Cases, for example, have been called "multi-purpose tools" (12, p. 11). In other words, those who use case methods do not necessarily limit themselves to one goal, but usually have more than one goal.

Those who use the case method also seem to define their primary goals in terms of some aspect of behavior—either rational, emotional, or social. Although considerable information may be imparted by the case method, no one uses it primarily for this purpose. It is also worthy of note that case-method users are generally more concerned with long-term goals and with goals clearly related to behavioral tasks. To put it differently, users of the case method have goals that extend beyond the time of telling students and testing them at the end of the course. Their chief concern is often with life problems and situations that students will encounter after the course is ended. Thus, in courses on administration, the primary goals have been defined in terms of future "on-the-job" behaviors.

Case-method users show considerable diversity in the specific kinds of behavior that they hope to develop in students. Behaviors that for one person have first priority may be of secondary importance for another teacher. Two basic classifications of instructional goals can be highlighted by posing two questions. One classification would follow from the question, "What should the student do with case content?" Another related but different classification would follow from this question: "What behavior should be developed through the social interaction resulting from case discussion?" Answers to both these questions would result in goals behaviorally defined. However, those who define goals in terms of the first question emphasize goals that are more rational in nature. For such persons, the development of social and emotional kinds of behavior is related but somewhat secondary to the development of rational processes. Those persons who define goals in terms of the second question are more interested in social skills and desirable emotional responses. Such goals become the primary focus, while rational processes are implicit or secondary.

Actually, the above distinctions are analytical to show relative emphasis. Most behavior in a classroom situation is, of course, a complex of rational, emotional, and social elements. These broad distinctions are useful in that some specific examples of goals that illustrate rational, social, and emotional kinds of behavior can be noted.

Goals emphasizing rational behavior. The rational goal of case-method teaching is often labeled *problem-solving* or *decision-making*. A careful analysis of the facts of the case to define problems and to arrive at logical solutions becomes a central consideration. Although a number of persons hold this to be the primary goal of the case method, perhaps Hunt's formulation (19, p. 178) of purposes is the most explicit. Four of the goals that he has set forth may be used for illustrative purposes: (1) "the power to analyze and to master a tangled circumstance by selecting the important factors from the whole set of facts and by weighing their importance in context"; (2) "the ability to utilize ideas, to test them against the facts of the problem, and to throw both ideas and facts into fresh combinations, thus discovering ways to make them appropriate for the solution of the problem at hand"; (3) "the ability to recognize the need for new factual material or the need to apply technical skills to a problem and the ability to assimilate such facts and skills as are needed for the solution of the problem at hand"; (4) "the ability to use later experiences as a test of the validity of the ideas already obtained, with flexibility to revise goals and procedures as experience is deepened."

Professor Hunt describes these as minimum goals for all students in his class. The ability to communicate, the ability to use ideas in theoretical form, and the ability to attain economically the four goals noted above are three additional skills in which better students should also gain facility. Thus, the goals applying to all students are defined by Hunt in terms of intellectual or rational behavior. Others have written about the use of cases for deductive and inductive reasoning. Stein (29, p. 22), for example, speaks of the use of cases "for suggesting and testing generalizations about behavior in public organization." On the other hand, Dubin (7) suggests that cases should provide opportunities for generalizations based upon an inductive approach.

Goals emphasizing emotional and attitudinal changes. According to Josh Billings, as quoted by Peterson (23, p. 256): "It ain't the things we don't know that make such fools of us, but a whole lot of things that we know that ain't so." The meaning of this statement would no doubt be accepted by those who emphasize emotional and attitude change through the case method. Unlearning may be more important than new learning if opportunities are provided for the student to become aware of and to examine negative and harmful attitudes. For example, a student might have a negative or fearful attitude toward authority figures, which could markedly interfere with effective administration. The case method might enable him to identify this attitude, to examine it, to develop insight into its effects, and, in the process, to change or partially modify it. The student's goal then becomes self-examination. In the words of Sargent and Belisle (28, p. 21), "Awareness and self-awareness grow throughout. Learning becomes increasingly a *self-conscious* process. The results of learning are bound up with the increased *awareness of all aspects of the experience*. . . . This implies growing awareness of one's own values, needs, choices, and achievements at the beginning, throughout, and at the conclusion of a particular learning experience."

Those who are committed to the goal of attitude change point especially to the unique capacity of the case method to produce a high degree of emotional involvement and, thereby, to provide opportunities to students for recognizing and understanding emotions. Actually Hennessey (18), in a carefully designed study, found that there was greater learning in social skills than in thinking and writing skills among participants in case-method classes. The study also revealed that the amount of social and attitudinal learning among students was positively correlated with the extent to which they perceived their instructor to be "human relations minded." Those who emphasize attitudinal learning, again, assume that telling is not teaching.

Goals emphasizing social skills. It is difficult to separate social and emotional aspects of behavior. There are two social skills, however, that have been mentioned frequently as goals of case-method teaching. The first of these is "co-operation" (15, p. 2). Since much of the administrator's work involves others, it is assumed that learning co-operative skills is essential. Individual problem-solving ability in working with groups, for example, might be seen as secondary to co-operative problem-solving ability. Behavior resulting from student-teacher interaction or student-student interaction is designed, then, to improve the social skill of co-operation.

A second social skill that some users of the case method seek to improve is communication. It is notable that, of the seven goals listed by Hunt, communication was the only one not primarily rational in nature. Those pursuing this goal assume that communication is a skill in which administrators need to be proficient if they are going to do their jobs effectively. They believe that the skill can be improved through case-method learning.

Some teachers who use the case method have formulated goals that are broad enough in nature to encompass social, emotional, and rational behavior. For example, Glover and Hower have indicated that a central goal in their teaching is to help students to "act responsibly" (15, p. 3). Donham has suggested that a basic goal is to assist students to "deal successfully with the unpredictable future"

(6, p. 145). He believes that change is proceeding at such a rapid rate in modern society that today's students must be educated to deal with unique situations that are continuously emerging.

The goals that a teacher selects for himself will, of course, affect the technique or techniques that he uses. The next task will be to consider some of the techniques that are used in case methods of teaching.

Case-Method Techniques

At least three important limitations confront anyone who wishes to describe instructional techniques for case-method users. For one thing, teaching technique is inseparable from individual personality, and for that reason is not and cannot be a strictly logical or precisely described procedure. It is well known, for example, that there is a great deal of artistry in effective teaching, and certainly the case method is no exception to this rule. Although teaching can be guided and shaped by following learning principles, it contains a certain element that is essentially creative. No one has arrived at a very precise formula for creativity in either the arts or the sciences. Who could have produced a formula for Beethoven to compose his *Fifth Symphony*? Would prescriptive suggestions alone have enabled Balzac to write his great novel *Eugénie Grandet*? Distinguished teaching is also, in one sense, an artistic product stemming, not from words or musical notes, but from the richly variegated, notably complex, continually changing, and markedly different personalities that make up a class.

A second factor that limits the precise prescriptions of techniques is the fact that the case method is an adventure that is never exactly repeated even though the same case may be used again and again. When a teacher lectures, he can predict what he will say at the beginning of the period, at the middle of the period, and at the end of the period. He can also make accurate guesses about the reactions of the students during this process. By contrast, the case method is a dynamic process whose structure is not easy to predict. Success depends to a considerable extent on flexibility and adaptability on the part of the teachers.

The third condition of case-method technique is that the method is dedicated to the experience method of learning rather than to verbal absorption. For this reason various persons who have written about the method have expressed reservations about their ability to communicate its meaning. The following quotation from Gibson is typical (13, p. 219):

> It is difficult to write *about* a teaching method which is dedicated to acquaintance. In fact, to do so is a contradiction in terms. I had to learn that no one could tell me about the case method. I had to experience it, and this experience on my part makes me fundamentally despair of successful expository communication to anyone else.

In spite of the limitations noted above, it seems desirable that serious efforts be made to make clear the procedures and results of teaching experience. The following techniques are offered as suggestions rather than prescriptions, and as flexible guide lines rather than inflexible procedures. Unqualified acceptance of a technique for imitation's sake cannot long be productive. A quotation from Glover and Hower illustrates the point (14, pp. 18–19):

> Some of us who have tried to copy what we took to be the teaching techniques of some of our older and more experienced colleagues have inevitably "come a cropper." We have found that, for better or worse, we have to be ourselves; and "technique," we now hold, must be a manifestation of one's true self—in teaching and in administration alike. If it is a kind of synthetic overlay without integral relation to the man, it can hardly be otherwise than uncomfortable, ineffective, and ridiculous.

Under what circumstances should the method be used? Perhaps some self-examination is desirable before one plunges wholeheartedly into case-method teaching. Several questions can guide the process, and the following are suggestive: Am I interested in developing behavioral skills in students, as well as in imparting information? Am I willing and able to be a co-learner with students in the examination of concrete cases of administrative experience? Can I play the role of stimulator in guiding student thinking? Do my attitudes allow me to be relatively unconcerned about maintaining teacher authority? Am I adventurous and willing to experiment? Do I enjoy and have some facility in group discussion? If a person can answer most of these questions in the affirmative, he can doubtless use the case method without much difficulty. If, on the other hand, he finds himself answering most of these questions in the negative, another interpretation may be indicated. Negative reactions do not mean categorically that one should not experiment with the method. However, those using the method under these conditions may meet with some discouraging experiences.

In this regard, Wengert has the following to say about the use of the method in teaching courses in public administration (32, pp. 65–66):

> . . . This is a cold water bath for students to be deprived of a nice, neat, orderly universe that the textbook pretends to describe. But the biggest problem that the Inter-University Case Program has found comes from the fact that any number of teachers in the field of public administration, and I might venture the guess that perhaps this is true also in the field of educational administration, simply cannot get comfortable with the idea of not bundling things up. Indeterminacy of the principle is one that we feel in this Inter-University Case Program is something that people teaching in administration need still to be made comfortable with. Thus, case teaching is tough on the teacher. It uproots him; it turns him upside down. Some of his fondest notions, perhaps, are exposed to some rather withering kinds of criticism through the case process.

Implicit in Wengert's statement is the suggestion that case-method instruction changes the thinking of teachers as well as that of students. It is a learning process that encourages teachers continually to test their own ideas against the facts recorded in cases. Even though it may at times be a trying experience, this is no reason to turn one's back upon the method. Undoubtedly the best way to learn the case method is to use it. The following testimony by Sargent and Belisle relate to this point (28, p. 4): "And we have found ourselves none the worse for venturing to develop and use cases long before we began to feel familiar or comfortable with the many nuances of possible case definition and use."

Preparing for the teacher's role. Teachers can take various steps that will make the transition to case-method teaching easier. Insight into the method can be developed through staff discussion of cases and the discussion of problems that arise from staff interaction. It is also desirable for more than one person on a staff to begin the use of the technique, in order that those using it may compare notes and experiences. The sharing of success and the mutual solving of problems have a place in using a technique that may be somewhat unfamiliar. Wallace Donham (6) has suggested that a very effective method for preparing teachers to use the case approach is to relieve them for a semester so that they can experience the method at some university where it is used. He notes that approximately twenty teachers have come to participate in the case method at Harvard University, and most of them were skeptical of the method's value in the beginning. However, involvement in the method convinced them of its value, and many returned to their own universities to institute the method there. A grant from the Kellogg Foundation has made possible a similar plan at the University of Oregon. Each summer during the years 1957–1960, five professors of educational administration from various parts of the country have been or will be selected to participate in an interdisciplinary case-method seminar. Data on the effects of this program are being gathered and a written evaluation will be made when it is completed.

It is also well to keep in mind that a gradual introduction to case-method teaching is sometimes desirable. A teacher, for example, may use the method as a suppplement to other methods used in a course. In this way a limited number of cases will be used in a quarter or a semester. By using this approach, the method can be learned without too much discomfort, and confidence in one's capacity to use it can be gained.

Preparing the student. As has already been intimated, the case method seeks to shift the responsibility for learning to the student. Various techniques have been developed to achieve this goal. One aspect of preparation has to do with stimulating and guiding students in the careful reading of cases. Students in the beginning, for example, often tend to read and to discuss cases rather superficially. What techniques can be used to guard against such a condition?

At the very beginning, the tendency toward uncritical reading of cases should be pointed out to students. They can be informed that persons often tend to read cases as stories, rapidly and, sometimes, superficially. Teachers can try to make clear that, in order to discuss and analyze a case carefully, thorough and systematic case reading is needed. One must not read just for the gist of the story, but for what lies behind the story—not just the black lines, but also for what lies between these lines. Only experience can show what part careful reading plays in the successful analysis of a case.

There are more specific techniques that can be suggested. Revzan (26), for example, has reported that he has students prepare a brief of every case that is discussed. This brief contains the name of the case, the type of general problem represented, a summary of the most important facts, a statement of the issues, alternative solutions to the problem, and the one solution considered most appropriate, with reasons for the choice. Whether this particular form or some other form is suggested to students, it is undoubtedly true that they can profit from some systematic approach to the study of the case.

There is some danger in over-specific and uniform guides for analysis. One way to achieve flexibility is to suggest different approaches to students and to encourage them to select or develop an approach that seems most appropriate to their own interests or purposes. After six or eight cases have been discussed by a class, students can share the techniques that they have found most useful in case analysis.

In small classes a student can be asked to present briefly his analysis of the case and to lead the discussion that follows. In larger classes it is sometimes useful to break up for discussion into smaller groups. Reports of certain aspects of the analysis of the small group can be reported to the total group for further discussion. Whatever approach to the problem a teacher takes, the importance of effective student and teacher preparation and participation should be clear. Experience also suggests that intensive exploration of a case is considerably more desirable than extensive exploration of several cases.

Setting the stage. Almost every person who has written on the case method has emphasized the importance of class atmosphere. A desirable atmosphere is usually described as one in which students are relatively free to think and express thoughts and feelings openly. Although every member of the class carries some responsibility in this regard, the role of the teacher is particularly significant. Verbal assertions on the teacher's part are not sufficient to achieve such an atmosphere. It is the teacher's behavior that carries to the student the real meaning of his beliefs, and discrepancies between the teacher's words and his actions are unerringly detected. For example, if a teacher states that there are no "right" answers and then behaves as if there are, this is quickly evident to students and will be disturbing to the communication processes of the group. Or, if teachers verbally encourage the expression of individual ideas and then their behaviors show that they do not wish to tolerate those that are different from their own, there will be interference with thought processes.

In creating a desirable learning atmosphere, the teacher needs to be an accepting listener. He must communicate through his behavior that he is a co-learner along with the others in the group. This is not an easy role to play. In order to stimulate and enrich the learning process, he also frequently needs to play the role of question-raiser and provocator. Instead of answering questions, he questions answers. Because of the teacher's status position, this role often requires deft execution in order not to cut communication processes. In the first weeks, until rapport is developed, he needs to be especially careful. This means that he should raise questions, not with the attitude of a prosecutor, but rather as a stimulator and clarifier. He should do this, not so much in the spirit of the master, as in the spirit of servant. If this can be done, learning can be stimulated and student-teacher rapport preserved.

Facilitating case discussion. As already noted, a central role of the teacher who uses the case method is that of question-raiser. This does not mean that he continually asks questions, or that he will have a clearly structured pattern of questioning. Many times he may decide to be silent instead of raising a question. On another occasion, he may decide to be silent as far as a particular individual is concerned, when under similar circumstances he would question ideas of another individual. On some occasions, particularly after rapport is established, he may express his own ideas for class members to examine.[3] In other words, in a dynamic discussion process the teacher must be

---

[3] The ideas that are presented relative to the teacher as a question-raiser are based mostly on the reports of experience that instructors have had in the Harvard Graduate School of Business Administration. For the most part, they have maintained that teachers should not impose their own views on students in case-method teaching, and it is well to be aware of this assumption in evaluating the techniques that they have recommended. Teachers in the area of public administration, however, have had more diverse views on the role of the teacher. This is largely due, no doubt, to the fact that the case method for educating business executives was born and flourished at Harvard University while the case-method approach in public administration has developed and grown in diverse climates in different universities. Five universities, for example, were involved in the original Carnegie grants for developing cases dealing with public administration. It is also of interest to note that teachers of public administration generally have not been as interested in making their instructional methods explicit in written form as have those teaching business administration. On the other hand, they have written more on the nature and preparation of cases than have teachers of business administration.

flexible and make the best use of learning opportunities through accurately timed and appropriate behavior based upon an assessment of factors affecting the teaching-learning process.

A class is often started by the use of a question—usually one that is general in nature. This may take the form of, "What do you make of the facts of the case?" or "Are there general reactions to the case?" or "What do you see as the main problems in the case?" Such queries are usually sufficient to get discussion started.

One kind of questioning is that which checks on communication. This may take the form of a teacher's restating in question form what a student has said to be sure that he and the others have understood it. Or a question may be directed to the class or to an individual by asking students to state what they understand a class member has said. This encourages more careful listening as well as more direct communication. There is always the danger, and especially so in the beginning, that a class will engage in a "collective monologue" rather than a "co-operative conversation," to use the terminology of Irving Lee (20, p. 11).

Another line of questioning is directed toward the solution of the case. Culliton has suggested a number of questions pertinent to this aspect of the method (5, p. 87): "What, if anything, should be done?" "Why?" "How would you get it done?" "What facts would you like before you decide?" "What facts can you get by the time you have to decide?" "What risks are involved in your decision?" Such questions are most approprite in those case discussions which present clearly defined problems.

A line of questioning that frequently precedes decision-making or solution-proposing is that which seeks to clarify the "why" of administrator, teacher, or the behavior of others in the case. Examples of this type of questioning are: "How do you explain Principal Smith's reaction to Teacher Y's suggestion?" "Can you suggest why Principal Smith made the decision that he did?" "Why did Superintendent Jones misinterpret the request from the teachers' organization?" "Why did Teacher X refuse to change her position about in-service training?" "Can you explain why Parent Brown did not co-operate with the teacher?" Such questioning focuses attention on human relations and motivational problems.

Control is sometimes needed to bring fallacious, unfruitful, or vaguely abstract thinking back to the facts of the case. In order to set forth more clearly some of the situations exemplifying student reactions of this kind, several of the directions that a discussion may take will be elaborated.[4] Most of these discussion tendencies are over-simplified or inadequate approaches to the solution of problems and, therefore, place some responsibility on the teacher for their correction. These tendencies are human and understandable in that neither teachers nor students react to a case as an objective thing but display their own feelings and attitudes as they grapple with it.

The following quotation from Glover and Hower illustrates the point (14, p. 17):

> Many instructors approaching the case method for the first time need to be forewarned, that from the moment a discussion starts, they will not be dealing with a case having an objective existence of its own, a collection of printed material which provides a secure base for reference whenever a difference of opinion emerges. Each person deals with the case as it appears to him. One student identifies himself with a character in the case; another projects his own feelings and attitudes into the situation; a third deals with stereotypes, rather than the people described; still another is responding more to his feelings toward the instructor than to the case situation; another seemingly says what he thinks the instructor wants to hear, or else what the majority of the class will approve, rather than advancing his own inner thoughts. Some talk principally in terms of reaction to other students' views rather than to case material; some go off on what appear to be irrelevancies; and some repeat ideas which have already been discussed, quite as if they were wholly fresh contributions. Students' views (and those of the instructor) change in the course of discussion—indeed, sometimes during the very act of speaking.

Because of these many factors, then, what are some of the specific directions that a discussion may take? A typical reaction that students have early in case discussions is that there are not enough facts in a case on which to make a judgment or to base a decision. Thus, students will often hesitate and even find it painful to make decisions about problem solutions. Under such conditions a class can be encouraged to make more effective use of the facts already available or to define more clearly the facts that are needed.

Describing dichotomies is another turn that a discussion may take. A student will pose an "either-or" kind of solution. A teacher

---

[4] The author is indebted to Ulrich (31) and Roethlisberger (27) for a number of the following ideas on student reactions to case-method discussion.

must be fired, for example, or she must be retained. Such kind of reasoning, of course, ignores all the possibilities in between the two extremes. The teacher's problem then is to help students discover and evaluate various other alternatives that can make the shortcomings of "either-or" reasoning clear.

A discussion may take the turn of what Roethlisberger has called "the hunt for the villain" (27, p. 186). The case is read with the idea of pinning the blame upon someone in the situation. Usually it is not easy to decide who the villain is or, at least, it is not easy to agree upon who the villain is, but sometimes a discussion will take a turn of assuming that "so-and-so" is to be blamed for what has happened in the case. Such an approach is usually another gross oversimplification that can provide the teacher opportunities to develop broader perspectives.

Still another turn that a discussion is likely to take is that of labeling or stereotyping. The students may conclude that John Doe failed as a primary teacher because men are really cut out to be high school teachers. Or Principal X was not successful because he had an inferiority complex. Such reactions are again understandable in that much thinking in higher education involves theorizing and classifying concepts that may be far removed from experience. To analyze a case on the basis of its facts becomes, then, a difficult and sometimes trying undertaking. Traditions, attitudes, and sentiments get in the way. Such barriers present a real challenge to teachers and students.

The "collective monologue" was referred to in a paragraph above. This tendency is more frequently observed at the beginning of a case-method course. It means simply that one student will recite certain reactions that he has to an aspect of the case, while another gives forth some of his ideas that may have little bearing on what has been said previously. When he is finished, someone else presents views on another unrelated topic, and so it goes. To achieve a "co-operative conversation" in dealing with a case is not always an easy undertaking. However, this condition usually improves as people become better acquainted and grow more accustomed to the method. Participants become more adept at listening to one another and to responding in a related way to what someone has said previously. Increasing skill in co-operative interaction allows students to have their views examined and is much more productive of learning.

Simple cause-to-effect reasoning can also be observed in class discussions. Although students may be able to verbalize that multiple causality rather than single causality is the rule in explaining social conditions, they may not actually transfer the statement to their analysis of cases. If Miss Jones's students do not measure up to the national norms in standardized arithmetic tests, then a person reasoning from simple cause-to-effect might say that the solution of the problem was to fire Miss Jones. Such reasoning, of course, can be checked and corrected through the use of the case method. The fallacy of such reasoning is usually made clear through the remarks of fellow students. Otherwise, questions on the teacher's part can help a student correct his thinking.

One other important direction that a discussion may take should be mentioned. This is the tendency for the students to turn to the teacher for answers. The case method, is, in a sense, a drastic departure from many kinds of learning that students have previously experienced. Thus, some frustration and a desire to become dependent upon the instructor may result. Roethlisberger has described this situation as follows (27, pp. 186–187):

> Now the class is filled with tension. The students have exterminated villains; they have played God; they have sought for a mystical authority; they have asked for more "facts"; and still the professor or leader does not seem to be satisfied. At this point their attitude is likely to be, "We've worked hard enough. You tell us. You give us the answer." Here is the toughest nut to crack. Being human and having also a nervous system, I would like to tell them "the solution." But so long as I am not too fatigued to hold out against them, I generally say, "The discussion has been very interesting. I am not sure I know just what should be done or how it should be done. I can tell you what I would do and how I would go about it, but that would not be *the* answer. It would be *my* answer. Perhaps we should discuss another case next time."

While it is unwise to frustrate students and add to their insecurities needlessly, the teacher nevertheless needs to guard against developing over-dependent attitudes in students.

An examination of the kinds of discussions noted above suggests that students' traditions, attitudes, and feelings have some bearing on their failure or inability to focus on a case critically and objectively. The teacher, of course, faces the same problem. This may mean that his own lack of objectivity will interfere with the success of his own questioning. Thus, he may raise questions that reflect his own interests and not the interests of students, or questions that students are not ready or competent to discuss. Or, he may raise questions at such times or in such a manner that thinking is interrupted rather than stimulated. With practice and self-evaluation, however, a teacher may improve his effectiveness.

Perhaps there are few teaching methods where the feelings and attitudes of participants are projected into the discussion situation as in the case method of teaching. While barriers to critical thinking and problem-solving result, at the same time unique opportunities for self-learning and concept development are presented. Such a situation gives participants a chance to recognize and to examine their feelings and attitudes for what they are. It brings opportunities to define the assumptions that underlie verbal expressions. It can be very fruitful in developing human-relation insights among students.

What Techniques Can Be Used to Supplement the Case Method?

A number of techniques can be used to supplement case study and analysis. Some of these techniques will now be briefly considered. Perhaps few people would use all these techniques in case-method teaching. However, some of them, no doubt, would be appropriate for most persons employing the method.

Supplementary reading. In the early days of case-method instruction, the importance of supplementary reading was not emphasized. Today there is almost universal agreement on the importance of related reading. However, there is less agreement as to precisely how this aspect of learning should be handled.

A central issue in this matter is the extent to which a teacher should define and guide the reading of students. In this regard, Sargent and Belisle (28) describe an approach designed to give the student considerable leeway in the choice of his readings. Narrowly prescribed study of concepts, in their belief, may do more harm than good. Their approach focuses on the self-direction of learning and on individual growth through the broadening of conceptual resources. The emphasis is on the quality rather than the quantity of experience. In their method the student is encouraged to select concepts to guide reading and thinking. These concepts they (28, p. 453) define as "terms which constitute basic building blocks in organizing and relating knowledge or experience."

After the students have studied cases for several weeks, the task of defining the supplementary reading is begun. The students are asked to select eight or ten concepts that have particular significance for the cases they have studied or for administration generally. At this point the instructors make no effort to give a precise meaning to the term "concepts." Rather, students are encouraged to think through the meaning for themselves and to select concepts accordingly. They are asked to have the concepts ready for the next week.

The next week's session then is devoted to outlining on the blackboard the concepts from the students' individual lists. This usually results in a list of 60 to 70 concepts. Then the students are asked to select one or more of these concepts for individual exploration. At a later session they talk briefly about the concept chosen, and at this time additional suggestions or clarifications are made by either students or teachers. "Communication," "group co-ordination," "personality," "culture," and "decision-making" are examples of concepts that might be chosen. The student then is on his own to read, to reflect, and to assimilate. No formal report is required of the experience, and only what is considered significant is shared in class.

Other teachers, of course, have used methods of guiding reading that are more structured and defined. Required readings may be assigned in connection with a series of cases, or students may be given a bibliography with the request that they select an area of interest for intensive reading. Formal reports may or may not be required. Another technique is to schedule specific class periods for the discussion of supplementary readings that are judged to be appropriate for throwing light on cases analyzed.

Although structure aids in focusing on selected materials, it may interfere with student spontaneity and the pursuit of individual interests. Another plan may be noted that tries to combine student interest and selected readings. In order to do this, interests are determined after the class has had a number of case discussions. When students have discussed six or eight cases, most of them will have been stimulated to formulate questions that have general significance. As examples, such questions as "What is leadership?" or "What is the basic function of the administrator?" typically arise early in case discussions. Students can be given an opportunity after the early discussions to write down the question they would most like to discuss. These questions can be consolidated in the form of an inventory, so that students can indicate in rank order the two or three questions that are of most interest to them. Tabulation can be made by the students and reported. Typically, certain general interest patterns will emerge from the responses.

At this point readings can be assigned appropriate to student interests and certain days can be set aside for discussing the questions that are of general interest. Sometimes brief presentations by resource persons from outside the class with follow-up discussions are also useful. Such procedure can be repeated at different times during the semester if an instructor so desires.

Lecture. The lecture is another technique that can be used to supplement case discussion. Some persons select three or four days during a quarter or semester for a full-period lecture. Others use the "lecturette" at the end of a discussion period to summarize or to bring out points that have been skirted or left implicit. The relationship of lectures to the case method of teaching have been set forth by Fuller (10) among others. Traditional lecturing as a systematic exposition of information or knowledge is considered out of tune with the method. In general, nothing should be introduced into a lecture that has not already been talked about or implied in previous discussions. This does not mean, of course, that the material should be presented in exactly the same way as it was treated in the discussion. Rather, the purpose should be to draw out implications and to develop meanings in line with the students' readiness for learning. This calls not only for careful assessment of what is happening to students, but also for a careful consideration of the content of discussions. For this purpose, as well as for others, it is useful to keep a brief diary of class discussions, which includes a summary of class progress. In addition to providing basic material for future lectures, it can give a teacher a better understanding of the whole case-method process.

Role-playing. Role-playing is a technique that is also adapted to the case method of teaching. The method has already been widely used in supervisory training and in the teaching of personnel administration (33). When used successfully, it can be very effective in promoting the understanding of human relations. A crucial situation may be re-enacted, for example, so that students are able to become involved and to project themselves into main characters in the case. This can heighten interest, sharpen discussion, and help students to understand themselves, as well as provide opportunities to develop empathy and understanding of others. It is less appropriate for dealing with general knowledge and concepts.

For those who have already used role-playing, cases will offer an excellent medium to continue this approach to teaching. For those who have not had experience with this technique, cases offer an opportunity for experimentation in that they are an excellent springboard for role-playing and role interpretation.

Searching for common patterns. Another approach to supplementing the analysis of single cases is to take a number of cases already studied and to see what common patterns, if any, can be discovered in these cases. Some teachers believe that all cases are unique and that it is dangerous to try to generalize on a limited number of cases. They say that students are likely to generalize too easily and superficially. Such an attitude seems to reflect a lack of faith in student judgment. It is also worth noting that others have come to opposite conclusions. Hunt (19, p. 189), for example, says that "students are inclined to be too ready to criticize generalizations, because they do not suit a particular of the cases they have seen."

In any case, it would seem that such an exercise should be fruitful for developing tentative hypotheses about certain aspects of administrative behavior, or for testing ideas already held. Although there are problems in scientific generalization, it must also be recognized that potential administrators need to develop a theoretical basis for action.

Student cases. Student preparation of cases is also a supplementary method of note. Such cases can be dittoed and used as a basis for discussion just the same as the more professionally prepared cases. Students at the University of Oregon have judged this aspect of the method as very valuable, and many of them have stated that they have gotten more from discussing student-written cases than from discussing professionally prepared cases. Ordering and objectifying one's own experience in written form can be very good for developing insight. In addition, there is a certain personal atmosphere that goes along with such case discussions, which adds to student motivation. If the cases are introduced into the latter part of the course, the decrease in motivation, which Castore (4) has reported as tending to occur during this period, may be partially avoided. Student-prepared cases can also be used for reports, for teacher-student conferences, and no doubt for other purposes.

Success in the use of student-written cases can be increased by following certain guides. First, it is important to see which students have experienced situations that have the makings of a case that would be profitable for class discussion. In small classes this can be done through brief interviews, and in larger classes students can be asked to submit an outline of their proposed cases with the sources of data available to them. For those persons who do not have an adequate basis within their own experience for writing a case, other arrangements can be made. For example, they can profit from gathering data and from writing cases that are available in nearby communities. Since students will be more unfamiliar with such a case than with one they have experienced, two to four persons can be assigned to a case, depending on the scope of the undertaking. It is also a good practice to read the first draft of such cases and suggest revisions for final drafts. While this practice takes time, it will make the case a more valuable instrument for class discussion.

A few suggestions about the discussion of student-prepared cases can be made. First, it is well to discuss these cases in later class sessions, after students have become well acquainted with one another. This will enable students to be more open and free, and the results generally will be better. Second, there are distinct advantages to having the writer of the case remain silent during most of the discussion. Otherwise, remarks in the form of questions are likely to be directed toward him so that general class discussion and interaction are minimized. Before the discussion period is over, however, it is a good practice to provide the writer an opportunity to make a statement. He may want to clarify, add additional information, or answer or raise further questions. A written analysis of the report of his own case *after* he has heard it discussed can be a valuable experience for a student. Finally, students should have the opportunity to collect the copies of their cases after they have been discussed, in case they have reasons for not wanting their reports to be generally known.

Evaluating Case-Method Learning

Little has been written on the evaluation of case-method learning. Almost all the persons who have discussed evaluation have emphasized the difficulty involved in the process. Perhaps the difficulty of evaluating case-method learning as compared with other methods of learning has been exaggerated. In other words, in what method of learning is evaluation easy and exact?

There are two general approaches to the problem of evaluating case-method learning. One of these is through examining the written analyses of cases, and the other is through observations of student behavior in case-method discussion. Both of these methods will be discussed briefly.

Written examinations. Written exams typically consist of the analysis of a case. Fuller (11) has set forth what he believes to be some of the characteristics of an unsatisfactory case analysis. One kind of unsatisfactory response is the failure or inability to distinguish between factual statements and opinion statements. Such a student might read the statement, "The principal thought that Miss Jones was incompetent," and conclude that Miss Jones was incompetent. Such an incorrect interpretation, of course, would lead to an unsatisfactory analysis.

Another characteristic of an unsatisfactory response, according to Fuller, is failure to analyze the case, because "Not enough information is given in this case to be able to do anything with it." Better students make a careful analysis of the existing facts and draw reasonable conclusions as to their meaning and limitations. A third unsatisfactory and limited approach is for the student to reject opinion statements as irrelevant. Such an attitude would be expressed in this statement: "These are just opinions, and an objective picture, which I can deal with, is not given in this case." With such an attitude the student is again unable to arrive at a satisfactory analysis.

There are other characteristics shown by students in unsatisfactory analysis. There is, for example, the problem of clear expression of ideas. Students presenting inadequate analyses will use words that they have heard or read but which have little meaning or application to the facts at hand. Such a student might recommend that the problem be solved through the "use of line authority." Or he might suggest "better school-community relations" without being specific. Such expressions fail to communicate proper relations between the facts of the case and the proposed solution. A related kind of unsatisfactory response is the stereotyped expression. Such statements as, "The principal is a perfectionist," and "The teacher has a maladjusted personality," would be examples of this type of response.

Students with less satisfactory papers sometimes show a tendency to think in terms of very limited alternatives. Such an analysis might revolve around the "either-or" orientation, discussed earlier. Another unsatisfactory response is to superimpose in an unanalytical fashion a long list of general principles such as could be found in the typical textbook upon the facts of the case.

The criteria underlying the shortcomings noted above relate more to a student's *approach* to problem-solving than to "right" and "wrong" solutions to problems. A correct approach on the part of the student implies the ability to distinguish between facts and opinions, the ability to establish concrete relationships between these facts and opinions, the ability to recognize alternative solutions, and the ability to evaluate and to draw some reasonable conclusions about the alternatives. These criteria, it will be noted, relate to rational aspects of behavior, as the latter is expressed verbally.

Observation. Although evaluation through written examination is more likely to be used in very large classes, the teacher in smaller classes can more easily form judgments about students through observations and thereby arrive at evaluations of learning. There are advantages to this kind of evaluation over written examinations. For one thing, written analyses are usually performed within narrowly prescribed time limits. Such prescriptions place limits on the nature and number of cases that can be treated even if the student is given opportunities to do the analyses of cases outside of class.

Hunt (19, p. 187) has enumerated other specific limitations to written analyses as a basis for evaluation. First, written analyses do not show the ability to select from a whole complex of facts those that are relevant and to relate them to an issue being discussed. Second, such an examination does not furnish accurate information on the *process* of considering various alternatives in analyzing a vague issue. Finally, there is a lack of opportunity to see how a student can build upon the ideas that others have proposed in a group discussion.

It is also evident that those who are interested in developing social skills cannot test such skills easily through a written analysis. Skills of oral communication, skills of co-operation, and skills in human relations may be observed much more adequately in an open discussion. Thus, for some purposes observations can provide more relevant data for evaluation than can written analyses. Even information on problem-solving or rational skills may be obtained through observation. The main limitation of observation lies in its inappropriateness for judging those who do not participate in discussion.

Issues and Problems in the Use of the Case Method

Several issues and problems that confront the user of case-method teaching have been implicit in the previous discussion. This chapter will be concluded with a discussion that focuses more sharply on a number of these issues and problems.

Which goal should receive most emphasis? Case-method users are faced with the issue of deciding on goals that are realistic and important. Should one be more concerned with social skills or with rational thinking? Should one focus on the development of self-understanding, the development of general insights, or the development of a point of view? Should one try to change the whole rope of personality, or should he concentrate on one or a few diverse strands? Are there other goals yet unstated that should take priority? For the most part, these are value questions, and every teacher who intends to use the case method should assess them rather carefully.

How much structure? Some believe that, if the teacher controls the direction of discussion, he will interfere with student interest and spontaneity. There are others who believe that if the teacher does not control the direction of discussion, learning may be inefficient and misdirected. Thus, practice has varied somewhat from teacher to teacher, some being more directive and some being less directive.

Actually, it is well to recognize that there is never a completely non-directive situation. By deciding to make a discussion situation non-directive, a teacher is imposing an important limitation on the direction of the class. Perhaps the real issue is a more basic one: How can the teacher best develop rapport among students in situations where there are varying degrees and different kinds of directedness?

How much teacher participation? An issue related to the direction of discussion is the teacher's proper role as a class participant. Should a teacher practice, in the words of Stein (29, p. xxxi), "a rigorous doctrine of pedagogic self-abnegation" or should he play a more active and assertive role in a classroom? Those who argue for self-abnegation believe that this is the best way to develop independence of thought and attitude on the part of the student. Expressions by the teacher in a position of authority create a barrier to the student's becoming his own authority or developing his own point of view, so the argument goes. On the other hand, the person who argues that it is desirable for the teacher to express his own views may have strong values that he believes are important to communicate to students. Or he may believe that students will be critical of whatever views are expressed, and that they will accept or reject views on the basis of rational criteria. Again, a broader kind of question might be asked—"How can status barriers be diminished so that students will examine teachers' ideas just as critically as those of their fellow students?"

How closely should discussion focus on the case? Should a case be viewed as a "take-off" field, whereby students may zoom into the blue to deal with issues not too closely related to the facts of the case, or should students consistently deal with case content, or are there conditions that would indicate some kind of intermediate position? Again practice varies in regard to this problem, but the tradition has generally been more oriented toward sticking to the case, analyzing the facts of the case, and drawing conclusions that are clearly relevant to the given case. However, there are doubtless some exceptions to this rule. Some cases by their nature make excellent springboards for general discussions. Others are much more limited in content and can be dealt with more quickly. Actually, many very fruitful discussions seem to hover between general concepts and the facts of a case. Thus, the teacher must continually make judgments about whether a given bent in a discussion adds up to effective and efficient learning and, if not, about how to change the discussion so that it will be fruitful.

How difficult is it for students to adjust to the method? The case method has been called a "lethal instrument" (1, p. x). It is lethal because it often involves some reorientation on the part of both the student and the teacher. It is a well-known fact, for example, that some students who have had brilliant records in pre-legal training encounter difficulty in analyzing legal cases. Much education deals with logically organized bodies of knowledge. Such material is often neatly wrapped in textbooks and is studied and absorbed without much reference to concrete experience. Since the case method departs from this pattern, it sometimes creates student discomfort. When the burden of the responsibility for their own learning is thrust upon them, some students would rather have the cup pass from them.

Difficulties in student adjustment to the method in the Harvard Graduate School of Business Administration have been reported in some detail (9). According to the reports from studies based on 600 students, approximately two-thirds of this number had some difficulty in adjusting to the method.

Three-fourths of those having difficulty were able to adjust to the method with the help of individual counseling with faculty members. Many problems encountered among members of this group were not personal adjustment problems, but involved such factors as the failure to understand social science concepts. Of the remaining one-fourth of those having difficulty, the problems were "non-medical difficulties of social orientation." These students showed unusual disturbance and bewilderment. About 10 to 15 per cent of this group needed psychiatric help. Generally, the remainder of the students required more time than a faculty member was able to give. The task of helping these persons generally fell upon a trained counselor.

No study was made to compare the adjustments of students to different methods of teaching. However, in Fox's opinion the case method brings to the surface one's basic inadequacies for successful living much more readily than does the lecture method of teaching.

The Harvard report dealt with students who had had little or no administrative experience. Undoubtedly students who have had administrative experience are much less disturbed by the method than those who have had none. The former students are generally more mature, and many of them have already come to accept the idea that there is no one answer to administrative problems. In addition, since they have held responsible positions, they are more ready to act responsibly in analyzing case studies. Even among students with administrative experience, however, the method sometimes demands a certain reorientation. Thus, some individual counseling with students may be necessary.

Does the method reinforce the *status quo*? The case method has been criticized because case content deals with what is and not with what should be; therefore, present practice is taught. Perhaps this criticism is more relevant to the use of cases in legal training than to the case method in the training of administrators. In the legal profession, cases do become precedents, which determine future actions. Heavy authority is attached to the legal decisions as contained in cases. Even here precedents do give way, however, as is shown by the 1954 Supreme Court decision on racial integration.

In administration, cases should not be perceived as precedents, as court cases are. They are not necessarily a sound basis for future action. Rather, the focus is on understanding, analysis, and problem-solving. Mistakes of administrators are studied, not to be repeated, but to be comprehended and avoided. In addition, in administrative cases, one is continually confronted with value questions. Precedents are not necessarily binding, because actual events reported in cases are continually evaluated. It would seem, then, that the danger of reinforcing the *status quo* through case study is not as great as it has been made. Nevertheless, the teacher needs to be aware of the problem so that efforts can be made to avoid confusing the actual and the ideal.

How expensive is the method? The case method has been described as uneconomical. In the first place, it takes a great deal of time to develop cases, and as yet there are not sufficient cases representing the various problems of school administration. The writing of cases can be an expensive process. The Harvard Graduate School of Business Administration, for example, is reported to have budgeted $65,000 annually for case writing for a number of years and as much as $170,000 in 1936–1937 (30).

Some argue that case-method learning is time-consuming. It reduces the time, they say, in the training program for other kinds of learning. When assessing such objections, one must consider economy not only from a short-term but also from a long-term point of view. Although cases are expensive to develop, they can be used many times. No method can do everything, and there are few short cuts to *changing* student behavior. In other words, is the problem accurately described by saying that the case method is a slow process, or does the problem stem fundamentally from the fact that significant learning by any method is slow? For those who come to value the case approach to learning and teaching, the expense of the method, as well as the other problems noted above, should make it even more challenging. The challenge is also heightened by the present social scene. In the words of Turner (30, p. 349): "In a world no longer static, in a society so unstable that we may hope for no more than a moving equilibrium, the adventure of case teaching is destined to find a larger place."

References

1. Andrews, Kenneth (ed.), *The Case Method of Teaching: Human Relations and Administration.* Cambridge: Harvard University Press, 1953.

2. ———, "Executive Training by the Case Method," in *The Case Method of Teaching: Human Relations and Administration* (Kenneth Andrews, ed.). Cambridge: Harvard University Press, 1953, pp. 193–212.

3. Bauer, Ronald, *Cases in College Administration.* New York: Teachers College, Columbia University, 1955.

4. Castore, George, "Attitudes of Students Toward the Case Method of Instruction in a Human Relations Course," *Journal of Educational Research,* Vol. XLV, No. 3, Nov. 1951, pp. 201–213.

5. Culliton, James, "The Question That Has Not Been Asked Cannot Be Answered," in *Education for Professional Responsibility,* A Report of the Proceedings of the Inter-Professions Conference on Education for Professional Responsibility held at Buckhill Hall, Pennsylvania, April 12–14, 1948. Pittsburgh: Carnegie Press, 1948.

6. Donham, Wallace B., "Why Experiment? The Case System in College Teaching of Social Science," *The Journal of General Education,* Vol. 3, No. 2, January, 1949, pp. 145–56. Copyright 1949 by the University of Chicago.

7. Dubin, Robert, *Human Relations in Administration.* Englewood Cliffs, N.J.: Prentice-Hall, Inc., 1950.

8. Ferguson, Hob, *How to Get Teamwork Through Discussion.* Chicago: The Dartnell Corporation, 1955.

9. Fox, John, "A Note on Counseling as an Adjunct of the Case Method," in *The Case Method of Teaching: Human Relations and Administration* (Kenneth Andrews, ed.). Cambridge: Harvard University Press, 1953, pp. 41–45.

10. Fuller, Frances, "The Use of the Lecture in a Case Method Course," in *The Case Method of Teaching: Human Relations and Administration* (Kenneth Andrews, ed.). Cambridge: Harvard University Press, 1953, pp. 75–93.

11. Fuller, Stephen, "What is an Unsatisfactory Examination Paper?" in *The Case Method of Teaching: Human Relations and Administration* (Kenneth Andrews, ed.). Cambridge: Harvard University Press, 1953, pp. 122–37.

12. Garceau, Oliver, "Ten Years of Cases: An Appraisal." East Boothbay, Maine: 1955 (mimeographed).

13. Gibson, Hilden, "The Case Method in Human Relations," in *Accent on Teaching Experiments in General Education* (Sidney French, ed.). New York: Harper and Brothers, 1954, pp. 205–20.

14. Glover, John, and Ralph Hower, "Some Comments on Teaching by the Case Method," in *The Case Method of Teaching: Human Relations and Administration* (Kenneth Andrews, ed.). Cambridge: Harvard University Press, 1953, pp. 13–24.

15. ——— and ———, *The Administrator: Cases on Human Relations in Business.* Chicago: Richard D. Irwin Company, 1952.

16. Gragg, Charles, "Because Wisdom Can't Be Told," in *The Case Method of Teaching: Human Relations and Administration* (Kenneth Andrews, ed.). Cambridge: Harvard University Press, 1953, pp. 3–12.

17. Griffiths, Daniel, *Human Relations in School Administration.* New York: Appleton-Century-Crofts, Inc., 1956.

18. Hennessey, John, Jr., *A Study of Some Aspects of Teaching and Learning in a College Case-Method Course in Human Relations in Business.* Unpublished doctoral dissertation, University of Washington, 1956.

19. Hunt, Pearson, "The Case Method of Instruction," *Harvard Educational Review,* Vol. 21, No. 3, Summer 1951, pp. 175–92.

20. Lee, Irving, *Customs and Crises in Communication.* New York: Harper and Brothers, 1954.

21. Llewellyn, K. N., "Case Method," *Encyclopedia of the Social Sciences,* Vol. III. New York: The Macmillan Company, 1930, pp. 251–254.

22. National Conference of Professors of Educational Administration, *Providing and Improving Administrative Leadership for Amercan Schools.* New York: Teachers College, Columbia University, 1951.

23. Peterson, Houston, *Great Teachers.* New Brunswick: Rutgers University Press, 1946.

24. Reining, Henry, Jr., "Case Method and Public Personnel Administration," *Public Personnel Review,* Vol. XII, No. 3, July, 1951, pp. 151–158.

25. ———, "The Preparation and Utilization of Cases in Teaching Public Administration," *Related Disciplines and the Study and Teaching of Educational Administration* (Theodore Reller, ed.). University of California, Berkeley, California, 1954 (mimeographed), pp. 60–65.

26. Revzan, David, "The Preparation and Utilization of Cases in Teaching Business Administration," in *Related Disciplines and the Study and Teaching of Educational Administration* (Theodore Reller, ed.). University of California, Berkeley, California, 1954 (mimeographed), pp. 69–76.

27. Roethlisberger, Fritz J., "Training Supervisors in Human Relations," in *The Case Method of Teaching: Human Relations and Administration* (Kenneth Andrews, ed.). Cambridge: Harvard University Press, 1953, pp. 175–192.

28. Sargent, Cyril, and Eugene Belisle, *Educational Administration: Cases and Concepts.* Boston: Houghton Mifflin Co., 1955.

29. Stein, Harold, ed., *Public Administration and Policy Development: A Case Book.* New York: Harcourt, Brace & Co., 1952.

30. Turner, Glenn, "Teaching Business by the Case Method," *California Journal of Secondary Education,* Vol. 13, No. 16, October, 1938, pp. 338–349.

31. Ulrich, David, "The Case Method," in *The Case Method of Teaching: Human Relations and Administration* (Kenneth Andrews, ed.). Cambridge: Harvard University Press, 1953, pp. 25–34.

32. Wengert, Egburt, "Comments on Cases," in *Related Disciplines and the Study and Teaching of Educational Administration* (Theodore Reller, ed.). University of California, Berkeley, California, 1954 (mimeographed), pp. 65–7.

33. Wolozin, Harold, "Teaching Personnel Administration by Role Playing," *Personnel,* Vol. 27, July–August, 1948, pp. 107–109.

Cases

The Rock and
Roll Ruckus

In addition to the usual problems of student discipline, the unusual incident of a student strike faced the administrators in the following case. The setting was a large metropolitan area, and the time was 1953–1954. At the particular place and time involved, the "rhythm and blues movement" was growing in popularity, a movement that was to become a national phenomenon known as "Rock and Roll."

The events included in the case raise various questions: How does the administrator deal effectively and ethically with the conflicts resulting from the clash of differing cultural values? What are the limits of compromise when administrative authority and student expectations brush against each other? How can the administrator, who, by the nature of his position, is somewhat isolated from the members of his organization, still maintain communication channels that will enable him to understand the problems that confront the organization for which he is responsible? These are a few of the many questions that the case poses.

The narrative is broken into four parts. The first part depicts the school strike. In the nature of a flashback, the second part recounts some events leading up to the strike. The events are depicted as isolated incidents in the manner and order in which they occurred. In fact, so separated in time were the incidents that the administration was largely unaware of the smoldering resentment slowly building up to the crisis of the strike. Part III includes a description of the community and the student body. In the final section, decisions and action taken immediately following the strike are reported.

PART I. THE STRIKE

"See ya later, alligator!"

"After a while, crocodile—at nine o'clock. Man! I can hardly wait to see ole Nielson's face. What a square!"

Fran Holm bounded through the door of her English class and slipped into her seat just as the 8:55 bell rang signaling the start of first-period classes at Los Robles High. Mrs. Calloway, her teacher, was taking roll at her desk in front of the class.

"There's going to be a strike at 9 o'clock, Mrs. Calloway," Fran announced. "You don't need to take roll."

"Oh, really?" said Mrs. Calloway without glancing in the direction of Fran's voice. "Well, I'll just go ahead anyway so there'll be sure to be some check on who the strikers are. In the meantime, will the second persons in each row get enough of the story books from the shelf for their row. Thank you."

"Mrs. Calloway, what will happen to the students who go on strike?"

That was Bob Adams's voice, and he looked concerned. Mrs. Calloway looked directly at him.

"In this class, any students who go on strike will fail for the days they're absent. I don't know what steps the office will take," she said.

And so sophomore English in Room 211 proceeded with its scheduled activities. Students opened their books in preparation for the day's discussion, but Fran Holm watched the hands of the clock move around to 9 o'clock.

Then—"We're going on strike!"

At the door, Fran stopped, looking up and down the second-floor hall of the main building. "Well, where is everybody? There's nobody out here, and it's time."

In a moment a few heads peered out of other classroom doors up and down the corridor, and approximately 15 students stepped into the hall.

"Here they are!" Fran Holm's voice was triumphant. "Come on, everybody!"

Two other students in Mrs. Calloway's class hesitatingly rose from their seats, entered the hall, and just as quickly returned, Fran Holm with them.

Mr. Gordon, vice-principal in charge of discipline and assistant to the principal, had appeared. At the sight of him, students immediately ducked back into their classrooms. As he slowly passed each room, all would-be strikers were in their seats and starting to work as if nothing had happened.

While the appearance of Mr. Gordon on the upstairs floor had had the effect of quelling any large-scale abandonment of classes in that part of the building, there was quite a different scene on the ground floor. Principal Nielson and his assistant, Miss Cobb, stood in the entryway of the main hall and waited as a group of about 100 students, led by student-body vice-president Jane Ramsey, approached them.

"Well, what's all this?"

The group quieted as Mr. Nielson spoke. In an even tone Jane Ramsey replied, "We're going on strike, Mr. Nielson."

"What for?"

"We're tired of the way we've been treated, and we don't like the way things have been going. . . ."

"What things?" Mr. Nielson broke in. "No one's complained to me about anything. Has anyone come to you, Miss Cobb?"

As Miss Cobb shook her head, Mr. Nielson continued. "I'd like to hear what's wrong. Why not give us a chance to help you before you do something that will put the whole school in a bad light? What's wrong with the Student Council? Have you brought these matters to their attention?"

"No . . . it wouldn't do any good," Jane's voice began to falter. "We . . ."

"Well, I'd like to find out why. Let's get the executive committee down here right away and have a special meeting in my office along with some of you people here."

As he finished speaking, Mr. Nielson quickly glanced over the group and began calling out the names of those students whom he knew commanded a following among their peers.

"Come on. Let's talk this thing over. Is there anyone else who would like to sit in on this?"

Mr. Nielson addressed this last question to Jane as well as to the group.

"Yes, I think there are, Mr. Nielson, but I don't know where they are now," Jane replied.

"I'll send the office monitors around to each teacher. The rest of you can leave this up to your representatives to speak for you, can't you?"

Mr. Nielson had the upper hand now. He had the leaders, and the followers knew that they were followers. Some looked distrustful and disgruntled; others nodded their heads, satisfied.

"All right," continued Mr. Nielson. "Return to your classes now, and we'll give a report to the student body over the public address system as soon as we come to some conclusions."

With grumbles here and there, the group milled about, broke into twos and threes, and dispersed. Some of the tension had gone out of the air, but it was not all gone.

PART II. IN RETROSPECT

The Soph Hop. There was a good crowd out for the Soph Hop. Since Los Robles was a new high school only a year and a half old, this was the second such dance to be given by a sophomore class.

The strains of "My Desire" drifted across the dance floor. The record ended; dancers paused, conversed. Then—"Money, Honey!" With almost a jarring note, the record blared forth with its accentuated, synocopated beat taking up a rhythm that was later to be known across the nation as "rock and roll." The goodly representation of Los Robles colored students who were attending the dance were on their feet at the sound of the familiar beat. A few white students continued dancing; but for the majority, the music and the style of dancing were unfamiliar, and so they took their seats.

When the record ended, a number of colored students dashed over to the student attending the music and requested another rhythm-and-blues number. Their request was granted.

The music was intoxicating—at least, Betty Lambert seemed to find it so. Grabbing her girl friend by the hand, she pulled her toward the dance floor. "Come on, Selma. Let's show these kids how to really rock."

Betty and Selma put on quite an exhibition, and the rest of the dancers gathered around to watch their swaying, undulating movements. When the students glanced about to see what effect the two girls' dancing was having on the chaperones, they could not help but note the looks of disapproval.

The music came to an abrupt halt. The honking saxophones and jarring piano chords were replaced by Eddie Fisher's baritone. The white students stepped onto the dance floor, and most of the colored students took their seats.

For the first time at any Los Robles dance, there was tension in the air, and, for the first time at any Los Robles function, a color line had unmistakably been drawn.

The Assembly. As the bell for the second assembly rang, the students poured expectantly into the halls. They met the students from the first assembly coming up the stairs, stopping at their lockers in the halls.

"Was he good?"

"Yeah, man, yeh."

"Wait'll you see his suit—solid gold threads, man. Solid gold!"

"That Swingin' Sam is the most. Wait'll he spins 'Cadillac Baby!' It'll really send ya."

"How did Nielson take it?"

"Are you kiddin'?"

The cafeteria, on Fridays serving as a makeshift assembly room, rapidly filled. When all the chairs were taken, the remainder of the students sat on the tables which were lined up around the walls of the room and dangled their feet over the edge. The student-control members took their places around the room. Some students got up from their seats and sat on the tables so that faculty members could sit in the chairs.

Student-body president Max Washington stood up and banged his gavel. A hush fell over the room. The student-body meeting began and proceeded in its customary, orderly routine of pledge to the flag, reading of the minutes, committee reports, old business, and new business.

The assembled students were courteous and attentive and excited. The business portion was fairly interesting, but this Friday it was almost hard to sit through it until the program. After all, it wasn't every day that one could see Swingin' Sam in person—Swingin' Sam, the most popular disc jockey among the students in the school.

Then it was time for the program. Swingin' Sam stepped onto the platform, impeccable mustache, dark horn-rimmed glasses, blue suede shoes, tan tweed suit flecked with gold, and all.

"Well, cats," said Sam. "You and I know what we like—money, all we can make. So here comes your first platter spinnin' . . ."

Once again, from the looks on the faces of Mr. Nielson and several faculty members, it was clear to the fans of Swingin' Sam that their idol, his running commentary, and his records were definitely unacceptable fare for a high school assembly program.

Afterward, the students remembered that Mrs. Berg, a counselor, and Mrs. Shelley, the attendance secretary, had walked out of the program, and they assumed that it was because the two staff members did not like Swingin' Sam and wished to let him know that they did not like him.

The all-school dance. The next all-school dance sponsored by the Student Council was held in the upstairs hall of the main building, as had been all the council's dances that year. Next year it would be a different story, with the new gym completed, so the students philosophically accepted the temporary cramped quarters. Only two couples of Negro students showed up for this dance, including student-body president Max Washington and his date. They stayed for approximately half an hour and left. There was no rock-and-roll music played at this dance.

Passing-time. At the sound of the 10:05 passing bell, the halls of Los Robles were suddenly flooded with students moving in a kaleidoscope of color. Mr. Nielson stood in the hall of the main building near the foot of the stairs watching the students pass by, as he did on one or two occasions a week.

"Hello, Mr. Nielson!"

"Oh, hello, Tom," answered the principal.

A few students called out or spoke to Mr. Nielson, but the majority gave little or no sign of notice.

But out of earshot . . . "Hey, did you get a load of the warden over there watching the inmates file by?"

"Yeah. What does he think this is—a grammar school or somethin'? I thought we were past that when we left Washington School. We might as well be back in the third grade, the way we get treated around here sometimes."

Student Council. "All right, let's move on here. We don't have much time before the period'll be over."

Max Washington, student-body president, was presiding over the weekly meeting of the Los Robles Student Council. The main business before the student legislative assembly this week was the spring formal scheduled a month hence. Student representatives from the advisory sections were reporting on their constituents' vote concerning the dance theme.

"Mrs. Stone's section," called out Max.

Don Jameson stood up. "Fifteen for 'Forbidden City,' ten for 'Cherry Pink and Apple-Blossom White,' and two for 'April Showers.' "

As the secretary marked her tally on the blackboard, the president called for the final representative, a student from a freshman advisory.

"Seventeen for 'Forbidden City' and twelve for 'Cherry Pink and Apple-Blossom White.' "

When the secretary had added the votes, Max announced the results. "Looks like 'Forbidden City' will be the theme for our next dance—403 votes for 'Forbidden City,' 310 votes for 'Cherry Pink' et cetera, and 59 votes for 'April Showers.' "

"Well! It seems you've got the most difficult theme to work on for your next dance." Mr. Small, faculty advisor to the Los Robles student-body government spoke, as he rose from his seat near the rear of the room and moved toward the front. "I hope you all realize the work this is going to involve. We'll have to make all new props. We can't use any of the stuff we already have on hand. This is going to run into money. You know, this is getting near the end of the year, and there isn't much cash on hand."

"Aw, Mr. Small, a bunch of us can make that pagoda from scraps in shop. Some of the kids are already through their big projects, and they'd be glad to work on decorations for the dance. I don't think it'll be so tough."

"Yes, and I've heard that before, too. But what happens? It's always the same ones who get stuck with all the work. At the end of the year there's always lots going on, and most of you just don't have the time. Now, if we had the 'Cherry Pink' theme, there wouldn't be anything to it. We have those flowers and trees from last year, and . . ."

Before he could go on, another student interrupted. "But Mr. Small, we've already voted on it. The kids don't want the 'Cherry Pink' theme. My advisory voted for 'Cherry Pink,' but I don't think we can go against the majority."

"All right, they've had their vote, and they're happy. All the

same, the executive committee, when they really get down to looking into this, may have to reconsider. This matter of time—and the
finances—may change things," replied Mr. Small.

A junior girl raised her hand and was recognized by the chair.
"Mr. President, since we don't have much time—about two minutes
left in the period, I think we should make plans to get organized—
for our 'Forbidden City' dance. I move that the executive committee
at their next meeting assign the dance committees and needed jobs
to the various advisory sections and inform us of the assignments at
the next Student Council meeting." Looking directly at Mr. Small,
the girl sat down.

The motion was seconded, voted upon, and passed as the bell
rang ending the meeting.

"Hey, Jim, wait up!" Don Jameson called to a friend. "What are
you going to tell your section? Wait'll mine hears what happened
today. They're already putting old Small down as a real square from
way back. This'll really tee them off."

"Oh, I don't know as I'll even bother to report. This is just more
of the same old stuff. It happens all the time. We get asked to vote
on something, and what happens? Mr. Small gets it his way every
time. My section doesn't hardly listen to my reports any more. They're
so fed up."

"Yeah, and you know what's going to happen in that excom meeting. We'll come back next week, and the theme will be 'Cherry
Pink.'"

"You're tellin' me! Well, just wait. Things are really gonna start
poppin' around here. Just wait."

PART III. THE SETTING

The community. Situated in a suburban area located not far from
a large, busy metropolis, the Los Robles school plant had been in use
only a year and a half. The plant itself was still in the process of completion, but it showed definite promise of being ready by the next
fall.

A large military installation, established in the community during the war and still in use by the United States Government, had
brought with it an increased and transient population including a

proportionate influx of Negroes, housing projects for workers and military personnel associated with the base, crowding of housing elsewhere in the community, cut-rate stores and installment buying, and the beginnings of a slum area in an old section of the city. It was from the housing projects and the transient military population that Los Robles largely drew its students. At the same time, the remainder of the student body represented families who had lived in the community for from 5 to 30 years. Many of the latter families, like those whose children attended the "respectable" old high school, resented the changes wrought in their city by the war and postwar years and resented the intruders. This attitude is reflected in the following statement by a Los Robles student:

"My house used to be in a nice, clean neighborhood. Now you ought to see it. Those old projects are right next to us. They're run down and the lawns aren't cut. It's noisy. It's crumby. I wish we could move over to the other side of town so I could go to West High."

Before the war, the area subsequently taken over by the government for military and housing purposes had been in truck gardens owned and farmed by persons of Italian or Portuguese descent. Little or no industry was associated with the community other than the truck gardens.

The suburban community in general was a desirable residential area. Its streets were graced with large, shady, well-cared-for trees and homes dating from the late Victorian era. Belmont Acres, the most plush residential section, made up a quarter of the community.

With the war years, many older residents died or moved elsewhere. A good number of the once fashionable Victorian homes in the center of town became apartments or flats to house the rapidly growing population. A small business area that formerly served the Italian residential and farming area at the eastern end of town now expanded and began to rival the older business section. At the same time, several blocks of moderately priced new homes were built in the "east end."

Still, the western section of the community "looked down their noses" at their neighbors to the east. Their attitudes were clearly reflected when the boundary line between the two high school districts was drawn. Even though Belmont Acres extended many blocks eastward, that area was included in the district for West High. Thus, instead of a more or less straight line dividing the two districts, the boundary line ran a very jagged course across the city. Old-time residents were thus assured that their sons and daughters could attend and share in the traditions of old West High and join one of the social fraternities or sororities that played a large part in teen-age life at that school.

At the same time, whether by chance or by plan, the line was drawn so that, without exception, all Negro children of high school age would be attending Los Robles. This was the case even though some Negro families lived as far west as some residents of Belmont Acres.

The student body. Approximately 25 per cent of Los Robles students were colored. The families of some of these students had been in the community for ten or more years, but the residence of most was short-term. The majority of colored students lived in the government projects, and the livelihood of their parents was dependent upon employment at the military base.

For many, both white and colored, living quarters were cramped —a situation that made for noise and little private or quiet space for such things as homework for students of high school age. Often both parents worked. Younger children were frequently the responsibility of high school brothers and sisters. For some, meals were eaten in two or more shifts. Without parental supervision at night, many students wandered at will. Some were in trouble with the police. Others took advantage of the projects' group activities, including the dances, parties, and athletic program. Still others formed their own social groups and planned get-togethers at each other's apartments. A high premium was placed on nice clothes and a big, flashy car.

At Los Robles the colored students, in spite of such previous handicaps as modest formal education and lack of economic security, for the most part made a significant and constructive contribution to the school. During the 1953–1954 spring term, four out of the five members of the Executive Committee were Negro students. Vice-President Jane Ramsey was the white student on the committee. The colored students were also well represented in the executive positions of almost every other club and organization in the school. Their contributions and participation in the school's total athletic program were outstanding. As a group they were, with few exceptions, well accepted by the white students. All the evidence seemed to indicate that integration had been achieved at Los Robles.

The white student body to a large extent also represented families of a lower middle- or upper lower-class economic status. Thus, the high school experience for the majority of Los Robles students was the end of their formal education. Some would perhaps take an additional two years in a junior college. Few would enter a university.

For a majority of Los Robles students, there was little or no pressure from home to master academic or college-preparatory subjects or to be included in any particular social clique. This situation was a distinct contrast to that at West High, where many students strove to excel academically and to be included in one of the long-established sororities and fraternities.

Student values and interests. While some Los Robles students resented not being able to attend West High, the majority welcomed the chance to attend a new school and to have a part in building the school's traditions. They expressed their disapproval of West High's "frat-rats" by placing a taboo on such articles of clothing as saddle shoes or white bucks for boys and cashmere sweaters for both boys and girls. Peg pants, ducktail hair cuts, gaucho shirts, thick-soled shoes, and narrow leather belts were popular with a large segment of the boys. With the exception of the cashmere sweaters, most of the girls dressed in the fashion of the day, although a substantive minority preferred the straight, tight skirt, near-hip-length blouse, dangling ear-rings, and "bop" boots or "baby-tear" shoes. Among the latter group were many students who were most outspoken in their dislike of "frat-rats" and who were in open rebellion against home, school, and, sometimes, community authorities. Fran Holm and her friends were of this category. Among the boys who were discontent, black peg pants, black shirts, crucifixes, and India ink tatoos were the outward symbols of their rebellion.

Some teachers at Los Robles at first found it difficult to adjust to the frankness and outspokenness of many of their students. An honest expression of opinion was often interpreted as rudeness or impudence on the part of the student. On the whole, a teacher could know how his or her students felt. Hypocrisy was not a general characteristic.

In addition, teachers soon discovered that homework assignments would rarely be completed on time or would not be turned in at all by a large percentage of their students, either because of lack of time, interest, or facilities for home study or for other reasons. Assignments that could be supervised and completed in the classroom were more acceptable to the students and were performed cheerfully for the most part.

If many of the students were not interested in academic pursuits, they were interested in radio station KRBA, Swingin' Sam, and the kind of music usually featured on his disc jockey shows. KRBA's broadcasts as a whole had a great appeal to the colored population of the area; and for a large group of Los Robles white teen-agers, the rhythm-and-blues music generally featured on the station was also very appealing. The dance steps that were a counterpart of rhythm-and-blues were either the "slow-drag" (quite an accurate description of the step) or "Bop." Although slow-drag was danced only by the colored students, bop was danced by both races but still by only a very small minority of students. Following the incident at the Soph Hop, rhythm-and-blues music was virtually outlawed by the administration at Los Robles dances. Members of the administration and Mr. Small, advisor to the student government, both expressed their disapproval.

Thus, in this realm of interest, there developed a definite rift between the students, their school administrators—especially Mr. Nielson—and some of their teachers.

Mr. Small particularly came under fire, although student censure of him was due mainly to what the students called "playing favorites." Mr. Small himself stated, "My policy in working with people is to reward those who are willing to co-operate and work hard for me. The rest I don't bother with."

There could be little doubt that Mr. Small practiced his avowed policy. As a result, he had a small group of students who were very loyal and dependable, and who worked hard for him. However, many students felt that such a sitaution in effect took the student government out of their hands and put it in the hands of Mr. Small. They claimed that matters and issues that did not have his approval did not pass in the Student Council. Even in such a minor matter as a dance theme and dance decorations Mr. Small often had his way. Thus, many students began to lose faith in the Student Council. In the advisory sections, they were heard to say that it didn't do any good to bring up issues at the Student Council, because Mr. Small would veto them.

Aside from a change in the administration's attitude toward rhythm-and-blues or rock and roll, many students at this time also desired for their school a spring carnival, a juke box for the cafeteria, and stag dances to be held either after school or at noontime. Although a lack of facilities and the approaching end of the semester precluded any possibility of a spring carnival, the word spread in school that the spring carnival, the juke box, and the stag dances had all been vetoed either by Mr. Small, Mr. Nielson, or both, apparently for no reason.

Thus, in the seeming rejection of values of importance to a large number of Los Robles students, the seeds of dissatisfaction and rebellion were sown.

PART IV. DECISIONS AND ACTION

Meeting with the strikers. Mr. Nielson's first step toward ferreting out and destroying the seeds of rebellion and discontent was his meeting with the student-body officers and the strike leaders. At the end of the second period on that fateful spring morning, the public address system came on all over the school. Students eagerly awaiting further news of the results of the strike and the meeting fell silent as Mr. Nielson's voice came over the loudspeaker:

"I have an announcement that I believe all Los Robles students will be interested in. Your student body officers and several other interested students have just had a meeting here in my office to attempt to clear up some misunderstandings apparently existing between members of the student body and the administration. Some matters I had heard little or nothing about until today, but I think we have arrived at some conclusions and understandings.

"One thing that evidently has been bothering a number of students is the matter of having a juke box in the cafeteria. I see no reason why the Student Council cannot appoint a committee to secure a juke box or a record player for the cafeteria, to raise the necessary funds, and to select appropriate records.

"Stag dances is another matter that was brought up. After some discussion, the group has decided that they would be willing to see the Student Council sponsor some stag dances next year on a trial basis. If they are successful, they should be continued.

"It was also reported to me at this meeting that students did not like to see me or other members of the administration standing in the hall observing the students during passing-time, that they think it is grammar-schoolish, and that the Student Control can handle anyone who might be out of order. I did not know until today that Los Robles students felt that way. Hereafter the other members of the administration and I shall refrain from 'standing guard' in the halls between class periods.

"These and several other issues were discussed at this meeting. Some matters will need further consideration by your student-body officers, your Student Council, working together with the administration. However, these are the conclusions that we have come to thus far. The student body will be informed of any further meetings or developments either by your officers or by myself. I hope that Los Robles students will see that understandings can be worked out through meetings such as these, and that they will report complaints to their Student Council and officers or to the administration rather than take some action that will reflect badly on the whole school—action that they might well be sorry for later.

"This is a new school. We can't do everything at once. It takes time for your various school groups to set up and organize activities. I think you'll find that next year, with a new gym, a cafetorium, and a bigger plant, you'll be able to plan and have many of the activities that you have missed this year. Only have a little patience, and things will work out. That is all."

Los Robles students on the whole seemed satisfied with this report. Even though the strike had been thwarted, they felt that they had achieved a moral victory. As one of Mrs. Calloway's advisees put it, "At least they listened to us and gave us some of the things we wanted. They wouldn't have listened if we hadn't gone on strike. And the thing that made it work was Jane Ramsey. When she was in it, too, they paid some attention."

Afterwards it was found out that student-body president Max Washington had also informed Mr. Nielson of the student's feelings about Mr. Small.

"Man, when Mr. Nielson said he wanted to hear everything, ol' Max, he told him everything," reported Ted Moore, one of the strikers who sat in on the meeting. "Ol' Max wasn't scared of Mr. Nielson one bit. He just told Mr. Nielson that the kids think Mr. Small plays favorites and doesn't accept the kids' ideas a lot of the time. Max told Mr. Nielson he thought the student government would be a lot better if they had a different advisor. And when Max talked like that, the rest of the kids, they agreed and told how they felt too. Mr. Nielson, he sat there and asked a whole bunch of questions, and he really listened to what we said. I think a lot of kids around here got the wrong idea about Mr. Nielson. He's okay."

CASE THREE

The Senior Trip

The ringing of the phone interrupted Superintendent Smith's work on the Mason School budget. A voice greeted him, "This is Ned Boltz."

"Oh, yes, Ned. I heard that you were back in town," Smith responded.

Ned continued, "I just want to call and tell you that everything was fine. We had no trouble. I have never seen a group behave better. I thought you would want to know."

Mr. Smith hesitated a moment, then replied, "Thanks, Ned, for calling me."

Mr. Smith returned the telephone slowly, leaned back in his chair, and glanced out of the window. "I wonder if the seniors did behave on their trip to Washington," he thought. "If Ned had any control over them, it was the first time." It was well known to students, parents, and teachers that Ned's students did as they liked in his classes. They threw erasers, stood at the windows while he lectured, left the room at will, and even tripped him in spite of his crippled condition. Smith, along with Bealson, the high school principal, had tried everything they knew to place Ned where he would work out well. One year he was assigned only three classes. The other three periods of the day he acted as a guidance counselor and a general community consultant. This had not worked out well. The two administrators had considered refusing his contract renewal, but this plan did not seem feasible, since Ned got along rather well with adults in the community. Various groups outside the school considered him a real scholar in international affairs. He was often asked to discuss national and international problems in various clubs and organizations. Also, Mrs. Boltz, who operated the Mason Telephone Exchange, was one of the best-loved personalities in town. The Boltz's three teen-age children were talented and popular, and the Boltz family was deeply rooted in the community.

Mr. Smith's mind wandered back three years to the time when he had accepted the Mason School job. He was happily employed as an elementary principal in a 15-teacher school in a city 100 miles away. A friend who taught in Mason told him of a serious financial difficulty in the Mason School and of the Board's decision to look for a new superintendent. He had gone to Mason without invitation in early August to visit the board members. They had told him they were looking for an older man with more experience. Mr. Smith was only 29 at the time. Besides, everyone seemed busy making plans for the approaching Homecoming and did not seem too serious about making a decision concerning the vacancy. Therefore, he had dismissed the position from his mind and had gone to another state to visit his family.

Mr. Smith still remembered the telephone call on Labor Day offering him the Mason School job. Sara, his wife, thought he shouldn't take it so late, but he had seen it as a chance in a lifetime to make a real jump ahead. He accepted the position for $4,200, which was $1,500 more than his elementary-principal salary. It was nearly a year later that he learned that the Board had agreed to pay up to $5,500, if necessary. At the close of the first year, the Board voted 4 to 1 to bring his salary to $5,500. He remembered how the dissenting board member spread the statement, "The other members of the board gave our superintendent a $1,300 raise." This incident had caused criticism from teachers and patrons which had embarrassed the Smiths.

He came to Mason highly enthusiastic about the educational possibilities in the school and community. There were 235 students in the upper four grades and approximately 800 in the school system. The town had a population of only 1,500, but considerable progress had been made in consolidating the schools in the surrounding territory. The people were proud of their school and seemed willing to support school functions. School facilities were a little limited in some ways, but generally were adequate. An important source of school-district wealth was a rich bean-farming area which had provided good incomes for almost a decade. Mr. Smith had felt from the beginning that there were many possibilities in the Mason School chief administrator's position.

Those first months in Mason were trying ones. He remembered the Board's surprise when he and the auditors, who he insisted should be hired, found that the school had a debt of $90,000. The debt included $10,000 payable to the Federal School Lunch Program for over-claims on lunches and $80,000 of illegal loans. The auditor's report did not reveal misappropriation of the borrowed funds. The situation demanded that the people vote an additional 20-mill tax for three years or lose their high school. The State Department of Education had already indicated that, unless the school district achieved a satisfactory financial condition within the next few months, it would be necessary to consolidate with one of the surrounding high schools.

The first two votes for the additional 20-mill tax failed. It was then that it fell to Mr. Smith's lot to say to the Board what everyone else seemed clear about: the people of Mason had lost confidence in two board members. Bill Acres and Milt Tunis were the only two remaining board members who were a part of the old board which had placed the school district in such deep indebtedness. If the people were to pass the 20-mill increase, these two must go. While Mr. Smith never indicated which board members were responsible for the low degree of confidence the people had in the Board, Bill Acres and Milt Tunis immediately offered to resign when the general problem was explained. However, they were less friendly after that. As a matter of fact, when public opinion later became hot on educational issues, Milt came out openly against him. Nevertheless, the tax passed overwhelmingly on the third try.

Blight Kelson, one of the two appointed board members on the reorganized board, was made president. Blight had the reputation for being against everything which cost money—especially superintendents. His reputation for close handling of finances was judged by many to be the sole reason for his appointment. He became a thorn in Mr. Smith's side from the very beginning. One was never sure where Blight stood on anything. He seemed to delight in "digging up" events, problems, and gossip which Mr. Smith did not know about and using these to embarrass the chief administrator during board meetings. Blight's farm implement store became a sort of cesspool of gossip.

As Mr. Smith looked back over his past three years, he wondered if he had been very effective in working with Blight. He found himself angry and defensive a lot of the time. He had spent hours talking about Blight to Sara. Teachers and principals were aware of and generally shared Smith's feelings toward Blight. The problem was aggravated by Sam Sabert, the school custodian, who took everything he saw or heard directly to the board president. Sam was especially interested in any student or teacher's behavior which might have sexual implications. He appeared to be the source of several stories that were found to have no bases. Sam had been with the school system for years and at times seemed to carry more weight with the Board than did professional personnel.

Mr. Smith turned his glance across the street to Blight's big brick home and was reminded of a problem involving Hal Jones. Hal, a local farmer, had been hired to teach English until a fully qualified teacher could be obtained. Three members of the reorganized board, especially Blight, were constantly critical of Hal. They said he had queer ideas and had carried out many crazy community projects. They were especially critical of a pageant developed by Hal in which a pageant participant was accidentally shot in the leg.

Mr. Smith knew that Hal's teaching was certainly unorthodox, and he did discuss the hazards of some of Hal's projects with him. However, Mr. Smith had felt that Hal was doing as well as anyone available, so he recommended him over the Board's protest the first year that he was superintendent. However, after continued board protest, especially on the part of Blight, Mr. Smith did not recommend Hal the next year. This was during the spring of the senior trip that Mr. Smith sponsored. When Hal asked Blight why he had not been rehired, Blight said, "Mr. Smith refused to recommend you." This made Hal furious. Later in the year, Hal was to add to Mr. Smith's worries as the latter grappled with problems arising from an ill-fated senior trip for which he, himself, was responsible.

Once more Mr. Smith found himself recalling the details of the three senior trips during his tenure in Mason. He wished that he could forget them all—just wash that part of his three years right off the slate. However, there was always something to remind him—a telephone call, a cold look from a person on the street, or the general attitude of certain students.

The Mason seniors had been taking trips to Washington, D.C., just prior to graduation for several years. There were numerous stories of drinking, wild sex parties, and dangerous pranks among past trip members. No one seemed to be very concerned about these stories. Many people said, "Boys will be boys," or "It's just story-telling—there's nothing to it."

The seniors went to Washington during Mr. Smith's first year in Mason. The sponsors were Mr. Pete Brown, the band instructor, his wife, Marjorie, and George Hen, the agriculture teacher and football coach. Mr. Hen was a very able teacher and a popular person among students and adults in the community. He was known to be a person liberal in his beliefs and in his expectations of students. In addition to Mrs. Brown's duties of housekeeper and mother of five children, she was an able musician and evangelist. She was a key worker in the local Evangelical Church and was particularly concerned with the morals of youth. Pete also seemed very much concerned with the morals of youth. Many felt that his appearance of rigidity was not so much how he felt as it was a reflection of his wife's views.

The behavior of the group on this trip did not remain in the undercurrent of public discussion. It was openly discussed and condemned, first from the pulpit of the Evangelical Church and, then, from all the Protestant pulpits in Mason. It was reported that drinking was common and excessive. Supposedly, Hen participated in drinking parties with class members. One girl, who reportedly had never taken a drink before, became so intoxicated that she attempted to jump out of a window. Some students, it was reported, were not sober during the entire Washington visit and sometimes failed to make scheduled trips. Many, it was further reported, participated in group sex parties. Some members were accused of stealing hotel property.

As a result of the community upheaval concerning the trip, the Board suggested that Mr. Smith personally sponsor the next senior group, which was scheduled to go to New York City and Washington,

D.C. Mr. Smith had always wanted to make a trip to the two cities, and he saw the problem as a challenge in working with a student group, so he readily consented to sponsor the trip. He assured the Board that he could organize the group so that there would be no trouble.

One of the first things which Mr. Smith decided should be done was to involve both senior members and their parents in the planning. His program for educational administration preparation in the State University had placed considerable stress on community involvement, and Mr. Smith was a great believer in this way of dealing with community problems. He felt that the senior trip could be approached best through the students and their parents.

Early in the fall, the senior group was called together to begin work on the forthcoming spring senior trip. Mr. Smith reviewed the problems of the past trip and outlined the Board's concern for the forthcoming trip. He said that he believed in the group's ability to develop sufficiently adequate guides for a successful trip. He further indicated that some clear understanding concerning the group's behavior was necessary if they were to make the trip.

Mr. Smith noted from the beginning that the students did not seem enthusiastic for the guide lines. As he looked back on it now, it seemed that they reluctantly discussed what they wanted this trip to be and what responsibility each person should take for himself. Although Mr. Smith did not notice it at the time, it now seemed that he and the students behaved as though they were sitting on the opposite sides of a bargaining table.

He had not felt very comfortable with the group during these discussions. He had attributed this to his limited contacts with them. After all, he had the key responsibility for the expenditures of $135,-000 per year, to say nothing of the administration of the school lunch program, a 15-bus transportation system, and a staff of 35 teachers. He also had an important leadership role with the board of education. How could he hope to know the members of the senior class well?

Later on, his critics had said, "You didn't gain the confidence of the group," "They didn't know or like you," "Your nickname was 'Stoneface'—no wonder you had trouble with the group," "Mr. Patterson, the former superintendent, used to hand trays to the children in the lunch line and wave good-bye to the buses as they left. Our children liked him." All of these comments had disturbed Mr. Smith very much. He knew that he hadn't spent much time with the students, but how could he do everything? Which was more important —being close to the students, or developing a good school?

Not all students resisted the development of guide lines for the trip. A set of rules did emerge on which there was agreement. The rules included items on promptness, places where smoking would be permitted, and some statements on over-all conduct. One statement was very clear: "There shall be no drinking of alcoholic beverages during the trip." The group agreed that anyone guilty of the infraction of this regulation should be sent home immediately. Mr. Smith was not clear whether the "punishment" was decided by free choice of the conservative element of the class or whether they agreed on such action because they felt such a rule was necessary before the trip would be permitted.

The students also decided that they would enforce their own regulations. The sponsors should not act as policemen but should hold the whole group responsible for the fulfillment of the regulations as agreed upon by the class and their parents. If any member broke the regulations, it would mean that either those who broke the regulations or the whole group would receive the appropriate punishment. The group was agreeable to this plan.

Parents of the senior class met four times to review the guide lines developed by the class. The first of the four meetings was a joint meeting with the senior group. It was readily apparent that few parents would express themselves freely with their children present. Therefore, the second and third meetings were with parents alone. It was during these meetings that parents admitted that they hesitated to speak out frankly because of the embarrassment it might bring to their child in the presence of his classmates. Mr. Smith had often wondered if this lack of free rapport between parents and children was related to the later problems.

Parents not only endorsed the regulations as set forth by the seniors, but they also agreed to an additional one. They felt that one of the adult sponsors should accompany members of the group during after-dark hours in New York City. This regulation was discussed at some length and was endorsed 100 per cent by those present, even though some thought that the rule might be unduly restrictive and unfair for the bigger and more physically mature boys.

The fourth, and the last, meeting involving parents included both seniors and their parents. This was primarily a summary session. It was at this meeting that Mr. Smith asked parents to study the rules upon which they had agreed and return them with their signatures to the school. This, he said, would indicate their approval of the regulations and their support of their enforcement.

Mr. Smith did everything possible to get all parents to attend the meetings. Seniors were asked to encourage their parents to be present and participate. Letters were sent to all parents prior to each meeting. Thirty-seven of the 42 seniors were represented by at least one parent during one or more of the four meetings. However, Mr. Smith soon realized that there was a definite lack of participation by the parents from the Pennibog region. Only later, however, did he get the full impact of what the absence of these parents meant.

Mr. Smith glanced at the big transportation map on his office wall. His eyes fell on the northeast extreme of the map. Yes, if he had known a little more about some of the past deep-seated community issues, perhaps he could have sensed the meaning of the limited attendance of Pennibog parents.

For years Mason and the Mason School had been under control of key members in the Evangelical Church. Bill Acres had been president of Mason's only bank, Sunday School president in the Evangelical Church, mayor of the town, and school board president for years. Only a few years before, either all or a majority of the board members had been strong Evangelical supporters. There had been many instances, Mr. Smith had been told, in which school staff members were expected to support the Evangelical Church and, in some cases, patronize "Evan" church members in their places of business. For years school policy had been shaped according to the beliefs of the Evangelical group. In the eyes of some persons, this group tended to be very conservative about what youth should and should not do.

One story had been told to illustrate the "Evan's" control over student activities and staff behavior. Sam Sabert, a strong "Evan," was sweeping in a classroom in which a new teacher was helping a group of sophomores plan a party. The teacher suggested that the class dance and play cards. Sam reported this incident to Bill Acres, who immediately called a special board meeting. The next Sunday, the Board invited the teacher to attend church with them. They sat as a group with the teacher in the front row while the minister preached an entire sermon on "The Evils of Cards and Dancing."

A few years previously, a consolidation movement brought Pennibog, a predominantly Catholic population, into the Mason School District. This new addition had shifted the heavy bulk of school policy power away from the "Evan" group but had in no sense given any significant power to the Catholic element. The balance of power was still primarily Protestant, but not so Evangelical-centered as it had been. The Pennibog Catholic group felt that they were not fully included in the newly organized Mason district. They reasoned that they were included so that Mason would be sufficiently large to maintain its secondary school. For this reason, the Pennibog residents did not always participate if they felt that their influence would not be considered.

There were sharp differences in the religious and moral beliefs of these two groups. The Pennibog group was generally more liberal in their homes, churches, and meetings. Most families in this area did not object to their children smoking, drinking in moderation, playing cards, gambling in limited ways, and dancing. Alcoholic drinks were available to many teen-agers in their homes.

The Protestant group, especially the Evangelical segment, was more exacting in their moral expectations about codes for their young. They were vociferously opposed to dancing, gambling, card-playing, smoking, and drinking. Not only were these restrictions strongly fostered in the church group, but they were also reflected in school policies in many ways. Annually, Bill Acres distributed Bibles in the schools and gave a talk to students on the evils of smoking. He also arranged for school-assembly lectures on alcohol abstinence.

One thing had puzzled Mr. Smith about so many of the key men in the Evangelical religion. They professed and appeared to sincerely believe in these moral codes while in Mason, but these same men behaved quite differently when out of town. This was especially true on out-of-town stag occasions. This behavior first became apparent when the local Rotary Club, of which Mr. Smith was president, went to baseball games in Central City. This had also become more clear when Mr. Smith went deer-hunting with a group of local men. Even Dr. Knox, who was considered a teetotaler, tipped the bottle on this occasion. Bill loved to smoke a cigar and drink scotch and sodas when he left town on these occasions.

Mr. Smith recalled how different life had been in his rural boy-hood community. He, with six other children, had been reared under high moral standards on a remote ranch. So far as he knew, his parents, brothers, and sisters and his neighbors lived as they said they believed. He had learned to place a high value on being consistent between what one said he believed and what he did. People who were known to deviate from moral conduct agreed upon by most people in Mr. Smith's boyhood community were not well accepted. Why were people so different in Mason?

He had recognized that there were inconsistencies between "professed beliefs" and rumored behavior of some of his fellow class-mates in high school. This had, at times, disturbed Mr. Smith deeply and had damaged his relationship with many of his schoolmates. He remembered how shaken he had been about stories of immoral con-duct concerning his fellow teen-agers. He recalled how puzzled he had been when his friends went to the altar during evangelistic meet-ings to confess their sins. What could these people be repenting about? What had they done that was so wrong? How could normal people be so inconsistent in belief and behavior? Why did people say they believed one thing but practice something quite different when they felt that they would not be discovered?

Mr. Smith knew that he could do nothing about the inconsistency between belief and action in Mason's adults, but he felt that the school could not permit such inconsistency in students while under the school's direction.

As Mr. Smith's mind returned to the Senior Trip, he remembered very clearly the Greyhound bus which pulled up to the Mason School at 5 A.M. on April 26. Since the seniors were scheduled to be in Niagara Falls on the evening of the same day, an early start had been planned. All but seven seniors had returned their signed "statement of rules" prior to the date of leaving. Four of the seven arrived and were ready to leave without their statements. They said that they had forgotten them. The party was anxious to get away, and, since it was believed that all knew the guide lines well, Mr. Smith had decided to permit the four to go without having their signed statements. Two of the four boys were from Pennibog. One was from Mason and the other from a farm near by.

That night the group stayed in a motel just outside Niagara Falls. After a look at the Falls, the party returned to their quarters around

9:30 P.M. That first night was a hectic one for all who wanted to sleep in the motel area. Three other guests in the motel left by 4 A.M. It was like an all-night celebration of the Fourth of July.

The rules said nothing about a curfew; therefore, at 11 P.M., when it was obvious that there was to be no voluntary retiring, Mr. Smith consulted the other two sponsors, Mrs. Osborne, a first-grade teacher, and Mrs. Bailey, mother of a sophomore boy. They decided to let the group go as long as they were not destroying property. The sponsors felt that there might be advantages in New York if the group "ran themselves out." As Mr. Smith reflected on that night's activities, he felt that the behavior of the group revealed more than an attempt to have a good time. In a sense, the group's behavior had a rebellious tinge to it. Mr. Smith felt that a rather large percentage of the fireworks went on directly in front of his motel door.

The group arrived in New York City at 6:30 P.M. the following day. They registered in the Taft Hotel, ate in a nearby restaurant, and agreed to meet in the hotel lobby for a tour of Times Square. The entire group, except Mrs. Osborne, who remained in the hotel with a headache, departed at 8 P.M. Soon after the group had left the hotel, Mrs. Osborne overtook the group to say that Mr. Bealson was trying to contact Mr. Smith by telephone. Mr. Smith returned to the hotel, talked to his principal concerning various items of business, and returned to the group. Upon his return, Mrs. Osborne and Mrs. Bailey said that just after he had left, several seniors had indicated an interest in seeing Dempsey's Bar. This, they said, had been one of their ambitions during their New York trip. Neither of the two women sponsors felt that they wanted to go to the bar with the youths, so Mr. Miles, the bus driver, who was a resident of Mason, said he would accompany the group. The sponsors said they could see no harm in it, since Mr. Miles was an adult and familiar with the regulations. Mr. Smith had agreed that this seemed entirely reasonable to him.

The whole group went to a TV show the next morning. After the show, all agreed to go their own ways for the remainder of the day. It was agreed that as many as three groups could be formed for various activities during the evening. One sponsor could go with each group. However, a survey of the class revealed two groups. Eight indicated that they would like to go to Coney Island and the remainder chose the theatre. Since Mr. Miles, the bus driver, said that he would like to go to Coney Island, Mr. Smith said that he would prefer to go to the theatre with the larger group. As soon as this was known, six more of the group switched to the Coney Island tour. When Mr. Smith learned of the increased number going to Coney Island, he changed to this group, feeling that one of the regular sponsors should accompany a party of as many as 14.

As the Coney Island party left the restaurant and proceeded to the subway, six boys, including the four who failed to bring their signed parental statements, turned up a side street and left the Coney Island party with no explanations. Seeing this, Mr. Smith asked Mr. Miles to go on with the remaining eight to Coney Island while he followed the six. Mr. Smith caught them at the door of the theatre. For the first time since the beginning of the trip, he lost his patience. He pointed out to the six that he was only attempting to go by the agreed-upon rules of the group and their parents, and that he expected all to abide by these regulations if they planned to continue the trip.

Back in the hotel that night, Mr. Smith turned to the job of getting the trip's financial matters in order. A senior girl had helped on financial details, but he found it necessary to do a great deal himself. The class had asked him to handle the class funds during the trip. He was still working on these accounts at 1:30 A.M. when there was a knock at the door. He opened the door to find two very disturbed seniors, Mary Potter and Harry Furnace. They had said, "Mr. Smith, we think you should know that there is a drinking party in Room 1232. Several of us tried to stop them, but they laughed at us. We are trying to take the responsibility which we agreed upon before this trip started. We think something must be done."

Mr. Smith asked, "Are you sure?"

The reply was, "Absolutely."

Mr. Smith hurriedly put on his clothes, reflected aloud to Mr. Miles, his roommate, what his procedure might be. "Of course, something must be done; these two seniors are quite representative of the majority of the class. They are fine students with high morals and excellent character. You can't ignore their warning. On the other hand, I hate to send anyone home. I guess I'll have to go to 1232 and see what goes on. I hope it isn't so."

On the way to the elevator, Mr. Smith had a new idea. He would contact the house detective and have him check Room 1232. The house detective might still settle the matter without making an unpleasant issue of it. The detective willingly made the trip, while Mr. Smith waited for him in the lobby. However, the detective reported that "He'd never seen a quieter room." Wasn't it strange that the party had broken up so quickly, if there was a party? As Mr. Smith walked back in his room, Mr. Miles casually asked, "What happened?"

"Nothing," Smith had replied. "I guess both they and I are off the hook tonight, at least."

Mr. Smith would never forget the next one-half day. He walked into the lobby, packed and ready for the Washington trip, at 8 A.M. He could sense at once by the expressions on the faces of the group waiting in the lobby that all was not well. It was not fatigue alone written on their faces. It was discord. As he turned, Harry spoke, "Mr. Smith, we want to talk to you." He had led them into a small room off the lobby and stood facing them. One after another, they spoke.

"There was drinking last night—a lot of it." "Several broke the regulations." "Something must be done." "Some of the people should be sent home."

Mr. Smith had asked again, "Are you sure?"

The reply was, "Absolutely certain."

He had then said, "If we begin an investigation and what you say is true, there is no turning back. Do you understand that?" They had said they knew it and they were convinced that there should not be any turning back. Some members of the party should go home.

Mr. Smith had inquired about who was included. He was told that all could not be identified, but they knew four who were definitely guilty and they named the four who had failed to bring their signed statements.

As the bus pulled out of New York, Mr. Smith talked to each of the four boys who had been reported. Each claimed that he and the other three had gone out for one beer after the group had returned to the hotel the night before. Each insisted that he had had nothing else to drink. However, even though it was now 10:00 A.M., the breath of the four reeked of alcohol.

After consultation with the other sponsors, it was decided that Mr. Miles and the sponsors should leave the bus and let the group decide what should be done. Therefore, the bus parked just outside

Philadelphia and the four adults waited in a nearby restaurant while the group grappled with their problem.

One hour later Harry, visibly shaken, came to the restaurant with his report. "We've decided to go to Washington, all of us." The sudden change of attitude surprised the three sponsors. After a period of silence, Mrs. Bailey was the first to speak, "I couldn't go on to Washington with the group now. Not the way they've been." Mr. Smith turned to Mrs. Osborne, "How do you feel?" he asked.

"The same way," Mrs. Osborne remarked.

Mr. Smith turned back to Harry, "Your decision is unsatisfactory to us. We will not go on to Washington with the group as it is."

Harry then asked, "This means that either we all go home or some of us must go?"

"That is correct," Mr. Smith answered.

Harry returned to the bus. It was nearly one hour later that eight of the group walked off the bus and reported that they were ready to return to Mason. When Mr. Smith saw who was included in the eight, he realized why the group must have had such a problem deciding what should be done. There were, of course, the four who had failed to bring their signed statements. Later he learned that they had purposefully left their statements at home and did not consider the rules applicable to them, since they were permitted to go under these conditions. It was also reported that two of the boys' parents had said to their sons, "Nothing or nobody can stop you from having a drink if you like." Another boy's mother had included a bottle opener for the occasion. No one was surprised about the four boys being involved. Also, it was no surprise to the group that Linda, one of the three girls to return home, was among the guilty.

No one expected to see Dave and the Roth sisters in the group. Dave was the only son of a key member of the Evangelical Church. His parents were devoted to the boy and felt that he could do no wrong. Everyone knew it would be a terrible shock to Dave's parents.

The Roth sisters were quiet, unassuming, average students. They were not outstanding in anything. Mr. Smith felt that they were typically unnoticed by many of their peers. They had come on the trip at great financial sacrifice. They were from a poor family and had had very limited opportunities. It hurt everyone deeply to see them involved. Everyone knew that they were innocently involved and that this was probably their first drink.

Five of the eight were Catholic. Mr. Smith had wondered whether this would be considered by the Pennibog group. But how could they—after all, this was certainly a self-selected group. He did not point a finger at any of them.

The eight were taken to the railroad station, tickets were purchased, and Mrs. Osborne consented to accompany the group home. All eight were very subdued and apologetic to the sponsors and other students. Without exception, they agreed that this was what had to be done, and they said that they did not have hard feelings toward anyone.

Mr. Smith called Mr. Bealson, explained the situation, and asked him to take each one home and explain to his parents what had happened.

The remainder of the trip to Washington and the return were very successful for the remaining seniors. Mr. Smith was rapidly accepted by the group and made close friends with many students, including Jean Jones, the released English teacher's daughter. Everyone recognized and openly discussed the complete change in the whole climate of the group. The group felt that all had been done that could have been done. They returned to Mason on Saturday afternoon in very high spirits.

Mr. Bealson met the bus and drove Mr. Smith home in order that they could talk about some school matters. Just before parting Bealson had remarked, "There may be some trouble over the returned seniors. There are some rumblings."

Mr. Smith had replied, "I am ready for them." He had felt confident that all was done that could have been done, and he felt assured that he could answer their questions to the satisfaction of all concerned.

The next night was Baccalaureate in the school. Mr. Smith approached Father Riley, priest from the Pennibog area, who was participating in the function to express his regrets about the returned group. Father Riley had remarked to him cooly, "One must gain the confidence and respect of youth if he expects to render leadership over their behavior."

Mr. Smith was disappointed about the Father's attitude, but after all, he represented a rather small proportion of the district's people. He would have to discuss it more fully with Father Riley after things cooled down, he thought.

Just before the Baccalaureate procession, Dave's father, drawn and worried, approached Mr. Smith and asked if the parents of the returned seniors could talk to him after the program. Smith readily consented and suggested that they meet in the social science room. When Bealson heard of the meeting, he offered to go with Mr. Smith to the meeting. As it turned out, Mr. Smith was most grateful that Bealson was there.

Mr. Smith found not only the mothers and fathers of six of the eight seniors at the meeting, but also the children involved. The Roth sisters and their parents were not present.

It was evident from the beginning that there would be no chance to examine the problem in a rational way. Mr. Smith felt the "mob" spirit among the persons present. The seniors, who had returned home with the recognition of their personal responsibility in the incident, now were openly defensive and hostile toward Mr. Smith. Both students and parents literally cursed Mr. Smith for more than two hours. He would have left the meeting, but he feared bodily harm if he tried. There was nothing to do but to listen and hope that they would talk out their aggressions toward him.

The group's hostile attitude toward Mr. Smith was based primarily on two things. First, they said he was cold and impersonal with students. They claimed that, since he was as he was, he had made the members of the guilty group want to put something over on him. They believed that it was Mr. Smith's fault that there were such "poor" relationships between him and the seniors.

The second argument was new to Mr. Smith. They had said, "Why didn't you send Rita home? She was drinking, too. You just sent part of the guilty ones home. You favored Rita." It was no use explaining that he had not decided who should return. "How was I to know Rita was involved?" Mr. Smith asked.

At this they sneered, "She was in the picture. That was evidence enough."

"What picture?" he had queried.

"The one taken in Dempsey's Bar. Sure we were there, but so was Rita—all with beer in front of us. But you let Rita go on to Washington. She was just as guilty as the rest of us."

The real blow came to Mr. Smith when he asked, "Where was Miles?"

They all laughed a jeering laugh at this question. "He was there in the picture, too—he bought our beers for us." It was Linda who followed. "Who do you think called us that night in the Taft while you were snooping on us? Mr. Miles is a decent fellow. He's our friend."

Apparently the parents were agreed that the blame was on Smith, not on their children.

The following days were hectic ones. Smith explained the details over and over to individuals and groups. Blight Kelson, the board president, had listened to the parents of the returned group and apparently had sided with them openly. A meeting initiated by other board members who had heard of his position and who backed the superintendent's action soon convinced Blight that Mr. Smith had clearly carried out their policy in the matter. Various groups asked Mr. Smith to explain the details of the incident so that they could be well informed. Many of these groups pledged their support to the action taken.

The incident became a clear-cut issue among many people in the community. Numerous persons and some groups were openly hostile to Mr. Smith. They said, "He demonstrated his inability to work with young people. He is not liked and respected by our children. They liked, respected, and behaved for Mr. Patterson." Others supported Mr. Smith clearly and openly, saying that it was time for some action. One of Smith's friends called him out of bed at 2:00 A.M. one morning and in a drunken voice asked about how he had handled some small detail of the incident. After he had explained, the voice on the other end of the wire said, "That better be true because I have just gotten a black eye over defending you."

Later Mr. Smith learned that some of his friends kept a close watch on him day and night because they feared that some of the seniors or their parents might do harm to him physically.

A few people forcefully defended the actions taken by Mr. Smith. Several senior members who completed the trip openly spoke out for Mr. Smith. Hal Jones, the released English teacher, was known to have contacted the parents of the eight students sent home and encouraged group action against the superintendent. Jean, his daughter, strongly supported Smith and openly criticized her father's action. The father and daughter were not on speaking terms for weeks after the incident.

One thing was clear: while the action was not criticized by the scores of calm, level-headed people in Mason, neither was it openly and forcefully supported. People in general seemed to neither condemn nor condone the behavior of the eight returned seniors.

The board of education's first reaction to the whole affair was to eliminate all future senior trips. Mr. Smith had responded to this by a positive and clear stand for continuing the trips. He had said that such trips could be a fine experience for young people—many of whom would never have the chance to go see the National Capital and other parts of the country again. "Why should we let the behavior of eight destroy the opportunities for all? We started a method of planning and control. Let us not turn back now." However, he had also pointed out, "If we in the school cannot have the backing of the school board and parents in planning some limits on individual behavior in these groups, parents should not expect the school to sponsor these trips. We must remain together and move forward if we are to make progress."

The board had reluctantly said, "Let's try it once more."

During the first faculty meeting in the fall after the ill-fated journey, the teachers raised the question of senior-trip responsibility. They were concerned about the lack of backing which the school representatives had gotten from citizens concerning the incident. All the staff except Mr. Boltz agreed that they would not be a part of any trip which did not clearly set out regulations on drinking and other types of behavior that the school could not condone or support. The teachers said that, in the light of public sentiment concerning the senior trip sponsored by George Hen and Mr. and Mrs. Brown and the second one sponsored by Mr. Smith, they felt that clear guide lines with teeth for enforcement must be agreed upon by parents and board members. Otherwise, they felt that parents should sponsor the trips and that the school should be absolved of all responsibility.

Ned Boltz, who became sponsor of the next senior group, did not take a stand on this issue. He had dreamed for three years of taking the group to Washington. He loved American History and he felt that a visit to the Nation's Capitol was vital for himself and the group. Even though control in his classroom was a laughing matter among students, faculty, and community people, he indicated that he did not feel that he would have any difficulty with the forthcoming group.

The Board of Education supported the faculty on their stand

and clearly asked Mr. Smith to work with the students on the development of a well-planned and controlled trip. They had said that Mr. Boltz could go with the group, but that he was not a person who could alone represent the school.

Mr. Smith, Mr. Boltz, and Mr. Bealson started meetings with the senior group early in the fall. The group was obviously opposed to any type of guide lines, either discussed or written. Such discussion was evaded carefully by the senior group.

The seniors took American History with Mr. Boltz, so they were in close contact with him day after day. Part of the history time was spent on Washington-trip plans. Of course, Mr. and Mrs. Bealson were not in these meetings.

At one point in the trip planning, the seniors became interested in a boat trip on the Great Lakes. Mr. Smith and Mr. Bealson heartily supported this idea. These trips were carefully supervised by the steamline personnel. Intoxicating drinks were not permitted on board during senior excursions. This seemed a reasonable solution to the problem in view of the difficulty encountered during the past two trips.

Mr. Boltz was sold on a Washington trip. Apparently he convinced the group that Washington was the better plan. At any rate, the class swung back to the Washington idea.

Mr. Smith never knew quite how it happened, but there was a gradual increase in support by the Board of Education for a trip without definite regulations and for Mr. Boltz, the only staff person who was willing to go with the seniors under such conditions. Perhaps it was because Board member Mrs. Northwert had a daughter in the senior class, or perhaps it was because the sentiment grew against the action taken with the eight seniors the year before. At any rate, when Mr. Smith recognized the Board's sentiment, he offered to remove himself from any relationship with the group. The Board agreed to this and officially turned the responsibility to Mr. Boltz. Mr. Smith did not participate further in the planning.

It was a clear May morning when the seniors boarded the bus for Washington. Mr. Smith approached the group on his way to the office. "That bus driver facing the other way looks familiar," he thought. As the driver turned to face him, he was astonished to see that Mr. Miles was the driver for the group. As Mr. Miles saw Mr. Smith approaching, he smiled widely, spoke and said, "It was thoughtful of this group to invite me to drive for them this year. I enjoy so much driving for these young people."

As Mr. Smith looked back on the whole incident, the selection of Mr. Miles as driver was the clearest indication of how the community accepted his role with the seniors the year before. After all, it was Mr. Miles who had bought beer for the group in Dempsey's Bar. He was the one who had drunk with the group at Coney Island, and he had protected the party in the Taft Hotel so that they would not be caught. Still, after all the difficulty Mr. Miles had helped create, he had been invited, with no apparent resistance from the community, to drive this senior group to Washington.

The clock on the wall was now pointing to 6:20. Sara would have dinner ready. Then, too, he had a meeting with a community school committee at 7:30. They were working on ways to improve the moral values of the Mason youth.

As Mr. Smith walked out of the school building, he met Russell Cook, the school coach. Russell approached him and in a confidential voice asked, "Have you heard what Sue and Herbert did on the senior trip? I just heard it from some of the boys downtown. They are really in a position to know."

Already the stories were circulating. "Rus, if you don't mind, I'd just as soon not hear about it. You know how these people talk."

CASE FOUR

The Sword of Damocles

Dionysius in all his power and glory sat on a "golden" throne, admired and envied by the courtiers and flatterers of the court, who extolled his grandeur and happiness. One day the most vociferous, a certain Damocles, was invited by the king to sit in the royal chair during a magnificent banquet, where he might enjoy all the royal honors and regal fare.

During the height of the entertainment, Damocles looked upward, and there he saw directly above his head, suspended by a single hair, a naked sword, point downward, threatening to cleave his skull. He had never seen the sword before. Only he who sat in the king's chair could see the sword.

His appetite lost, Damocles was filled with dismay, for he realized that the price of splendors and privileges of royalty were paid for by the sacrifice of personal security and mental peace.

In his private office, the superintendent of schools settled back in his chair, put his feet on his desk, and relaxed. This was not a pressing day—no appointments, and no deadlines. School was out for the year. Most of the teaching staff had checked out the day before. Although there were some of the old timers still around, they would be no bother. Of course, the principals were still on the job, but that was a different matter. They, too, would be glad that the pressure was off.

By appearances it had been a good year. The graduating class had received an unusually large number of scholarships. The athletic teams had won most of their games. No one was after the coaches. The budget for the coming year had already passed by a vote of five to one. One of the former directors had been re-elected to the board of education. The schools had been evaluated and commended for their program.

This was the summer for which the superintendent had been waiting. He sat contemplating fishing streams and camping trips. He *must* go back to the place where he lost the "big one" last summer. This time he knew just what to do.

Suddenly his daydreams were interrupted by his secretary, Mrs. Jones. The morning mail was in her hand. She smiled as she handed him letters, circulars, and advertisements. "The usual," she said. Then added, "It looks like we are going to have a quiet summer. Maybe we can do that study you suggested two years ago."

Kennedy grinned and shook his head.

Kennedy, with trout on his mind, began to open his mail. About halfway through, he picked up an ordinary envelope and happened to notice that the address was printed. This was not unusual, since occasionally letters were so addressed. He opened the envelope, unfolded the page, and began to read, and as he read his body stiffened, his face turned pale, and from his lips there came a spontaneous exclamation, "Oh, No!"

MR. SUPERINTENDENT:
WHAT KIND OF TEACHERS DO YOU HAVE IN YOUR
SCHOOL THAT THEY APPROVE IMMORALITY? YOUR
BAND MAN IS KEEPING COMPANY WITH A HIGH SCHOOL
GIRL. SHE IS TRYING TO BREAK UP HIS HOME. HIS POOR
WIFE IS ALONE MOST OF THE TIME. WHY DO YOU ALLOW
THIS TO GO ON? THE SCHOOL IS RESPONSIBLE FOR THE
MORALS OF ITS TEACHERS. WHAT KIND OF AN EXAMPLE
DO YOU WANT TO SET FOR YOUNG PEOPLE? YOU HAD
BETTER DO SOMETHING ABOUT THIS.
                                                          A TAXPAYER

He read the letter again, not believing what he had read. He
snapped on the inter-com. "Mrs. Jones, get me the high school principal at once. Tell him to drop whatever he is doing and come down
here." He added, "At once."

Jim Kennedy had 18 years of experience behind him. This was
his fifth year as superintendent of this school system. He had come
to Mountain View from the southern part of the state. There he had
served several years as a teacher, a high school principal, and superintendent. He believed that the school was responsible for the children's safety, health, and education while in school, and in that order.

Mountain View was a community of about 5,000 people. Its
economy was chiefly dependent upon agriculture and lumbering.
It was the county seat for Alpine County. The community had not
grown during the years of World War II, or the years following. It
was proud of its culture, its schools, and its traditions. The town supported 15 churches, a very fine library, and a modern hospital.

While waiting for the principal, he examined the letter and envelope very carefully. The envelope was an everyday one. The letter
was written on a plain piece of typing paper. The message was
printed in large letters. He suddenly realized that only he had touched
the letter. Very carefully he set it to one side on his desk, and made
a typewritten copy, word for word and line by line.

Mr. Johnson hurried in. Kennedy motioned him to close the door
and then pointed to the letter lying on his desk. "That came in the
morning mail. Don't touch it. I don't want anyone else to handle it."

Johnson's shock and disbelief were as great as Kennedy's. "Who
do you think sent this?" He asked, and then added, "I don't think
White is the type to get mixed up with any high school girl."

According to the high school principal, Mr. White was a quiet

man. He had always co-operated with the faculty and the administration. On the other hand, he had no close ties with the faculty members. White always came to their meetings but contributed very little
in the discussions. His department had shown good organization and
the band was much better than it had been the year before. He
evidently could handle the "kids," since there had been few disciplinary problems brought to the office. From all appearances and
the comment around the school, he was liked by teachers and students. The Whites had left town yesterday. Mr. White planned to do
some additional work at the college.

"What do you know about his wife?" asked Kennedy.

"I really can't say. She had a baby this spring. Remember the
staff bought them a layette." Johnson paused, "I am trying to think.
But I don't remember any girl in the band that has been a problem."

Both men talked at some length and decided that they should
make some discreet inquiries about White. If there were any undercurrent of gossip, the sooner they ran it down, the better. Johnson
would sound out some of the older faculty members who were still
around and who could be depended upon. Kennedy would go downtown that afternoon and see if there were any rumors "floating"
around on "main street." He would also make it a point to "drop in
and have a friendly chat with a couple of the board members."
Kennedy pointed out that their responsibility was to seek information,
to protect White, and not to ask questions which might make anyone
suspicious. This could be a very delicate situation. After all, White
was married and he had a contract with the school district for the
coming year. There was also the girl to think about. If this accusation
were true, it could mean a nasty mess. If it weren't, and White were
innocent, they were duty-bound to stand behind him.

After Johnson left, Kennedy looked at the letter again. He would
like to know who sent it. He picked up the page by its edges and with
the aid of a pair of tweezers placed it back in its envelope. These,
together with the typewritten copy, he placed in the "confidential"
folder in the vault. He went back to his desk. He tried to concentrate,
but he could not. Under his breath he cursed the writer of the note
and White as well. It did not help. Tension was already building up.
They were doing all that was possible at the present. Why could he
not forget it until this afternoon? If the faculty members knew any-

thing, Johnson would get it out of them. He was a good man, intelligent, dependable, and well liked by the teachers.

On his way home, Kennedy tried to recall what he knew of White and his wife. This was White's first job. He had been properly screened like all the other candidates for the position. He had excellent references from the music department and from the school of education. Kennedy had liked the man's appearance. He was quiet, but in Kennedy's mind that was an asset. White was not temperamental. He was young. Perhaps he had been indiscreet or maybe he had done something in all innocence and his actions had been misininterpreted. There were troublemakers in every community. Who would write a letter like that, and for what purpose? Kennedy did not remember much about Mrs. White. He would broach that subject to Mrs. Kennedy after lunch.

Kennedy did not enjoy the noon meal. He cautiously asked his wife, "What do you know about Mrs. White? Isn't she a member of the women's group at the church?"

"Is there something wrong?"

"No, I was just curious. That's all."

"Well, she does belong to the church auxiliary. I haven't seen her for some time. I don't know whether she is shy or what. She doesn't mix well with the other girls in that group. Sometimes she makes the most inane remarks, clear off the subject of conversation. Just like last fall when we were getting ready for the church bazaar. She picked up one of the Kewpie dolls we were making dresses for and said, 'Poor little pregnant doll, and no one to wash your back.' We were just floored. She hasn't been to a meeting for a long time now. She had a baby boy the first part of February."

Kennedy remembered a little of Mrs. White. Rather a colorless personality, he thought, and with as much sex appeal as a fence rail. He could not believe that White would be stupid enough to get mixed up with a high school girl. He thought of the letter. To say that it was disturbing was an understatement. It was the first anonymous letter he had ever received. It kept gnawing his insides. He could not remember what he had eaten for lunch: it felt like lead.

That afternoon Kennedy stopped along "main street." There he talked with businessmen, had coffee, bought a shirt, and did some errands for the district. He discussed school, athletics, children, and teachers, and each time mentioned, "The band certainly had a good year." He included two of the school board members in his stops. Not a whisper about White. If there had been any rumor on "main street," he was satisfied that he would have heard it by now. Whatever the men at the "listening post" downtown did not hear, their wives would pick up at bridge club.

At the office Johnson was waiting for Kennedy. He had talked to one of the older teachers, Mrs. Evans. She had overheard some of the girls in her home economics class discussing Mr. White and one of the girls in the band, a Jean Graham. This was about a month ago. Mrs. Evans had discouraged the girls from talking about Mr. White. She had mentioned this incident to one of the other women teachers, and they had decided to say nothing about it. However, during the last week of school she had heard some more "talk" among the youngsters.

After a week Johnson and Kennedy had found out there was a "story" going around about White and the Graham girl. They believed at this point that the "talk" was largely confined to some of the high school students over at the swimming pool. However, eventually it would get to the parents. Some of them might have heard a version already. Gossip of this kind just didn't die out. It would be repeated and retold many times over, probably with additions.

Kennedy had thought about the anonymous letter for several days. It seemed to him that he was going in circles. He worried about who wrote it. When he tried to concentrate on his work, he would find himself thinking about White, the girl, and what the writer of the letter knew. He had first thought of taking the letter and envelope to the postal authorities, but cast that idea aside. He was not going to let any more people know about the letter than he had to. The risk of promoting more "talk" was too great. He also remembered his sister-in-law who had worked in a post office: she had known everyone's business and a lot more. There could be some legal aspects in this case—slander against White, contributing to the delinquency of a minor, and White's contract with the district. He would go talk to Brown.

Mr. Brown was the attorney for the school district. He enjoyed a good reputation in the community. When he talked, most people listened. He was considered an "honest" lawyer. Kennedy regarded Brown as his best friend. When Brown was shown the copy of the letter, he was surprised. "We haven't had any cases of anonymous letters for a long time." They speculated as to the source of the letter. Brown pointed out that hearsay was no evidence. One had to consider the possibility of slander, and a man's reputation, family, and career. There was also the girl and her family. The best course of action was to sit tight and wait.

When Kennedy mentioned that he might sound out the Sheriff, Brown agreed. "If there is anything going around, he might know about it. He won't go off the deep end. His ears reach a lot farther than ours. I think it would be safe."

Kennedy had worked with the Sheriff before. The Sheriff was a man you could trust. Furthermore, he generally knew what was going on in the community.

In a couple of days, Kennedy dropped in at the sheriff's office. He had to take the tax levy notices to the assessor. This would afford a good excuse to be in the courthouse. The Sheriff waved him into the private office and motioned him to close the door. "Say, Jim, what goes on up at the school? I understand one of your high school teachers is running around with one of the girls." Then he laughed when he saw the expression on Kennedy's face. Kennedy felt that the ground had just been cut out from under his feet. "Now, don't get excited, Jim. You're not the only one who has problems."

According to the Sheriff, high school students had seen this fellow taking the girl home at night on several occasions. He had also been reported as "parking" with the girl. The Sheriff said, "We have been watching the situation and we will continue to do so after school starts. I don't think you're in trouble now, but you might be if some of the parents hear about this, especially if they have girls in the band. If anything happens, we'll let you know."

The Sheriff was given the original letter. He did not think there was a chance in a million of finding the writer. However, there was always the possibility of a second letter. In a way Kennedy was glad the Sheriff already knew, for if anything serious happened, someone else in authority would be in on the case from the first. If White were guilty, there certainly could be some legal complications. Two years ago an adjoining district had had a case of a homosexual teacher and the Sheriff had cleaned that problem up very quickly and efficiently.

Kennedy had found out a little about the girl. Jean Graham, a junior the preceding year, played in the band and kept track of the music for White. She had been in the Whites' home several times, as a babysitter. Her family lived on a small farm on the edge of town. She had never been in any kind of trouble in school. Rather a plain-looking girl, she was not the flashy type who attracted the high school boys.

Kennedy remembered that he would have to inform the board. When? Maybe he could wait until August. Why "put the fat in the fire now?" On the other hand, suppose one of the school board heard the "story" and brought it to the next meeting? Or suppose a board member should be stopped on the street and asked by one of the parents, "What is this we hear about the band instructor and one of the high school girls?" Kennedy and the board had developed a mutual understanding, over a period of years, that information regarding any problem which could put any of them "on the spot" would be passed along as quickly as possible so that they would not be caught "flat footed." The next board meeting would be held in two days. Kennedy felt that he had no choice. He must inform the board.

"If White had to have an affair, why couldn't he have one with a grown woman instead of a high school girl? Why couldn't he have picked on someone in the next town?" Kennedy could see all kinds of complications—angry parents, newspaper publicity, an hysterical wife, reactions in the community. This could have the "making of a nasty mess" and even end in the courts. Kennedy did not relish the last thought. Concrete proof was one thing: hearsay was another. But public opinion did not always rest on facts.

In spite of the letter, Kennedy believed that White had just been indiscreet. Even though he were innocent, vicious rumor and gossip could hurt a man's name for a long time. This boy was just beginning his career. You had to accept some responsibility for a beginning teacher. But suppose he were guilty? What was one's responsibility to the students in White's classes? He was beginning to feel the horns of the dilemma.

The school board completed their regular agenda. Kennedy waited until the meeting was officially closed, then he asked if he could have a few minutes. He did not wish this matter to be written into the record.

Kennedy explained that he and the high school principal had carried on a quiet investigation. There apparently was no "story" on "main street." However, one of the high school teachers reported that some of the students had been talking about White and one of the girls in the band, just before school was out. He believed there was a "story" slightly circulating at the present. He doubted if it were widespread. He said he did hear that White had taken the girl home at night, when she babysat for them.

The school board did not like the letter, its contents, or its writer any better than Kennedy. "This is an administrative matter, Jim. You can take care of it in the fall."

As the summer passed, Kennedy heard a word here and a word there about White and the girl. He doubted if the "story" was getting around very fast. Maybe it was dying out. He began to think of what he was going to say to White. During the last days of August, Kennedy reviewed the approach. He should be careful. There was no evidence that White had done anything wrong. He had better play it close. White could insist that he was being slandered. Kennedy could also have the girl's parents on his neck, right or wrong.

The teachers returned to school three days before the pupils. Kennedy waited a day before he sent word to White that he would like to see him. Kennedy knew that one misstep could lead to the point of no return. He did not wish this to happen. A cautious questioning with an indication of an open mind would be best.

After White and Kennedy exchanged greetings and shook hands, White settled into a chair. They discussed summer school and then turned to the subject of the band and its record of the previous year. Kennedy asked how the registration of band members was progressing. White admitted that he was having some difficulty with students who were in band last year, due to scheduling and conflict of classes.

Kennedy remarked that he thought they had a mutual problem and gave White the typewritten copy of the anonymous letter, saying, "I received this through the mail just after school was out last June."

Not a muscle moved in White's face as he read the letter. He did not change his expression. It was completely "dead pan." He seemed to have absolutely perfect control of himself. He very calmly handed the sheet back to the superintendent and just looked at him.

Kennedy began, "This is only a copy. I have the original in a safe place." (White never asked to see the original, nor did he ever express doubt that it existed. Kennedy, on the other hand, was sure that if he had been in White's shoes, he would have wanted to see the original.) "You realize," Kennedy went on, "it is very disturbing to receive an anonymous letter with such content." (He bit his tongue on the word "charges", and it did not come out.) "Also, I have heard that there was some talk among the high school students last spring." . . . A long pause. . . . "You know, a man can innocently place himself in a position where his actions can be misconstrued." . . . A pause. . . . "Well, like taking a babysitter home." Kennedy was getting desperate. He had hoped for a man-to-man talk; to settle the whole affair right here and now. At this point he believed that White had probably been indiscreet—maybe the man had been a fool—but this could be straightened out—after all, there was the whole year ahead.

White just sat there, devoid of all expression. He did shift his position in his chair.

"Well, what do you think about it?" Kennedy was determined to force the man to express himself.

White said, "I don't know."

Kennedy took the step, "The word going around indicated the girl was Jean Graham." He waited and looked White straight in the eye. "Isn't she in the band?"

"Yes, the girl is in the band," confirmed White. She was a friend of his wife. She babysat for them last spring. He did not see anything wrong in that.

Kennedy pointed out the danger of being too friendly with high school girls. People could misinterpret teacher-pupil friendships. Besides, there were always those willing to condemn on the basis of gossip. After all, White was young; he should think of his career and family. "I don't think that any 'talk' has been widespread. But I do think you must watch your relationships with *all* the students in the band room."

White very quietly remarked, "I cannot see where I have done anything wrong."

Kennedy warned him that since there was "talk," people would be watching him, and not to place himself in any position where his actions could be misjudged. He also told White that no one was accusing him, and certainly they were all satisfied with his work. However, the district simply could not tolerate the situation of having its teachers running around with high school girls. If that ever happened, the teacher would have to leave. Kennedy said, "I don't think you would want to place yourself or the district in such an awkward and embarrassing position."

White assured the superintendent that there was nothing to worry about. He and his wife liked Mountain View and the school. They wanted to stay. White then excused himself and left.

Johnson came to the office later that same day. He brought word that twelve former band students, juniors and seniors, were resisting the signing up for band on the excuse that they wanted another course which conflicted. All these pupils had signed up for band during pre-registration last spring. He asked Kennedy how he got along with White.

"I don't know," said Kennedy. "That fellow is very hard to talk to. I am inclined to think there isn't very much to the 'story.' But if there is, this boy is certainly smart or awfully dumb. Either way, I would hate to play poker with him. I don't think you would ever be able to tell what he held in his hand. We should watch him very closely. What's the word with the staff?"

"I don't think we will have to worry about the staff if trouble develops," stated Johnson. "I'll talk to those we can depend upon, within the next week. If any 'talk' should start among the students, they will hold it down and let us know. And I think they will do the same on the outside. A number of them belong to some kind of a community organization or church group. I think the staff will do all they can to protect White and the school district."

"Don't say anything to those three new teachers," said Kennedy, "and I don't think it should be mentioned to Cummings, either. His wife talks too much. The grade people probably don't know, and I can't see that they should. However, if anything further develops, I'll have to tell the other principals. Loose talk is hard to fight once it gets started. If White is innocent, as he claims, and watches his step, I think we'll be all right. If he isn't and he continues to give this girl too much attention, we'll have real trouble on our hands."

All fall they waited. Nothing happened. Tension eased. There had been a murmur here and there, nothing serious. Then it began. It started about the last of November. One of the faculty wives had been "asked" about White and the girl at a bridge party. Kennedy's reaction when he heard was, "Maybe some of those women are just getting around to talking about the gossip of last June."

Kennedy began to worry after he heard that White took the Graham girl home after the last band concert. A few days later, one of the school board called him. "Say, Jim, Mr. Smith came into my office this morning and asked me what we were going to do about this high school teacher who is running around with one of the girls. John says his daughter told him it was 'all over school.'"

"I don't think it's all over school," answered Kennedy. "Yes, I'll look into the matter and see what I can do about it." He thought— "If Mrs. Smith knows, the 'story' will soon be all over town."

During the next two weeks, Kennedy and Johnson were certain that the "story" was spreading fast. One could not pretend otherwise. Christmas vacation was three weeks off. That would afford a breathing spell. Johnson had a conference with White and got no further in his efforts than Kennedy, even though he spent a longer time. "It was like talking to a blank wall," Johnson related. "I hope we can hold together until school is out. I think the faculty is getting concerned, too. They don't say much, but the feeling is there."

Kennedy was still not certain what was fact and what was fiction. He had heard reports all during the month of December that White was with the girl at nights. One fact for sure, the district could not afford to have White another year. The matter of contracts would have to be settled by the first of April. It would be better for both Mr. White and the district if White would resign at the end of the school year. The question was, "Would White resign or would the district be forced to let him go?" If the district did not renew his contract, what would be the specific reason, if a reason was demanded?

At the January school board meeting, the superintendent was asked what he was going to do about White. Two of the members of the board said that they had been approached by parents with that question. "You just can't sit there, Jim, and do nothing."

Kennedy smiled to himself. He knew they expected him to do something. What could he do? Both he and Johnson had talked to White. Fighting rumor was like fighting in the dark, or stopping the running of water through a sieve with your hands. He couldn't ask for White's immediate resignation—there was no factual evidence. The only way was to live with the situation and attempt to get White's resignation effective at the end of the school year. He had thought up to now that White would stay "in line," owing to the fact that White had stated, "My wife and I want to stay here." Perhaps White had stayed "in line."

Kennedy now experienced pressure from three parents, and in addition was asked by a couple of his friends on "main street" what the district was going to do about "this teacher." He answered that the district and he were aware of the situation and "had it well in hand and there was certainly nothing to worry about."

All during January Kennedy felt the tension grow. The next move was up to him. That was expected. That was his job. The board expected it, the faculty expected it, and he felt the community expected it. Johnson stood on the edge ready to help. But this was his move, not Johnson's. If this affair backfired, the less Johnson were implicated at the present the better. Johnson's contract came up for renewal next month; his own had two years yet to run.

In February the superintendent resolved to act. Either one of two things would result. White would resign and leave at the end of the year, or he would stand and fight. If he stood and fought, he could ask for a board hearing, or he could ask the state teachers association to step in. It could evolve into a very nasty uproar. He thought of the possible reaction of the girl's family, and of Mrs. White; angry parents and hysterical women were not pleasant. This was a true "hot potato" he held. It was certain that White had been seen with the girl. Did that convict him? It had been reported that White had parked with her at night. But when the chips were down, would this stand up? On the other hand, suppose the worst happened and the girl became pregnant. Could the school be absolved of all responsibility? The affair had been called to his attention, first by the anonymous letter, and by others since school began last fall. It could be said that he knowingly stood by. Could he be judged for "aiding and abetting"? Where did his responsibility begin, and where did it end?

Kennedy thought he should seek the advice of attorney Brown before he approached White about resigning. Brown advised him not to press the man too hard. "Don't back him into a corner. You'll probably have better results by a friendly manner. Don't push him. And above all, don't accuse him in any way. You could get your neck stuck out a mile in a case like this." He smiled, "Not that it isn't out to some extent already."

The conference with White was not exactly satisfactory. Kennedy began by a review of all the events leading up to the present. He said that under the circumstances he thought that White would be acting in his own interests if he resigned at the end of the school term. He pointed out that with the "feeling and talk" in town, it would be a mistake if White stayed with the district. Also, he mentioned the fact that some of last year's band members had not returned to the band. Furthermore, community pressure might force the board not to renew White's contract. Kennedy said that he realized that it was a difficult decision, yet many teachers resigned their positions. White had been with the school for two years and his work had been very good. Kennedy said that he did not see that it would be a reflection on White's record if he left the school at the end of the year.

White was not receptive. He stated that he and his wife liked the school and the community and wanted to stay. He did not admit nor did he deny that he had been seeing the girl.

Kennedy told White that he should keep an open mind and give the matter of resignation a great deal of consideration. "Frankly," he said in a friendly voice, "I think it would be your best course of action. Come back in and see me in a week or so. I don't think that you would have any trouble getting another job."

By March 10 Kennedy was concerned. There had been no word from White. Time was running out. The second conference was no better than the first. White seemed to be more determined to stay than ever before. In fact, he saw no reason to submit a resignation. Furthermore, what he did was his own business. (Kennedy began to wonder—was the man really innocent, or was he guilty and did not want to go home and explain a resignation to his wife?) The conference ended by Kennedy saying, "The board meets on the 30th of this month. I would like to have your resignation by then. Effective, of course, at the end of this school year."

White did not answer as he left the office.

Johnson came to the office the next day. "Did you get any place with White?"

Kennedy shook his head. "I don't know whether I got through to him. Most of the time when I try to talk with him, he just sits there. I am afraid the only course will be to let him go through board action."

Johnson wanted to try to convince White, "Maybe I can make him see that it is the best action he can take."

Kennedy thought it wouldn't hurt. (Johnson, by this time, had signed his new contract with the district.) "Be sure to tell him that I want his resignation, not you. That will place you in a better position to deal with him."

Johnson returned in three days. He didn't know whether he had made any progress either. "I may ask one or two of the faculty to help me. Some of them believe that they are in this as deep as we are. They think it might reflect against the entire staff. I don't understand White any better than you do, and I am beginning to think there might be something between him and that girl."

March 30th, the board-meeting date, arrived. White had not turned in his resignation nor was there any indication that he would. Kennedy knew that Johnson was working. Noon came, and still no word. That afternoon Kennedy tried to concentrate on some problems which were on the evening's agenda. Three o'clock, three-fifteen, three-thirty, came as he caught himself watching the clock. He must forget about White. Either the resignation would come in or it would not.

At four-thirty Johnson walked in. "Here it is."

"What did he say?"

"He didn't say anything. But you could tell by the way he acted that he didn't like it."

"When did you get it?"

"Just now."

"Well, that's over with." Both men looked at each other; strain had left its mark, and now relief had set in.

"Let's go out and have a smoke."

The tide had reached its highest mark. But there was still the backwash that could knock their feet out from under them. White would be with the district two more months. Whatever control there had been arising from the fact that he said he wanted to remain with the district had vanished. Kennedy did not celebrate any hour of triumph. He had a washed-out feeling, almost like failure. Perhaps it was failure. Perhaps they should have taken more time with White when he first came to the district. He still thought that White was a good man in his field and deserved another chance. What had made the man place himself in a position for public censure? Kennedy could not get rid of the feeling that somehow he, or all of them, had failed. He tried to forget this guilt feeling. After all, White was an adult. He had to face up to the problems of life sometime.

A modest news story carried the report that four teachers were leaving the school system at the end of the year. White's name was mentioned among them. The next day Kennedy was stopped on the street by a friend who, owing to his job, was involved in a great many community activities, and who had two children in school.

The friend said, "Jim, I think your timing was about right in White's case. If you had waited any longer, I think the board would have been visited by a delegation of parents. I was about to tip you off about their plans just before I read the announcement in the paper. I think it is a dead issue now."

After school was out, the Whites moved away. During the summer Kennedy heard they had separated, and later he heard they were living together. His mind was still filled with unrest. Had he, by his actions, pushed White into a web of entanglement? Could he somehow have extricated him? Was White innocent, or was he cunning and actually having an affair with the girl? Whatever the answers were, he did not know. He doubted if he would ever know. His feelings were such that he hoped he would never hear of the Whites again.

Two years later Kennedy opened his mail one morning. A letter from a state teachers' association drew his attention.

Dear Sir:
   Will you kindly verify the experience of Mr. White who taught in the Mountain View high school.
   To your knowledge was there any extracurricular teacher-student relationship on his part while he was with your school system?"

Kennedy stood up. He walked over to the window and looked at the top of the mountain. "Now what do I play, defense counsel, public prosecutor, judge, or Pontius Pilate?"

CASE FIVE

Democracy: Riverbank, U.S.A.

The 1949 graduating class members of Riverbank High School had the unique experience of receiving their entire high school education in a gymnasium where classrooms were separated by thin, eight-foot-high partitions. The following case describes some of the persons, actions, and events behind this unusual situation. During the extended time span of the case, a few persons took important action regarding the apparent issue of school-site selection, but the voting public, representing a small portion of the total strength of the community, made the ultimate decision. The high school students, who were most affected by the turn of events, had no formal voice in the matter. Also of interest is the fact that natural disasters in the form of a fire and a flood strongly shaped the course of the decision.

Involved directly in the resulting controversy were two school superintendents, a succession of school board members, and a number of "prominent citizens" of the community. One of the administrators was forced under considerable pressure to make what proved to be a crucial decision. He then failed to gain acceptance for his decision among the voters of the district. Was his decision a valid one and, if so, why did the community reject it?

Riverbank

Riverbank, in 1945, was a rural community of approximately 900 persons. The outlying community, enclosed on three sides by steep, wooded mountains and on the fourth by a large river, contained 2,100 additional residents.

Riverbank's first settlers arrived before the Civil War. Until the beginning of the twentieth century, the town was largely isolated from the rest of the state, since the chief means of transportation to Riverbank was the stern-wheelers which served the river communities.

During Riverbank's earlier days, logging had been the principal occupation. As the logging moved back into the hills, small farms began to appear. Commercial fishing also became important as the state's population grew.

About 1915 an enterprising native saw the possibility of diking the river bottomland. As a result, a number of dikes were constructed, thousands of acres of land were brought into use, and farming on the dikelands became profitable. For many years, dairying was the principal type of farming, but during the Second World War the growing of peppermint became a highly lucrative agricultural pursuit. Many people made small fortunes from peppermint farming, and some of these fortunes were really sizable. World War II also brought some light industry to the town.

Riverbank's population was and has remained largely Northern European. Many Swedish and Norwegian people came for the logging, and a number of Finnish people came for the fishing. There are still many homes in the community where a foreign language is preferred, and many of the older people speak little English. The "second generation" is well dispersed throughout the community, however, and its members take part in some phases of community life.

In 1945, about 30 to 50 per cent of the high school students had surnames of Finnish origin. At that time, a newcomer might have received the distinct impression that there was some discrimination against the Finnish people by certain elements in the community. This discrimination, which in recent years has diminished considerably, was confined largely to a failure to associate with the Finnish people rather than an active segregation. An observant high school principal might have noted that certain groups of students voted together, that Finnish boys or girls, as a rule, did not date boys or girls of other nationalities. The same pattern existed in the community in that membership rosters of fraternal and service organizations did not include Finnish names.

Riverbank's Decision-Makers

In the eyes of many citizens, the important affairs of Riverbank were controlled by a comparatively small group of individuals. Thus, the well-known label, "The Big Five," signified the persons who were the holders of community power. These men were residents of the town, although their interests in most cases extended far beyond the community.

Forrest, a very short, middle-aged man whose family had for years controlled the largest timber company in the area, was one of "The Big Five." As second in command to his elder brother, he did most of the "fronting" for the organization. He was also a director in the local bank, an active participant in church and civic affairs, and for many years a Riverbank school board member. He was the wealthiest person in Riverbank.

There were some who said that Forrest simply did what his older brother told him to do, but on this matter the evidence was not entirely clear, as certainly he was a man of firm and definite opinions. Frequently, when appointed to committees, he simply went ahead and did things on his own without consulting others. Argument failed to change his opinion. He always listened politely and seldom took the trouble to refute opinion. His home and that of his brother were showplaces, and only a small circle of friends were invited there.

Downey, a second member of the group, was a farm-owner and a tavern operator. He was also a director of the local bank and was active in the one Service Club of the town. He spent most of his time supervising the operation of his farm and tavern and playing cards in the tavern. He seldom attended public meetings other than those of the Service Club.

Martin, owner of several farms, was also proprietor of the town's largest grocery and market. Fully as active in community affairs as Forrest, Martin was a member of the Service Club, had served a number of years on the school board, had run unsuccessfully for county commissioner, was a director of the bank, and consistently had attended all important community meetings and gatherings. He was almost always a member of the school budget committee.

Ingram and Worth, the two remaining members of the "Big Five," took little part in the life of the community except for the affairs directly related to their business. Ingram was president of the local bank and Worth owned and operated a large mint farm. He had also been a director of the bank.

In addition to their individual holdings, the "five" were reportedly associated as a group in several business enterprises. Presumably, they jointly owned, among other things, a lucrative automobile agency and several eastern Oregon ranches.

While not a member of the "Big Five," Thomas, the editor of the local weekly newspaper, *The Riverbank Times,* was a brother-in-law of Worth and was closely associated with the five influentials socially. He was a highly respected and highly vocal member of the community. In the early stages of the site-selection process, he was mayor of Riverbank. He was a very active member of the Service Club and at various times he had been a member of the school board. He had been most effective in such activities as securing better roads for the area. Blunt and forceful, educated at Yale, Thomas never left any doubt as to his position on any issues. He was especially vehement on matters affecting the welfare of Riverbank. Apparently he owed allegiance to no particular group but was more or less a power unto himself. Many observers believed that he found it difficult to tolerate people who did not agree with him.

The Service Club was an important organization in the community of Riverbank. No person connected with Labor was ever a member, and no Finnish names were heard at roll call. The "Big Five" were always represented on the Board of Directors. Most major community activities were sponsored by the Service Club and very few, if any, were successful without "Big Five" support. At any meeting held in the city of Riverbank, the Service Club was always represented, regardless whether it was a school board meeting, a church meeting, the city council, the United Fund, or the Boy Scouts.

Some of Riverbank's decisions were influenced by persons in the outlying community. In this regard, the Finnish people, who were a closely knit group, were important. Also of significance was the fact that the farmers in the community felt that the townspeople would place their own interest ahead of that of the community as a whole.

The most influential person among the farmers and the Finnish people was Inor. Of Finnish descent, he was the largest peppermint grower in the area. He also headed the co-operative association which marketed most of the peppermint crop. For several terms he had served on the Beaver District School Board, which sent a proportionately large number of students to the Riverbank High School. A "second-generation" American, he had been active in many Beaver Community enterprises throughout the years. He also distrusted the town's leaders, but was willing to co-operate whenever possible. He was loved and respected by the people of his community, and his advice on farming, marketing, and community affairs was sought by many. He was independently wealthy.

Norman, another citizen of Finnish background, and owner of a grocery store in Louville, was also highly influential. He had served several terms on the Louville school board. He visited a lot with people in the local community and was quite vocal in expressing his opinions. He was much interested in the athletic program of the high school, as well as in the other phases of the school program.

The Riverbank School System

In 1945, the Riverbank School System operated two schools. One was an elementary school of 270 students in grades one through eight. Constructed in 1929, the elementary school building was rapidly becoming overcrowded.

The second school, the Riverbank High School, contained about 140 students in grades nine through twelve. About one-third of the high school students were on a tuition basis from Beaver, Burntwood, and Louville, three smaller districts which were three, five, and ten miles from Riverbank, respectively.

Urvine, superintendent of the district, also acted as principal of the high school. Directly under the supervision of Urvine were the six high school teachers, the elementary school principal, and the elementary staff of ten teachers. Originally, Urvine came to Riverbank as a teacher and coach in the high school. Because he was well liked and was judged by some to be a good schoolman, he was promoted to the high school principalship and then to the superintendency of the Riverbank schools. A man of definite opinions, Urvine sometimes made enemies because he had a strong determination to get things done and did not always cater to the opinions of others. Urvine was able to get along with Forrest, the member of the "Big Five" who was on the school board during his administration, because he felt he had a system for dealing with him. As Urvine expressed it, "You could get most anything done if you could get Forrest to think that it was his idea." Urvine was well aware of the various factions in the community. For example, when he resigned his position in 1947, he suggested to his successor that he would be wise to become affiliated with a particular church in the community.

The high school plant consisted of three buildings. The main building was quite old, having been constructed about 1898. The Industrial Arts building, commonly known as the Shop, was the first school building in Riverbank, and even the oldest living resident hesitated to estimate its age. The gymnasium building had been erected in 1910, and a stage and bleachers had been added to it during W.P.A. days. All three buildings were in excellent condition for their age, having received excellent care from the custodian, a veteran of many years of service.

Notwithstanding the age of the school buildings, the community seemed satisfied with its schools. They felt that the educational facilities were adequate, the staff well qualified, and the administration sound. The basketball team had recently won the state "B" championship, taxes were bearable, income was high, and almost everyone was happy.

In addition to Forrest, the Riverbank School District had two other board members. One was cashier of the local bank and was directly under the supervision of the "Big Five." He was a very pleasant but very quiet man who seldom ventured an opinion. The other member was also very pleasant and quiet. A devout churchman, he disliked controversy of any kind. As a result, he was generally seeking to compromise any difference of opinion. He had risen to the highest rank in the district organization of the Service Club and had served a term as president and several terms on the Board of Directors. It was common knowledge that Forrest seldom bothered to consult either of the other two board members regarding school matters.

A Catastrophe Creates Problems

On November 1, 1945, the Riverbank High School main building was completely destroyed by fire. When discovered near midnight, the fire was well under way. The volunteer fire department, hampered by low water pressure, was unable to save any portion of the building. The fire department did, however, save the gymnasium building without loss, and the shop building was largely saved; only about half the roof was burned, although there was a considerable amount of water damage.

Immediately after the fire, partitions eight feet high were erected on the gymnasium floor, so that the space was divided into five "classrooms." The two small dressing rooms back of the stage were made into a superintendent-principal's office, a secretary's office, and a library. The shop building was reroofed and the shop machinery cleaned and repaired. One room of the shop building was made into a typing and/or commercial room. All agreed that these were not the best conditions, but no one realized that the high school freshmen of that year were to spend all their school days in that environment.

After the immediate and pressing problem of housing the high school students was alleviated, Urvine and Forrest turned their attention to the location and erection of a new high school building.

Two major problems arose immediately, the first of which was financial. With building costs so high, it was immediately impossible under the existing law for the Riverbank School District to bond sufficiently to build a new high school. The assessed valuation of the Riverbank District was $1,226,370, which gave a bonding capacity of approximately $61,000. With the additional $50,000 fire insurance money, a total of $111,000 was available—which, of course, was inadequate. The only solution that seemed feasible was to join with outlying districts and, thereby, increase district bonding capacity. One approach was to form a union high district in league with the Beaver, Louville, and Burntwood districts. The other approach was to form a consolidated district of grades one to twelve. Either approach would result in sufficient bonding capacity to finance the building of a new high school.

Second, the question of the location of the high school site arose almost immediately. One group, for whom Forrest was the spokesman, favored the so-called Hill Site. This was the site of the old building. Thomas, Urvine, and others favored a location known as the Park Site. From the beginning, many of Riverbank's citizens held strong opinions about the desirability of these sites.

The Hill Site, which was the location of the old building, comprised approximately four and one-half acres. It derived its name from the fact that it was located on the side of a steep hill. This location was favored by Forrest and many others of the community because they contended that the new building could be erected there at considerably less cost since it would not be necessary to build a new gymnasium and shop. Many residents felt also that, since this was the location of the old school, the new one should be there, too. Forrest even contended that the concrete floor of the burned building and some of the old water and sewer pipes could be used. The plans which Forrest drew for the new building were predicated on the location and use of these items.

Opponents of the Hill Site insisted that it provided no room for expansion or for athletic facilities. Many of the firemen felt that they could have saved the old building had the water pressure been adequate, and that the conditions would not allow adequate water pressure in a new building. Others argued that a new gym was needed for additional physical education space.

The Riverbank City government owned approximately 15 acres of land called the Park Site, which was located just two blocks from the business part of town. This area had long been operated as a city park and was used as a baseball, football, and physical education field by the high school, even though it was located about a half-mile from the high school buildings. The site was low, filled-in land and was subject to flood. It was level, however, and would have placed all of the high school facilities in a convenient location. This location was favored by a considerable number of people in the community. A large number of these persons felt that the Park Site would be more convenient for administering the athletic program.

Urvine held the Park Site to be the most desirable, and he was seconded by Thomas. These two worked together and, because of Thomas's standing in the community and his influence through the newspaper, they made a powerful pair.

A third alternative, the Conyers Site, was to enter the picture later. Located one-half mile outside the city limits and seven-eighths of a mile from the business district, the site contained 25 acres of ground, on two levels, about equally divided as to acreage. Several other sites were mentioned at various times. However, none of these received serious consideration, although a few reached the ballot by write-in votes.

Consolidation or Unionization?[1]

Forrest moved quickly to solve Riverbank's school building problems. Without discussing matters with the other members of the Board or the Superintendent, he secured the services of a consultant on district organization problems. Previous to this, Urvine had suggested unionization, but this had received little consideration from the district board. The consultant conducted his survey and in a report to Forrest on March 31, 1946 recommended consolidation. Forrest immediately mailed letters to the members of the district

---

[1] Consolidation in Riverbank's state meant unifying its elementary schools and those of the outlying districts with the high schools all under one administration. Unionization, on the other hand, is a method whereby several independent elementary districts form a district for high school purposes only. In this arrangement, the elementary school districts are left undisturbed.

board and several interested citizens giving the essentials of the report. In brief, the report recommended the consolidation of the Riverbank, Beaver, Louville, and Burntwood districts. The Riverbank Elementary School was to operate as a six-year school, as was the Beaver School. The Burntwood and Louville students were to be transported to Riverbank, and all students of seventh grade or above were to attend the new six-year high school.

On April 26, 1946 a meeting was called for the boards and interested patrons of the Riverbank, Beaver, Burntwood, and Louville districts to discuss the question of consolidation. According to Urvine, "The Board members of the outlying districts were told by the consultant that they could consolidate or send their kids elsewhere." Apparently the consultant and Forrest had conferred previous to the meeting and agreed on this statement. Forrest spoke later in the meeting and said essentially the same thing. Urvine later remarked, "Some of those Finns stood up and said, 'they just might do that.'"

A vote for consolidation was held on May 20, 1946 and was defeated overwhelmingly.

Urvine, on his own initiative, asked and received permission from the Riverbank School Board to approach the smaller district boards and discuss unionization with them. He approached Inor and Norman on the unionization idea and received their support as individuals. However, a cooling-off period apparently ensued, for there is no record of any formal action until February 21, 1947, when a joint meeting of the four school boards was called. All board members expressed themselves in favor of unionization, and on April 4, 1947 voters in the various districts approved the unionization by a large majority. Immediately following, on April 30, 1947, a public hearing on the proposed Riverbank-Beaver-Louville-Burntwood union high school district was held at the County Courthouse. There was no opposition, and the Union High School District was officially formed. A five-member Union High Board was appointed, which included Inor, Norman, Forrest, and the other two members of the Riverbank School Board.

A New Board Makes Decisions

The legality of the unionization was questioned soon after the Union High Board was seated. Forrest had insisted that he and

Urvine could draw up the necessary papers, notices, and petitions for the unionization and had proceeded on that basis. There was also some discussion as to whether or not the Union High Board should pay for the services of the consultant, since he had been employed by Forrest. According to Urvine, "Forrest was given to understand that henceforth all actions were to be taken by the Board as a whole in regular meeting."

The insurance money also proved to be a sore point. Forrest contended that, since unionization had taken place instead of consolidation, all money from insurance should remain in the hands of the Riverbank Elementary District. This would mean that the Union High District would not benefit from the insurance money. Inor and Norman bitterly opposed this idea, contending that the other districts had contributed to the insurance program through their payment of tuition over the years. However, the other two Riverbank board members sided with Forrest, and the Union High District never did receive any of the insurance money. The loss of this money would have seriously handicapped the building program had not the legislature later raised the bonding capacity to a point which allowed the Union High District a bonding capacity of $255,000.

In May and June, prior to the annual district meeting, the Union High Board held several meetings. The architects' firm of Graham and Inman was employed to conduct preliminary surveys of both the Park and Hill sites. Mr. Graham reported that a building could be constructed on either site, but that the Hill Site would be approximately $50,000 cheaper, since it would not be necessary to erect a gymnasium immediately. Mayor Thomas sat with the Union High Board on at least one occasion, and verbal agreement was reached between the Union High Board and the City regarding the use of the playing field. Mr. Graham told the Union High Board that such an agreement would have no legal status, but Thomas assured them that the city would never take the field away from the kids.

The Board also agreed that a test vote would be taken at the annual meeting. The vote was not to be legally binding.

According to an earlier agreement, the seated members of the Union High Board were to serve only until the annual meeting, at which time candidates were to file petitions for election. Two incumbents refrained from filing, but Forrest, Inor, and Norman did file. The week before the election, Forrest reportedly spent much of his time buttonholing everyone to urge them to vote for the Hill Site.

In the selection of Union High Board members, the Riverbank District was to have two directors and the other three districts one each. Inor was re-elected from the Beaver District, as was Norman from the Louville District.

Orkkla, a prominent peppermint grower of the community, who had been a member of the Burntwood District Board, was a third member. Forrest received only eight votes and was not re-elected. Norwood and Thurston were the board members selected to serve Riverbank's citizens.

Besides owning large tracts of land in the area west of Riverbank, Norwood had many other business interests in the community. He dealt in beef cattle, sheep, and grain. In addition, he owned "heavy" equipment which he leased or sold to those who needed it. Norwood was prominent in the beef cattlemen's state association and was also interested in local politics.

Thurston owned and operated an oil distributorship in Riverbank. He was the only member of the Union High Board with a child in the high school. While Inor had a daughter of high school age, she attended a private school in the state's largest metropolis.

In the straw vote on site location, the count favored the Park Site over the Hill Site. The vote was 105 to 95.

Prior to the annual school meeting, preparations had been made by the Union High Board to hold an election on July 8, 1947, at which time the voters were to decide whether or not they wanted the Park Site for the new high school building. Two months earlier, the City Council of Riverbank sold three acres of the Park area to the Union High District for $3,000. The title to the remaining 12 acres was to remain with the city, but the Council agreed to use this sum for lighting the athletic field. The vote was to be binding, and all steps were presumably taken to make it legal, although no attorney was employed to handle the details. When the election was held, the Park Site was defeated by 164 to 152 votes.

When the Park Site was defeated, the Board tentatively set another election for August 18, 1947, at which time voters were to decide whether they preferred the Hill Site. In addition, they were to be asked to approve bonds to construct a high school building on whichever site was chosen.

The board also agreed that the bonds should be approved by

Mr. Taylor, an attorney, who approved most of the municipal bond issues in the state. Reportedly, Mr. Taylor had built such a wide reputation with bond buyers that few, if any, bond houses would bid on bonds unless they were approved by him.

A Change in Superintendents

Shortly after the tentative date for the election was set, Urvine announced his intention to resign and accept another position. The board then delayed the election until after the selection of a new superintendent. After a fairly rapid screening procedure, Garnett was selected to replace Urvine as Superintendent-Principal of the Union High District. Garnett had been an elementary principal for eight years in small to large schools, and just previous to his selection by the Union High Board had been a superintendent-principal of a small union high school in another part of the state. Although he had had only two years of experience in dealing directly with school boards, he had every confidence in his ability to handle the situation. Later he wondered to what extent the varied work experience and the difficult financial problems which he met during the depression years affected his success in Riverbank. Because of his depression experiences, he almost automatically distrusted people with money and people who attempted to influence others unduly. As a person, Garnett found it difficult to make acquaintances easily. However, over a period of time, his acquaintances frequently became his good friends.

Since Garnett was not selected until about ten days before the opening of school, his first concern was to get the schedule and other things in order so that school could start smoothly. Owing to these demands on his time and the problem of getting his family moved, it was not until the October meeting of the Board that he really began to understand the site problem.

During the first month, the site problem had been called to his attention. For example, when Thomas and Garnett first met, the former asked Garnett to indicate his position regarding the site question. Garnett replied that he had not had time to acquaint himself with all the facts and that he supposed the ultimate decision would rest with the people. Thomas's reaction to this was blunt and profane. He remarked to Garnett that any school administrator worthy of employment could see that the Park Site was superior. This initial contact set the pattern for the relationship between Thomas and Garnett for years to come. Each time Garnett's contract was up for renewal, Thomas would contact one or all of the Board members to urge Garnett's removal. Fortunately for Garnett, Norman was apparently the only member of the Board who took Thomas's complaints seriously. Inor treated the relationship as a big joke. At almost every Board meeting, he would inquire of Garnett about his "relations with the press."

Previous to the October Board meeting, Garnett had talked to the architects several times concerning Mr. Taylor and his report. Each time they stated that no report had been forthcoming.

At the Board meeting, Garnett volunteered to see Taylor and determine the cause of the delay. This he did, and Taylor informed him that, owing to a number of irregularities in the procedures used in forming the union high district, the district was not legal. Taylor further suggested that the procedure under the circumstances was to go into circuit court and attempt to have the district validated. Garnett returned this information to the Board and suggested that it was imperative that an attorney be retained to handle this and other legal problems that were sure to follow. The Board accordingly retained an attorney from a neighboring town. It was estimated that the proceedings, including the preparation of papers, the waiting period, and the validation would take about three months. Actually, it took five.

The New Superintendent Makes a Commitment

In the meantime, Garnett began to get better acquainted with the Board and the community and to clarify his thinking on the subject of sites. It soon became evident that the Board was favorable toward the Park Site—with the exception of Thurston, whose greatest concern was to get the building started. It also seemed clear to Garnett and to the Board that there was strong sentiment in the community for the Hill Site. This sentiment appeared to be based largely on the undeniable fact that it would be cheaper to build on the Hill Site, since there would be no immediate necessity for the construction of a gym. Garnett, however, felt that at least half of the $50,000 difference in cost as quoted by Forrest would be offset by the expensive work required to make an adequate physical education play field. The architects further assured him that it would cost from 10 to 15 per cent more to build on the Hill than it would to construct the same building on a level area. Further, no one had been able to refute successfully the theory that the low water pressure had contributed to the loss of the old building. However, the Hill Site did have the gym and perhaps the leveling could be spread over a period of years, so that the money saved on the gym could be used on the main building.

On the other hand, the Park Site did offer a level tract of land which could provide excellent athletic and physical education facilities. However, the low ground worried him with its possibility of flooding. Also, while some of the businessmen saw the proximity of the site to the business district as an advantage, Garnett felt this to be a disadvantage and would have preferred to keep the students near the school during the noon hour.

As time wasted, cost became an increasingly important factor. The architects were now quoting ten dollars a square foot, as against the seven to eight dollars quoted in their original estimates. This meant that, from the very beginning, a building on the Park Site would be more cramped for classroom space.

Garnett was puzzled as to the continued and firm opposition of Inor and Norman to the Hill Site. Inor once hinted at the reason for his position by saying, "They promised us that if we came in, they would not put the school on the Hill." Just who made the promise is not known. Actually, no one could have made such a promise legally. Nonetheless, Inor definitely appeared to feel that his District had been doublecrossed—presumably by Forrest and others in favor of the Hill Site. To a lesser extent, Norman and Norwood seemed to feel the same way. Orkkla never expressed an opinion to Garnett, and Thurston was willing to put the building anywhere just so long as construction was started.

It seemed to Garnett that he had three choices. He could recommend the Hill Site and probably lose the confidence of the Board. Second, he could come out in favor of the Park Site and work actively for it. This he could not do conscientiously, since he felt that the Park Site would place decided limitations on the school program that could be offered. Finally, he could endeavor to locate a third site and try to get Board and community acceptance. He decided upon the third alternative.

Garnett, at this time, also thought an advisory committee might be helpful. The Board did not appear receptive to this idea, however. They believed that such action would only complicate matters when the issue was already sufficiently confused. They did, however, agree to look at any new sites that might appear to show promise. Finding a site was not easy, as much of the surrounding terrain was either swampy or hilly. State Department personnel, the Board, the architects, and Garnett viewed various plots of land. Only one appeared to have possibilities, namely, the Conyers Site. Several reasons could be offered in support of the site. Its cost did not exceed that of the other two sites. It met State Department requirements for size, with its 26 acres of land. Finally, it had no major drainage problems.

The Conyers Site was not acceptable, of course, to proponents of the other two sites, and these persons raised various objections. They said that it would still be necessary to build a gym, it was too far from town, it was outside the city limits with no fire protection, it was too far from public utilities, it had drainage problems just as severe as those of the Park Site, and it would prevent older persons from walking to the basketball games.

With the exception of the need for a new gym, none of these objections seemed valid to Garnett. Power lines ran right by the property and the water and sewer lines ended only a few hundred feet from the site. The fire department had frequently and successfully combatted fires outside the city limits. Finally, he thought that most of Riverbank's senior citizens could obtain automobile transportation to athletic contests; certainly, the site would provide ample parking space.

In order to clarify the situation, Garnett attempted to secure a definite statement from the State Department concerning the Hill Site. On March 12, 1948 he received a letter from the State Department which stated in part, "The site of the old building is entirely inadequate for reasons which were pointed out in previous letters. It, therefore, cannot be approved by the State Department of Education." Another letter from the State Department written on the same day stated, "A check of the proposed site known as the Conyers Tract reveals that it is probably the best location viewed so far. It apparently satisfies the requirements for a site and can be developed for use at minimum expense." The Board went on record as favoring the Conyers Site. Garnett then regarded the Hill Site as "out of the picture."

Armed with this support, Garnett threw himself wholeheartedly into the campaign. He spoke before civic organizations, prepared a leaflet stating the facts concerning the proposed sites, and got as much material into the newspaper as he could. Thomas, in spite of his regard for the Park Site, never refused to print information offered him by Garnett.

Thomas and Forrest, however, did not take the proposal for the Conyers Site at its face value. Whatever cost figures were presented by Garnett, other figures were offered by Forrest and Thomas. Garnett used only figures or estimates given him by the architects. The opposition used figures provided by local "experts" who had had no technical training or school building experience.

During this period one of the architects spoke at a meeting of the Service Club. Thomas called him a liar and accused the firm of padding the figures to increase the firm's commission. After telling the Service Club members that they were all a "bunch of hicks" and that he would never set foot in Riverbank again, the architect walked out. The meeting broke up in what may be mildly described as a state of confusion.

An election was called for April 4, 1948, with only the Conyers Site and the Park Site on the ballot. By law, a space was required on the ballot for write-in votes. In the balloting, the Conyers and the Park Sites each received 142 votes, the Hill Site received 23 write-in votes, and several other sites received one or more votes. Including some spoiled ballots, there was a total of 321 ballots cast. Since a majority of the ballots had to be cast for one particular site to make the election results legally binding, no decision was reached.

At the Board meeting following the election, Thurston stated in strong terms that he thought this thing had gone on long enough and that it was imperative that some sort of compromise be reached. He suggested that an election be held in which voters would choose between the Park Site and the Hill Site. This was refused. He further made a motion that the Board attempt to secure from the City the entire Park area and then back the Park Site. The motion lost. Thurston then moved that the Board withdraw its support from the

Conyers Site and support the Hill Site. The motion lost for want of a second. A motion was then made by Norwood and seconded by Orkkla that the Board continue to support the Conyers Site and make a further concerted effort to get out the vote. The motion carried, three to two, with Thurston and Norman voting against it. The board also decided to ask the State Department and the County Superintendent to make a reappraisal of all sites. This was done, and again the Conyers Site was named as the most suitable of the three.

At Thurston's request, Garnett visited the State Department with him. Thurston then inquired as to what would be necessary to make the Hill Site acceptable to the State Department of Education. Garnett and Thurston were told that the Hill Site would be adequate if a minimum of 135,000 square feet of ground suitable for a play field area were developed within a period of five years.

Garnett, at this time, was bitter about this decision of the State Department. He felt that, having once made their decision, they should stand by it, inasmuch as they had once declared the Hill Site as unsuitable and still regarded it as less desirable than the Conyers Site even with the addition of the 135,000 square feet of play area.

A Flood Influences the Decision

On Memorial Day, 1948 an unusual flood disaster swept the state. Riverbank was not spared, as its entire populace was endangered by high water. Some dikes in the surrounding communities broke, and a considerable amount of land was flooded. The Park Area was covered by water to a depth of from three to eight feet and remained so for several weeks. No water was observed on the Conyers Site.

For many days no one had any time to worry about school sites. Nearly two hundred sailors were quartered in the high school gym, and Garnett was working in the truck dispatcher's office at night and was helping to care for the gym during the day. It was not until June 30, 1948 that the Board reconvened for another meeting.

As a result of the flood, the Park Site became a dead issue. Only Thomas continued to back the area, and then without much force. This left the Board with two choices. Thurston was decidedly in favor of the Hill Site, and Norman had changed his point of view in favor of the Hill Site. Inor and Norwood still favored the Conyers Site, as did Garnett. All knew that many of the former supporters of the Park Site would give their vote to the Hill Site if given an opportunity. There was reluctance, therefore, on the part of Inor, Norwood, and Garnett to place both sites on the ballot.

Early in the meeting, Norman made a motion that was seconded by Thurston to place both names on the ballot. Several weary hours of debate followed. As Garnett recalls, Orkkla did not once express an opinion during the entire period. Several efforts were made by both sides to secure a statement from Orkkla, but he did not respond. Garnett reviewed the advantages and disadvantages of both sides as he saw them. At two o'clock in the morning, Garnett suggested that they would have to take a chance on Orkkla. Norwood called for the question. Thurston and Norman voted for the motion to place both sites on the ballot and Orkkla voted with them.

An election was called for July 30, 1948 to decide the school bonds and school site problems. The bonds were approved by a large majority, and the Hill Site received 181 votes while the Conyers Site received 103.

Following the election, the construction of the building proceeded with only normal delays. Plans for the building on the hill were completed, bonds sold, bids called, and contracts let. The low bid was $239,000, which was somewhat lower than had been expected, owing to a favorable winter market. On the basis of this figure, the Board authorized a building containing approximately 32,000 square feet of space at a cost of about $7.50 a square foot. Thus, ample classroom space was provided. Construction began in March, 1949, and the students moved from the gym to the new building during Christmas vacation, 1949, four years and two months after the fire.

Garnett drew and presented to the Board a "five-year plan" for the development of the play area and grounds around the school. Five years after the plan was presented, a portion of the area had been leveled but nothing further had been done regarding the play area. The Board and Budget Board consistently refused to budget more than token sums for the development of the play area. At the end of the five-year period, the State Department of Education ordered the Board to show cause by August 1, 1956 why the work had not been done and to indicate future plans. The Board delayed action until the September, 1956 meeting, at which time word was received from the State Department that Basic School Funds would be withheld until another improvement plan was presented.

Garnett accordingly submitted another plan to the Board and to the State Department, which was accepted by both. This plan called for the expenditure of $1,500 annually on the play area until the original plan was completed. During the fall of 1956 the plan called for a portion of the area to be leveled and seeded; in addition, the construction during the summer of 1957 of two concrete or asphalt play courts was planned. When the 1957–1958 school year opened, contracts for constructing the play courts had not been let. During the same year Garnett resigned his position as Superintendent of the Riverbank Union High District to attend the State University and pursue further graduate work.

CASE SIX

A Coin Has Two Sides

The following case aroused no community-wide repercussions, The position and leadership of Principal Jones, the central character, were never challenged. Within the school where the events occurred, there were undercurrents of feelings, but never any seething whirlpools of emotion.

Why, then, is the case reported? The story is told because it deals with one of the most disturbing problems facing a principal today—that of fairly evaluating a teacher who is neither an outstandingly good one nor so grossly poor that it is readily apparent to everyone. This problem becomes all the more crucial in districts with teacher-tenure laws, in that the decisions made may have long-term implications.

The case also has value in that it recounts two views of teacher evaluation. The principal's view, told through the eyes of Principal

Jones, was written one year after Norris's release. The teacher's side of the story was obtained through careful interview with Teacher Norris three years after his dismissal. The person who interviewed and wrote Teacher Norris's side of the story remained totally unfamiliar with Jones's report until after he had written his own. Thus, the reader has the opportunity to examine differences and similarities in the perceptions of values, events, and persons, and to weigh the implications for teacher-administrator interaction.

JONES'S STORY

Principal Jones had spent several weeks working on the 1951–1952 budget for the Andrew Jackson Junior High School. Except for typing, it was now complete. With relief he turned to the next task, namely, the preparation of a preliminary schedule. It was mid-January, and the central office wanted information on the kinds of teachers needed for the next year.

Working on a schedule had always appeared to Jones to be a challenge. In a way, he viewed it as an enjoyable game. As he contemplated his task, he reviewed the various factors with which he would have to work. Next year's enrollment promised to be larger than that for the current year, but probably the increase would not be more than 30 to 40 students. To meet this anticipated increase, another teacher would be added to the staff and, in addition—and this really pleased him—two portable classrooms were to be moved to the Jackson School. This should help an otherwise tight scheduling problem. Now he must decide the area of the instructional program that would benefit most by adding an extra teacher.

Beyond a doubt, the physical education and health classes were becoming too large. There was only one rather moderate-sized gymnasium, so the physical education and health classes were alternated, and girls and boys used the gym on succeeding days. The 1951–1952 enrollment would be between 650 and 675 in the seventh, eighth, and ninth grades. Jones did some quick calculating and concluded that in the seventh-grade classes, at least, there could be as many as 60 students in each section. Sections of this size were very large, at least for the health education part of the combination. This part of the program, then, certainly needed relief. The problem he faced was a very practical one: how to use one additional teacher to give relief to both the boys' and the girls' classes. Perhaps the idea suggested by Mr. Schrader, the boys' physical education instructor, of turning all health classes over to another teacher, should be considered. The more Jones thought about it, the better he liked the idea.

After further deliberations, the proposal was approved by all concerned, and Assistant Superintendent Watson began his search for a health instructor. The plan was simply to take one-fourth of the boys and one-fourth of the girls out of each physical education class each quarter for a class in health instruction. This meant that health instruction would be carried on in mixed classes, and Jones wondered about that in view of some of the units in the state course of study. However, everyone assured him that his fears were groundless and that there should be no trouble. Since there was only one gym, the three-fourths of the class in physical education would alternate with a study hall rather than with health. Both Mr. Schrader and Mrs. Rogers, the girls' physical education instructor, believed that this time would give them an opportunity for group testing and counseling. Because he had a great faith in both instructors, Jones was also enthusiastic about these possibilities.

Teacher Hired

During the month of February, 1951, Dr. Watson, the Assistant Superintendent, was busily concerned with activities attendant to the hiring of a teacher: interviewing, corresponding for references, studying credentials, conferring with principals about possible selections, and finally recommending his choice to the superintendent. He did not immediately find someone for the new position at Jackson Junior High School. The position probably wouldn't be the easiest one in the world to fill, and he had told Jones so. However, he felt that the new plan was a good one, and continued his search. In March, during spring vacation, a break came. A young man who had filed an application for a physical education and health position in early February called and asked for an interview. Watson made the appointment for later in the week and called the college to have the applicant's credentials sent for study. By Thursday, when his secretary announced that Herbert Norris had arrived for his interview,

Watson had checked the confidential papers carefully. Norris introduced himself with a reserved smile, and the interview proceeded. Norris, a finely proportioned and handsome young man, made a very good impression during his 15-minute interview, and Watson mentioned the new health position at Jackson Junior High. Norris seemed interested. He told Watson that he was anxious to return to Auburn, his home town. Watson gathered that he had been quite successful at the small town of St. John, where he had been teaching in the high school during the past year. Ordinarily Watson sent likely-looking candidates to see the principals with whom they might have to work, but Jones was out of town attending the annual convention of the state teachers association, so a meeting was not possible. After the interview, the assistant superintendent had his secretary send some reference blanks to some of Norris's former superiors. Returns indicated that during his three years of experience Norris had pleased his former employers, for they gave him a hearty endorsement. Later, when Jones studied Norris's credentials, he agreed with Watson that he seemed qualified. Norris was subsequently appointed and accepted by letter on April 19. Jones was pleased to know that the position was filled and proceeded with his plans for the next year.

Teacher Rated

Principal Jones remained in Auburn during the summer and, as usual, spent some time in his office each week taking care of requisitions, invoices, and other routine work. By August 1 he had met all the new teachers except Herbert Norris. Some time in July he learned that Mr. Schrader, his physical education teacher, had taken a position with the F.B.I. He would have been disturbed had not Watson recruited another very acceptable applicant who had taught previously in Auburn. Mr. Johnson, the new recruit, was hired for the physical education position and soon called on Jones to renew his acquaintance and begin planning for the next year. Jones felt pleased that such a promising replacement had been found so quickly and was doubly impressed by Johnson's willingness to spend some extra time at school checking over equipment and getting ready for the opening of the term. The principal explained his desires for the new "health department" to Johnson and hoped that Norris, too, would drop in soon to talk over his assignment. He was disappointed in this hope, however, and did not meet Norris until the fall workshop for new teachers.

After a brief group meeting in the fall with all the new teachers, Jones talked with Norris alone. He was anxious to outline to his new teacher what he had in mind, and he enthusiastically told him about the new plan. He explained that, since there were no precedents, Norris could have virtually a free rein. The principal discussed his feeling that health instruction could be made much more functional if classes met every day, and he mentioned some areas in which the class might set up some projects. He suggested that Norris might help organize the annual physical inspections that were made at the beginning of every year under the direction of the school physician, Dr. Brandt. Jones explained that Dr. Brandt was a bit fussy about this activity and liked to have everything go off like clockwork. Last year's inspection had been organized by Mrs. Rogers, but Jones thought it would be splendid if Norris would help this year and then perhaps use some of the results of the inspections as a basis for units of work in his health classes. The principal had other ideas, too, but before going any further he asked Norris his reaction, and was disappointed again. Norris was not nearly as enthusiastic as his principal and reacted in a way which sounded to Jones almost like "Whatever you say—after all, you're the boss." At any rate, he thought he perceived a coolness to his ideas and decided to drop the matter for the present. Later he met again with the teachers in the physical education and health department and was glad to find that all three seemed to have their work pretty well planned. Norris had checked out his books from the librarian and was all ready to go.

Several weeks after school started, Jones got out to check on his new teachers. He liked to give them a little time to get settled before visiting their classes and, besides, he had been very busy in the office. In addition to the two new teachers in health and physical education, there was a new science teacher and a new social living teacher. The latter teachers were stationed close to Jones's office, and he had a good feeling about them almost immediately. They appeared to have everything well organized and seemed completely at ease and in full control of their classes. Norris had been assigned to one of the portable classrooms west of the main building and was thus further removed from Jones's casual observation. Sometime during the first month, however, the principal visited his classes. As Jones was to report later, he was not particularly impressed, but he suspended judgment and expected to visit again soon.

In the meantime, Norris had failed to send some enrollment cards to Dr. Brandt's office. The request for the cards came from the doctor's office to Mrs. Rogers. Since the matter involved the pupils enrolled in Norris's classes, Mrs. Rogers notified Jones, and he went out after the cards. He was sure that Norris had merely forgotten to turn in the cards and, knowing Dr. Brandt's summary requests, he approached the portable in a charitable mood. Norris had the cards in his desk all right, and gave them to the principal with an air which made Jones uncomfortable. Although the cards were overdue, there was no explanation of any kind, and Norris seemed almost flippant as he handed them over. The principal returned to his office with a little less charity in his heart.

Before the end of the first quarter, Jones had several other occasions to visit Norris's classes and to talk with him. But, try as he would, the principal could not break down the apparent reserve with which the new health teacher treated his superior. In only one instance had Jones really been satisfied with the results of a meeting between the two. On this occasion Jones had called Norris in to discuss a matter of procedure in the health class. Inasmuch as this was the first experience in Auburn with a mixed health class, the principal was anxious that things should go smoothly. There were several units involving sex education in the course, and Jones shuddered to think what might happen if they should be handled injudiciously. He resolved to trust Norris's judgment and asked him only to report at the quarter's end on how things had gone. Shortly after the end of the nine-weeks period, Norris gave the principal a number of questionnaires on which he had asked parents to express their opinions about the mixed classes. The reports were most encouraging and Jones was delighted. As he was to recall later, this was about the only time the two had met on a warm and congenial plane. It was to be the last such meeting.

During the second quarter, Norris was visited by Dr. Brandt. The visit turned out to be an unpleasant one, but Jones never was quite sure what had happened. He was inclined to believe Norris's version that the doctor had disagreed openly with him about some points of information he was giving his class. Naturally, the teacher was embarrassed and resentful. Jones knew how the doctor behaved, and tried to soothe Norris's feelings. He pointed out the lady's eccentricities and the many things she had accomplished for health education in Auburn and concluded with "We all have to live with her, so let's make the best of the situation." Again the principal noted Norris's curtain of reserve and knew that the teacher resented the attempt at peacemaking.

At about this time, too, the nurse became critical. Jones reasoned that this was probably a partial reflection of Dr. Brandt's attitude toward the new teacher, but he could not believe that it was entirely so. The doctor could be a tyrant all right, but Jones had every confidence in the nurse. He knew, too, the pressures under which she worked as she tried to carry out the doctor's many directives. He agreed, therefore, that Norris could have been of much more help in distributing and returning the many forms which the doctor's ambitious program of "corrections" entailed. Jones felt that here was another chance to make health education more functional and reasoned that Norris should have welcomed the opportunity to do something beyond purely textbook teaching. He could understand, therefore, when the nurse complained about how Norris treated her "courteous suggestions."

By Christmas, criticism of Norris came from yet another source. The noon-hour supervision crew, with the vice-principal as chief spokesman, complained that Norris was not discharging his supervisory duties in a very satisfactory manner. Jones pondered this complaint, and decided to check for himself. Mr. Harvey, the vice-principal, was in his second year at Jackson Junior High, and Jones knew that he could be most impatient at times with anything that he regarded as slipshod. Harvey was several years older than Jones and, prior to coming to Jackson, had spent a number of years as a manager of a local business office. Before that, he had spent at least 15 years as a high school principal. Jones felt that he was a bit severe and sometimes even abrupt with people, but he was doing his job well and his experience had been a big aid to him in the supervisory assignment he had been given.

Harvey, Johnson, Mrs. Rogers, and the shop man usually ate their lunch together at the cafeteria, but Norris generally went home for lunch. There was the best of rapport between Harvey, Johnson, Rogers, and the shop instructor. About once a week Jones would eat lunch with this group, and it was at this time especially that he began to hear the criticism of Norris. After several different observations of his own, he concluded that Harvey was right perhaps. There was usually more horseplay and other noise in the area allotted to the health teacher's supervision. Several times Jones found, too, that Norris was missing from his post and the activities assigned to him were unsupervised. On a pretext he called the entire group together in the cafeteria to discuss the whole noon-hour program. He hoped by this method to improve conditions without causing any embarassment to Norris. He was unable to observe much change, however.

This was the state of affairs in January when Jones made his preliminary ratings of his probationary teachers. As usual, he extended to each teacher the privilege of a conference at which the rating sheet was jointly completed. His session with Norris was not pleasant, but neither was it very trying. After the formal rating was completed, the principal indicated the areas that were not covered very satisfactorily by the rating sheet and discussed these with the teacher. He told Norris that he would write a supplementary page to the rating sheet and asked him to come back later in the week to hear what he had written. The statement which he read to Norris follows:

Andrew Jackson has this year inaugurated a new schedule for health classes. Mr. Norris has been given this assignment. Since the class is new and there are no precedents upon which to base an evaluation, generally Mr. Norris's work has been acceptable but not outstanding.

At present there are twenty-one sections of students at Andrew Jackson Junior High School. Mr. Norris has each section one class period a day for a period of nine weeks. This, of course, presents some handicaps. In the first place, he must cover the material quickly. Since there is a course of study to follow, he is definitely limited; and, since time is short, instruction is likely to become stereotyped. Neither can he learn to know individual pupils very well in the short time allotted. Student-initiated projects must also be kept at a minimum. In spite of these restrictions, he has been able to rouse a good measure of interest among the students of his classes. With more time he might be able to carry out projects which would make the class even more interesting.

Because of the organization of health classes described above it has been necessary to present the unit on Social Hygiene in mixed classes. This was a cause of concern to principal and teacher alike. However, reaction among students has been generally good and, according to questionnaires returned by parents, they, too, have generally reacted well. This is, indeed, a credit to Mr. Norris's manner of presentation.

The extra class activities that have been assignd to Mr. Norris have been either neglected or discharged in a perfunctory manner. He seldom extends himself in the discharge of these assignments and on occasion gives the impression that he is doing no more than necessary to get by.

Those who work with Mr. Norris in the health department seem to have this feeling. The nurse has expressed the opinion, for example, that much closer co-operation between her and his health classes would be desirable. Dr. Brandt feels much the same way.

Mr. Norris, along with several others, had been assigned to noon-hour duty. It is in the capacity as noon-hour supervisor that he does his poorest work. The teachers assigned with him feel that he often fails to assume the responsibility that should be his. They complain that he shows no initiative in the arrangement or supervision of student recreational activities. They feel that he does not assume his fair share.

Several people who work closely with Mr. Norris feel that he treats lightly many of the ideals, habits, and skills which the school is trying to instill. According to their evaluation, he sees everything as a big joke. The writer could not be that severe in his statement, but a sincerity of purpose does seem to be lacking.

Mr. Norris is being recommended for re-election in spite of the observations because he has done fairly acceptable classroom teaching and it seems that, with proper help from the office, improvement may be expected in the future.

After finishing the reading, he asked Norris to comment. Again the teacher's reaction disappointed him somewhat, but he was encouraged when Norris said with some feeling, "Well, I'll see to it that you'll never have to write another report like that." Jones was glad that he had spoken frankly and believed that there would be improvement.

Teacher Fired

In spite of Norris's statement in January, 1952, things did not improve very much. As Jones was preparing the 1953 evaluation (Norris did not come in for this one), he pondered what to say. He remembered the several conferences that he had had with Norris and admitted rather ruefully to himself that they had not done much good. He admitted to himself, too, that he really had never given

Norris any very concrete suggestions, and reasoned that maybe there still was a chance if ever he could get through to him.

Dr. Brandt, the nurse, Mrs. Rogers, and Harvey continued to be critical. Dr. Brandt felt that Norris was "just plain lazy," and that Jones was silly to even think of keeping him on. Harvey and Mrs. Rogers both decried the fact that Norris often left his post in order to have a smoke with some of the younger men teachers in the boiler room. Mrs. Rogers thought it improper for a health teacher to smoke, and Harvey did not think that any teacher should smoke. Jones did not feel as strongly about it as Harvey, but he did wish that the fellows could abstain while they were on the job. He had not had any difficulty about smoking until two years previously, when some of the younger ex-servicemen had joined the staff. He knew that several of the older teachers did not approve at all. His two shop men regarded smoking as sinful and were critical of the principal for not stamping out the evil immediately. Jones had also had a little difficulty with some of the eighth- and ninth-grade boys' smoking in the neighborhood of the school, and, when talking with their parents about it, had been chagrined by their reference to the teachers' smoking in the boiler room. He had attempted to talk with one of the younger teachers about the situation, but had bungled it somehow and only gained their resentment for his effort. He sighed as he thought of the alternatives, and prayed that he might avoid a rift between the two elements that were becoming apparent on his staff.

Shortly before Christmas, an idea came to Jones that could provide a solution to the problem of what to do about Norris. At any rate, it would provide him with an opportunity to view another facet of the teacher's work and could give him a clue as to what to do next. So he proposed that Norris and Johnson, the physical education teacher, exchange assignments for a quarter. Johnson readily agreed, since he had decided to accept the health and physical education position at Auburn's fourth junior high school, which would open the following September. Harvey also thought well of the experiment, since he was to be principal at the new junior high school and felt that the experience would strengthen Johnson. The experiment had been under way only about two weeks when Jones's ratings of his teachers were due in the central office. He did not feel that he could judge Norris's work in physical education very fairly on such short notice, so wrote simply:

Mr. Norris's work is still not entirely satisfactory. I believe, however, that he should be re-elected for his third probationary year. He has made an effort to improve in the areas where a weakness has been indicated to him.

Presently, during this third quarter, Mr. Johnson and Mr. Norris have exchanged assignments. Mr. Johnson is teaching health classes. Mr. Norris has the physical education classes and, on alternate days, a study hall. It is still too early to make a very reliable observation of his success in these areas.

Jones viewed the experiment as a sort of last resort. He hoped that it would pay off, but he was dubious about it. He was pretty sure that Norris also viewed it as one more chance. When the proposition was originally made to him, Norris had not commented upon it in any way, but had only shrugged and agreed to do it.

Norris now worked in the gym just across the hall from Jones's office. Many times Jones left his work and crossed the hall to have a look. It was difficult for him to understand how Norris could remain undisturbed by the apparent confusion and horseplay that he often saw. At the end of the quarter, Johnson and Norris returned to their original assignments, and Jones had pretty much decided what he must do. Sometime in May he had definitely decided to inform Norris that he would not be able to recommend him for permanent tenure after the next school year. Notification at this time would give the teacher an opportunity to seek employment elsewhere during the summer.

Jones wondered what kind of reaction his decision would have on the faculty. He was positive that Norris had been seeking sympathy from the "boiler room gang," and he was quite certain that they were solidly behind the health teacher. And this was not hard to understand. Norris had an engaging personality and a sharp, though cynical, wit. Jones had always wished that they might be closer friends, and hoped somehow that even at this late date he might find another way out. But such thoughts were fleeting, and whenever he wavered in his resolve, he remembered his first year as principal at Jackson, when he had recommended a teacher for tenure against his better judgment. Well, that had been eight long years ago. The teacher had never learned how really to control a classroom, and there was never a year without some kind of an incident.

He thought, too, of the two other times when he had failed to recommend a teacher for tenure. In each case, the replacement had been able to do a much better job and the move had proved to be a wise one.

On June 1, 1953, he sent the following communication to Assistant Superintendent Watson:

> Dear Dr. Watson:
>
> Herbert Norris is now completing his second probationary year as instructor of health classes here at Andrew Jackson Junior High School. He has been re-elected for a third year. Since his work has not been entirely satisfactory, however, I have informed him that I shall not recommend him for tenure after he completes his probationary period. I have informed him of my intention so that he may seek another position during the summer if he so desires. Dr. Hunt has asked me to make a written report of my reasons for this action. Will you look this report over, add any comments of your own, and pass it on to him?
>
> My reasons for not recommending for tenure follow:
>
> 1. The teaching of content material.
>
> Dr. Brandt has been critical at times of his knowledge of the facts necessary to teach a health course. She does not feel that he is properly qualified to teach the subject. I feel that he lacks competence in the teaching skills and that, therefore, he has failed to get his ideas across.
>
> 2. Co-operation with fellow teachers.
>
> When I reported on Mr. Norris's effectiveness during his first year of work here (January, 1952), I pointed out both Dr. Brandt and the nurse had expressed the opinion that a much closer co-operation between him and them would have strengthened the health department. They still feel that way.
>
> 3. Noon-hour supervisory duty.
>
> I reported, too, in January, 1952, that Mr. Norris had been given this particular supervisory duty, along with several other teachers, and that in this assignment he had done his poorest work. At that time he saw the report I made and stated that he would assume more of his noon-hour responsibilities. I have been able to note little improvement, however. He still shows no interest in the arrangement or supervision of noon-hour activities. He has left all of the planning to others and has often failed to be on hand for his supervisory assignments.
>
> 4. Attitude toward work.
>
> Mr. Norris still seems to treat lightly many of the habits, ideals, and skills which the school is trying to instill. Perhaps this is just a part of Mr. Norris's philosophy of life, but those who work with him feel keenly that it is not the proper attitude to bring to his classes.
>
> Because I had been critical of Mr. Norris's work as a health instructor and in order to observe his work in another field, I assigned the physical education classes to him during the third quarter of this

year. Immediately the fine organization of the class and the spirit of the boys began to deteriorate. In fact, on some days the class got so noisy that I felt the boys must surely be alone. Upon investigation, however, I found Mr. Norris there with the boys, apparently oblivious to the confusion.

On the other hand, the health classes which were assigned to Mr. Johnson in the exchange were strengthened. There seemed to be a definite plan, the classes seemed to have purpose, and there was much less strictly "textbook teaching."

I had hoped, by the institution of a "health department" here at Andrew Jackson, that we might strengthen the functional teaching of health habits. It seemed to me, also, that the health instructor might work closely with the nurse and school doctor in the direction of such "health" activities as the annual physical inspections, the school's immunization program, audiometer testing, etc. Although I believe these programs have been very successful here at Jackson, they have had to be organized by others. Mrs. Rogers, girls' physical education instructor, has usually been charged with the responsibility of planning for these activities. I've talked with Mr. Norris about this, but he has never been able to seize the initiative or make the plans necessary.

Herein, I believe, lies Mr. Norris's greatest weakness. He simply lacks the initiative and drive necessary to be a good junior high teacher. He seldom extends himself and, in fact, often gives the impression of just getting by. I feel that, in the best interests of the school, I must recommend that he not be placed on tenure and that an effort be made to find someone who possesses more of the qualities necessary for a teacher of young adolescents.

Very respectfully,

/s/
Arthur H. Jones
Principal

Dr. Watson appended this note and sent the letter to Dr. Hunt:

I consider Mr. Jones's statement about Mr. Norris to be fair in tone and based on good evidence.

I cannot personally document the objections. On the occasions of my visits to Mr. Norris's classes the work which was going on was neither worthy of praise nor of condemnation. I think that Mr. Jones's objections grow out of a more consistent observation than I have given.

Knowing Mr. Jones's essential fairness, and his demonstrated willingness to "lean over backward" to give a teacher a fair chance, I certainly will support his recommendation.

/s/
George L. Watson

On June 3, Dr. Hunt made the action official with the following letter:

Dear Mr. Norris:

The purpose of this letter is to convey to you officially and in writing the fact that a report made to me today by Mr. Arthur H. Jones, Principal, and Mr. George L. Watson, Assistant Superintendent, is such that it will not be possible to recommend you for permanent tenure after another year of probationary teaching. It is my understanding, from Mr. Jones's report, that he has previously conveyed this information to you orally.

Briefly, the report from Mr. Jones indicates that you lack adequate knowledge of subject content material, do not co-operate well with other members of the health staff of the school, have not adequately assumed your noon-hour supervisory responsibilities, and that you treat lightly many of the habits, ideals, and skills which the school is trying to instill in youth. Mr. Jones further indicates that he reached his decision concerning your teaching effectiveness reluctantly and after considerable observation of your work over a two-year period.

In bringing this matter to your attention a year ahead of the time that you need to be notified that you cannot be recommended for further employment by the district, it is my purpose to provide you with ample opportunity to obtain other employment if you wish to do so. Although Mr. Jones has discussed your lack of teaching effectiveness with you, we will discuss the matter further if you so desire.

Very truly yours,

/s/
Donald Hunt
Superintendent-Clerk

Jones felt that this action would solve the Norris problem because he was certain that the teacher would seek another position during the summer. When Norris checked in at the end of the spring term, he gave no indication of his plans, but Jones wished him luck.

Teacher Departs

September brought a new school year and the return of Herbert Norris. Jones did not understand why Norris had chosen to remain, but since he had, the principal determined to view him like any other third-year probationer and to make an effort to observe his work in that light. This proved to be difficult, however, and when he visited the health classes, the situation always seemed quite tense. He asked the assistant superintendent and the director of secondary education to look in and to make their evaluations, which were also reported to him. The new vice-principal observed Norris's work on the noon-hour supervisory assignments and reported his impressions to Jones. He evaluated Norris's work as lackadaisical and half-hearted. None of these observers believed that the decision of the previous spring should be changed, and, in addition, the nurse and the doctor had not changed their minds. Accordingly, in January, Norris was again told that he would not be placed on tenure.

All in all, Norris's "lame duck" year at Jackson was much the same as the previous two years had been. But then, under the circumstances, Jones had not expected anything noticeably different. There were, though, several little things which annoyed him and to which he gave considerable thought. There was, for example, the matter of the teachers' room. Because the room was large and contained a number of comfortable chairs, Jones scheduled faculty meetings there, only to receive complaints because some of the teachers were smoking. Jones moved the faculty meetings to the library. On another occasion, a homemaking teacher was talking with Jones and mentioned that she had been visiting with Mr. Hardy, a new science teacher. She recounted their conversation, saying that Hardy had remarked that he understood one had to be careful to stay in good with "old man Jones." She reported that she had told him that if he tended to business, he would not have anything to worry about. Jones did not like this state of affairs much and supposed that Norris had been talking. This could be expected, of course, but he wondered how widespread ideas similar to those held by Hardy were. He could not be sure.

When Herb Norris came in for his final check, Jones tried to be pleasant and cheerful and asked him about his plans. Norris only intimated that he had a job, but did not offer any further information. He thanked the principal for his check, turned, and walked out of the office, leaving Jones with that same old uncomfortable feeling. He sighed as he shuffled through some papers on his desk, suspicious once again that he had "goofed" and certain that he had better take a long, searching look at himself before next fall.

NORRIS'S STORY

Herbert Norris completed work for the Bachelor's degree at the State University with major concentration in health and physical education. For some time he had looked forward to teaching one or more phases of this broad field, and he keenly anticipated a professional career. Previous to university work, he was journeyman pipe fitter, a sawmill employee, and a businessman; he was content with none of these. He concluded that by completing his degree and the state requirements for teaching, he would realize his primary vocational desire.

During his first three years of teaching, he considered himself quite successful. He felt that he had enjoyed the wholehearted support of the administration and community during these years. But St. John High School, in which he gained these years of experience, was in a rather inaccessible area of the state—especially during the winter months when heavy snows occasionally isolated this mountain community. Besides, he had spent half of his life at Auburn in another part of the state, and he considered it his home. He had attended the public schools there and had a strong desire to return to his home community as a teacher.

Teacher Hired

In February of his third year at St. John, he wrote a letter to the superintendent of schools at Auburn to inquire about possible vacancies in health and physical education. Upon learning of a vacancy for the following year in health instruction at Andrew Jackson Junior High School, he asked for and was granted an interview with the assistant superintendent. He was also to meet Mr. Jones, the principal. The day he arrived, however, Mr. Jones reportedly was out of the city.

Mr. Norris soon learned that the unfilled position was quite atypical. Mr. Watson, the assistant superintendent, explained that the new position was experimental and that it stemmed largely from the fact that Jackson Junior High School had extremely large physical education sections. The new teacher would provide health instruction for classes composed of both boys and girls in successive nine-week periods. During the course of a school year, the teacher would have every junior high school boy and girl, totaling approximately 650, in his various health classes. To Norris, the position presented some problems, especially with the increasing emphasis on sex education, but he felt confident that he could handle the situation. He indicated an interest in the position and was subsequently employed.

Teacher Rated

In his first interview with Principal Jones, he was questioned concerning his smoking habits. This seemed to be a concern of Mr. Jones, possibly all the more so since Norris was teaching health. However, Norris considered his smoking to be in moderation. He would try to avoid being offensive with the habit, but he "didn't feel it improper to smoke in public, and he had no intention of hiding the fact that he smoked." Later, he learned that the principal also smoked, although he did not do so freely in public. In addition, several other teachers on the staff smoked.

As for the position, it presented a challenge to Norris. He tried to organize instruction in keeping with the state course of study and considered his efforts in this regard quite acceptable. As for classroom control of the various groups, he considered it to be good. At first he had been somewhat apprehensive about potential problems that might result from the presence of mixed sexes in the classes. However, control was never a problem during his three years at Auburn: "I wouldn't say I had any discipline problem. I recall only one boy who was a problem case during the three-year period. I tried to keep the pupils busy; I believe I expected a lot from them, but they seemed to feel that it paid off. I had youngsters come to me and say that they'd learned more under me than any other teacher they'd had. Also, during my first two years at Auburn, I was in charge of the student court. I thought that my work with this group was quite satisfactory."

Norris and the boys' and girls' physical education teachers were assigned to supervise noon-hour activities of pupils. The vice-principal assisted with these activities occasionally. However, Norris recalled that the two physical education teachers usually stayed inside the building and left the entire playground for him to supervise. He judged this to be more than his share of the total responsibility and felt that his experience with it was generally unpleasant.

Mr. Norris was disappointed with the supervisory help he had received. One person on a district-wide basis was employed presumably to assist with the over-all program of curriculum improvement. Norris had relatively few contacts with this individual, however, and he felt that the contacts he had were practically useless. Speaking of his supervision in general, he said, "I never once received any constructive help from any supervisor. I had taken a course in supervision at the University taught by our superintendent, and he told us how supervisors worked with teachers and how they held conferences with teachers after observing them. However, never once do I remember having anyone who visited my classes talk with me afterward about my teaching. They usually got right out after the class—oh, except for possibly speaking to me about something unrelated to teaching, such as the weather."

Norris was not aware of any particular rating procedure except for visits to the classroom by Mr. Jones and Dr. Brandt, which finally culminated in a completed rating sheet filled in by the principal. He recalled that the first time the rating sheet was completed by Jones it was done over coffee together. However, he did not recall having seen the completed form. He did not know precisely what procedures were used with other teachers nor whether they saw their completed rating sheets. He was most aware of visitations in his classroom by the departmental supervisor and occasional visits by the principal. However, in his own words, "Before it was over, I had everyone in my room up through the assistant superintendent."

Dr. Brandt, the health and physical education supervisor, had taken over Norris's class on two occasions because she did not agree with his treatment of the material being discussed. The first time she arrived after he had begun an explanation about muscles. He had always felt that she misunderstood the approach he had made. The second time, he made an error in the use of terms. This occurred during a discussion of the effect of poison oak. During the period a boy asked why some persons were affected without touching it. Norris said that it was because the "oils" from the plant were carried by the wind. He knew he should have said "resin" instead of "oil." At that point, however, Dr. Brandt corrected him and then took over the class for the rest of the period.

Dr. Brandt was a medical doctor, but in his estimation she knew little about teaching methods and classroom problems. In spite of this fact, he gave her the highest credit for her understanding of the technical aspects of health. He also had a high regard for the program she provided in health services.

As for the relationship between Norris and the principal, there were several significant things which stood out in his mind. For one thing, there were recurring references to the fact that he smoked. Now, he knew that he could have hidden the fact that he smoked, but at the time he did not consider it the thing to do.

It was during the second year that Norris learned from the principal that he "didn't fit into the happy family" of teachers. Although this accusation bothered him considerably, he tried to overlook it. It became clear to him, however, that through this inference by the principal he now had two "charges" against him. In spite of this fact, he did not consider them to have the potential effect which they later proved to have. Obviously, they did not loom as large to him as they did to Mr. Jones.

It was never clear to him why he did not fit into the happy family. He did recall that he met his classes the first year in a portable building located away from the main building. Because of this physical arrangement it was not always convenient for him to share in the coffee breaks, nor was he always aware when coffee was available. However, he attended all of the faculty meetings and all faculty social events.

Another incident stood out in his memory: "After a local staff member had been arrested for being intoxicated, the principal called a faculty meeting and in the course of it announced that he would not tolerate the use of alcohol by any of his faculty. He could not defend any teacher who drank, nor would he defend any teacher seen in a place that sold the stuff. Yet shortly after announcement, the men of the faculty, including the principal, had a social event in which all men except Norris drank beer. Norris "did not refrain from drinking because the principal had said what he had, but simply because he did not like the taste of beer." Norris had always found it hard to reconcile the announcement with the event that followed.

In one of the conferences with the principal, an additional factor that apparently entered into his rating was introduced. After the principal reminded Norris that he had not given up smoking, he asked him what church he attended and what organizations he was active in. Norris guessed that Jones did not approve of a local civic group to which he belonged—a group which sponsored recreational activities. Again Jones made it clear that Norris did not "fit into the happy family."

Teacher Fired

Norris was notified at the end of the second year that he would not receive tenure. Mr. Jones explained that if Norris desired, he could teach the third year to have time to look for a new position. This he did, and at the end of the third year Jones thanked Norris for co-operating as he had. Norris stated later that he "wouldn't have wanted to do otherwise."

Adjusting to the loss of his job was not easy for Norris. As he stated later, "Well, it was quite a blow to get fired. I felt that I could teach reasonably well, and I wanted to teach at Auburn because I liked it there and it was my home. I've been a journeyman pipe fitter, and I'm sure I could make more money doing that than teaching; I've worked in a saw mill and I could make more there; I've been in business and I know I could make more there. But I felt I wanted to teach. So I can tell you, it was quite a shock to have things go as they did. I wondered if I had wasted several years of college."

Norris also wished that he had a clearer picture of the reason for his release. He was not sure why he was fired. The only reasons he clearly recognized were that he smoked and that he "didn't fit into the happy family."

Teacher Departs

When Norris was released, he was not sure at first how to go about getting a new position. However, he learned through a colleague at Jackson School that a man whom Principal Jones had dismissed the year before he came to Auburn was a school principal in the state and that he needed a teacher. So he went to him and was fortunate enough to be offered the position; he accepted it with relief. In the interview, Norris was very interested to learn that the new principal felt he had experienced about the same kind of situation at Jackson as Norris had experienced.

His teaching field in the new position was not health and physical education but math and science. He held this position for three years, and at the beginning of his fourth year remarked, "I like my job and I feel I'm doing a pretty good job of teaching. But I hope sometime to go back to Auburn. I'm beginning to feel that I'd like to talk to someone at the central office in the school district to see if I might be able to get back into the system. By now I have six years of good recommendations and perhaps three of the other kind. I believe I could show that I can do a satisfactory job now. After all, Auburn is my hometown. Also, my oldest boy will soon be entering the public schools."

CASE SEVEN

Alice Smith, Transfer

It was the middle of May. School for the children of the United States Armed Forces personnel in Stratford, England, was hurrying to a close. Individual assignments for the next school year had arrived in the mail. During the coffee break, teachers were eagerly exchanging notes on where friends and acquaintances were to be located.

Jane Adams, principal of this eight-grade elementary school of 450 children, looked sadly at the group of 16 teachers with whom she had worked so closely. All but four were soon to be scattered to various countries in the world. How wonderful it would be to keep these same teachers who had done so much to cement community relations and to provide rich experiences and security for these children who were to move so often, she reflected! What a difference this school had made in the community of 600 American families who had so few facilities for family recreation! This was the second group of good teachers to be disbanded in her two years as principal of this school. But one had to be realistic. Many of the teachers were on leaves of absence from jobs at home. Others were eager to see more of the world. Miss Brown, an exceptionally good teacher who had been with Miss Adams for two years, was to transfer to a Navy base in Italy.

Jane Adams was brought back to reality with this remark, "And guess who is coming to Stratford? Alice Smith."

"Oh no! You don't mean that. Things will be different next year," chorused a startled group.

Although Miss Adams listened to casual remarks about the prospective member of the faculty as she was discussed informally from time to time, nothing too startling was disclosed. One teacher did say, "We must be careful not to influence Jane. Give her the opportunity to form her own opinion."

In the busy days of closing the school for the summer and bidding farewell to faculty friends departing to the States, assignments and new teachers were forgotten. It was not until Jane Adams arrived in Paris at a graduate school attended by more than 200 American teachers from Europe and North Africa that the disconcerting subject was again brought to mind.

Unexpected Information

While waiting for a room assignment in the dormitory, Miss Adams sat next to two strangers who were carrying on an earnest conversation in clear voices. "Yes, I'm going back to Plymouth, but I'll be much happier next year. I had the misfortune of having Alice Smith for a roommate for two months. Was I unhappy! Fortunately, I was able to convince my principal that either I was to have different living quarters or I was going back to Wisconsin. And even more fortunate for all of us, she has been transferred to Stratford."

"Poor Stratford," was the reply.

Jane Adams's curiosity could stand no more. "I couldn't help overhearing your conversation," she remarked. "I work in Stratford and am wondering about this person, Alice Smith. She is to be a member of our staff."

"It's nothing you can put your finger upon. She's a good enough teacher, I guess, but she doesn't fit in. She's the laughingstock of Plymouth. She was transferred to our school after three months in Rome; so you see that something is wrong."

Immediately after she received her room assignment, Jane Adams wrote a letter to Mr. Finley, the regional superintendent of the Area Command. She stated the rumors she had heard and emphasized the fact that, in spite of her effort to be objective and open-minded, she was bound to let what she had heard influence her thinking. Miss Adams also stated that the Stratford area had achieved outstanding community-school relations through great effort and that she was eager to maintain that relationship. She suggested that Mrs. Smith be transferred to a large school system where her private affairs would not be exposed to the gossip of a small officers' club. Miss Adams pointed out that both communities to which Mrs. Smith had previously been assigned were twice as large as Stratford, and that placing her in a smaller community would create even greater problems.

A polite letter from Mr. Finley stated that much thought had been given the transfer of Mrs. Smith to Stratford. Since it was her request to come to Stratford, and since he felt that Miss Adams could do much to help Mrs. Smith, the assignment would not be changed. Mr. Finley mentioned also that he had visited Mrs. Smith's classroom briefly and had not seen anything too much out of the way, except possibly her attire. He was certain that a woman supervisor could help her in that respect.

Knowing what a brief first-hand picture Mr. Finley must have of Mrs. Smith's work since his area included 20 schools within a 100-mile radius, she was not much comforted. As a matter of fact, she resented the decision which her superintendent had made. It did not help solve *her* problem.

Resigned to her fate and determined to listen to no further gossip, Jane Adams settled down to her work. In spite of her determination to forget the whole affair, comments about Mrs. Smith were heard again and again. She was well known over a wide area!

At an administrators' conference following the summer school session, the Director of the Area Command announced that hereafter there would be *no transfer* of personnel who might be misfits during the school year. It would be each administrator's responsibility to guide the teacher and to document unprofessional behavior.

The Teachers Arrive

August came, and with it the new teachers who had just arrived from North Carolina, Missouri, Florida, Pennsylvania, California, and other places. The first four young women arrived on the same day and chose their rooms in the big house that was to be their temporary home until the new billets were completed. They had met aboard ship on the way across the Atlantic, and they began immediately to form a close, closed attachment that was to last throughout the year.

Other teachers in the school were not slow to note the tight relationships, and soon the group was given the name "sorority gals." They were all between 25 and 30 years of age and had similar interests. In the eyes of their colleagues, they had come to Great Britain to have a good time. Their fellow teachers also felt that they were interested mostly in social activity, particularly with male companions. Jane Adams soon concluded that all of them valued social activities more than educational activities.

Three older women arrived singly in the next three days. They were quiet and retiring and immediately sensed the exclusiveness of the first arrivals. Although these older teachers were different in personality and outlook, they soon became friendly with one another. They also formed a relatively closed group and isolated themselves from other faculty groups.

Mrs. Alice Smith, a young divorcee of 28 years, dressed in a tight sweater and shorts, was the next to arrive—not by staff car, which was the usual procedure, but in an army truck with all of her possessions and two GI's at her beck and call. How she had maneuvered this unique arrangement was never known. It certainly was against Army regulations. Her first request to Jane Adams, who had personally escorted each teacher to her new home and who had just arrived with another new teacher, was that Miss Adams provide a night's lodging for these two companions who had worked so hard. Since according to official regulations there were no facilities, it was impossible to comply with this request. Mrs. Smith then took matters into her own hands and used the two remaining rooms in the house for her guests.

Mrs. Smith and her guests proceeded to make themselves at

home. They enjoyed coffee in the kitchen and a social time in the living room. Not caring to join Mrs. Smith and her guests, the other occupants of the house retired to their rooms in stony silence. "This was shocking—men in women's billets!"

The four young women who had been on the Stratford faculty the previous year were the next to arrive. One of these teachers had returned to Michigan for the summer. The other three had taken advantage of the summer vacation to travel extensively on the Continent and in the Scandinavian countries. This was the third year that two of these teachers were to be under the supervision of Jane Adams and the second year for the other two teachers. They had already developed very close relationships. All of them were very much interested in travel. They also shared such interests as plays, books, and operas. Jane Adams saw these teachers as mature people very much interested in teaching. In addition, they were interested in good faculty relationships. Jane Adams judged one of these teachers to be exceptionally talented in handling problems of human relations.

Among those arriving to begin the work of the school year was the one and only male faculty member. Jim Turner, both handsome and eligible, came just before school started and took his quarters in the house where the army officers lived. The "sorority gals" became interested immediately and for a few weeks monopolized his time. Before long, however, he discovered a friend in town who was more to his liking and, even though he remained friendly to the "sorority gals," he spent little time with them.

There were three other faculty members who were already on the scene and ready to begin the year's work. Two of them were kindergarten teachers and one a third-grade teacher. These teachers were of English background and lived with their families in Stratford.

Inharmonious Relations

Early in the year, Principal Adams became very disturbed by the cliques that were evident among her faculty. This was especially upsetting, because her previous faculty groups had been such congenial colleagues. To remedy this problem, she brought the faculty together in a series of social affairs. Early in September she provided a steak dinner for the teachers and the P.T.A. officers at the Army Club. To all outward appearances, the affair went well, she thought. There was considerable intermingling on this occasion and Jane Adams was encouraged.

Later the faculty was invited to Miss Adams's apartment for dessert. Faculty members arrived in groups, sat with their particular clique, and left with their own group. Little interaction took place. The guests seemed, to Jane Adams, just to be paying an obligation. No one stayed long. Apparently it was not the type of party in which they were interested. Alice Smith sat through the affair seemingly not in the least perturbed by the obvious rejection which she received from most of the other faculty members. Although the four former teachers made an effort to talk with each group and especially with Alice Smith, Jane Adams thought that the affair was a failure.

Another approach to improving faculty relationships was to serve refreshments at faculty meetings. Birthday cakes were baked by Miss Adams for faculty members and brought to the morning coffee gathering, but, as one of the former teachers remarked, "It's like trying to make one big, happy family out of an assortment of personalities that you wouldn't find in a faculty three times the size of this one." A few of the outsiders quit coming to the coffee hour, but Alice Smith enjoyed her cigarette and participated in the conversation as if she belonged.

A social committee composed of a representative group planned additional gatherings. The first affair was a shower for the third-grade teacher. After a quiet evening, most of the guests, including Jane Adams, departed early. The "sorority gals" planned to have a party afterward just for themselves and some male guests. Sensing the possibilities for a gay evening, Alice Smith crashed the party, monopolized one of the guests, and had a gala time. "They thought they could put something over on me," she boasted to one of the former teachers.

Jane Adams was discouraged that her various efforts to improve relationships through social activities had produced almost no positive results. The "sorority gals" continued to reject all friendly overtures from the former teachers. They also rejected and sometimes expressed open hostility toward Alice Smith. Jane Adams wondered if the "sorority gals" felt that Alice Smith was competing with them for masculine attention. Certainly she was a very aggressive opponent. This was illustrated the very first week that the teachers arrived, when a party was planned by the "sorority gals" and only male guests were invited. To make certain that others would know that this was a private party, the doors to the living room were closed by the "sorority gals." Refusing to miss out on a social affair, Mrs. Smith remarked, "Who do they think they are? The living room belongs to all of us. I am going to that party." She did crash the party, and this experience and similar activities undoubtedly increased the hostile feelings which she incurred.

This hostility was sometimes expressed through rude remarks addressed to Mrs. Smith. During discussions of educational issues at faculty meetings, one of the "sorority gals" on different occasions screamed at Mrs. Smith over seemingly trivial matters.

Although the older teachers did not reject Alice Smith as openly and as strongly as did the "sorority gals," they formed no close attachment with her. From her first arrival in Stratford, they displayed cool feelings toward her. Even though she visited the older teachers from time to time, they maintained an impersonal attitude toward her.

Early in the school year the former teachers came to talk to Principal Adams about the "sorority gals'" clique. They tried to break down the barrier between the members of this group and other faculty personnel. They did this because they thought that the "sorority gals" were mostly responsible for pulling "the whole faculty to pieces." All of their overtures were ignored, however.

The former teachers suggested that they might voluntarily move out of their apartment into the new billets where most of the teachers were. Jane Adams discouraged these teachers from making the change, since she believed that the move would do little to improve interpersonal relations. They made the move anyway, however, even though they regretted it later. In spite of all their efforts to establish a more cohesive faculty, they were quick to admit that their efforts had availed almost nothing.

The former teachers felt sorry for Alice Smith. They regretted the strong hostility evidenced toward her by the "sorority gals" and the lack of acceptance among other faculty members. Therefore, they tried in various ways to treat her kindly.

Alice Smith Creates Problems

Since there were no cooking facilities in the living quarters, it was necessary for the teachers to eat their meals at the Officers' Club, which had an adjoining bar. Alice Smith, carefully made up and dressed in a form-fitting cocktail dress, frequently fluttered into the bar. She would choose a seat next to a prospective friend, roll her big brown eyes, and begin a lively conversation. Always the helpless one, she would drop a handkerchief or her purse and purr her thanks when the object was returned. "This is the way to meet people," she quipped.

At the dormitory Alice began to have guests at unusual hours. Since the dormitory was in the center of the housing area, the community began to react. Before long, two mothers who formerly had been most co-operative and helpful appeared with complaints. It was stated that Mrs. Smith had been a guest for tea in one home and had spent the time discussing the immaturity of her sixth-grade class in comparison with other classes with whom she had worked. She also had told an "off-color" story in the presence of the sixth-grade son. The other mother, whose daughter was an outstanding student, stated that her child hated school. The daughter had complained that the whole class was losing physical education periods because a few students were not co-operating. Jane Adams explained to the mothers that the class of 36 pupils was the largest in the school and that there were a few who did need firm handling. Thus, the situation was smoothed over. It was suggested that the mothers go to Mrs. Smith to talk over their problems.

More complaints were registered. Children who formerly had liked school began to request permission to stay at home. Students who had done a high quality of work were just getting by. The slow learners were doing nothing, according to reports, except wandering around the room and getting into trouble. Teachers began to complain about the lack of discipline, the running and shouting in the halls, and the long, noisy sessions in the lavatories.

Observations brought to light that Mrs. Smith attempted some modern practices. The class elected officers and chose some activities. It was divided into two reading groups to meet individual differences. However, her late arrival to the classroom every day, both in the morning and at noon, encouraged the children to get off to a disorganized, rowdy beginning. There seemed to be little teacher-pupil planning for the use of leisure time. By the time the students were settled, much valuable time had been lost.

In an attempt to help Mrs. Smith meet the needs of her students, Miss Adams provided an American youth association instructor for the boys' physical education classes. The boys were enthusiastic over the opportunity to receive instruction in football, basketball, tumbling, and other activities.

But this did little to solve the problem. Conferences with Mrs. Smith also seemed to bring negative results. The problems could not be solved, according to her, because of the type of class she had. This group was "impossible." She knew, because she was a former teacher in Philadelphia with cadet teachers under her supervision. (Mrs. Smith did express herself exceptionally well and could verbalize about the latest educational practices.) When the enrichment of the curriculum with the use of community resources such as the Anglo-Saxon ruins was suggested, she remarked that it would be impossible, as a certain supervisor from headquarters would expect her to be on a certain page at a given time.

Miss Adams searched for ways to make Mrs. Smith feel secure. She invited her to her apartment on several occasions. She wrote letters of commendation to the teacher and students praising *any* noteworthy activity or improvement. This brought only temporary results. The sixth grade maintained the status of being the worst room in the school.

In addition to her late arrival daily, Mrs. Smith was absent frequently. A succession of substitutes contributed little to the stability of the group.

As is common in Army schools, a complete upheaval took place in late October. One whole unit was moved from the Stratford community to the Plymouth community. Another unit was moved from Plymouth to Stratford. This was disastrous for Mrs. Smith, as the new arrivals were ready to spread the details of Mrs. Smith's life in Plymouth. Of course, the children overheard these discussions and spread this information among themselves, especially on the school busses.

When this gossip became malicious, Miss Adams called Mrs. Smith into the office for a friendly conference. She explained what was happening and agreed that Mrs. Smith was innocent as she claimed. However, since this new group was maligning her reputation, she advised her to be more discreet in her actions, and to go outside the immediate community for her entertainment. Miss Adams suggested also that she dress more carefully, as her students were at a very impressionable age. She stressed that she would believe in her until it was proven that there was a reason to believe otherwise. Mrs. Smith agreed to be more careful, but new rumors and complaints continued to come to Miss Adams.

Early in the month of May, these rumors were climaxed when a colonel's wife, the mother of one of Mrs. Smith's students, came with the tale that Mrs. Smith was breaking up a home and that the wife had appealed to the Inspector General. Again Miss Adams stated that she must support Mrs. Smith until there was reason to do otherwise. The colonel's wife said that she would send a gentleman who could bring definite proof.

When Mrs. Smith was informed of the last accusation, she became very angry. She accused Miss Adams of not supporting her and demanded that she be called from her classroom the moment a complainer arrived. To this Miss Adams agreed. The young gentleman never did arrive, and somehow the school year ended without further serious incidents.

Alice Smith Receives Her Rating

Ratings were due in the central office in the latter part of May, and personal conferences were arranged with each teacher to discuss these ratings. Jane Adams had spent much thought on Alice Smith's rating. If she gave her an unsatisfactory rating, she had been told by other principals that she would have to document it with reams of proof, because of official regulations. Although it hurt her conscience, the easiest way out was to give a satisfactory rating.

When Alice Smith glanced over the rating, she began to pace the floor: " 'Satisfactory'—this is disgraceful! I've never had such a low rating before. I deserve and must have a much better rating than this!"

"I'm sorry, but it will be impossible to change this rating."

"I won't sign it! What will happen if I don't?"

"Your signature does not mean that you agree with the rating. It means that you have seen it and discussed it with me. If you do not care to sign it, it will be sent to headquarters without a signature but with an explanatory note stating why the signature is missing."

Alice Smith continued to pace the floor. "This is disgraceful. It is your fault that this year has been such a difficult one. I certainly have had no backing, not from you or the personnel at headquarters. I'll be glad to return to a school where my work is appreciated." She picked up a pen hastily from the desk, dashed off her signature, and flounced from the room.

It was the second week in June. School was over, and once again the members of the faculty were to be dispersed to a wide area. Each came to the office to say his farewell. Alice Smith had the most exciting plans of all: a trip around the world—that is, if she made the right connections. She had a good beginning: a free ride to London with a civilian.

Alice Smith, the Individual, had arrived in Stratford in a unique manner. Her departure would not deprive the community of one last choice bit of gossip.

CASE EIGHT

The Gifted Child Committee

Early in March, Assistant Superintendent Lark, of the Shadyvale Elementary Schools, called Dr. Fine, Curriculum Director in the neighboring Hillview School District, to ask, "Would you folks be interested in a joint study of gifted children, if we can get the county superintendent's office to help pay for some consultant services?" The director of curriculum replied affirmatively, and a chain of events began, leading to a joint, two-district study of programs for gifted children.

Hillview and Shadyvale elementary school districts, serving

large families in the middle and upper socioeconomic levels, were in suburban communities. They were served by a separate high school district. Adjacent to a large metropolitan area, they had almost no industry. Most of their inhabitants commuted to work in the nearby cities.

Both Hillview and Shadyvale were unincorporated, with populations of 15,000 and 10,000, respectively. During the last ten years both communities had changed from small villages serving a farming area to small towns with homes replacing cattle pastures and hillside orchards. Enrollment in the Hillview and Shadyvale elementary school districts had increased to 3,500 and 2,500 pupils. Mr. Smith, district superintendent of the Hillview schools, had served since the district was very small with only one school. Mrs. Jenkins similarly had served the Shadyvale schools as superintendent through most of the years of its growth.

Vocations were pursued generally by only one family member. Doubtless this was partially owing to the many small children found in most homes and to the relative lack of economic pressures. Occupations were of the skilled, semiprofessional, and professional types. Educational levels were rarely less than high school graduation, and most had some college education.

Previous Study Groups

Various district activities preceded the committee on gifted children and they undoubtedly gave impetus to it. Both communities had active and independent citizens' committees. Administrators in charge of instruction, rather than the superintendents, worked with the citizens' committees. Shadyvale's committee had been centering its attention for at least a year upon the curriculum and was quite interested in reorganizing the upper-grade program so as to offer greater challenge to the more able students. Hillview's citizens' committee had operated for about three years and had focused attention on various aspects of curriculum. Committee leaders found considerable interest in gifted children's programs, although concerted study had not resulted.

Parent study groups were also organized at several of the Hillview district schools under the sponsorship of the school principal with the co-operation of P.T.A. units. The director of curriculum took the initiative to encourage the formation of these study groups. Some of these study groups selected topics dealing with reading instruction; others, those with adolescent problems. In one instance, a study group investigated the nature and needs of gifted children.

Both school district staffs were concerned about educational problems that were directly or indirectly related to gifted children. The fairly recent establishment of upper-grade schools in both districts suggested an interest in providing a diversified program for this age group, with no small concern for ability differences. A policy of "heterogeneous" grouping in elementary classes was being questioned by some principals and teachers in the Hillview schools, with considerable talk of "homogeneous grouping." Many staff meetings had been devoted to this question.

Organizing the Committee

Weeks elapsed before the Hillview curriculum director heard anything further about the proposed joint committee on gifted children. Almost two months after the telephone call, he received word indirectly that Mr. Smith had presented to the Hillview school board a proposal for a steering committee to study gifted child programs. This proposal had been developed in the intervening period by Superintendents Smith and Jenkins. They proposed a joint steering committee to guide the study of programs for the two districts.

The board of Hillview received this with considerable enthusiasm, and the minutes of the meeting recorded their action.

> Authorization was given to the superintendent to proceed with the setting up of a joint committee of the Hillview and Shadyvale districts to study developing a program for gifted children.

This board action stirred considerable talk in Hillview school circles. The director of curriculum discussed with Superintendent Smith the advisability of having citizen representation on the committee. Miss Rankin, a school principal with a strong interest in gifted children, called the director of curriculum the morning after the school board action to inquire about more details.

"What is this I hear about the board authorizing a gifted child committee? . . . I hope this committee will not rush into one program and eliminate the chances of others. Who will represent us? . . . I hope the work of our parent study group will not be lost. . . . Will this school get some representation?"

Planning progressed as the two district superintendents met with Mrs. Cunningham from a nearby university and made preliminary arrangements for her to act as consultant to the joint steering committee. Dr. Cunningham was a specialist in curriculum development and had had experience with other school districts in planning gifted child programs.

Further planning involved a few additional persons from each district and from the office of the county superintendent of schools. It was proposed that the county assist with financing and provide some staff time to co-ordinate the work of the joint committee as it progressed in the two districts. The county agreed to co-operate as far as it could, but final commitments were withheld until further developments indicated just what was involved. The county superintendent expressed some concern about just what a committee including lay citizens was going to attempt to do. He expressed, however, a cautious desire to co-operate.

When the Shadyvale School Board followed the example of the Hillview Board in authorizing the joint committee, there was a problem of determining membership. In discussing possible members for the committee with his director of curriculum, Mr. Smith commented: "I talked to Mrs. Jenkins in Shadyvale. She has a citizens' group already studying this thing. I think she would like to have them serve on this committee. There are about ten in the group."

After some discussion between Mr. Smith and his director of curriculum, they agreed to suggest a committee of about 18 people —four school representatives and four citizens from each district, a representative of the high school district serving both communities, and at least one county representative.

The Members of the Committee

When the committee began its deliberations in June, it included eight parents and eleven school persons, with three other school representatives from the county office in attendance. The balance of

membership hoped for was often upset even further by the attendance and participation of visiting school personnel at many of the
meetings.

The parents representing the two school communities offered
varied backgrounds of experience and sentiment. Board members,
ex-school teachers, and vigorous critics of the schools were included.
All came to this committee with some prior experience in school
affairs beyond that usually found among parents. Only one parent
in this group would be regarded as having only recently become
involved in school activities. Five of the eight parents were house-
wives.

Mrs. Haines was a member who had been very active in school
affairs for a number of years. She had attended many meetings where
educational problems were discussed. Having one child enrolled in
primary and one in upper grades gave her an opportunity to see something of the school program at these different levels in two different
schools. Mrs. Haines was a housewife with four years of college education. She commented on her view of gifted children after the committee had been organized for about eight months:

"I have changed my mind. . . . I now accept the view that the
gifted child cannot be taken care of in the regular classroom. . . .
Perhaps I didn't want to accept it. . . ."

Mr. Lock was a businessman. He appeared to be a leader of influence in the community, and he had served as the head of an advisory committee to one of the school boards. In his thirties, with
three years of college education, he was probably wealthier than any
other member of the committee. His three children were all rather
young. He expressed some reluctance to judge teachers or school
results.

"Educators are the ones running the schools. If they don't know
what they are doing—who does? . . . So, I've sort of kept my nose
out of it. . . ."

Mrs. Johns was the parent with the least experience in school
activities. She had been a member of a parent study group but reported almost no other activities. Her two children were in the primary and middle grades. She had had private school education when
in high school. She appeared very enthusiastic about being a member
of the committee and expressed some concern about not having more
opportunity for school participation. She gained courage to visit a

school and observe in some classrooms while she was serving on the committee. She remarked:

"You asked me about contact with the classroom. . . . I have tried that—. As long as you are not a nuisance and show an interest, they don't mind. . . . There is a stronger understanding of what the child is doing; better parent-teacher understanding, too. . . ."

Mrs. Morse was a parent who had rather extensive past experience with the schools. Her two children were in the middle grades and in high school. She had contacts with the schools as a room mother, in civil defense work, and in a citizens' committee. Over a period of about five years she had seen the school district grow, had come to know much about its problems, and had taken part in a number of projects directed toward the problems of the schools. Many of her concerns about the school program were expressed in terms of criticisms of not enough breadth, challenge, and variety. A housewife who had been a teacher for a brief period, she was in her forties and had more than four years of college education. Mrs. Morse was a critic, but she saw much that was good in the schools also.

"They are certainly improving their methods. All the visual aids, the use of other materials—resource materials,—I like this. . . ."

Other parents included an architect, a research chemist, and another housewife who had also been a teacher in earlier years. The average education of the parent group was over four years of college. Their children ranged from preschool age to college. The majority of their children were junior high school age or older. All had either two or three children.

High school district representation on the committee was sought because of a desire expressed by both elementary school officials and parents that any program developed should continue into high school. The high school district superintendent designated Mrs. Brown as their representative. She acted primarily as an observer during the first two meetings, speaking briefly at the first meeting and not at all at the second. She did not attend the following eight meetings. Thus, the high school district was a non-participant in most committee meetings. This situation was openly referred to by one parent:

"Isn't there a chance that we could get more active participation by personnel from the high school district? I know we are supposed to have a member, but. . . . Has there been any communication to her that we might be doing something that would be quite appropriate for them to be engaged in?"

District school representatives, after some early changes, included two teachers, two principals, a director of curriculum, an assistant superintendent, a high school district curriculum co-ordinator, and the two superintendents. One superintendent met regularly with the committee; the other, for reasons of health, met the committee only twice.

The chairmanship of the committee was given to Dr. Fine, director of curriculum of one district, and Assistant Superintendent Lark of the other district on alternate meeting dates. The committee co-ordinator was designated to serve as recording secretary and liaison person among districts, the county, and the consultant.

Early Activities of the Committee

Activities of the Gifted Child Committee formally began in mid-June. It was hoped that starting at that time would permit study over the summer months and hasten committee activity in the early Fall. The first meeting was held in the library of one of the Hillview schools on the evening of June 17. Two parents were absent, along with one of the teachers. The agenda called for a general orientation by the two district superintendents, followed by a presentation on "Operational Design for the Study . . ." by the consultant, Dr. Cunningham.

First, Mr. Smith of the Hillview district reviewed past activities of the schools in planning for the education of gifted children. He emphasized earlier studies and program modifications that had resulted. He cautioned about the need for money for any proposed program and the lack of special state monies for this purpose. Superintendent Jenkins of Shadyvale made similar points in reference to that district. She cautioned about the possibility of detrimental effects of a program for the gifted on the whole educational program. She emphasized the responsibility of the schools to all children and urged that the committee study the needs and ways of meeting them in this context. Both district superintendents expressed opinions about the need to involve a wider segment of the community in the study.

Consultant Cunningham reviewed the current nation-wide interest among educators and citizens alike in gifted child programs. She cautioned against expecting to find simple, pat answers. She pointed up the issue of pupil segregation, and suggested that partial segregation had value in meeting the needs of gifted children. As to working procedures, Dr. Cunningham suggested that the committee had an "over-all guidance function" which indicated the need to obtain background, possibly establish subcommittees, and make written reports to the school boards that might include recommendations. She identified areas that should be considered:

1. Assumptions and agreed-upon principles.
2. The problems of identification of the gifted.
3. The problem of appropriate terminology.
4. The role of the school.
5. The problems of public relations.
6. Possible ways of working with the gifted.

The county superintendent attending this first meeting raised questions about the specific purposes of the committee, the nature of the decisions appropriate to such a body, and the particular problem of the committee. He expressed the view that these questions should be clearly answered from the beginning. He was especially forceful in asserting that there were certain decisions that rightfully belonged to the profession:

"I have an official concern as county superintendent of schools. . . . Therefore, whatever happens . . . whatever ideas that are usable, that we can discover here in these two communities, I hope will be such that they will be useful elsewhere. That is my principal excuse for having such a concern over these activities. . . . As you know, the courses of study . . . are developed and adopted under the authority of the County Board of Education. . . .

"I come to some questions: What is the purpose of this group? What is the nature of the decisions for which this committee is to become responsible? There are certain decisions that belong to the profession! There are other decisions of comparable importance that belong to the people as a whole! . . ."

Dr. Cunningham objected to this point of view and expressed the opinion that all considerations about gifted children were legitimate. Later expressions of both school personnel and parents indicated this this was one of the areas where differences in thinking were significant. Some school personnel, perhaps most of them, shared the concern that a committee with parents participating on it might encroach upon activities which should in their judgment be reserved to the profession alone.

Another meeting one week later also had good attendance. How the committee members could best become well informed and the appropriate relationships of the committee to the community and the schools were the main problems considered. Subcommittees were again mentioned as a desirable opportunity to involve more people. Superintendent Jenkins expressed the hope that interest could be stimulated rather widely in the community. Superintendent Smith mentioned the possible need for taxes for a gifted child program and the significance of this for good community relations.

Several suggestions for initiating the actual study were made. One parent urged that some common understandings were needed within the committee. Mr. Boyd specifically asked that problems of program planning, subcommittees, and finance be postponed in favor of a period devoted to the study of the general problem, thus formulating committee thinking to some degree. Another parent was interested in contacting the parents of gifted children for their ideas.

These various ideas were not crystallized at this point. Another meeting on committee organization was planned for the fall, when terminology, the nature of the gifted group, and some basic principles were also to be considered. Study materials relating to these and other topics were made available for committee members to take with them.

Inquiry and Discussion

When the committee met in the fall, it began an exploration of numerous aspects of gifted children programs. The meaning of "giftedness" was discussed. Basic principles were considered. Reports on programs in other school districts were heard. A survey of opinion within the committee was taken. And reports from teachers in the Shadyvale and Hillview schools on existing programs for the gifted were presented.

At the end of the fourth general meeting in late October, all committee members were given a questionnaire on which they could designate their thinking about certain problems and issues that had been raised during previous meetings. At the following meeting these opinionnaires were tallied. The tallies showed considerable agreement even at this early date on basic principles, the nature of the pupils to be considered, methods appropriate for identification of pupils, and next steps for the committee. A list of eight basic principles were accepted almost unanimously. Emphasis was on the intellectually able pupil. There was substantial interest in the talented pupils as well, but almost no agreement on what talents were important. Strong interest in identification procedures using intelligence and reading tests indicated the focus of the group on intellectual giftedness. Program planning was strongly advocated which would include identification, enrichment in regular classroom, provision of additional books and resources, and attention to raising standards and expectations of gifted students.

Items on which there was no substantial agreement revealed some of the major obstacles of the committee. Terminology acceptable to most committee members presented a problem. No consensus was found on the talents that should be cultivated, although "leadership" and "creative writing" carried heavy favor. Acceleration of pupils seemed an issue on which there was considerable uncertainty. This was also true of the formation of special classes or groups.

Three meetings provided background on gifted child programs in Shadyvale, Hillview, and two other districts. Hillview representatives reported their findings on the program of group intelligence testing over recent years. A group of teachers used about half of the meeting to report on the kinds of activities they were currently providing for gifted children. Shadyvale also had a group of teachers report briefly on existing practices.

These reports were well received and prompted questions and discussion. Hillview's director of curriculum, Dr. Fine, commented:

". . . It is quite evident to me, and I'm sure to the rest of the members of the committee, that we are not starting from scratch in this matter of a program for the gifted child. A lot of things have already been going on; . . . and are going on for the good of the gifted children in our schools. So we're not stirring up anything entirely new here. We're just trying to get it co-ordinated so that . . . we can put it in the records. . . ."

Consultant Cunningham seemed anxious to be sure that this comment was not to imply the narrowing of the scope of the committee's work at this early date:

"Well, let me add one thing to this. We might be trying to find some other things . . . !"

At two other meetings, much of the time was devoted to presentations by visiting officials of two other school districts about their programs. A short discussion period followed each of these presentations. Still further background was provided to many members of the committee as they attended a special December meeting. In this session, the director of a statewide research study on gifted children outlined the plans for such a study and discussed its possible implications for Shadyvale and Hillview.

During the various discussions, the parents seemed to be more observers than discussants. There were times when this was distinctly not so, but these were few and of limited duration. Some parents sat through entire meetings without speaking. Although Mr. Boyd did not speak at three of the five meetings he attended between June and January, he was considered a reasonably outspoken person. Mrs. Morse, Mrs. Johnson, and Mrs. Masters did not speak during the meetings they attended. In the first meeting, parents spoke only four times, in contrast to the 88 times for school personnel. Parents spoke more frequently in subsequent meetings but did not approximate the frequency of school personnel. In final meetings, when some disagreements arose, parents spoke a great deal more frequently than at other times. It was still very limited verbal participation in comparison with that of school personnel.

From the very beginning, parents strongly believed that the needs of the gifted children were important and could be better met. Thinking about ways of providing for the education of the gifted was not so clear, although modification of thinking resulted. Mrs. Haines, for example, acknowledged her change in view:

"I'm aware of having changed . . . I have come to accept the view that the gifted child cannot be taken care of in the regular classroom. . . . I'm concerned with too much separation. . . . They still have to get along. . . . They shouldn't be separated too much from the other children. . . ."

Perhaps this problem of segregation was among the more perplexing, for it was referred to frequently. Mr. Boyd expressed concern for the able pupils' being held back:

"As long as you retain the most gifted with the least able, you are going to have trouble. . . . There is trouble with using a common approach for all. . . . The better students try to go ahead. The others hold them back. . . ."

Mrs. Jones was not sold on segregation. In the beginning she commented:

"The bright . . . They should be kept with the regular class, but given lots of extra things. I don't believe in segregation. . . ."

Later on, Mrs. Johns continued with similar ideas:

"It all depends on the teacher. It is a wonderful thing if a child can go along . . . be with a class and still be ahead on their own! . . ."

As parental opinions crystallized, Dr. Fine also expressed stronger views:

"Teachers feel that when they have a group of children who are homogeneously grouped according to their potential . . . that . . . these children can grasp the basic skills so much more rapidly that the base of presentation can be broadened much more. . . . These students can take it more effectively than having a group of children who range all the way from the bottom to the top. . . . This is the feeling of the teachers, anyway. . . ."

Consultant Cunningham cautioned against oversimplification in response to Dr. Fine's statement:

"Yes but . . . the question involved in grouping . . . is a complex business. We have oversimplified it in practice. . . . You group one way for one purpose; and you group another way for another purpose. We probably have at least half a dozen sets of purposes that relate to this how-you-group thing. . . ."

Dr. Fine responded:

"However, we wouldn't want to say that grouping is poor all because we haven't done the best job of it. Therefore, it doesn't mean that we shouldn't continue the effort."

In the January and February meetings, school personnel expressed concerns about too much participation of parents in school affairs. Parents sensed these concerns and were not entirely happy about them. In interviews, one parent stated that the school administration always fears "too much participation." Another expressed concern about the defensive attitudes of teachers toward parents. Still another queried, "Why can't they listen and realize that we are sincere in wanting to help?"

In January, as specific aspects of programs for the gifted children were being considered, Shadyvale's superintendent commented:

"I don't know if this committee is going to decide for us what we are going to set up or not. This kind of bothers me. . . . It seems to me that the machinery should be planned entirely through the local school district and its teachers. . . ."

The curriculum director from Hillview held a similar view of the proper role of the committee:

"We will propose that certain factors be included in a program. . . . say, the enrichment of the science or mathematics program. . . . We are going to have to tell them (the governing board) something about how we plan to do this, since I don't think that is this committee's responsibility. . . . I think this is the job that is going to be dropped back in the lap of the administration. . . ."

Moving Toward Decisions

By early January the district superintendent at Hillview was encouraging the committee leaders to think in terms of a report on which the school board could initiate a program for gifted children for the following school year. The members of the committee from Hillview met in a special meeting and agreed on a list of program possibilities with priorities and a plan for publicity to go to their board.

A meeting late in January of the entire committee devoted its attention to outlining a report to go to the boards late in January. Cautions were expressed about going too fast into new programs. A school representative suggested that more emphasis on present programs with no new programming for the coming year would permit time for more careful planning. Some administrative concern was expressed about a single report serving two separate districts. Mr. Smith expressed a desire to have recommendations sufficiently specific so that he could give them consideration in terms of budget allocations. But controversy over the proper function of the committee persisted here and became more intense. Dr. Cunningham reviewed her thinking about the nature of the committee's report to the school boards:

"I must confess that up until tonight I was thinking entirely of this group suggesting to the boards that 'We think these things are important aspects of the program' . . . ; and then saying to the boards, 'We hope you will come up with some machinery, mechanics, for planning the details, and do it pretty quickly'! Now we would offer our services to help in doing that planning in detail. . . ."

Dr. Fine responded to this:

"Neither one of these boards is familiar with what we have been doing. . . . This group . . . owes it to the respective boards to make some recommendations for the first-year program. . . ."

Superintendent Jenkins had other convictions:

". . . Well, now—the boards don't know what's been going on, but somebody has to make a recommendation. The one who is going to make the recommendation is the one who sits with the board to recommend!"

Mrs. Jenkins emphasized her view: "It's got to be up to each individual district to make a recommendation. . . ."

Dr. Cunningham looked to others in the group for ideas: "Well, what do others have to say?" Silence followed.

Finally Mr. Lark ventured a view: "It (the report) should be as close to what the committee thinks as can be."

Superintendent Jenkins replied, "I agree with that. You have to have the report to show what the commitee has done. . . ."

Silence prevailed again. Consultant Cunningham suggested that no final decisions need be made at this meeting. However, one of the parents, Mr. Boyd, a school board member, injected a new view:

"As a board member, I would expect to have certain things in a report. . . . One thing would be a complete report of the various things we have talked about—and a firm recommendation for a program, not considering time.—I would also expect a practical report from the committee on how it could be approached on an immediate basis extending, say, over a two- or three-year period—something a little bit tangible. And, third, I would want something specifically from the school administration concerning how it expects to proceed today into next year. I don't see how the board could act at all without these three things."

Mrs. Jenkins objected, "I don't see how this committee, . . . could give you what your administration is going to do."

Board member Boyd clarified his view, "The third thing was not for the committee to do. It was the administration.—"

Mrs. Jenkins pressed her point: "The problem here is, what can this committee present that will fit the needs of both school districts?"

Mr. Boyd's reaction was strong, "That is right. But—I think that the report should be divided into two branches. One, the over-all, gifted child program. . . . Secondly, bringing it down just a little bit so that it is presented on a practical basis, so we can start.—Otherwise, I'm afraid that we might not get started in a manner that will be a spur to keep on. I feel that there is a danger—of not getting off the ground at all. . . . A tangible recommendation from this group on how to get started is of very great importance."

No real conclusions were reached in this January meeting. A meeting in early February pursued further the problem of the nature of the report to the boards. Dr. Cunningham used a questionnaire to arrive at a consensus about ". . . what we think the school boards should consider. . . ." This formed the basis for a report outline.

A draft of the proposed report to the boards was presented to the group at its meeting late in February. At this point there was considerable dissatisfaction with the proposed report among parents and among some school personnel. The issue appeared again to be how much specificity. A parent expressed the view, "After all these months, we are just telling the boards that they ought to do something. We could have done that much months ago."

Apparently the recurring problem of lack of agreement as to what should be the role of the committee had not been resolved. In the February 26 meeting, parents objected to a proposed committee report to the two school boards because they felt specificity was still lacking in the recommendations. Some school-personnel members continued to argue that this was only proper, since it was the responsibility of the administration and not the committee to make specific proposals. A parent's reaction to this was expressed in an interview:

"There is no idea of taking over. . . . This feeling of teachers of being defensive, and the profession's move to close off the profession from public influence. . . . I know they are doing this! . . . It is very disconcerting."

A member of the Hillview staff who had expressed interest in pushing ahead with recommendations and requests for funds at earlier meetings was now counselling slower movement:

". . . It seems to me that the first year we are not ready to employ a full-time person. . . . We don't know what the program is going to be yet. . . . We are not ready. . . . The first year is going to be spent pretty much in identifying youngsters. . . ."

Mr. Boyd, noting the recommendations were for a slow-moving program, commented: ". . . Isn't that almost what you are doing now? . . ."

Dr. Cunningham likewise seemed concerned about the cautious approaches being suggested by some school personnel:

"I hear a modification of our thinking of last time that I'm not sure I share—the conviction that, if you were in the first year to attempt this or that, that it would fall on its face. . . . Learning comes from the doing, not just planning. . . ."

School personnel seemed torn between the desire to get specific proposals with committee support before their boards and the desire to retain for themselves the authority for detailed planning of any such a program.

Mr. Boyd continued to express his views even after other parents seemed reconciled:

"I think that this committee will not be carrying out its responsibility . . . if it drops it and puts it in the hands of individual school administrations and boards. It is going to result in floundering. . . . We go through all this and come up with some kind of over-all conclusions. . . . I don't think that we have carried out our responsibilities if we don't bring it down to a somewhat tangible basis as something that can be carried out in the next two or three years. . . . I think we should stick it out until we can make a firm recommendation. . . ."

A committee report to the school boards of the two districts was drafted during the month of March. It remained largely a statement of principles with general recommendations, rather than a set of proposals for program development. Subcommittees which were originally planned and periodically discussed never came about. The survey of the opinions of parents in the communities was not undertaken. A bulletin was developed to provide information to school personnel on the work of the committee, since communications from the committee to other district staff members seemed quite limited. Newspaper releases were also planned in hopes of providing some community-wide orientation. Each district staff proceeded to develop its own specific proposal for a gifted child program for the coming year.

Conflict in Alton

The Alton school board meeting in August 1956 marked the beginning of an "open battle" between the school superintendent and certain school board members in that community. The first big surprise of the meeting was Superintendent Brown's offer to "sell" the unexpired portion of his contract. This offer brought to light a number of facts, and the disclosure of these facts in turn set off a series of events that had many implications for Alton's citizens.

Since Superintendent Brown's unexpired contract was not purchased by the board members, he found himself entangled in the decisions that followed. Did he wisely resolve the choice situations which faced him? Why did he choose the courses of action which he pursued? Could the deterioration in superintendent-board relationships have been avoided? To what extent, if at all, were the individual citizens of Alton responsible for the undesirable events that transpired? What were the relative effects of personal pressures and information on the official decisions of school board members? These and related questions are posed by the case that follows.

The Community

Alton is a small, semi-agricultural community located northwest of a New England industrial center. Many of the residents are descendants of the early farmers who settled there in the colonial days. Some of the land about the village is still used for agriculture.

During the postwar employment boom, many people moved into this quiet little town because of the easy commuting distance to the ever-growing employment market of the industrial center. The daily 7:30 A.M. exodus of automobiles and workers dramatizes the fact that Alton has become a suburban, "bedroom" community.

Not all the citizens are self-employed farmers or commuters to the large industrial center. Alton also has several smaller industrial plants. About ten per cent of the wage earners are employed by industries in Alton; a majority of the latter group work for a firm which produces automation machinery. This particular firm pays a substantial portion of the community's taxes for education.

Six thousand people are included in the Alton School District, but only 2,600 actually live in the village of Alton. The remainder live either in one of the three housing developments adjacent to the village or on outlying farms. Most of the early settlers belonged to the Lutheran faith and their descendants have carried on the strong church program of their forefathers. The Lutheran church is not only the largest and most prosperous church in town, but it also has its own elementary school, attended by most of the children whose parents belong to the church.

Superintendent Brown and the School Board

Mr. Brown first came to Alton in 1944 as a social studies teacher in the high school. After a very successful year of teaching, he accepted the principalship of the Mt. Eden High School in the nearby community of Mt. Eden. There he spent four very successful and happy years. In 1949 he was offered and accepted the position of superintendent of Alton.

Mr. Brown did not establish residence in Alton when he became superintendent but lived in a larger community some 12 miles away. When he was appointed superintendent, he already knew a number of Alton's citizens because of his experiences as a social studies teacher there. He judged Alton to be a friendly place and, on one occasion, stated that he could not walk around town without someone's stopping him for a social chat.

When he became superintendent, he joined the local Lions Club and was a member of the Board of Directors. He was asked to run for vice-president of the Lions, but declined because of the time it would take. Mr. Brown joined and was very active in both the Exchange Club and the P.T.A. About once a month he and his family came to Alton to attend the Lutheran Church. Mr. Brown judged that he divided his out-of-school time about equally between the town's social and educational organizations.

Some of Alton's teachers did not feel close to Superintendent Brown. They attributed this feeling partly to the fact that he lived outside of Alton and, therefore, was not a member of the community. In addition, many of them believed that the tasks which Superintendent Brown performed and the decisions which demanded his time were far removed from the instructional problems that they faced. Consequently, when they visited his office, he was not able, in their own view, to understand accurately the concerns which they had. Few, if any, of the teachers viewed him as a friend, and some thought of him as cool and aloof. It seemed that it was not easy for him to be friendly and outgoing. Perhaps this was the reason he spent a great deal of time in his office.

In the seven years from 1949–1950 to 1955–1956 inclusive, things went along quite smoothly for Mr. Brown as he energetically pursued a program of new school construction and curriculum improvements. In his own words, "The first five years were excellent, and the next two were quite good. I had a very good relationship with my teachers and an excellent relationship with my school principals. In all the time I was in Alton, I never lost a bond issue for school construction nor a proposition to increase the operational millage."

During the first seven years that the superintendent was in Alton, there was very little turnover in school-board membership. In 1956 the five men representing the educational interests of the community were all self-employed and none had children attending school.

Mr. Jones, chairman of the board, owned his own machine shop and specialized in making precision-machined goods. He was a middle-aged man of medium height who appeared to be very wiry and healthy. His grey hair, conservative dress, and well-modulated voice generally created favorable first impressions. He seemed a most affable person. In a group he did not stand out immediately. Some persons thought that his apparent control over himself and the impression he created—that his only motive was to improve conditions in the school—helped him greatly to obtain his objectives.

Jones established his local machine shop in 1956. Much of his work came from Acme Gauge, owned by an old friend, Ken Bond. Bond owned not only Acme Gauge but also the local sewage disposal plant recently completed at a cost of $190,000. To add to this small empire, he was also the president of Bond Enterprises, a housing development and construction company. Such holdings had made it possible for him to promise the donation of a substantial piece of land to the school district as an elementary school site.

Mr. Abbott was an accountant in business for himself. He was heavy-set, had a ruddy complexion, and walked with a noticeable limp. He impressed people as one having great leadership capacity. Although he was not overly cordial, he was articulate and made people feel quite comfortable with him.

Mr. Wilson, a publisher, was tall, quiet, and definitely a listener. He did not have an outgoing personality. He was not very articulate under normal circumstances, but under pressure he could ask some very thought-provoking questions.

Mr. Deal was a retired appliance dealer and salesman. His appearance resembled the stereotype of a man who had dealt with the public in business over a number of years. His flashy clothes, loud voice, and heavy build all helped to support his egocentric personality and the impression that he knew his way around in business.

Mr. Katz was a salesman who did much traveling. He appeared to be very cautious and reserved. His heavy build and ruddy complexion helped to give him an air of a judge who would listen to all sides of a case and then, in a quiet and persuasive voice, hand down a decision.

Over the years, negative feelings toward Jones had developed among some of the board members. Abbott, for example, felt very hostile toward Jones. He judged the latter to be vindictive and cunning, and he openly opposed Jones both inside and outside the meeting. Wilson had known Jones for most of his life, and he strongly desired to work with him co-operatively. Although he came to challenge Jones more and more, he never completely withdrew his loyalty.

While the other two members objected to Jones's actions, on most issues they were strongly influenced by Jones. Deal made vitriolic statements out of board meetings about Jones, but he frequently went along with him on official decisions. Katz sometimes questioned Jones's behavior but, in the eyes of some observers, was greatly concerned with the balance of power and, therefore, tended to vote with the majority. Since Jones controlled most decisions, this meant that Katz typically voted to support him.

In spite of Jones's powerful control, his colleagues made their first concerted move against him in the spring of 1954. They voted to relieve him of his position as school district treasurer. Without prior notice he was notified of his dismissal during a regular meeting of the board. A majority of his fellow board members charged Mr. Jones with willfully withholding payments to the teachers and with being lax in discharging his responsibilities as treasurer. In the election one month later, he lost his position as school board member in Alton. However, two years later, in June of 1956, Mr. Jones sought re-election to the school board and was successful by a margin of 202 to 175 votes. A week after the election, his opponent brought suit against him, charging that he had violated a state law by filing late and, therefore, could not legally take office. Owing to legal complications, a decision on this matter was delayed indefinitely and, in the meantime, Mr. Jones was elected chairman of the school board.

A Rift Is Revealed

Superintendent Brown's decision to offer for "sale" the unexpired portion of his contract was largely motivated by experiences he had had with chairman Jones. Specifically, the move stemmed from an "unpleasantness" with Jones over the purchase of $1,500 worth of chemical lawn fertilizer and soap. Jones had charged that the purchase was unauthorized and had told Brown that, as president of the board, he was notifying him that he should resign. Brown's motives for offering to sell his contract seem mixed. He wanted to avoid more unpleasantness, sought to place Jones in an untenable position with the other members of the Board, and was confident that he could justify his action and thus gain status. Furthermore, he was embittered by the whole affair. The board members were aware that the superintendent had had a very bitter dispute with Jones prior to the meeting, although they did not know the details.

As reported by the *Valley Herald*, Mr. Abbott immediately jumped to his feet when he learned of the pressure upon Superintendent Brown to resign and demanded of Jones: "What right did you have to consult with Mr. Brown about any kind of resignation without first talking it over with the board?" At this point Jones further charged Superintendent Brown with having given the fertilizer and soap to his church in the community where he lived. Mr. Jones said that he had investigated the matter and had learned that Brown had made the donation under the pretext that the goods were "surplus property" and available to him personally at an absurdly low cost because of quantity purchasing of surplus property by the school system. After a bitter debate between Jones and Brown, the meeting settled down to the routine matters at hand without having acted on Mr. Brown's offer to sell the remaining time of his contract. This is what Brown had hoped would happen. Later in the evening a lawyer was hired to defend Jones in his coming court fight over the legality of his election.

Commenting later on this unfortunate course of events which resulted from his relationship with Jones, Mr. Brown said, "I guess it all started when I joined the Lions Club. Two members of the school board, Mr. Jones and Mr. Wilson, had been trying for years to join the Lions but had been rejected by its members. Up to the time I joined, I had remained quite aloof from the members of the board in all matters that were not school business. I really didn't get much closer to Abbott, Deal, and Katz, but we did work together on Lions Club projects such as raffles and Christmas parties. I guess Jones and Wilson, especially Jones, resented the fact that I belonged to the Lions. During my first four years in Alton my relations with the board members were very good and the next three years they were good with some of the members but not so good with others. Most of my trouble was with Mr. Jones."

The Sewage Disposal Problem

In 1956 the Alton school district began constructing a new 1,000-pupil high school. Since the community did not have a municipal sewage disposal system, one of the problems facing the board of education and the contractors was that of finding adequate facilities for sewage disposal. At first the superintendent and the board negotiated with some nearby farmers for the purchase of land to be used as a drainage field but, for reasons which were never disclosed, the farmers decided not to sell.

At a board meeting when the sewage problem was discussed, Jones mentioned the possibility of negotiating with his friend, Bond, about the possibility of tapping into the sewage system which he had recently completed. Fortunately, and interestingly enough, the sewage system was sufficiently large to accommodate the number of taps required for the new high school. A further argument for utilizing Bond's sewage system was the fact that one of the main trunk lines leading to Bond's facility was very conveniently located directly at the rear of the school property. After some discussion it was agreed that Mr. Jones should request Mr. Bond to present a "firm" bid to the board at the next meeting.

At the next board meeting a bid by Bond Enterprises was presented. The bid stipulated $76,000 as the cost for taps into the sewage disposal system. This bid, according to Mr. Bond, was based on water consumption used in homes in the area. The unit amount of water consumption per home was then multiplied by the number of pupils (600) to be housed in the new high school the first year. He indicated further that, should the school population increase to the recommended capacity of 1,000 pupils, an upward adjustment for cost would be made when such increase in pupil population occurred. The superintendent told the board that he thought the cost was "way out of line" and that they should get more information by using the consulting services of several engineering firms in the area. However, no formal action was taken on this recommendation.

During the next few weeks the superintendent decided to consult some engineering firms on his own. At the next meeting he mentioned again that the cost, as estimated by Bond, was excessive, and advised that the board should not accept the bid. He further emphasized that the board would be making a serious mistake if it entered into any contract which left the unit cost for additional facilities as undetermined as Bond's proposal implied. Furthermore, Superintendent Brown said that not only was the cost high, but such a negotiation would also set a precedent for similar services for future construction in the area.

Jones came to Mr. Bond's defense by saying that he had gone over these figures with Bond and thought that they were not out of line. Apparently all the members of the board, except Wilson, were then willing to go along with Jones. Mr. Wilson said that he thought the entire matter needed review. The superintendent suggested that a fact-finding committee should survey other localities in the area and compare costs. Only in this way could the board arrive at a just price.

A fact-finding committee was established to examine costs in similar communities. After their study, the committee reported that they considered $76,000 an exorbitant price. Bond was asked to appear at the next session, and the price which he demanded was dropped to $48,000. When this price was not accepted, Bond lowered his price to $28,000. By a three-to-two vote the board accepted this latest bid. The superintendent, still confident that $28,000 was too high a figure, tried to convince the board that they should rescind their action until further facts were assembled. However, the board had accepted the bid of $28,000 and would not listen to further arguments.

Without consulting any of the board members, Superintendent Brown on the next day sent a letter to the State Department of Public Instruction, with a copy to the Governor and to the *Valley Herald,* stating that the board was not functioning in a legal manner and that the whole thing "smacked of intrigue and smelled to high heaven." His choice of words he was not soon to forget. Although the wording of Superintendent Brown's letter to the State Department might be regarded as unfortunate, he was acting in what he thought was the best interest of the school. He had analyzed the problem objectively, and as a professional educator thought it was his responsibility to bring the situation into the open lest he be charged at some later date with a lack of courage and leadership.

A few days after the superintendent had written to the State Department, board members Abbott and Katz called a special meeting of the board to discuss the matter of the sewer taps. Both Abbott and Katz said that they had found that the cost of the sewer taps was indeed excessive and that something should be done about it. Jones, Wilson, and Deal failed to appear for the special meeting, which had been called in strict compliance with State Law regarding special meetings. Each of the three board members claimed that prior commitments had not permitted him to attend the meeting.

Jones, acting in his official capacity as president, then called for a special meeting which was attended by all the board members. However, there was no discussion of the sewer taps, since this item had not been included on the agenda. Legally, since all members were present, the item could have been discussed, but Jones ruled that discussion on any item not appearing on the agenda for a special meeting violated previous board policy.

The next regular meeting of the board was well attended by parties interested in the sewage disposal. After a series of charges and counter charges, the board rescinded its motion to accept the bid of $28,000 for the sewer taps. Jones and Deal abstained from voting on the motion. At this meeting tempers ran high, resulting in statements reported in the *Valley Herald*, many of which were later regretted. Developer Ken Bond stormed out of the room in the middle of the meeting.

During the heated discussion, Mr. Brown said that officials in the State Department of Public Instruction had advised him that no school system in the State had ever paid as much as $28,000 for sewer taps. After the board voted to rescind its previous action on the bid, Deal remarked, "Now we don't have a sewer system. Will Katz, Abbott, and Brown assume all the responsibility for the sewer problem in the new school?" According to the *Valley Herald*, Mr. Deal's remarks brought Abbott to his feet crying, "We called a special meeting for Monday night. You were asked to attend. You never showed any willingness to extend us the courtesy of attending this meeting." Abbott continued to berate Deal while Jones pounded his gavel calling for order. After things calmed down a bit, Wilson suggested that a thorough study should be made before final action was taken.

Leave Without Pay

At the next board meeting, according to the *Valley Herald*, Mr. Jones told Mr. Brown that he was being placed on an "unpaid leave of absence" status. Mr. Jones said that the suspension was the result of sending the letter about the sewage disposal debacle to the State Department and for releasing it to the press without notifying the board. When the resolution to suspend Brown was put to a vote, Abbott and Katz voted against it.

Previous skirmishes with the Board had always left Mr. Brown with the feeling that such occurrences were just a part of being a superintendent of schools. He had been annoyed a number of times and had been known to be caustic in his reply to criticism. He felt that Chairman Jones was making a concerted effort to destroy his professional career. Until recently he had taken the attitude that he must fight for what he thought was best. Increasingly, however, the impact of developments began to weigh heavily upon him. He became defensive, found it easy to project blame upon others, especially Mr. Jones, and in general found himself preoccupied with finding ways for revenge. The forced leave, without pay, brought him to the "boiling" point. The interest of the school, his staff, and the community became unimportant. In its place there developed intense bitterness and a feeling that he had been the victim of the calculated cunning of evil men.

At least three of the board members had not anticipated that Superintendent Brown would respond with bitterness. They remembered particularly that in the early years of Brown's tenure he had seemed affable and friendly. They had not suspected that he had the potential for such bitter responses. They were also somewhat surprised that he recently had "clammed up" in his relations with them while, at the same time, he had mentioned an open policy with the press. As for Jones, he consistently stated that his actions were guided by what he considered to be the welfare of the school.

A short time after Brown wrote the letter to the State Department, Jones, Deal, and Wilson, without board approval, notified the local newspaper that they had visited the State Department of Public Instruction relative to the sewage disposal and that they had been completely "vindicated." Following a series of charges and responses at the next board meeting, Brown claimed, "I have earnestly tried to work with the board this year, but it has been not only virtually impossible to work with Mr. Jones and Mr. Deal, but has been extremely unpleasant." Brown also charged that Jones acted improperly as a board president when he organized the local teachers into the A.F. of L. Brown announced to the members in the audience, "After I objected to this labor activity, Mr. Jones went over my head by tampering with the curriculum, restricting my purchasing power, and interfering with the staff." Jones denied these charges of Mr. Brown, but Katz testified that each was true. Katz continued, "I think what they (Jones, Deal, and Wilson) have done to Mr. Brown is inexcusable. I think boards of education should merely determine policies and should depend upon the superintendent to handle administrative and educational matters in the district. Mr. Brown merely wrote that letter to the State Department to protect his professional reputation as an educator. He did not want to be a party to the gross misuse of public funds which the bid for $28,000 or above would represent. In fact, the letter was written in the interests of the school district."

Many townspeople spoke up in sharp criticism of the dismissal. One of the parents said, "It's a dirty trick. Should this man be crucified for trying to save the taxpayers some money?"

After strong feelings had been expressed on both sides, Abbott reminded the board that it now had another problem. It had not discharged its superintendent. He had merely been suspended. Who was to "run" the school now?

In an attempt to place someone in charge of the schools, the board majority suggested that the principal of the high school be asked to take over the position as acting superintendent. Although the principal did not refuse, he did ask time to "think it over.'"

Mr. Brown decided that he was not going to accept his suspension without some kind of resistance. He contacted his lawyer and was told to report to the school each day even though he did not do any work. The high school principal continued to "think it over" and never assumed the title of acting superintendent. The superintendent reported at his office each day but discharged no responsibilities. With no superintendent and no acting superintendent, the president of the board, Mr. Jones, took over the reins of the school. Under his "leadership," the school board bought a fleet of new buses, a move that Mr. Brown had opposed for several months because of a lack of funds. Also during Mr. Jones's "reign," the board decided to invest $650,000 of the building fund through a private investment firm. This investment proved costly to the district.

During Mr. Brown's suspension he went to the State Department of Public Instruction, where he talked to the administrative assistant. Said Mr. Brown: "I told the assistant that the board majority had invaded the right of the board by calling on the State Superintendent of Public Instruction without the knowledge and consent of Mr. Abbott and Mr. Katz."

In a few days, matters were further ensnarled by the serving of an injunction on three board members by Mr. Brown to show cause on or before the 11th of the next month as to why they should not be restrained, enjoined, and prohibited from enforcing the suspension without pay. Also, on the same day, Mr. Jones was to appear in court on his disputed election.

When contacted by the local newspaper about further details on the sewer taps, Jones said, "The number of taps required to service the new school has not yet been determined. When such a decision is reached by competent authorities, then and only then will the board be able to determine the actual cost of sewage disposal and negotiate a price for the service."

Mr. Jones went to court on the 11th and admitted that he had failed to file his application for school board candidacy until ten days after the June 9th deadine. He claimed that he followed the June 19th date appearing in a legal advertisement under the signature of Mr. Deal. Deal stated that Mr. Brown had given him that date. "The preparation of the advertisement is a responsibility of the board secretary," said Mr. Brown. The court ruled that the election was legal on the grounds that Alton was a registered district and not a fourth-class district.

In the case of Brown vs. Deal, Jones, and Wilson, the judge ordered a "Status Quo" for the present and, over a board plea, ordered and set a trial date for the 15th of the following month. The judge also stated, "The court is distinctly of the impression that any public board must, before it can remove its officials, give notice of charges and have a hearing on it." Mr. Frank, the lawyer for the board members, stated. "Mr. Brown is not under tenure so he must sue for money, not the illegality of the board procedures." Mr. Summers, the lawyer defending Mr. Brown, contended that the superintendent should have protection from such an arbitrary or unreasonable dismissal.

In the meantime, construction of the new school neared completion. However, the sewer-tap problem had not yet been solved. It became clear that, if the February deadline was to be met, the sewer-tap problem had to be solved without further delay. The board members had often mentioned the possibility of asking Kingston, a nearby community, for permission to tap into their sewer system, but Mr. Jones had always balked at this proposal. He claimed that the board should not get "involved" with Kingston and should solve its own problems. At the next board meeting it was again suggested that Kingston be "sounded out" on a proposed sewer tap. To everyone's surprise, Mr. Jones agreed.

Kingston agreed to a sewer-tap request and quoted the figure of 30 taps for $9,000, but only if all the Alton board was in agreement and if Bond Enterprises was willing to relinquish all rights to the sewer taps. The Board of Education issued a check to the City of Kingston for $9,000.

A Temporary Reinstatement

In a few days Mr. Brown received a letter from the board asking him to meet with them for a special hearing. Mr. Jones, who wrote the letter, told a reporter, "The board unanimously authorized me to write to Mr. Brown and ask him to come in and talk our troubles over."

After consulting his lawyer, Mr. Brown attended the meeting, where he was notified that by unanimous approval of the board he had been reinstated with all rights and back pay. Mr. Brown said, "The reinstatement is personally gratifying to me." This statement, however, did not reflect all of Mr. Brown's feelings. Still embittered by the experience, Mr. Brown's mission seemed to be the ousting of Mr. Jones from the Board of Education. He could hardly mention Mr. Jones's name without giving the impression that he wanted to find some way of eliminating him. In fact, as a condition of reinstatement Mr. Brown insisted that an impartial study of Superintendent-Board relationships be initiated. Mr. Brown's hope was that he would be reinstated and his opponents on the Board, especially Mr. Jones, would be recalled from board membership.

Mr. Jones would not comment on the reinstatement except to say, "Enough has been said already."

A few days after Mr. Brown was reinstated, he received a phone call from the construction foreman of the new high school telling him that a man from Bond Enterprises was on the school grounds cementing all the sewer taps. Mr. Brown immediately called Bond and learned that the latter was going to fight the sewer-tap contract being given to Kingston. Mr. Bond also stated that he had called Mr. Jones to tell him that he was going to cap and cement the sewer taps, and Jones had told him to go ahead.

Shortly thereafter the board of education received a check for $9,000 from the City of Kingston with an explanation that they could not consider the sewer-tap contract if it meant a court fight with Bond Enterprises. The Alton board met in a special session and agreed to hire a lawyer and to bring suit against Bond Enterprises. This placed Mr. Jones in the very awkward position of bringing suit against something he had instigated. Furthermore, Ken Bond had been his friend, and it was through this friendship that the promise by Bond to donate land for an elementary school had been made. At this point, the land had not yet been deeded to the school district. Mr. Jones was unusually quiet during the whole meeting.

In an unexpected move, Deal sent out about 1,500 letters to the voters of Alton. The letters informed them that he was not acting as a board member but as a private citizen in requesting information from them. Would they please show him by returning the enclosed card that they were in favor of settling the sewage disposal problem at a figure of $23,000? The voters were led to believe that if a majority of them were in favor of negotiating for the figure of $23,000, Deal would take it upon himself as a board member to see that their wishes were carried out. He would do this by getting a motion passed at the next board meeting.

At the next meeting of the board, Mr. Deal stood up and told the board and audience that, as a result of his letters, he thought that the board should negotiate with Bond to settle the sewage disposal problem for $23,000. He moved a resolution to that effect. Mr. Abbott asked him how many people had answered his letter. Deal's answer was, "My phone has been jingling all day." Deal was pressed by members of the board to reveal how many postal cards were returned to him, but he refused to cite any number. In fact, contrary to Deal's intention of canvassing the electorate, he sent letters to only about half of the electorate.

Still more confusing to the electorate was the fact that the day following Deal's letter to them he had announced in the *Valley Herald* that he was going to resign. Said Deal, "Everything is in a mess." He cited changes in the architect's plans, the dispute over the suspension, and constant threats of court suits as reasons for leaving the board. "I don't want to be party to all these delays," he said. Deal never indicated when he was going to resign. Actually, his resignation took place several months later.

The community was completely aroused by this time, and under the leadership of the parents, a recall movement to get Jones off the board was started. The charges were:

1. Failure to work in the best interests of the school,
2. Failure to implement additional elementary school facilities,
3. Illegal suspension of the superintendent,
4. Dictatorial conduct,
5. Repeated lack of support of educational objectives,
6. Constant wrangling with other board members.

A petition, incorporating the charges, was signed by 600 people in the community, and when Jones was asked about his reaction to this by a reporter of the *Valley Herald,* his only comment was, "I don't know. I don't get mad easy."

A Partial Solution

At the next board meeting, which was attended by 50 electors, the largest turnout in school board history, the committee submitted its petition for recall. They were told that Mr. Deal, the board secretary, had 30 days to check the signatures. Prior to the expiration date, Mr. Deal announced that the petitions were not prepared in compliance with law and were thus not valid. This action resulted in a suit brought against Deal by the citizens. In the course of the suit, it was revealed that the petitions were legal. However, a number of months elapsed and the school year of 1956–1957 closed without the recall of Jones becoming effective.

At the same meeting at which the petitions were submitted, Jones sidetracked all moves to answer any questions from the floor. People soon began to leave in disgust, murmuring veiled threats as to what they would like to do to Mr. Jones.

The superintendent and his principals were asked to attend a meeting of the board, which was to deal with contracts and salary raises. The principals were told the amount they were to receive. The superintendent, without having been responsible for recommending them, was asked to approve the raises. The principals were asked to leave the room. Mr. Brown was then notified that his contract was not being renewed for the next year on the grounds that it was in the best interest of the school that he not remain in Alton.

During the next few months, the credentials of applicants for the position of superintendent were reviewed. By July a new superintendent had been hired, the courts had fixed the figure of $12,000 as a reasonable cost for the sewer taps, and the petition for the recall of Jones was still in the courts.

CASE TEN

Salem Secret Societies

Caesar rose to speak. Twelve members came to respectful attention. "Brothers, if there is no further business to come up, the meeting is adjourned. May brotherly love go with us."

Caesar started on his right and shook hands with all the members, saying as he grasped each hand, "Friendship." Each brother in turn answered, "Forever." Caesar was followed solemnly by the brothers in turn until all had shaken hands. They gravely filed out.

The above ritual signaled the closing of a regular meeting of the Julius Caesar Fraternity. It was taken from a copy of the ritual and constitution of that organization used in 1916 in the Salem, Oregon, High School. Activities of the Julius Caesar secret society at this early date precipitated action by the school board against the society's expanding activities in the high school and marked the start of a struggle that was to last until 1952. The true signature of "Caesar" was attached to the 1916 ritual copy. Near the end of the struggle in 1949, another boy by the same name, possibly the son of the first signer, was expelled from Salem High School because of his membership in a secret society.

The above account of the Julius Caesar Fraternity represents a problem in American secondary education that goes back at least to 1866. Legal action has been taken against secret society movements in most states. Oregon, the scene of the present case, passed a law forbidding secret societies in 1909. Expulsion or suspension from school was provided as the student penalty for membership, and administrators could be fined for not adhering to the law.

Secret societies still operate in the schools of many states, and they raise various issues which the school administrator must face. Among the questions which the present case poses are the following: Could the problem have been solved at all had all the former fraternity members remained "in the fold"? How far can out-of-school cliques and social groups develop without being classed as fraternities? Are school organizations in which ability is a membership prerequisite subversive? Why did Salem's secret societies persist for decades although they were clearly illegal? In the face of the responsibilities legally assigned to the administrators, were there alternatives other than coercion for meeting the problem?

At the climax of the secret societies' struggle in 1950, Salem, the capital city of Oregon, had a population of 43,000. About 15,000 more people lived in the suburban areas. State government activities and the rich agricultural farms in the surrounding valley were the main economic supports of the city. Located on the main line of the Southern Pacific Railroad, the city was bordered on the east by Highway 99, the direct route from Seattle to Los Angeles. The broad Willamette River flowed quietly by on the west. The city's industry was limited to sawmills, canneries, and flax-processing plants. The surrounding regions raised great amounts of fruits, vegetables, berries, and nuts.

As befitted its rural character, Salem was judged conservative by many persons. Basically a middle-class town, it had many wealthy people who had earned their fortunes from the commerce of the community or on the farms that surrounded it. It was one of the last communities of its size in the United States to adopt secondary education through the twelfth grade. It did so only after the voters had voted against it three times. The fourth vote was successful and the first four-year high school class graduated in 1906.

Early Phases of the Struggle

The official struggle against secret societies in Salem High School began in 1916, when the school board ordered all such societies within the school to have a faculty adviser. Holding true to the secretive nature of its society, the Julius Caesar organization presented a statement to the board refusing an adviser and refusing to disband.

Setting a pattern for future caution and discretion in dealing with such societies, the board requested an opinion from the attorney general on the legality of its position. The attorney general refused to rule. Thereupon the director of the board summoned the society as follows:

> . . . . . Now, therefore, you and each of you are hereby cited to appear at said time and place and then and there to show cause if any of you have or if any exist why an order shall not be made suspending you or expelling you from the Salem High School. It has been found that a secret society exists among the pupils in said high school, contrary to law, and that you are engaged in the organization or maintenance thereof. . . . . .

Sensing the seriousness of the board's intention to expel them, the society capitulated and a faculty adviser was appointed. Gradually it became clear, however, that the societies were not playing fair with their faculty advisers. Problems developed over the hazing activities connected with initiation. For example, the case is recorded of a girl initiate who was forced to drink a mixture of castor oil, cold cooking grease, coffee grounds, raw oysters, and mackerels' eyes.

By October 1919, the school board was sufficiently concerned to pass a resolution against hazing. The resolution was ineffective, and on April 14, 1921 a new resolution was passed. It provided that all clubs in existence must submit their by-laws and constitutions, oaths and pledges, to the school board. Continued violations of this policy between 1921 and 1933 resulted in 19 boys being expelled.

Toward the end of the 1921–1933 period, the secret societies, according to many observers, were in control of student activities. They became an integral and most powerful force in the Salem High School community. A former member of the Julius Caesar fraternity gave a word picture of the secret societies' influence on Salem High School during their heyday:

"As one entered the front door before school started, small groups of boys or girls huddled in noisy but private seclusion. One group of boys, the Friars, all wore identical pants with wide inserts of a different color in the lower leg and lined at the edge with pearl buttons. The mass of students passed along the hall giving wide berth to the self-reserved areas of the secret societies. In the assembly hall each group sat in a section permanently reserved for it. Student officers were all club members, since a non-member had no chance to gain office. All members of the basketball teams belonged to the same club. The same was true for football and other athletic teams."

Membership on the ball team did not entitle a boy to membership in the club; membership in the proper club had to come before a boy could turn out for a sport. A vice-principal of Salem High cited the case of a student who turned out for football without being an active member in the proper club. The next day he was taken by his teammates out on a lonely road, brutally beaten, and left in a ditch seriously injured.

Different observers have reported that club members, during the 1921–1931 period particularly, were student leaders and tended to come from prominent families. Thus, the sons of such officials as the state governor, state treasurer, and the mayor of Salem belonged to the secret societies during the 'twenties and early 'thirties. Reportedly, there was a change in the quality of the leadership in the secret societies during the 'forties.

In September 1933, a student was injured during secret society hazing activities. Because it wished to give the fullest consideration to the matter, the board held two hearings during 1933 and 1934. Former secret society alumni defended the societies at the meetings, but civic organizations of Salem backed the School Board in its stand against these organizations. Based upon this support, the Board rejected the proposal for continuing the societies.

At least one Salem newspaper held up the banner by publishing the following editorial.

WHY THEY ARE BARRED

Capital Journal Salem, Oregon Oct. 24, 1934

Partisans of high school secret societies have appeared before the board of education asking why the societies are being fought and their members barred from school activities. They demand the devising of some scheme for countenancing their societies. Their proposal was deservedly rejected.

High school secret societies are barred because the state law bans them and the board is only living up to the law. It would be in violation of statutes they are sworn to uphold, if societies are officially countenanced. That they exist is the fault of alumni and parents.

These societies are barred because experience proves them a demoralizing influence in school life, breeders of dissension, favoritism, discrimination, and snobbishness. They are an undemocratic influence in the foundation of our democracy—the public schools.

Further evidence of the thought and consideration given by the school board to the problem of secret societies is shown by the development of a plan for control. The preamble to the plan of action follows:

The one hope of a permanent correction for the secret society evil is that the attitudes of the boys and girls toward these organizations will change. The influences that will be most effective in bringing about such a change will vary with the individual. Some will respond to advice and friendly council, especially if it can be clearly shown that there are evil results; others will be influenced by a strong public sentiment; while others need a redirection of their energies. We should first give each one a chance to drop out of his club. Then bring stronger pressure on those who are left.

In effect, the plan provided for study to determine the effects of club activities, and outlined a controlled campaign to eliminate the clubs. Furthermore, authorized school activities to effect a redirection of student energy were planned.

The attitude of the school board during the mid-thirties is indicated in the following policies, which they adopted to guide their actions:

1. There must be complete confidence and agreement among ourselves at all points. The entire high school staff should be given time to think through the problem and should be kept informed of the purposes and progress of the campaign.
2. The co-operation of the press should be enlisted. That type of publicity can have a decided effect on our results. It will probably be best to have no mention of the early stages of our work.
3. We should avoid entangling alliances. Also, we must preserve the dignity and authority of the schol staff, and remain independent of other agencies that may operate along similar lines.
4. The fact that such work will take time and energy should be faced. It should be considered part of the services that the district is paying for.
5. Elimination of secret societies should be recognized as only part of a bigger work the school should be doing in training boys and girls to live in a changing world.

New personnel. In 1937 a new vice-principal was assigned to Salem High School. He was selected because of his marked ability to maintain classroom discipline, and was instructed to do his best to get rid of secret societies. He embarked upon an ambitious program of investigation and was instrumental in having all members and even those who were suspected of membership eliminated from sports and other activities. This action apparently helped to curtail activities during the year. However, the new vice-principal left at the end of the year to accept a principalship in another part of the state.

Frank Bennett became Salem's school superintendent in 1939 and remained until the climactic struggle against the societies apparently ended in 1952. Grave concern about secret societies was expressed by school board members when they interviewed Dr. Bennett for the position. He accepted the superintendency pledging to eradicate the secret society problem. From the time he took office, the school board members never wavered in consistently maintaining a policy of opposition to the secret societies. Bennett later stated that the main reason for the successful elimination of the secret societies was the board members' willingness to support established policies regardless whose children were involved.

Although the strict procedures employed by the vice-principal in 1937–1938 seemed to have immediate effects, the results were not permanent. In the early years of Bennett's administration, secret society activities continued unabated. For example, the following news item appeared in the *Capital-Journal* newspaper in 1942:

> Nine police officers were called into action early Sunday morning to break up a riot near the Marion Hotel where, according to police reports, the anual banquet of the Julius Caesars was held earlier in the evening, and before the row was over six young men were arrested on charges ranging from plain drunk to inciting a riot.
>
> During the melee bottles of ketchup were wielded and hurled and a series of individual fights broke out. Several of the officers were struck by fists and other objects including bottles; many car windows were broken.

Such actions stimulated the board to issue a public declaration of policy. This policy was to set the pattern for future action by the board regarding secret organizations in the Salem Public Schools. The policy which is quoted below guided the board through ten years of critical decisions:

SALEM PUBLIC SCHOOLS
Salem, Oregon
May 21, 1942

Declaration of Policy
Relative to Secret Societies in the Salem Schools

This policy is hereby adopted by the Salem School Board and shall be effective immediately, except as hereinafter provided in Section 8.

1. A bulletin shall be prepared and placed in the hands of each 9th grader as he registers for Senior High School, and new students coming in from outside the Salem district as they register. This bulletin shall carry general information to the students concerning the privileges in the Salem high school and a caution against membership in secret organizations, and a brief statement of Board policy in such matters.

2. The Senior high school administration shall maintain a regular committee and organization to deal consistently and persistently with this matter. The Chairman and personnel of this committee shall be named by the principal and confirmed by the superintendent. Such committee shall meet regularly, receive reports on students suspected of membership, pass upon eligibility lists (so far as secret societies are concerned), prepare memorandum to be attached to permanent records, and recommend to the principal action on secret society cases. The responsibility for action on secret society suspensions shall rest with the principal, and of expulsion with the Board.

3. All students who, by their conduct and association, give sufficient suspicion of "secret society" membership, shall be barred from participation in all school activities except attendance at classes, beginning September, 1942. The responsibility to keep himself/ herself free from suspicion of membership shall rest with the student if the student is to enjoy the privileges of student activities, such as student body officers, student body tickets, school dances, and other social functions, club membership, participation in athletics, and participation in the commencement exercises and receipt of a diploma.

4. Students who have been denied participation in student activities because of suspected membership, may not be returned to the eligible list until more than one semester of probation has elapsed, after formal affirmative action by the committee and approval by the principal. (Except in cases in which the committee find their own action incorrect.) This would mean that a student, after being placed on probation, must serve on such probation the balance of any semester in which that probation is granted, and the following semester, before he/she may again

become eligible. For instance, an individual wishing to participate in commencement exercises would have to have received such probation by the end of the junior year in 1942 to be eligible for participation in commencement exercises at the end of his/her senior year in 1943. Any student once reinstated who is again declared ineligible, may be expelled or returned to the ineligible list, if deemed wise, provided that such student shall not be given this consideration a second time. Any student on the ineligible list, must sufficiently remove such question so as to be placed on the probation list within a period of eighteen weeks or be subject to expulsion as a "secret society" member. Any student completing high school or leaving high school for any reason, who still remained on this ineligible or probation list, shall have a memorandum of such facts made a part of his permanent record.

5. Any student barred from student activities for reasons of suspected membership who engages in activities or becomes a party to episodes that bring reproach to the school, or who conducts himself in an antagonistic or unco-operative manner with school officials, shall be suspended by the principal, and, if proper attitude is not evidenced, shall be expelled by the Board.

6. "Secret society" members will be expelled from school by the board. The committee shall recommend suspension and expulsion from school of any student whose conduct, associations, behavior, or concerning whom other evidence is sufficient to convince the committee of a student's membership. Upon receipt of such recommendation, the principal shall review the case and act. If he feels there is insufficient evidence, he shall immediately refer the case to the committee for further study and recommendation. If he concurs in the recommendation of the committee for expulsion, he shall make his recommendation to the Board for final action.

7. No student, completing high school work and still remaining on the probation or ineligible list because of suspicioned "secret society" membership, shall be admitted for post-graduate work.

8. Students now in school and expecting to return next year, and known to be or suspected of being members of "secret societies," shall be contacted by the Dean of Boys and the Dean of Girls immediately and given an opportunity to declare their intentions, after explanation of the new policy, and to make affidavits with their parent/s to that declaration. Upon *satisfactory attitude* and a completed affidavit by parents and students, they may, by committee recommendation, be placed upon the probation list as of this semester. Those who fail to do so must do so before they may be admitted to school in the fall of 1942. Fall probations shall date from the fall semester. Seniors of the 1942 class now in school and known to be members of, or suspected of being members of, "secret societies," shall be given a like

privilege of declaration. Upon a satisfactory *attitude* and a completed affidavit of parents and students, they may be allowed all privileges of graduation. Otherwise, they shall receive only their credits and be denied all graduation privileges and diplomas, and memorandum of facts shall be attached to their permanent record.

9. Students graduating in the class of 1942, and thereafter, or leaving school for any reason, of whom it may become known that he/she has since become or were members at date of leaving school, shall have such memorandum made a part of their permanent record with the school.

10. Nothing in this statement of policy shall be construed to mean that equal standards of conduct and behavior shall not be expected of students other than "secret society" members, and that like action shall be taken for like conduct.

Note—The terms "eligible," "ineligible," and "probation," as used in this statement of policy are restricted to "secret society" relationships.

The committee, established by action of the board, took a vigorous stand with reference to its outlined responsibilities. In April 1943, the committee reported further activity in the Julius Caesar Society. Three boys were expelled for attending an annual banquet and dance sponsored by an alumni group of the society.

Such diligent scrutiny by the committee paid dividends, and before the end of the school year the assistant principal was able to report favorably to the school board: "There is no question but that the activities of secret societies are at a low ebb at the present time in Salem Schools. . . ."

On February 2, 1943 the Salem School Board placed a bulletin in the hands of each ninth-grader which warned against membership in secret societies. The bulletin was addressed to the parents of new students of the Senior High School and urged the participation of students in school activities. It quoted Oregon School Law regarding secret societies. The signatures of both parents and students were required as evidence that they had received the bulletin. Selected portions from the bulletin follow:

Each student should avoid membership in so-called "secret societies." They are illegal in Oregon, and their members are subject to suspension or expulsion by the Board. Students known to be members will be expelled and those strongly suspected of membership because of their associations or conduct, are barred from all other activities other than school attendance. They are ineligible for student body membership, or to hold student body offices; to be members of regular school clubs or activities; to participate in athletics; or, to participate in the Senior High School commencement exercises.

Once declared ineligible in such cases, individuals shall remain ineligible for one whole semester beyond the semester in which they may be placed on probation for re-admittance to activities. Students finishing or leaving school and still on the probation or ineligible list because of suspected secret society membership, shall have a memorandum of such facts made a part of his/her permanent record.

We call your attention to these societies because involvement with them may deprive your child of the opportunity of school participation and affect his permanent record. Students are often sought for these clubs. They feel flattered by the attention and join without realization of the full implication of their act. Students wishing to withdraw have found themselves so treated that it makes the withdrawal more difficult than they have the strength to command. Stories of terrorized youth who have joined, or indicated interest in membership, and later decided to stay out, are common.

Experience throughout the country has evidenced the undesirability of such organizations. Sufficient social and group activities are provided within the regular school program. We therefore urge all parents and students to co-operate with the Board and the school administration to the end that our school may be free of the charge of harboring illegal organizations.

Another Period of Concentrated Secret Society Activity

Early in 1946 Principal Carleton held a discussion meeting with parents in an attempt to create a better understanding of the problem. He described the nationwide pattern of the secret society problem and dwelt on its history in Salem. He explained to the parents that condoning such societies was a direct violation of school law and that leniency on the part of the school board would only foster more activity. He said, "Meetings let go with just a warning only cause new groups to start." In attempting to point out the reasons for the severity of the Board's policies, he dwelt on the fact that the secret society philosophy was "Once a member, always a member," and that even parents found that they had little control over this.

He pointed out that students who joined secret societies soon formed undesirable patterns of conduct. He noted that secret society members habitually stayed out late and participated in unchaperoned parties and trips. Parents were advised to check with the school authorities immediately if any such behavior was noticed.

On May 30, 1946 Principal Carleton received an anonymous phone call at his home. The voice said, "This is an alumni member of the Julius Caesar Club. I am calling to say that we will never cease to support the Julius Caesar Club. We will do everything in our power to keep it going." Superintendent Bennett and others believed that the alumni activity during this period was largely responsible for the continued activity of the clubs.

On November 27, 1946 members of the school administration advised the board that investigation had again disclosed secret society activity in the High School. This time nine members of the "Friars" and eight members of the "Julius Caesar" had been discovered. Mr. Harland, a member of the school board, moved that letters be sent to the parents of the boys involved advising them of the position of the board and of the law. In addition, the written communication was to make clear that secret society membership and school attendance were incompatible.

The letter which was sent also urged the parents to use their "good influence with other parents of boys of the same organizations" to insure the permanent dissolution of the illegal clubs. Briefly, the letter offered three alternatives:

1. Boys with membership in such organization could dissolve their organization.
2. An individual member could withdraw from such organization and give acceptable evidence of permanent withdrawal. This alternative was not open to any boy already in violation of written agreement relative to membership in such organization.
3. A member could exclude himself from the Salem school as of December 7, 1946.

The letter closed by stating, "Whether there shall be hardship must rest upon the choice of the student himself." Carleton later stated: "All through this we were attempting to salvage the individuals, and until we felt that the only way to save the school was to take action, we didn't do anything drastic." All 17 boys chose the second alternative.

On March 14, 1947, however, the Board was notified that the 17 boys had, in fact, violated their pledges and had continued their secret society activities. They were subsequently expelled from school. Mr. Chandler Brown, representing the "Julius Caesar," and Mr. Bruce Spaulding, representing the "Friars," met with the Board on March 22, 1947, to urge leniency for the boys. The Board, however, could find no reason to change its action and issued a statement reaffirming its policy on the matter.

For the remainder of this school year, Principal Carleton and Vice-Principal Flesher were constantly investigating the activity or alleged activity of secret society members. Several boys were on suspension and they were interviewed periodically to see whether they were keeping faith with their agreements. One such interview by Vice-Principal Flesher revealed that a new organization was functioning with two former "Friars" forming the nucleus. Flesher kept a written record of the ensuing investigation:

> May 26th, 1947.
> This morning I talked to a boy about whether or not those boys who had been suspended from school for membership in secret societies were keeping faith with the agreement which they made when they were allowed to return to school. He offered a suggestion that although he did not know what they were doing, he did think it wise that I know that there is a new secret society organized and that he knew that two former Friars had attended the first meeting and had assisted in setting up the new organization.
> I asked him if he could give me the names of the boys who were members of this group and he said that he knew that J.M., brother of B.M., was the acting leader and that (six other names) were associated.
> I then called D.J. into my office and questioned him at length in regard to this group. D.J. stated that he knew there was a secret organization patterned after the former Friars and Julius Caesars. He also stated that the members did not now have a closely knit organization but they were planning to set up their charter and make a very intensive membership campaign during the summer and early fall. I then asked him for a list of the members and the above names were given. I asked him if he was aware of the penalty for having anything to do with such an organization and he said that he knew. I then asked him why he joined and he said he really did not know.
> I then called in D.M. I asked him if he knew that there was an organization called "The Rooks" and asked him if he knew they were an illegal group and if he knew the penalty for belonging to such an organization. In all three cases he answered that he did. I then asked if he would give me the list of the members. He gave me the same list as D.J. and verified the report D.J. made, adding that they had no official membership list. He noted that they had no initiation and that their meetings were informal and held in automobiles in

different places. I asked whose automobile and he replied, "In J.M.'s." I asked, "Do you mean to tell me that seven of you met in one automobile?" He answered, "Yes."

I asked him what his parents would think if he received the same penalty for belonging to this group as that which had been given to members of former illegal groups? He said they would be very unhappy. I asked him what type of penalty could he expect, and he said he could not see why he could receive any different than any other.

Tuesday, May 27th.

I talked to A.H. this morning in regard to this new organization. I asked him if he had ever heard of the Rook organization. He said, "No." I then asked what he would think if I were to tell him that I have information which had convinced me of the fact that he not only knew of this organization but that he was also a member. He replied that I could not prove that he either knew or was a member. My reply was that I was not now attempting to prove either, this was merely a discussion.

He then said that I nor anyone else would have a legal basis upon which we could act because of the fact that this group apparently had no membership, no initiation, and no regular meetings. Also that since they met out of school they were not a school organization. He then quoted Oregon law, attempting to convince me that it would be necessary for me to prove that they were a secret society before any legal action or any school action might be taken. He then gave me a lengthy discussion on how unfair the school board action in regard to the former secret society had been, and that we had only made matters worse. That we were the only city in Oregon who persecuted worthwhile societies and that we had made some errors which had best not be repeated. I complimented A.H. upon his stand for his convictions and asked if he would like to discuss the source of his legal advice, which he refused.

I am quite firmly convinced that this is an outgrowth of the Friars Secret Society and that they are attempting to evade court action by tactics which are advised by adult leaders. I have contacted no other members of this group because I am now sure that they have had adult advice and that questioning would get nowhere.

May 28, 1947.

For some time I have been checking quite carefully on the actions of the boys who were members of secret societies and are now in school. I have questioned many boys and have come to the conclusion with one exception, that all of the boys who were former members are either now active members or are lending their full sympathy and support to the secret society movement.

It was necessary for me to call H.D. into my office recently and in my discussion with him, the subject of his stand on secret societies came up. I might add as a preface to this that I had heard from a very reliable source that when H.D. went to J.M., the president of the Friars, and told him that he was withdrawing his membership, that Jerry said, "You can't withdraw; once a member, you are always a member." H.D. replied, "Like hell I can't, I quit." I complimented him on his stand and asked him point blank if he felt that any other members of his group were keeping faith, and he replied that he knew that B.L. was attending meetings. I was not surprised as I had heard this on several occasions. He said that H.C. and D.K. were attending parties given by the Friars.

To me, this is conclusive evidence that they are not acting in good faith. He then told me that it might be well for me to be aware of the fact that in the near future the Friars beach party will be held. He could not give me the beach at which it would be held but told me he would inform me later. This party, he said, is terrific and is a boy and girl party, whose chaperones shall be older members of the organization and their friends.

On May 28 Carleton and Flesher notified the Board that seven boys were participating in secret society activity. The Board voted to expel all of them. On June 3, 1947 the Board held a special meeting to hear arguments from the parents and an attorney for the seven students. The Board refused to alter its position.

Only one incident involving secret societies came before the Salem School Board during 1947–1948. January 19, 1948 Carleton and Flesher reported that the societies had reappeared. Eleven boys were involved. The Board commended Carleton and Flesher for the report and expelled the boys.

The Court Makes a Decision

During the summer of 1949 a student from Portland, who was attending Willamette University in Salem, organized a club variously known as Alpha Beta Chi, American Boys Club, and Associated Boys Club. The young man belonged to such a group in Portland. The Salem chapter, with a charter membership of 13, tried to avoid being classed as a secret society in the legal meaning of the term. Superintendent Bennett later reported that the attorney advising the boys gave them some inaccurate advice in that some of the steps they took placed them in direct violation of the Code. The secret status of this group was proven in the court action which ensued.

In order to avoid drastic action by the school board, the group planned to organize quickly to develop a large membership, and in that way to "get their foot in the door" with a group so large that the school board would not expel the members even if the society were proven to be illegal.

Principal Carleton and Vice-Principal Flesher, however, had their respective sources of information, and shortly after the opening of school an investigation was in full swing. After gathering as much information as possible, the boys were called into Carleton's office for conferences. Following are exerpts from a written record of these conferences:

> Boys were brought in, in two groups of five and one group of three. Boys first were asked if any of the group were more responsible than others in the formation of this group called Alpha Beta Chi. They all were equally responsible.
>
> When asked if they didn't have some doubts as to the legality of the group, they said that some questioned it, but that they were assured by the Portland boy (named) that it was legal because it was a Portland High School group they were seeking to affiliate with.
>
> When asked if they had a charter from the Portland group, they said "No." They were operating on a period of six months' probation, and they would receive their charter and be a chapter on February 1, 1950, which would indicate that they had made application on or about August 1.
>
> When asked if they would withdraw from school rather than be expelled, every one of the 13 boys interviewed said he would withdraw. The fact that they made no argument whatever at the time asked indicates that every one of them knew he had been wrong in joining or helping in the organization of this group.
>
> There was considerable discussion in one group as to the purpose of the club; social activity seemed to be the only object, with semimonthly dances forming the major activity.
>
> When asked why they called a meeting of all parents for a special meeting about the middle of October, the reply was that they wanted to have the parents appeal to the School Board to have the group reorganized as a legal club. There was a great deal of uncertainty as to the exact date of the parents' meeting. In my opinion this meeting was not called by the boys until after their leader had been called into the principal's office and questioned as to the organization.
>
> It was also brought out in the questioning that the group was operating under the laws of Alpha Beta Chi. They had a copy of the by-laws and were presumably using them. They did not state that they had officially adopted them by vote.
>
> When asked if they did not know that there was a state law forbidding high school fraternities and that the School Board had adopted a policy of expelling students connected with such organiza-

tions, every one said he knew it, but did not believe their group to come under the law as a secret society. They admitted that it was to become an active chapter of an already established high school fraternity.

Subsequently, on October 6, 1949, Carleton and Flesher reported the results of their investigation to the Salem School Board. The Board then called a meeting of the parents of the 13 boys involved for the purpose of discussing the activities. The Oregon School Law regarding these activities was read to the parents and they were asked to comment. This meeting was held October 10.

On October 11, 1949 the following statement was released by the Salem School Board:

> The Salem School District Board, after a series of conferences with parents, students, and other parties concerned, and after very careful consideration and investigation, have definitely determined that the organization of High School students formed during the summer falls within the type of organization banned by the state laws of Oregon, which organizations school boards are charged with the responsibility to suppress.
>
> In the light of this decision, it becomes impossible for the school board to permit the continuance of any of the students involved in this organization in the Salem Public Schools for the balance of the school year. This latest organization has sought to pattern itself after a Portland club, believing thereby that it could evade the legal ban. The Salem School Board feels that the law is very clear in its charge to the School Board to suppress any such organization. The Salem School Board, over a period of years, has kept constant pressure on such organizations and are determined that any student wishing to have the privilege of education through the Salem Schools must definitely make their choice between such organizations and the school. The board is sorry to be compelled to use such drastic measures, but the insistence of such organizations to evade or disregard the law, and the oft-repeated policy of the Salem Schools, makes necessary such drastic action.

The Board expelled the 13 students on October 13, 1949. Immediately thereafter the parents employed an attorney and obtained a temporary restraining order against the action of the Board. On October 21, 1949, the Salem School Board employed three attorneys to present their side of the case, which was legally known as "Gene Lebold and others, Plaintiff versus School District No. 24CJ, Marion County, and others." Worthy of note is the fact that two of the board attorneys were ex-members of Salem High School's secret societies.

The case was heard in the Circuit Court of the State of Oregon for the County of Marion. The Plaintiffs alleged that:

1. They had not violated Oregon State Law within the meaning of the law, nor were they members of a Secret Society.

2. The defendants in taking the action of expelling the students were "committing an abuse of their discretion."

3. "The defendants acted in an arbitrary, capricious, officious, oppressive and discriminatory manner towards these plaintiffs."

In his Memorandum Opinion Dal M. King, the Circuit Court judge, pointed out that there were three main issues raised in the trial. They were:

> 1. Have we an organization that is actually disbanded and dead to administer on?
> 2. Did the School Board act in an arbitrary, capricious, officious, oppressive and discriminatory manner and in excess of their authority?
> 3. Was the organization, which the plaintiffs organized and to which they belonged, in fact secret or was it prohibited by Sections 111–3004 and 111–3005, O.C.L.A.?

In passing judgment on the first issue, the judge held that the organization was not in fact dead, since it had at no time indicated a willingness to disband and even planned to meet at a later date with the Portland club. On the second issue it was held that the Salem School Board was entirely within its authority to act as it did. It was pointed out that the School Board gave ample and plentiful warning of its position both in writing and in meetings. With reference to the third issue, it was held that Alpha Beta Chi was in fact a "secret" society and was in violation of Oregon State Law.

Thus the legal aspects of the case were resolved and the position of the Salem school authorities was upheld. On March 17, 1950 the Board added a final note to the case by allowing credit to those students who attended school while the restraining order was in effect. At that time they also recorded in their minutes that the boys were permanently expelled.

It appeared, for the moment at least, that the spirit of the secret society movement was broken. In August of 1950 a handbook was prepared for distribution to parents which explained the history of the conflict and referred to the ". . . untold heartache to students and parents."

Yet, while the court case rocked the community and while the school authorities were doing all they could to prevent a repetition of the tragedy, another organization was being formed. In November 1950, while Flesher was investigating the absence of some boys from school, he came across evidence that another secret society was active. This time four boys were organizing a group called the "Anglo-Saxons." Minutes of the meeting were found that showed eight other boys had been contacted and asked to join but had refused. The four organizers withdrew from school in preference to being expelled.

Epilogue

Two years passed quietly after the episode involving the Anglo-Saxons. In October 1952 still another group was being quietly pulled together. The "Van Dykes" had apparently been organized during the early spring, and investigation showed they were fully aware of the illegal nature of their activity. Their parents did not know about the club. The investigation was thoroughly made. The group, as usual, had a pledge:

> I . . . . promise to obey all rules and regulations set down by the club. Under no circumstances will I reveal any facts or information given to me by this club. I realize this is a life-time fraternity and will do everything in my power to keep it a good, and strong organization.

Despite this pledge, the boys when questioned separately over a short period of time told all they knew and furnished Mr. Flesher with a copy of the oath, the by-laws, the constitution, and a complete list of members. The boys were given the chance to withdraw from school rather than to be expelled. This opportunity they took. Twenty boys were involved in this affair.

Six years have passed without further secret society activity. Frank Bennett, now President of Eastern Oregon College, recently noted that the opening of a second high school in Salem (1953) and a strengthened program of officially organized school activities in both schools provided students with opportunities to satisfy social needs without violating the law.

Mr. Carleton has stated that informal gangs of boys have been observed from time to time but they have not had secret organizations. He refused to say that the problem was solved, however. The policy, he said, was to continue to wait and to watch.

Heartaches and Headaches

The school system of Lakefork County, an agricultural area of the great Midwest, was consolidated and organized as a single administrative unit known as Independent School District No. 21. The school district included seven small communities, ranging in population from 1,800 to 3,000 persons. These typical American townships were located six to eight miles apart, and almost all their inhabitants knew one another. No one lived a life unto himself. Each town was a municipality and maintained its own local government. The general municipal services were available and included a fire department, police department, and various other community agencies. The inhabitants were proud of the individuality of each town or village. The leadership and pressure of the State Legislature accounted somewhat for the consolidation movement, but apparently the main reason they were willing to join forces in educating their children was financial. These people had accepted consolidation as a means of providing a better program more economically for elementary and secondary pupils throughout the entire area.

Independent School District No. 21 was governed by a five-man board of education elected by the people. The board appointed a superintendent of schools, who was responsible for the over-all administration of the schools in the district. Each town had an elementary school, but the one large high school for the entire area was located in the largest of the communities, Laketown. Thus, the pattern of school organization was 6–6; this arrangement had proved to be most satisfactory for the area.

The administrative offices for the district were located in the high school building. Elementary teachers were assured of some help in curriculum planning, inasmuch as one supervisor was employed as a member of the administrative staff. This supervisor traveled from school to school observing the teachers at work, assisting in program planning, curriculum development, the testing program, personnel problems, and, last but not least, keeping the superintendent informed on developments in the various schools. Indeed, the superintendent had been most fortunate in securing the services of Miss Wright. Needless to say, Miss Wright was a very busy person. "If I only had more time to help the teachers," she would say. "It seems as if I cannot accomplish anything."

Mr. Davis, who had served as District Superintendent for a period of seven years, had just finished meeting with a group of irate citizens from Millville, the smallest of the towns in the district. They had visited him as a delegation from the Parent-Teachers Association to protest the building of a new elementary school in Laketown. All attempts to persuade the visitors that the responsibility concerning the matter resided with the Board of Education fell upon deaf ears. "You're the superintendent here, and you ought to be looking out for the little fellow." The superintendent finally concluded by saying: "I suggest that you present your case and views to the Board. I shall be happy to recommend further study of the situation." With a few more pertinent remarks about "Laketown trying to run the whole school district," the delegation departed.

Mr. Davis wiped his brow and settled back in his chair for a moment of relaxation. His moment was of short duration. The telephone on his desk rang. Mr. Barton, Principal of the Afton Elementary School in the next town, was on the line. The superintendent listened.

"Mr. Davis, I've about reached the end of my rope with Miss Simms, the sixth-grade teacher I was telling you about. She has been out of school more than she has been in during the past two weeks. When she is here, she doesn't seem to care whether school keeps or not. It is beginning to show up in her class, and frankly, I'm worried about it. I have tried to talk to her about it, but I can't get anything out of her except that she's getting to be a nervous wreck. Can you come up and talk to her? Or do you suppose that Miss Wright (the elementary supervisor) could come up and help me out with this? Perhaps the case needs a woman's touch."

Mr. Davis assured the principal that he would get busy on the problem and send for Miss Wright immediately.

Miss Wright was informed of the situation and agreed to reschedule her visits for the next week in such a way as to enable her to spend the next day in Afton.

Mr. Davis felt better. He was happy to shift the responsibility to a competent staff member. Yes indeed, Miss Wright was an excellent supervisor. Undoubtedly, she would investigate the problem and report to him within a few days. Although he hated the thought, in case Miss Simms were ill, perhaps he could replace her.

And with thoughts of supervision on his mind, Mr. Davis remembered another problem in the High School. Jack Larson, new English teacher, was a graduate of the local high school. He had completed his work at the University and had obtained the necessary teaching credentials. Mr. Davis had recommended his appointment to the high school faculty and felt a personal responsibility for his performance. Jack had experienced some difficulty during the first week of school, however, and Mr. Sawyer, High School Principal, had suggested that Jack might need constant supervision during the first semester. The superintendent had insisted, therefore, that Miss Christensen, a senior faculty member, be assigned to help Jack. After all, Miss Christensen had been a successful English teacher for twenty years. Certainly, she would be able to supervise Jack—or, for that matter, any new teacher.

Mr. Davis reflected on these supervisory problems. In his professional training, he had been told that supervision was the primary task of the school administrator. Perhaps this concept was right. At least from the standpoint of an instructional program, he felt he could make a professional contribution. And yet, he had hoped to graduate from this type of work. He believed that a superintendent of schools had more important things to worry about. His was an executive position demanding training, experience, and a considerable amount of insight.

What about that delegation from Millville? He would have to think of something to thwart the plans of that delegation. As educational leader of the community, he should be allowed to recommend the construction of school houses where he thought they were needed.

Supervisory problems and the instructional program would take care of themselves. Indeed, supervisors and principals were hired to do this type of work.

Before Miss Wright left her office the next morning, she consulted her files to refresh her memory on past visits with Miss Simms. She found from the personnel records that Miss Simms had completed two years of successful teaching in another district before coming to District 21. This was her second year at Afton, and the records indicated that she was experiencing a successful career. Miss Wright had visited her classroom three times during the past year, and the notations made at the time of these visits were all favorable. There was special mention of the excellent rapport between teacher and pupils. The classroom was described as being exceptionally cozy and attractive. Obviously the children had been happy. What could have happened in such a short time to change the picture so completely?

When Miss Wright arrived at Afton, she went to see Mr. Barton, the principal. She reviewed the information about Miss Simms which she had obtained from her files, and asked Mr. Barton if he had any idea at all concerning the change in Miss Simms.

"I haven't the remotest idea," confessed Mr. Barton. "I have tried to talk to her about it, but it seems that every time I open my mouth, I put my foot in it! She seems to be on the defensive all the time. The last time I called attention to her frequent absences, she replied that she didn't enjoy being sick. I assured her that I did not mean to appear unsympathetic, but my concern was for the children in her classroom. Her repeated absences were very hard on them. With that, she burst into tears and left the room."

"When did you first notice the change in her, Mr. Barton?" asked Miss Wright.

"I would say about a month or so ago. Some of the other teachers mentioned to me that something must be bothering Miss Simms, but no one seemed to know what it was. Things have been going from bad to worse, and I would appreciate anything you can do to help straighten things out. She is too good a teacher to lose. And especially in the middle of the year."

"I certainly agree with you and I shall do everything I can to help her," said Miss Wright. "I'll get to her classroom later in the morning. I wouldn't want her to feel that I am here specifically to see her."

Miss Wright first visited Miss Carson, a third-grade teacher. She knew that Miss Carson and Miss Simms belonged to the same bridge club, and that they were seen in each other's company quite frequently. She hoped that Miss Carson would give her some lead to open a discussion about Miss Simms. The children left the room to attend a physical education class, and as soon as they were out of hearing, Miss Carson said, "Have you seen Gladys (Miss Simms) lately? If you haven't, be prepared for a shock. She looks just terrible. I've been trying to get her to see a doctor, but she keeps shrugging her shoulders and saying, 'There's nothing the matter with me that any doctor could cure!' I don't know what she means by that, but really, Miss Wright, I'm worried about her."

"I'm sorry to hear that," said Miss Wright. "Do you have any idea at all what could be wrong?"

"Well, confidentially, I think that she had some trouble with her fiancé. His company transferred him to South America, you know. He left about a month ago, and she's been 'down in the dumps' ever since. I shouldn't think that would make her look so sickly, though, would you?"

"One cannot be sure," replied Miss Wright. "Many times personal problems become very difficult to solve. Well, let us hope it is nothing really serious." Miss Wright looked at her watch and then remarked, "Perhaps with a little encouragement from all of us, Miss Simms will solve any problem facing her." With that, the conversation turned to Miss Carson, and some specific questions she wanted to discuss with the supervisor.

Miss Wright waited until the morning intermission before she went into the sixth-grade classroom. She knew she would have an opportunity to talk to Miss Simms alone at that time. When she walked into the room, Miss Simms was sitting at her desk staring into space. She rose hurriedly when she saw Miss Wright, and said, "Oh, I didn't know you were in the building. You really caught me in a mess. My room is so—, I—I'm really not prepared for visitors—I—."

Miss Wright interrupted her gently, "Don't worry about that. If you would rather I didn't stay, I'll just move along to some other classroom. We all have our ups and downs, you know, and I guess I might have caught you in one of your 'down' times. I've been in your classroom several times, you remember, and I know that you are what people call a 'born' teacher."

"That's just it, Miss Wright!" exclaimed Miss Simms. "That's what is causing all my trouble. I'm a 'born' teacher."

"Oh, are you having trouble that is connected with being a born teacher?"

Miss Simms hesitated a moment, and then said in a determined voice, "I haven't said anything to anybody—not even to Joyce (Miss Carson). I have always taken pride in being able to keep personal business to myself. John agreed with me on this point. John is my fiancé, you know. I think I introduced him to you at a P.T.A. meeting, didn't I?"

"Yes, you did. I remember what a fine-looking man he was."

"He is handsome, isn't he? To my way of thinking, he has only one fault, and that is he's very stubborn. His stubbornness plus my being a born teacher are the things causing my trouble. You see, about a month ago John was transferred to South America, and he wanted me to give up my job here to get married and go with him. I didn't feel that I wanted to give up teaching, and we had several heated arguments about it. The night before he left, he told me if I would rather play nursemaid to a bunch of kids the rest of my life than to be his wife, it was all right with him. He would just walk out of my life. And, Miss Wright, (here Miss Simms burst into tears) he did just that! I haven't had one letter from him since he left—just one postcard giving me his address."

"Where in South America is John stationed?" asked Miss Wright.

"Bolivia. I guess there are plenty of new things to see in that country."

"Well, that little postcard is quite valuable, isn't it, Gladys? Perhaps it's John's way of saying, 'I'm waiting to hear from you.' After you received the postcard, did you write to him?"

"No. I didn't know what to say. I have nearly lost my mind the past few weeks trying to decide what to do. It seems that every time I look at the children, I hear John saying, 'Play nursemaid to a bunch of kids the rest of your life,' and it hurts me all over again. I know that he didn't mean it the way it sounded, but I guess it is too late to worry about that now."

At this point Miss Wright noticed that it was nearing the time for the children to return to the classroom. She suggested that they move to the teachers' lounge to continue their discussion. Miss Simms asked Miss Smith, the teacher in the next room, to look after the sixth-graders until she returned. She indicated that the pupils were working on an arithmetic assignment which could be completed.

When they arrived at the lounge, Miss Simms said, "I suppose this sounds awfully silly to you, doesn't it?"

"No, indeed, it doesn't sound silly! You had a very important decision to make. I'm not at all surprised that it upset you. As I see it, you had to decide between a teaching career and marriage. Isn't that about it?"

"Yes, and the trouble is that I want both. Or, at least, I thought I did. I have just about decided that I want John more than I want my job, but I don't know how to tell him."

"You could tell him about it the same way you told me. I'm sure he will be happy to hear the good news, and it won't make a bit of difference to him how you tell it. He is probably having just as rough a time of it emotionally as you are, and, when one is upset emotionally, it affects every part of his life, including his work."

"How well I know that! My heart just hasn't been in my teaching. Even the children know it."

"The children know it better than anyone else, you can be sure of that."

"I'll make it up to them before I leave, Miss Wright. I don't know why I let myself get into such a mess. You know, I've actually been sick. How foolish can one be!"

"Not foolish, my dear,—in this case,—just human."

"I don't know why I told you all of this, Miss Wright. All I do know is that a load has been lifted off my shoulders. If only you could come oftener. I would have probably spilled all of this out much sooner, and saved myself, and poor Mr. Barton, a lot of grief. By the way, Miss Wright, you won't tell Mr. Barton anything about this, will you? I am going to write John right away, and tell him the whole story—how desolate I have been, and, too, how inconsiderate I have been of the 'bunch of kids' he talked about. I am going to ask him if he will wait long enough for me to get my classwork up to standard and for Mr. Davis to find another teacher before I leave for South America. Maybe I could leave at the end of this semester. I want to restore Mr. Barton's faith in me, but I would really feel better if he didn't have to know all about the details. He would probably feel that it was a case of 'much ado about nothing.' And surely you won't tell Mr. Davis, the superintendent. I would never want him to know about my apparent failure this year. I wouldn't want him to know anything about my personal problems; he would think it only weakness. Please don't mention anything about me to the superintendent."

During the years that he had attended college, Jack Larson had been a conscientious, above-average student. He was inclined to be somewhat shy and idealistic. A number of classes stimulated him greatly, but also a number bored him, almost beyond endurance. In his own mind, there had never been much question about his becoming a teacher. For a little he had cherished some illusions about a career in law, but he had later realized that he probably was not personally aggressive enough to be successful in that highly competitive business. And then, he had always felt that teaching afforded one an opportunity to provide real service. He liked this thought. And, finally, the idea of controlling a captive audience also appealed to him. Jack rather fancied himself as a "leader of men" and a "molder of youth."

Now that he was actually a teacher in an American high school, Jack was assailed by doubts. He had experienced difficulty in preparing the appropriate lessons. High school pupils were not, apparently, interested in English. His discipline problems were increasing. Indeed, he had overheard the remark that he had lost control of his classes. Finally, the principal had re-assigned a difficult class, and had suggested that Miss Christensen would spend considerable time with him during the next few weeks. The principal had indicated that Superintendent Davis had suggested that Miss Christensen help Jack in a supervisory capacity. Miss Deborah Christensen, by reason of her seniority and strong personality, had long reigned as "dean" of high school English. She was known in professional associations throughout the state. She commanded the respect and admiration of the professional and layman alike.

Although Jack had graduated from the same school that produced the formidable Deborah (the disrespect was not his own; once graduated, Miss Christensen's students never referred to her by any other name), Jack felt that he didn't really know her. He was familiar enough with the folklore and myths perpetuated in the community, and he reflected that Deborah's students placed high on the university English placement tests. "They had better," Deborah would tell them. Deborah could read the whole of *Hamlet* without recourse to the play lying open on her desk. Deborah's voice was perfectly adequate for all the parts, although she confessed a distaste for the naïve Ophelia. Deborah's classes never had Christmas parties, because she "hated parties." Deborah's tests struck terror into the hearts of even the most conscientious students. Deborah was fond of telling her classes that in her room they were not part of a democracy, but a benevolent autocracy.

Foremost in Jack's mind as he anticipated supervision by Miss Christensen was the question, "How will I make out with her?" In addition to this immediate problem, Jack hadn't been sleeping too well lately, nor did his food seem to agree with him. In fact, something had been definitely wrong with his digestive system ever since he had started teaching.

It was no wonder that Jack appeared flustered and nervous when he walked into Miss Christensen's classroom at the appointed hour. He felt the cynosure of all eyes. He was sufficiently composed, however, to notice that Deborah—Miss Christensen—did not seem as aloof or hostile as he had feared. She seemed somewhat preoccupied, but certainly not hostile.

"Good morning, Jack. I'm happy to work with you. Teaching isn't an easy job, you know. We learn as we grow. Above all, we must professionalize our calling. Now, let me see. You've been having some difficulty in motivating the students. They must be taught the proper use of the English language and a proper respect for our literary giants. This is your free period, isn't it? Why don't you remain in my room during our literature discussion. I'm sure you will pick up some pointers."

Jack thanked her for the encouragement, and quietly took a seat. Strangely enough, he felt exactly like a cadet-teacher approaching the first experience as an observer.

From his position in the back of the room that day, Jack half-heard the discussion of John Milton's *Paradise Lost*. (It was evident that Miss Christensen admired Satan more than any other character in the epic.) The other half of Jack's attention was centered on his own forthcoming class of 11th-grade English. He always anticipated trouble in the 11th grade. The girls with pony-tails were cute, but the boys afforded no end of trouble. Miss Christensen made an as-

signment, and as the class settled down to study, she approached
Jack. Her arms were full of gifts.

"Here are six lesson plans, one supplementary text, and a seating
chart for difficult classes. I no longer use the chart. Study these plans
and see if they will help you. And here is a copy of one of my examinations in literature. (At a later date, Jack took the ten-page examination, and found that he ranked with the "B" group.) Don't hesitate to supply the student with sufficient information and assignments
to keep him busy."

Once again Jack thanked Miss Christensen for her help and advice. Loaded down with "supervisory aids," he trudged out of the
room. Yes, indeed, at times he felt like a school boy again.

Miss Christensen and Jack met several times during the next
month to discuss Jack's role as a teacher and his particular subject-
matter responsibilities. Miss Christensen informed him that all teachers must accept the new philosophy and become pupil-centered. But
they must not forget their responsibility to the subject.

During the month, Jack experienced fewer discipline problems.
He suddenly felt that perhaps he had reached a plateau of semi-suc-
cess. He was covering the material. He was obtaining a measurable
response. Teaching was not as difficult as he had at first experienced.
Miss Christensen visited his room occasionally and always suggested
that "good" teachers never had problems in classroom management.
Her recommendations were always direct. Jack had to admit that
she made teaching sound professional and precise. And yet, he had
some difficulty in utilizing techniques she suggested as the most appropriate to obtain the "best results." Miss Wright, the elementary
program supervisor, had chatted with him on an occasion or two.
She encouraged him, and this always made him feel more successful
than his consultations with Miss Christensen. Well, perhaps he would
be a "molder of men."

His expectations were short-lived. Without any notification, all
semblance of discipline seemed to vanish. Every boy in the 11th grade
was bringing flippers and beans. Open war seemed to have been declared. Students could not concentrate on O. Henry when at any
moment they might receive a mortal wound. The old familiar symptoms returned, and his insides were once more reduced to water.

Only yesterday, Miss Christensen had suggested that he invite

the principal and Mr. Davis, the superintendent, to visit this particular 11th-grade class the next morning. She indicated that she would
try to attend also. Jack would then be able to show the administrators
that he was a successful teacher and, undoubtedly, that the "constructive supervision" he had received had been most helpful.

As Jack prepared to meet the Junior Class the next morning, he
turned to face Miss Christensen and the administrators. He was surprised to find Miss Christensen calm and smiling encouragement to
him. Mr. Davis seemed pleasant but nervous. Jack wondered if the
superintendent would last the hour. The principal seemed tense and
apprehensive about the whole affair. Even the expressions on the students' faces were entirely different. Their eyes seemed to penetrate his
inner thoughts, and their glances indicated that they knew he was
being appraised.

Jack summoned all of his resources to begin a lecture and discussion, but with his first words these resources left him treacherously.
He stumbled, faltered, digressed, retraced, and contradicted himself until he was rescued by the bell fifty minutes later. All of this
happened despite the fact that he had spent considerable time in preparing this particular lesson and had even discussed it with Miss
Christensen.

Mr. Davis had left the room after a few minutes. Mr. Sawyer and
Miss Christensen remained until the end. Surprisingly enough, they
did not criticize his teaching. They seemed sympathetic to the performance, but maintained a definite parental relationship. Mr. Sawyer did not indicate that he wanted to speak with him about his teaching. Jack wondered what they actually thought.

During the next few weeks, Jack labored valiantly, but with
rather diminishing success. His presentations improved, but he remained diffident and unsure of himself before the Junior Class. Conferences with Miss Christensen sometimes helped, sometimes did
not. At first, Jack was encouraged by her positive comments, but later
he hesitated to tell her about half of his problems.

The students, who were orderly and attentive at first, became increasingly difficult. Tardiness to class increased. The attention of
most students was superficial, and even some of the better students
in the class, Jack was sure, went out of their way to "put him on the
spot." Class participation and discussion became almost nil, and

finally, when Jack would ask the question, "Who can explain these lines?" only Mary Kathryn would raise her hand. In desperation, Jack resorted more and more to class assignments and study to control the class. The students seemed happier with this arrangement.

It seemed as if the principal, Miss Christensen, and other faculty members were determined to remain friendly, but Jack often wondered about his situation. Would he continue until the end of the school year? Why was he having trouble? He was a university graduate and was trained as a professional educator. What help should beginning teachers expect from a superintendent of schools, a principal, and older faculty members? Although Miss Wright was an elementary supervisor, could she have helped him more than Miss Christensen? Did he make a mistake in coming back to his home town? If he completed the school year, should he really consider remaining in such a profession?

The Christmas Season was almost upon Mr. Davis before he realized it. Taking care of school-plant planning, the business management of the district, and handling public criticisms took all of his time. He enjoyed the work—he reveled in the challenge the position created. He always felt that he did not have time for personnel problems. And yet, he knew some problems existed in the district. Miss Simms, sixth-grade teacher in the Afton School, wanted to be released from her contract at the end of the semester. He had decided not to allow this. A contract was a contract, after all, and good teachers were hard to find. And then he had been wondering about Jack Larson in the High School. How was he making out? Mr. Sawyer always seemed to avoid talking about Jack. Mr. Sawyer should realize that, in view of his personal interest in Jack, some report should be made now and again on the boy's progress.

Mr. Davis checked his calendar and noted that a principal's meeting was scheduled for December 18. Among other things, he would ask for a full report on the Miss Simms affair and inform Mr. Barton that the board could not release Miss Simms during the school year. Miss Wright could help in supervising her program. And he would tell Mr. Sawyer to afford Jack Larson all the help he needed. The boy must be encouraged to take advantage of the wisdom and professional skills of Miss Christensen and other older teachers in the High School.

Mr. Davis jotted down a few notes as an agenda for the scheduled meeting, then hurriedly locked up his desk. He remembered a meeting with an important and highly recommended architect. The new building program must get under way.

Dr. Cook Survives[1]

In the spring of 1947 what had been a quiet Cincinnati suburb markedly changed its character. In late May, one writer described the community thus:[2] "Outwardly North College Hill is a peaceful community of small homes. Inwardly it is trembling on the verge of an open outbreak of civil strife. Already violence has occurred. . . . Life-long neighbors refuse to speak to one another or to permit their children to associate. Property values are falling sharply, although there is no such slump in communities nearby, and real estate dealers have more houses on their hands than they can sell. People even divide their purchases in accordance with the communal differences, which have split the town in two, and several undeclared boycotts are in force. This splitting apart of an American town has resulted from what the National Education As-

[1] Special appreciation is expressed to Richard Kennan, Secretary of the National Commission for the Defense of Democracy through Education of the National Education Association, for making available the voluminous materials which the Commission collected in its original investigation; the results of this investigation were published under the title *North College Hill, Ohio* (November, 1947) and the present case study has drawn upon the facts contained in the report. Appreciation is also expressed to Henry Butler, legal counsel of the National Commission, for reading and commenting on an earlier draft of the present report. He is not held responsible, of course, for the present content or form of the report.

[2] Harold Fey, "Preview of a Divided America," *The Christian Century,* Vol. LXIV, No. 22, p. 682. Copyright 1947 Christian Century Foundation. Reprinted by permission from The Christian Century.

sociation, after an investigation on the spot, calls 'probably the most serious school situation current in the nation.' "

Citizens began to express serious concern in February 1947, when three out of the five North College Hill School Board members voted not to renew the contract of the superintendent of schools, Dr. William Cook, at its expiration on July 31, 1947. The decision was followed by violent community protest in the form of extended student strikes, disorderly board meetings, riots, and mass resignation of teachers. Feeling became so strong that, on at least one occasion, local policemen had to protect certain board members.

North College Hill's plight had a history that preceded the February decision to discharge Dr. Cook. Many observers saw beginnings of the problems seven years earlier in 1940. During the 1940–1947 period, sharp differences of opinion on educational policy were expressed. These differences were closely related to the religious backgrounds of North College Hill's Catholics and Protestants.

A Problem With a Past

In 1939 North College Hill, with a population of approximately 5,000, was classified as an Exempted Village School District. In 1940 three Protestant and two Catholic school board members voted unanimously to incorporate the St. Margaret Mary Parochial School into North College Hill's public school system. Under the arrangement, the school district agreed to lease the parochial school building for the following two years and to pay the salaries of the Catholic teachers. The name "St. Margaret Mary" was changed to "Public School No. 3." While the newly named school officially operated as a public school, its personnel and curriculum did not change.

Some months after the agreement was effected, the 1940 census showed that North College Hill was large enough to become a city school district. In 1941 North College Hill became a city school district, which necessitated the election of a new school board. The central issue in the spirited election campaign which ensued was whether Public School No. 3 should remain in the public school system. When the decision was first made to incorporate the Catholic school in 1940, there was no clear-cut opposition to the idea. However, a few months later a number of non-Catholic citizens raised objections and began to prepare for the 1941 board election. Their goal was to return the newly incorporated school to its previous status.

At the same time, Catholic citizens organized to preserve the existing arrangements. Letters were sent to Catholic parishioners urging them to vote in the school board election, and a suggested slate of candidates was included. The argument for preserving the status of the newly incorporated school was based essentially on financial benefit. The point was stressed that if the parishioners did not elect the suggested candidates, they would lose the money paid by the Board of Education to the Sisters as salary; second, they would lose the $3,500 received as rental for the school; third, they would lose the $500 paid to the parish by the Sisters as rental for the cottages in which they lived; finally, they would lose the privilege of free textbooks.

The election resulted in a new board of four Protestants and one Catholic. Approximately three months after the election, the new board voted to separate Public School Number 3 from the public school system. Consequently, the agreement with Catholic authorities, which expired in June 1942, was not renewed. Apparently this action was not highly disturbing to the voters, since two Protestants were elected to fill school board vacancies in 1943. During the same year, the superintendent of schools resigned, and Dr. William A. Cook was appointed to fill the vacancy.

Dr. Cook Accepts a New Position

Dr. William A. Cook possessed both thorough training and wide administrative experience. After receiving his Bachelor of Arts degree from the University of Illinois in 1902, he served as principal in three different Illinois high schools. In 1911 he was awarded the Master's degree from the University of Illinois, and two years later the Ph.D degree from the University of Wisconsin. After teaching at the University of Colorado and the University of South Dakota, he accepted a position as Professor of Education at the University of Cincinnati in 1926. He remained there until his appointment as North College Hill School Superintendent in 1943.

Dr. Cook encountered no major difficulty during the first two years of his administration. However, he entered a new phase of his North College Hill career in 1945, when a school board election was held to fill the vacancies of three persons whose terms were expiring.

In the campaign, the central issue was whether to re-incorporate the parochial school into the public school system. An organization called the Citizen's School League supported the Catholic candidates and emphasized the financial benefit to the parish which would accrue from re-incorporation. Not only was the financial relief for Catholics emphasized, but also the fact that all of North College Hill's citizens would benefit from the increased amount of state aid that would become available if the school were re-incorporated into the public school system.

The election resulted in a school board composed of three Catholics and two hold-over Protestants. The majority membership consisted of the board president, a maintenance man for the Bell Telephone Company, the vice-president, an electrician for the Good Samaritan Hospital, and a paper cutter for a local printing company. A purchasing agent for a department of the Procter and Gamble Company and a field superintendent for the Herschede & Hall Clock Company were the minority members. There was no change in board membership until June 1947.

During the latter part of 1945, before officially resuming office, the newly elected majority board members met in the home of Superintendent Cook. At this meeting they agreed informally to re-incorporate the St. Margaret Mary School into the public school system. In a letter written to Dr. W. B. Bliss of the Ohio Education Association dated March 29, 1946, Dr. Cook described the agreement as follows:

> Shortly before taking office the new members came to my home for a long conference, in which they disclaimed any intention to interfere with the existing public school system, but reiterated their desire to secure financial relief in their own school. Learning that the State Department of Education could give us additional aid effective from January 28, the beginning of the first school month after these men took office, I recommended the certificated teachers (eight nuns) of the then parochial school for appointment as public school teachers from the above date. I took no position with reference to their salary, because the new members of the board declared they did not expect to pay them as much as the lay teachers receive. I did secure one lay teacher for that school, to replace a lay teacher there who was not certificated. This additional teacher was placed on our regular salary schedule.

In late January the parochial school building was re-incorporated into the public school system. The arrangements were quite similar to those which were in effect for 1940–1942, except that this time the school was called the Grace Avenue School. Thus, what seemed to have been a major issue in the election campaign was settled amicably. The decision was one of the very few which the school board and Dr. Cook were to resolve harmoniously.

Superintendent Cook Encounters Difficulties

Approximately three months after the new members of the school board took office, the relationship between Superintendent Cook and some of the school board members became noticeably strained. On March 29, 1946, Dr. Cook wrote to Dr. Bliss as follows:

> I observed small sinister signs from time to time, but I continued full co-operation with the new Board and its new secretary, extended the same attention to the newly adopted school as to the other schools, brought its teachers into contact with our local education association, provided them with Every Pupil and other tests, attended regularly all meetings of their PTA, etc. I was most considerately treated by their teachers and PTA.
>
> In early March the president of the board asked me to prepare the list of teachers for next year, so that before the close of the month any necessary action could be taken on termination of contracts, and so that the teachers might know what salary they would receive next year. Thus, he said, our losses could be lessened. With this I heartily agreed.
>
> At a regular meeting shortly afterward I asked the board to set the tuition to be paid by non-residents attending the new school, so that I could better estimate revenue for salary commitments. This the board refused to do, and the president directed me to draw my report on the basis of the salary item in the budget adopted *before* the new school had been brought in. That could have required me to cut salaries several thousand dollars from the present level, because the added teachers had to be included.
>
> I did not conform to this ridiculous request, but shortly placed in the hands of each board member, in preparation for a special meeting, a careful balance sheet covering 1946 and 1947. It recommended an average salary increase of $300 for the lay teachers. I did not touch the nuns' salaries, first because I shall do nothing which can be construed as approval of a double salary schedule, and second, because the president of the board had assured me in January that no increase in the salary of the nuns was contemplated.
>
> When the special meeting was held last Tuesday night, the president presented a counter proposal to mine, advocating an average increase of $150 for the entire staff *including* the nuns. Then fireworks began.

Superintendent Cook was responsible for administering teacher salaries in five schools. There was a high school (9–12), a so-called junior high (4–8), and the Goodman Avenue School (K–3). In addition, there was the Steele School (K–8), which served a section inhabited by Negroes. It was staffed entirely by Negro teachers and only Negro children attended. Apparently the situation existed because of geographical reasons, since the high school freely admitted Negro students. Finally, there was the Grace Avenue School (1–8), previously named the St. Margaret Mary Parochial School. The total population of the school district was slightly less than 8,000, and approximately one-fifth of the inhabitants lived in the Steele subdivision.

About the time that the salary problem arose, another event transpired that placed further strain on superintendent-board relationships. At the March 20 meeting, the majority members approved a motion to remove the incumbent junior high principal. In addition, a motion was adopted to replace the principal with the teacher whom Superintendent Cook had demoted from the principalship the previous spring. Superintendent Cook strongly protested, maintaining that he had a legal right to recommend and assign personnel. His stand was based upon a section in the Ohio General Code, which became effective in September 1943 (Section 4842–6):

> The board of education in each city, exempted village, and local school district shall employ the teachers of the public schools of their respective districts. In making appointments teachers in the employ of the board shall be considered before new teachers are chosen in their stead. In city and exempted village districts, no teacher or principal shall be employed unless such person is nominated therefor by the superintendent of schools of such district; provided, however, such board of education, by a three-fourths vote of its full membership may re-employ any teacher whom the superintendent refuses to appoint.

Superintendent Cook described the interchange on the junior high principalship in the March 29 letter to Dr. Bliss as follows:

> The board then passed 3-1 a motion that the former principal be reassigned to her administrative post. Next they asked me if I would so recommend, and I replied, "I will not." They then wished my reasons for recommending her demotion a year ago. I gave the reasons which satisfied me but which did not satisfy them, for there is evidence they have a campaign debt to pay her. The president stated that the charges against her would be heard at a public meet-

ing. I served notice on him that I would have no part in the unprofessional act of stripping down a teacher's reputation in a public meeting.

Then came the crowning gesture. Because of my refusal to recommend the restoration of the demoted principal, the president suggested that they rule that "The superintendent is insubordinate if he refuses to recommend Miss — for the principalship." I began to write it down, and the minority board member insisted that the secretary of the board "get that wording." The upshot was that one of the majority decided he "could not exactly stand for that," and so it did not come to a vote.

In addition to giving Dr. Bliss a detailed report on the salary and principalship problems in the March 29 letter, Dr. Cook also made a request. He asked that an Ohio Education Association representative attend the school board meeting of April 8: "I think it would be a great service to our teachers and the schools if OEA had a representative here to counsel us at the forthcoming meeting, and to tell some of our small town fellows that 'I represent 42,000 organized teachers of this state, and as their servant I am checking both the professional ethics and the legality of your actions.'" Dr. Cook also invited a representative of the National Education Association, who resided in Cincinnati, to attend the same meeting.

The board meeting of April 8 was well attended. The large attendance and the tenor of the meeting apparently provided Dr. Cook with another idea for coping with the very difficult situation which confronted him. On the following day he wrote to Dr. Bliss: "After sleeping over the matter, I am of the opinion that one way to hold my board in leash is to have about fifty-sixty interested citizens and teachers right there at every board meeting, regular and special, until they have acted on salaries for next year. They were mighty mild when their critics were so well represented, as last night. It will now be up to the friends of decent schools to see that each meeting is well attended. That is not *my* responsibility."

Conditions in the North College Hill School District were further complicated during the spring of 1946, when 13 vacancies in the teaching staff occurred. The board then refused by a three-to-two vote to accept nominations by the superintendent to fill the vacancies. The majority maintained that, until Dr. Cook submitted his applications to the board for review, they would not approve any nominations. The minority members, on the other hand, maintained that the

board did not have the power to take such a position. Dr. Cook agreed
to supply organized information about the candidates but strongly
opposed the idea of the board reviewing the individual applications
of teachers. The president of the board in turn rejected Dr. Cook's
offer to supply information. Finally the board passed a resolution, on
a three-to-two vote, which demanded that Superintendent Cook turn
over the individual applications to the board members.

On May 29 the clerk of the board gave Superintendent Cook a
letter which stated that all applications "must be made available to
the Board for review on this date for consideration in establishing a
salary schedule." Superintendent Cook replied to this letter on June
6 as follows:

> Referring to a letter of May 29 calling attention to a certain
> resolution, wherein applications for teaching positions are requested,
> for consideration in establishing a salary schedule:
>   (1) Since names of applicants are submitted to a considerable
>   degree in confidence, and
>   (2) Since these are personal memoranda of mine, and
>   (3) Since legal counsel informs me that there is no compulsion
>   to reveal names before I recommend individuals for em-
>   ployment,
> I am submitting on an accompanying sheet (copy herewith) in
> concise form all other data, to assist in setting a salary schedule, in
> compliance with the above letter.

An earlier analysis by Dr. Cook of the alternatives open to him
with respect to this problem was contained in a letter of May 21,
1946, written to Dr. Bliss of the Ohio Education Association:

> Two problems soon will demand a decision here. Suppose my
> recommendations are rejected as to personnel. My reaction is to
> offer a second recommendation for a specific position if one is re-
> jected, then possibly a third if the second is rejected, and then to
> sit tight indefinitely. At what point, if at all, should I ask the board to
> explain its rejection of my recommendations?
>   The other question concerns the request which is surely coming,
> to enter my file of applicants. I assume the purpose of such an ex-
> amination is (1) to enable the board to pick its candidate if not al-
> ready selected in rump meetings of the board, and (2) to ask my
> reason for not picking each of those not recommended. My reaction
> is that this is *my* file; it contains applications sent to me and not to
> the board. Therefore I may lean backwards to permit a board mem-
> ber to go through it, but it must not be taken away from the office.
> I wish to have it there for purposes of consultation.

Both the majority board members and Dr. Cook remained firm in their positions on the review of candidates' applications throughout the spring and during the early summer. The only exception to this policy was the employment of two athletic coaches. Both parties maintained that their positions were legally justified, as is shown by an analysis of the legal aspects of the situation in a report by the National Commission for the Defense of Democracy through Education as follows:

> The legal contention of the board majority was that under the Ohio General Code a board of education could require a superintendent to submit all applications to the board for review and an opinion to this effect was secured from local counsel. It is not proposed here to enter an extended legal discussion of the matter. The Ohio courts have not passed on the question, nor has the attorney-general. Whether the opinion in question would be upheld by the Ohio courts on the facts presented in this case is, to say the least, a moot question. It may well be that under certain circumstances and conditions a board of education may properly request a review of applications. The validity of the request, if tested, would probably turn in part at least on the motive and purpose of the board. It is doubtful if the Ohio legislature intended, for example, that a board could review applications for the sole purpose of selecting certain candidates on a basis of considerations other than merit. To so hold would in effect deprive a superintendent of his nominating power and would under such circumstances make the pertinent provisions of section 4842–6 of the General Code a hollow gesture.

Temporary Solutions Achieved

The stalemate on the review of applications was not resolved until late summer. The minutes of the August 12 board meeting, for example, show the following exchange:

> Discussion on hiring teachers came up, the audience taking an active part in the discussion.
> Mr. —— said the superintendent has the power to recommend. . . .
> Mr. —— read from the law book concerning hiring of teachers furnishing the superintendent power to recommend. Mr. —— asking when did the board ever deny the superintendent the right to "recommend."
> Mr. —— continues and charges that Mr. —— is a one man board, he has refused Dr. Cook the privilege of opening the mail and drawing up annual budget without consulting the board.

President ——: I am going to give you a true picture of the situation. I have charged Dr. Cook with insubordination. Mr. —— read report of his own making charges of irregularities.

Three weeks before school opened, owing to mounting public pressures, one of the majority members switched his vote to the minority. The switch resulted in a three-to-two vote in favor of filling the teaching positions. However, only 11 of the 13 vacancies were filled. A music position and a kindergarten position were left vacant. Since the problem of the junior high school principalship was never satisfactorily resolved, Dr. Cook served as principal of the school during the year 1946–1947.

Owing to the extremely strained relationships between Superintendent Cook and the majority of the school board, many persons during the fall of 1946 began to question whether the superintendent's contract would be renewed. That Superintendent Cook recognized the tenuousness of his position as superintendent is suggested in a paragraph of a letter which he had written to Dr. Bliss on July 26, 1946: "No stenographic record has been kept of any board meeting, but with the assistance of the minority I am preparing a catalog of possible illustrations of misfeasance, malfeasance, and non-feasance. We have an early appointment with our attorney to put them in form, and have him evaluate them, for the purpose of bringing charges against the president of the board. Sooner or later charges will be brought against me, and some of our leaders feel that we should beat them to it. If you have any suggestions or information as to procedure, we should be most happy to have it now."

However, a letter written to Dr. Bliss on September 28 suggests that Superintendent Cook had changed his strategy:

It is two months to a day since I wrote you. In the interim, we have had a very large and belligerent regular meeting in August, with 175 people present, and another for September with about 240 in attendance. The crowd is over 90 per cent completely antagonistic to the president of the board. . . .

On legal advice we have decided not to attempt removal proceedings against the President of the Board. The alternative adopted is the heat of public opinion, as evidenced by the large attendance at the meetings. Even at a special meeting two weeks ago over 60 were present. Perhaps this will work *if* kept up. Certainly in the bitter discussions it is the one man against the crowd, his colleagues keeping quiet.

In a letter written to Dr. Bliss on January 17, 1947, Superintendent Cook again noted that popular indignation was running high and that the board meetings were large and disorderly. He also foresaw the possibility of student strikes and the mass resignation of teachers in case his contract should not be renewed. In addition, he noted that local pressure might be supplemented by an expression of outside interest in the situation. In this regard, he reported that he had written to Donald DuShane of the National Commission for the Defense of Democracy through Education about the matter, and he suggested that the Ohio Education Association might look at the situation again. The uniqueness of Superintendent Cook's strategy is suggested by the following quote from the January 17 letter:

> In fact, it seems to me that our state association might investigate the first case of reprisal, and if our board is found guilty, proper publicity should be given that fact in *Ohio Schools,* following the technique of the American Association of University Professors. I am aware that would be a large responsibility and in some ways may be a new field of action. . . .

Superintendent Cook Dismissed

At the February meeting, the majority of the board decided to give notice that they would not renew Dr. Cook's contract. The minority board members were allowed only ten minutes to make their case. Afterwards, by a vote of three to two, Superintendent Cook's position was declared open after July 31, 1947. The incumbent was charged with "insubordination." On February 20, two days after the board meeting, Dr. Cook wrote Dr. Bliss saying: "The board assumed to pass a resolution giving me notice of intent not to renew contract, while a minority member had the floor defending me. Legal test of this will at once be instituted, since this board has no rule limiting debate. . ."

The community reacted quickly to the board's resolution. A protest in the form of a petition was circulated among the teachers of the North College Hill Teachers Association. All except three of the 32 teachers in the Goodman Avenue School, the high school, and the junior high school signed the petition within 24 hours. It read as follows:

To the North College Hill Board of Education: We the undersigned protest the action of the Board of Education in its attempt to
dismiss our present superintendent, Dr. William A. Cook. We consider this action a threat to our personal security and welfare and
to the good administration of the North College Hill Schools. If
the board persists in this attempt, we will take further action.

Teachers at the Grace Avenue School and at the Steele School
did not sign the petition. According to reports, teachers in the Steele
School did not sign the petition because they allegedly construed the
last sentence in the petition as a threat.

The day after the board meeting, a group of high school students called on Dr. Cook and the high school principal and reported
a widespread desire among students for a protest strike. Dr. Cook
persuaded them to forego their immediate plans. Nevertheless, during the next month additional efforts were made to achieve a student
strike. However, widely organized efforts to promote a strike did not
develop. A different type of action occurred before the next school
board meeting: three-fourths of the student body at the high school
signed a petition requesting that the board renew Superintendent
Cook's contract.

A similar petition, which was circulated among the citizens of
the community, obtained 1,100 signatures. This petition, which was
presented to the board at the March meeting, read as follows:

As citizens of North College Hill, Ohio, who are vitally interested
in the welfare of the school system which you have been elected to
supervise, we, the undersigned, wish to express our satisfaction with
the manner in which the school system has been administered by
the present Superintendent of Schools, Dr. William Cook. We
further wish to express the urgent wish that your honorable body
will retain the services of Dr. Cook as superintendent as long as he
is available and willing to serve.

On March 18 the majority of the board, at a regular meeting, refused to reconsider the dismissal of Superintendent Cook. This
action again precipitated strong community reaction. The next day,
more than 90 per cent of the high school, junior high school, and
Goodman Avenue School students struck. The strike at the high
school lasted for four weeks. It finally ended through the efforts of a
staff representative of the National Commission for the Defense of
Democracy through Education, who persuaded the students that
their strike had already served its purpose of protest. Some 400 ele-

mentary school students remained out of class for more than two months. Extensive picketing took place daily. Undoubtedly there was parent support for the students' actions. During the strikes, Superintendent Cook stayed at his post and teachers instructed the few students who did come to classes.

Much of the parent and student reaction was undoubtedly influenced by an organization in North College Hill called the Schools Improvement Association. The 1947 report of the National Commission for the Defense of Democracy through Education described the organization and its work as follows:

> Prior to 1946 it had been the practice of a small group of citizens to meet informally on occasion to consider problems affecting the welfare of the local school system. However, early in that year, when the trend of the majority board policy became apparent, a group of leading citizens organized themselves formally and founded the Schools Improvement Association. Beginning with less than thirty citizens the association now has a membership of more than four hundred.
>
> The association vigorously fought the majority board members in their attempt to reinstate Miss ―― to her former position as principal and in their prolonged refusal to appoint teachers in the summer of 1946. It also strongly supported a proposal to increase teachers' salaries. Following the board's action against Dr. Cook, the association took an active part in enlisting community support for him by circulating petitions and by urging all citizens to attend board meetings. Due to a considerable extent to the Improvement Association's efforts, the citizens of the community became thoroughly aroused over the policies and actions of the board.

When the board refused to consider renewing Dr. Cook's contract, almost all of the teachers decided to resign. The resignations were attended with this statement from the President of the North College Hill Teachers Association:

> Having seen how the board has acted in connection with efforts to control nomination of teachers, culminating in Dr. Cook's dismissal, the teachers felt these actions by the board to be a direct threat to their personal security and professional status. Furthermore, we regard the proposed reinstatement of Miss ―― ――, a former principal, demoted on recommendation of the school superintendent for cause, as an indication of an utter disregard of the prerogatives of the superintendent and of professional standards.

In addition to the influential forces operating within North College Hill, decisions were being made outside the situation which were to have their effects. On March 2, 1946, the National Commission for the Defense of Democracy through Education met in Atlantic City to discuss the North College Hill case. They decided that the urgency of the situation was such that an investigating committee could not be convened soon enough to meet the requirements of the emergency. Therefore, they decided that a staff investigation should be conducted.

Late in March, representatives of the North College Hill Teachers Association, the Ohio Education Association, and the Defense Commission of the National Education Association met. As a result of their discussion, the representatives proposed that the executive committees of the National Education Association and the Ohio Education Association jointly declare the North College Hill system "one in which no professional teacher can carry on his work efficiently and happily."

The Climax Comes

The April school board meeting convened in an emotionally charged atmosphere. One writer described the meeting as follows:[3]

> Both the Schools Improvement Association, which supported the Protestant minority on the board, and the Citizens School League, which supported the Catholic majority, had urged citizens to attend. They came, over 1,000 in number, crowding a school gymnasium. First an attempt was made by a member of the minority to present more petitions in support of the superintendent and to move reconsideration of his dismissal. This failed. Then the secretary of the board read, one by one, letters of resignation from 29 of 33 teachers in the system. The cumulative effect of these letters on the impressionable students produced an amazing scene.
>
> When they realized what was happening, all over the room these youngsters began to cry. By the time the last letter was read, literally hundreds of people, students and their parents, were in tears. One man who was present told me that not 200 people in the room were dry-eyed, and he said the only way he kept control of himself was by leaving the room. "I never saw anything like it," Superintendent Cook said to me. "I have seen children cheer for their schools and work for their schools, but I never before saw hundreds of children cry for their schools." At the end of the reading, a

[3] Harold Fey, "Preview of a Divided America," *The Christian Century,* Vol. LXIV, No. 22, p. 683–84. Copyright 1947 Christian Century Foundation. Reprinted by permission from The Christian Century.

minority member once more attempted to get the superintendent reinstated as the only way the teachers could be retained. This failed and a majority member stood and said, according to the report given me, "Well, now I hope you understand that Dr. Cook is not going to be your superintendent any longer."

This was too much for one citizen, who jumped to his feet. "How can you be so heartless?" he cried. "Don't you see how much these children care? Can't you see their tears?"

Under such inflammatory circumstances, emotions got out of control. Members of the audience approached the school board member and a fracas resulted. Others became involved, and the police had to intervene. The meeting closed without any formal adjournment. Two of the majority members were physically harmed and one required medical attention.

Approximately one month after the April school board meeting, the executive committees of the National Education Association and the Ohio Education Association released a joint statement, which concluded as follows:

> 1. We declare that the attitude and actions of the three majority members of the Board of Education of North College Hill, Ohio make that school system one in which no professional teacher can carry on his work efficiently and happily.
> 2. We call upon all worthy members of the teaching profession to refuse to accept a position in the North College Hill School System as long as it remains under the domination of the present Board of Education majority and until it is clearly evident that it is under the administration of a board of eduction that observes its primary responsibility for the public schools of the community.
> 3. We urge that school administrators give preference to applications for positions to the teachers from North College Hill who have set such a fine example of high professional conduct.

The statement also included ten specific charges against the three majority members of the school board. Among other things, the three board members were charged with ignoring the protests of the majority of students and parents in North College Hill, and of interfering with the efforts of the citizens of the community to solve educational problems. The statement also contained commendations for the minority members of the Board and the many citizens and parents of North College Hill for their support of the public schools. While the strikes were deplored, the students were

commended for their support of Superintendent Cook. Finally, the
North College Hill Teachers Association was congratulated for its
"professional unity, strength, and integrity."

In a delayed reaction to the joint statement by the executive
committees of the National Education Association and the Ohio
Education Association, the Chairman of the Citizen's School League
in North College Hill wrote a letter on January 10, 1948, to the National Commission for the Defense of Democracy which said in part:

> We find it hard to believe that a group professing the noble
> aims and purposes such as yours professes, would deliberately adopt
> and employ tactics such as you so ingloriously exercised at the North
> College Hill School dispute. . . .
> We cannot help but question your motives in so viciously con-
> demning three former board members, whom (sic) investigation will
> prove have been as fair and conscientious in their relations with the
> teaching personnel as any member who has ever had the privilege of
> serving in the North College High School System.

Shortly after the joint statement of the NEA and the Ohio Education Association was issued, the five members of the board resigned.
The move was welcomed by the minority members, who had offered
to resign if the majority members would take the same action. Undoubtedly the majority members were influenced in their decision by
the great difficulty which they were having in securing a competent
superintendent and a staff of 29 teachers. In line with Ohio legal provisions, the school district came under the control of the probate court
when the school board resigned. The court immediately renewed Dr.
Cook's contract for a three-year period. Shortly thereafter the Ohio
Education Association and the National Education Association withdrew their statements about the undesirable professional situation in
North College Hill. In looking back on his experiences in North College Hill from the vantage point of 1956, Dr. Cook in a letter to one of
the authors of this case wrote:

> It was a high landmark in my little life when NEA and OEA
> issued their joint statement in the spring of 1947, declaring North
> College Hill an "unfair" place for a professional person to seek em-
> ployment. For professional organizations in service to their member-
> ship, I feel this was a precedent of great importance in the history of
> American education. . . .
> The only alternative was to fight singlehanded. As I look back

now, it seems to me that we used on the opposition about every weapon possible. For the most part I refrained from making statements as to my projected course. I gave a corrective statement to one Cincinnati newspaper which had been guilty of very misleading publicity. With the large attendance at board meetings, this gave me the best opportunity to strike. This I would do whenever the majority of the board left an opening. . . .

Because throughout the many trying months I felt up to the last that I would lose, I had taken steps to secure another position, and had been successful in locating nicely in a fine denominational college. When the NCH board all resigned in June, 1947, under tremendous public pressure, my first reaction was to go on to the college job. Friends dissuaded me. Had I gone, other professionals would have said, "He fought them and whipped them, but they cut his throat." Instead I remained, and they could say, "He fought them, whipped them, and lived to tell the story. What he did, others too can do."

CASE THIRTEEN

The Rotating Librarian

At the end of the day, the administrator can close the door on problems of maintenance, finance, and curriculum; but those problems that deal with human relationships somehow manage to get in the car and ride home with him. Consequently, he must learn to live with inter-staff problems on and off the job, and these problems often give him his most uneasy moments.

Sometimes these problems flare up suddenly and just as quickly subside. At other times they come in so unobtrusively that the situation is well developed before the problem is recognized. In the case of the "Rotating Librarian," Mr. Evans, a young principal in his fourth year of elementary administration, saw the problem coming. It was never a big situation, and only four persons beside himself were ever involved. But it was one of those headaches of the migraine type—the kind that you cannot shake off.

Appointment of the District Librarian

The problem began when the district decided to assign a librarian for one-half day per week to each of its elementary schools. Up until this time each school had handled this duty in its own way, and in several of the schools the library was rather a nebulous thing. Mr. Evans's school, Belmont, however, was fortunate in having Mrs. Danner, a sixth-grade teacher who took great interest and pride in the library and who had for eight years managed it successfully. In so doing she had, in addition to the two assigned periods per week, given much of her own time and effort. There was no doubt in Mr. Evans's mind that she identified herself very strongly with the library.

After the part-time librarian service was officially approved, Mr. Hall, the district superintendent, called a meeting of the elementary principals. At this session the functions of the new librarian were discussed at great length. It became evident, however, that there was a great difference in library organizations and needs among the different schools. The superintendent concluded that each principal would have to evaluate his own particular situation and use the new librarian to the best advantage.

After the meeting, Mr. Evans stayed to talk to Superintendent Hall about his own particular situation. He didn't want to predict trouble, yet he anticipated some difficulties in initiating the program in his own school. He wondered how his teacher-librarian, Mrs. Danner, and the rotating librarian would get along in sharing the library responsibilities. Although he did not mention it to the superintendent, he was thinking of a remark by Mrs. Danner to the effect that only one person could ever be in charge of the library. This comment was made at a time when the rotating library service was only in the discussion stage. But the firmness of her statement stuck in his mind.

Soon after he met with the principals, Superintendent Hall arranged for them to meet with the librarian. At this session, which Mr. Evans attended, Miss Carpenter, the new rotating librarian for his school, gave a detailed picture of the program she hoped to bring to the four elementary schools to which she was assigned.

Evans was familiar with some of her background, for she had

been a teacher in a junior high in that district for the past 13 years. She was well liked and respected by her students and was considered successful by her fellow teachers. She devoted endless amounts of time to her school work and particularly to the library. In fact, she customarily came to work a week early and rearranged the library in her school without compensation.

Her previous assignment had been one of teaching seventh- and eighth-grade English classes one half-day and maintaining the library during the other half-day. Her new assignment would be to continue working in the junior high library one-half of her time and to spend the remaining time rotating among the four elementary schools' libraries.

She seemed to Evans to be a forceful, outspoken woman. Her tall, large frame and commanding voice would make it easy to locate her in a crowd. The preciseness of the organization of her materials and the manner in which she used her hands while speaking gave Evans the feeling that she had everything under control.

Miss Carpenter explained the system they used at the junior high school. Several times it was pointed out to her by the principals that there was more organization at the junior high school level than on the elementary school level, and that it was questionable whether some of this would be applicable to the latter. Miss Carpenter said, "I can't answer that, as I have never worked on an elementary level. I will explain the program I am now using, and then with your help we can determine what is applicable to the elementary grades."

Before anyone realized it, two hours had gone by and they were still discussing the junior high school program. It was then decided that the principals could discuss their own particular situation with Miss Carpenter when she came to their buildings. Once again a statement of the specific functions of the librarian had been postponed.

Mr. Evans deliberately stayed after the meeting to talk to Miss Carpenter. He explained how the library in his school operated and added that it was in better condition than the other libraries in the district. This, he said, was entirely due to Mrs. Danner's efforts. Miss Carpenter said that she had an opportunity to attend meetings at the Belmont School Library from time to time and was impressed with the organization, and she also felt that it was in much better condition than any of the other libraries. "I only wish that the other libraries were as far along as yours is," said Miss Carpenter.

Evans said, "I would like for Mrs. Danner to help us formulate plans and be consulted before any changes are made. She has been very capable and interested in the library and has practically run it for the past eight years. Also, she is much more familiar with the details than I am." He didn't know what Miss Carpenter's reaction would be to this arrangement, but was relieved when she said, "I understand your concern for wanting Mrs. Danner included and I will be happy to do anything I can to co-operate."

Mrs. Danner, the Belmont teacher-librarian, an attractive woman in her mid-fifties, was an excellent teacher with a good background in elementary education. She was a reserved, poised woman who had the respect of all her associates and the community. Although she was quiet and never tried to draw self-recognition, she was still looked upon by fellow teachers as a leader. She had a bachelor of science degree and considerable extra training in library work.

Mrs. Danner had been at Belmont 12 years. Before that, she had taught in one of the other schools in the district and had acted as teacher-librarian. There she had what was generally recognized as one of the best-organized libraries in the district. She had been a widow for the past eight years and had given freely of her time to school work and the profession. As mentioned earlier, her present position was teaching sixth grade and taking care of the library.

Mr. Evans relied quite heavily on her, not only as a librarian, but in all phases of the school program. She acted as assistant principal in his absence, as she had done for the two previous administrators. This responsibility was discharged without additional compensation.

Making Plans

When Miss Carpenter made her first visit to Belmont School, Mr. Evans told her to spend as much time as she needed to familiarize herself with the library. He suggested she make notes on things she felt needed attention and also prepare recommendations for future planning.

The same afternoon, Mr. Evans talked to Mrs. Danner about the library, explaining that he would like her recommendations for improving the library in view of the added help.

At that time Mrs. Danner said, "I can't see where we are getting much help if Miss Carpenter will only be in the building one half-day per week. You know, very little can be accomplished in this short period of time."

She also made the remark, half in jest, that she wished that, in place of the additional service, they could have the extra money for more reference books. Mr. Evans felt slightly uncomfortable about this remark. He didn't feel it fair to Miss Carpenter to have to contend with this attitude. He wanted to say something but he remembered that it was only recently that he had had to prove himself to this same person when he moved up to principalship from a sixth-grade teaching position at Belmont.

Two weeks later, Evans met with the librarians and each person expressed his ideas about future plans for the library. Mrs. Danner voiced a desire to continue with the day-to-day operation of the library. This involved working with student librarians who checked books in and out to their own rooms, keeping track of books, collecting fines, shelving books that were checked in, and handling periodicals. She said, "I would like to have some help processing new and rebound books or turn it over to you, Miss Carpenter. Also, I would like to have some help mending books. As you know, this job takes hours of work and always demands more time."

There was no comment when Mrs. Danner finished talking. Evans had hoped there would be some discussion on what she had said. From time to time Evans glanced at Miss Carpenter while Mrs. Danner was speaking. He saw no signs of approval or disapproval. Miss Carpenter sat very straight and emotionless. It appeared she heard very little of what had been said or at least felt it wasn't worth commenting on. Evans had the uncomfortable feeling that here were two people with their minds firmly made up.

When Miss Carpenter began to talk, it was in a very formal and dignified manner. "I also feel that the processing of books is most important," she said, "and I will be glad to do this. I do think, though, that we should have more information than just the Dewey decimal number on the outside of the books. The other things I have listed that I feel are important for us to be doing are: use more cross-reference cards; set up, in addition to the author and subject files, a title and shelf list file; classify the film strips under the Dewey decimal system; buy a larger card file cabinet; start a picture file; and have more attractive displays in the library."

Miss Carpenter went through this list in a very matter-of-fact manner, as though she were reading a grocery list. There were no stipulations as to how long she thought it would take or which things she thought were the most important to do.

Perhaps Miss Carpenter did not notice the irritated and amazed expressions on Mrs. Danner's face when she read this. Mr. Evans expected Mrs. Danner to make some comment about who was going to do all this, but there was only a moment of awkward silence.

Mr. Evans pushed his chair back from the table and felt he must change the atmosphere of the meeting. He reviewed the library program in general and made several attempts to draw the two librarians into a discussion, hoping to eventually reach some form of agreement. However, neither person contributed to the discussion beyond their initial recommendations. After some time it became obvious there was going to be no meeting of minds at this session. Evans knew that he was going to have to strike a happy medium in order to please either one. Finally he made the decision that Miss Carpenter would process all new library books, add additional information she felt necessary, take care of displays and the bulletin board in the library, transfer cards from the old file cabinet to the new one, mend books once a month, and, when these items were completed, start work on a subject index file.

Mrs. Danner was to be relieved of processing all books. Otherwise, she was to continue taking care of the daily operation of the library as she had previously.

When the meeting was over, Evans felt that each person was just as formal at the end as when the meeting began.

Complications

Miss Carpenter's half-day period was set for Wednesday afternoon. In the early weeks she developed a habit of arriving at 12:30 and of discussing and reviewing library problems with Mr. Evans when he returned to his office from lunch. She usually discussed discrepancies she had noted in the library and reviewed what she thought needed to be done. Evans listened, but was not certain why she wanted to go over and over what had been discussed previously. He did notice that each time she indicated her dislike for mending books. It did not seem so much a matter of reviewing as it was getting Evans to listen. Miss Carpenter usually did most of the talking and, when Evans did speak, he wasn't sure he was being heard.

Finally, after two months of reviewing library problems each Wednesday with Miss Carpenter, Evans decided it would be more convenient to eat a little later and avoid the office until she had become involved in her work. Since the discussions usually took 45 minutes, Evans felt that there were many times when he did not have that much time to spare.

Evans also noted that Miss Carpenter frequently became upset when her plans were not accurately executed. The district carpenter, for example, made a new file cabinet, but when it arrived, each drawer was one-eighth inch too small for the cards. Evans could see that this upset Miss Carpenter very much. She tried to fit some cards into the file. Finally she turned to Evans with tears in her eyes and said, "I can't understand it. This is the second time the carpenter has made this mistake."

Evans noted that other things were disturbing her. She said that the secretary was having difficulty following directions she left for her, and asked that the secretary work in the afternoons the day she was there. The secretary was on duty only in the morning. Evans could see that this was important to Miss Carpenter, and had the secretary change her schedule temporarily.

Soon after this, the secretary went to Evans and said she was finding it difficult to work with Miss Carpenter and Mrs. Danner. Evans knew the situation must be serious if the secretary wanted to talk about it. He felt that one of her good qualities was her ability to work with people.

The secretary said that Miss Carpenter had told her to mark biography books, but Mrs. Danner had come in and stated that it wasn't the way it had been done in the past. The secretary pointed out that this was only one of many disagreements they had on how to do detail work, and said, "I don't know who to turn to."

When Evans talked to Mrs. Danner about the situation, she said, "Perhaps Miss Carpenter's suggestion on how to mark biography books is desirable, but is it a must? After all, there are many things that are desirable in library procedure. This is an elementary school and I question whether we want to get into too much detail. You realize, if we mark the new books differently, we will have to pull all the old biographies on the shelf and change them. Personally, I would like to see for myself what procedure is recommended for the elementary grades."

Evans said, "Just a minute, I will call the city library and see what procedure they use." He found there were several ways to mark biography books.

Mrs. Danner said, "If we are going to change, and there are several methods to select from, I would like to see in writing just which procedure is recommended for the elementary grades." Evans was disturbed by her insistence on "proof in writing" but felt that it wasn't an unreasonable request.

He called Miss Carpenter and explained the difficulties he had encountered. He said, "I am lacking in library experience and would appreciate it if you would bring some of your professional books explaining library procedure for the elementary grades so that we can see to what extent we should mark our books."

He could not determine from the sound of her voice what her reaction to the request was, although she acknowledged it.

The Conferences

When Evans returned from lunch, Miss Carpenter was in his office with several books to substantiate her method of marking biography books. He explained that he might ask her for information or reference material about library procedure from time to time, for he wanted to learn as they went along. He also observed that it was much more difficult to talk to her now than ever before.

Finally he asked her how she felt she was coming along with the library.

"Frankly," she said, "I feel like I have been wasting much of my time. The past few months I could have been working on a subject index file instead of mending books once a month. Also, I feel the library bulletin board should become the responsibility of all the teachers and not just mine."

Evans replied, "Well, for the time being just let the mending go." Before the meeting was over, he assured Miss Carpenter that her efforts and suggestions were bringing about a definite improvement in the library. He added, though, that she needed to be patient.

"You came from the junior high school which is the same size as this school, but they have a full-time secretary and you could get more accomplished with her help. You must remember our secretary is here on only a half-time basis. The things you are attempting to do may take two or three years to accomplish, and you shouldn't become discouraged. When you came, everyone was under the impression that the library work would decrease, but actually it has increased."

He pointed out that under the new system it was taking from three to four times as long to process books as it had before.

After the meeting Evans sat staring out the window. He felt that this was the first time that Miss Carpenter and he had had an understanding. Was it something he had said, or was it the fact that she would no longer be mending books?

＊   ＊   ＊

Superintendent Hall came to the school a few days later to have lunch with Mr. Evans. They discussed some school problems. Finally Superintendent Hall asked, "How is the new library program coming along?" Evans thought it rather odd that he would ask about the program at this time.

"Frankly, not so good. Have you talked to Miss Carpenter lately?" asked Mr. Evans.

"Yes," replied Hall, "I have. She came to my office the other afternoon very much upset and said she felt her competency was being questioned here at Belmont."

"Yes, I suppose you could say her competency in social skills and getting along with other members of the school could be easily questioned from what I have seen. Also, I think there is evidence to question the practicality of her library work. I feel she knows her material and is following the procedure to the letter very well, but on the other hand there are accepted elementary library procedures which do not require so much detail and time."

Mr. Evans continued, "I feel there is more to this problem than questioning Miss Carpenter's competency. As I explained to you before, Mrs. Danner and Miss Carpenter are both somewhat inflexible personalities and they need time to get accustomed to sharing the same responsibility. Mrs. Danner has been very reluctant to turn over so much of the responsibility to Miss Carpenter, and in return Miss

Carpenter has been disturbed because she wasn't in complete charge."

"Yes," replied Mr. Hall, "she did say that all other schools had turned the complete responsibility of the library over to her, except Belmont."

"You see," said Mr. Evans, "Mrs. Danner ran the library very efficiently for a long time and still does most of the work. From the beginning she didn't think we needed a librarian, and Miss Carpenter hasn't helped to 'sell' her program. I want Mrs. Danner to have a voice in what is done in the library. After all, she could become discouraged and ask me to assign the responsibility of the library to another teacher. There isn't another teacher on the faculty who could take care of the library as well as Mrs. Danner, nor is there anyone who wants the job."

Mr. Evans reviewed the conference that he had had with Miss Carpenter and what had been worked out. Superintendent Hall said, "I am glad Miss Carpenter was taken off mending, for the program is too expensive to justify this. I think you have done everything that can possibly be done, and I am in complete sympathy with your situation."

The following day Evans discussed the recent developments with Mrs. Danner. He explained that, in the light of Miss Carpenter's success in the other school libraries, they must do something to correct their own situation. He told her that he had counted upon her support and was relieved when she said she felt above the situation and would give him her complete support to correct the problem.

When budget-making time arrived, Miss Carpenter submitted a library order to Mr. Evans with the explanation, "We had these at the junior high and I feel they are necessary for up-grading the elementary library program." Evans studied the order and found it to be seven times larger than any order of previous years. Since no limit had been set on materials for this new department, he decided to call the Superintendent before making any disposition.

Superintendent Hall replied that he would like to see the items and talk to the librarian before making a decision. He asked Miss Carpenter to compile her library order and submit it directly to him. Later, upon receiving this, he called her in and explained that her library order had to be cut by at least one-half. This apparently settled the issue and, as the end of the year approached and preparations were made for closing school, the librarian issue seemed temporarily to subside.

When the year was over, Evans, in reflecting on the issue, did not feel that the problem had been solved. In addition, he knew that the intervening summer would not change the basic personality patterns of Miss Carpenter and Mrs. Danner. However, he hoped that each, in being removed from the scene of the conflict, would have an opportunity to look back and gain a little more perspective on their mutual problem. As he locked the school for the summer and stepped into his car, his special rider seemed a little less conspicuous.

CASE FOURTEEN

The Case of a Tenacious Superintendent

John Ash—forceful, forward-looking, well-prepared as a professional educator—assumed his new position as superintendent of Brashtown's schools with confidence and enthusiasm. He came with a state and region-wide record as an able, progressive administrator. A man of high professional ideals, he was soon to become an integral part of both school and community life, readily accepting leadership responsibilities inherent in his professional and civic environment.

Brashtown, a southern city, was characterized by a sort of restless uncertainty; underlying this uncertainty was a peculiar paradox of conservatism on the one hand and progressivism on the other. Reflected were the values which today, to a less or greater extent, still oppose each other in various parts of the South—namely, preservation of the *status quo* in one instance, and acceptance of industrial and social change in the other.

This lack of stability was reflected in many aspects of community life. Cultural change within was reflected by threatened shifts in power structure. The social and "control" positions of "wealthy" merchants, "landed gentry," and "established" professional people were being challenged by the rise of industrial capitalism, which accompanied the large-scale movement of industry into the city of Brashtown and the surrounding territory.

Within Brashtown, as never before, nonmaterial aspects of the culture were being changed as artificial barriers were being challenged and broken down by rapid advances in modes of transportation and communication, as well as by rapid population changes. For some time, manufacturing had been replacing mining, lumbering, and the production and marketing of farm products as the principal source of livelihood and as a major source of wealth.

Such well-established composites of the culture as the city-management form of government and boards of education appointed by city councils were being subjected to open criticism with respect to their appropriateness and effectiveness. The concept of a ruling class limited to property owners and wealthy citizens was being challenged by a new proletariat demanding a voice in the conduct of municipal affairs.

Shifts in values were not evolving easily or rapidly, however. Cultural innovations that departed from familiar concepts and patterns were viewed with suspicion and alarm by controlling forces within the community. Change in the social structure was viewed as a threat not only to personal and group status, but to vested interests as well.

As John Ash, the new superintendent, began to identify himself with organized groups in the community, a rather distinct cleavage in community forces became more and more apparent to him. As he later said, "I could sense the struggle between the 'old' and 'new' in this community. I felt a rather strong sense of identification with the 'new' group, yet a sense of restraint as a result of my feeling of responsibility to the 'old' power structure."

Not only did Ash perceive change and resistance to change as characteristic of the social milieu in which he found himself; he was caught up in the struggle. He perceived the existence of the centrifugal forces seeking to produce change, as well as those centripetal ones resisting it. In spite of the sense of personal identification with the former that he was experiencing, he saw that positive identification with one group might provide him with a feeling of professional fulfillment and personal satisfaction at the expense of security and companionship with the more conservative element that, to date, had retained the upper hand in the struggle that was taking place.

Ash had become convinced that "stagnation and intolerance bred of vested interest" was a characteristic of the more conservative group to which he was indebted for bringing him to Brashtown. He was certain that the best interest of the school and community would be served if this conservative element either relinquished control or gave voice to groups more responsive to the progressive values that were beginning to make themselves felt.

At this point, Ash was perplexed by several questions: What was the role of the superintendent in this cultural conflict? What was the role of the school? How far did his professional responsibility to the conservative element go? The board had not issued a mandate when he was hired. Its only directions to him were, "We want a good school system for our children, and we believe you are the person to accomplish the job." He now wished that at the time of his acceptance he had sought clarification from the board as to what they meant by "good school system" and "accomplish the job." Would this have helped clarify what was now expected of him and point the way out of his present dilemma?

Did he have the ethical right to align himself with the progressive element, with whom he felt strongly identified, when he owed his very presence in the community to the more conservative faction? Should he evidence a detached point of view, ignore the basic conflict within the community, and attempt to keep the school isolated from the ebb and flow of events in the community? If this were a wise course, was it possible to follow it under existing circumstances? Should he work for the change he felt desirable? These were some of the unresolved questions that plagued Ash during the early weeks and months of his tenure.

Time did not lessen the significance or the immediacy of these questions. The lack of community stability came to be reflected more and more in its social institutions. The school system did not escape unscathed. Although conflict and confusion were not so readily apparent in the school system during the first year of Ash's regime, later developments brought the conflict to the surface with an explosion that rocked the entire education profession within the state and, to a less extent, within the entire southern region.

The crisis came when Albert Benson, immediate past superintendent, became a candidate for reinstatement and Ash was asked to resign as superintendent for "malpractice of office." Benson, after his retirement, had maintained his residence in Brashtown, where he had powerful political connections with community leaders engendered by family wealth and "family ties." His tenure of office as local school superintendent had lasted 23 years. A local merchant stated, "For twenty-three years the school and Mr. Benson had not changed."

Benson and the conservative element with which he was identified seemingly had interpreted every attempted improvement or change within the school during Ash's tenure of office as an adverse criticism of Benson's prior administration and, more generally, as a threat to accepted community tradition and mores. As Benson later related, "Ash seemed to be identified with every attempt, organized and otherwise, to change the old way of life in our school and community. We resented him and the change he brought. Why didn't he work to preserve it as he found it?"

Thus, as Ash reached the termination of his first two years in office as superintendent of schools in Brashtown, he was confronted with a rather complex situation. When conservative elements in the community were raising issues questioning the ethics of his administrative behavior and were seeking to remove him from office, should he utilize his skill and insight in identifying, utilizing, and even manipulating formal and informal groups in order to retain his control? Should he resign? Did this sort of situation invariably develop when a forward-looking superintendent tangled with a conservative board? As superintendent, what were his recourses against the seemingly unethical behavior of the opposing groups? Could his conflict with the board have been avoided?

The foregoing questions may more satisfactorily be considered in the light of additional data. Subsequent sections are devoted to (1) additional biographical data relative to Mr. Ash, (2) descriptive data relative to Brashtown and Brashtown's schools, and (3) a chronological sketch of events believed pertinent to the case. From these additional facts and the foregoing description of the setting in which the case occurred, the reader may identify for himself the sources of conflict and the alternatives for action, as well as the basic underlying value questions.

Superintendent Ash

John B. Ash was graduated from the state university in 1930. He worked for two years in his father's lumber business. In 1932 he began his career as an educator, teaching in a rural elementary school for one year. The following year, he taught mathematics in a secondary school in South Carolina and subsequently was named principal of this school. He served in this capacity for six years and during this period took his master's degree in mathematics. In 1941 he entered the Navy and was discharged in 1946. He re-entered college and received the Master of Education degree with a major in school administration. He served for one year as assistant superintendent of schools in a small, independent school system in eastern Tennessee.

In 1948, Ash was named superintendent of a small, independent school system in northern Alabama. It was here that he attracted much attention and professional acclaim as an authority on curriculum development and school plant construction. The school system of which he was superintendent became a pilot center for experimentation for the State Department of Education and the State University. The services of Ash as a consultant in curriculum development were much in demand by lay and professional school groups throughout the state.

While in this position, Ash delivered a public address in which he strongly advocated that the total number of administrative school districts within the state be drastically reduced. This came at a time when district reorganization was a statewide controversial issue and when his local board had recently gone on record as being very much opposed to reorganization. The actions of Ash were openly criticized by the board. An apparent conflict between Ash and the board ensued. There is strong indication that this conflict was largely confined to a "clash" between Ash and the board chairman. This resulted in Ash being openly and officially censured by the board for his address favoring reorganization at a time when it was, at least to the board, a controversial issue.

Ash resigned from this position on June 30, 1950 to become superintendent of schools in Brashtown. He states his reason for resigning as, "The board of education stated that I was overactive in advocating district reorganization, and I refuse to work where my professional ethics are seriously questioned." Ash seemed to feel that his resignation was an effective way of avoiding conflict, but that "this is not always the best course to follow in incidents such as these."

Brashtown, 1950

Brashtown was a distinctly southern town of 18,500 inhabitants. It was the county seat. Also located in the county were two small towns of about 500 people each. An additional 13,000 rural farm and rural nonfarm population gave the county a total population of 32,-500 in 1950. Population increase between 1940 and 1950 was 15,000 with about 75 per cent of the increase due to the rapid industrialization taking place within the county.

Agriculture, mining, lumbering, and supporting business and professional services provided the major source of income in the area for many years. The location of industry in Brashtown and adjacent communities during and immediately following World War II resulted in industrial payrolls comprising over 60 per cent of the total yearly income of the county.

Residential areas adjacent to the city began to develop as more and more rural families migrated to the city and became dependent upon industrial employment. Families from other rural areas of the state and skilled labor, both from the north and from southern industrial centers, began to swell population trends. These new arrivals were generally not regarded by established residents as integral parts of the community. It is worth noting, for example, that the corporate city limits of Brashtown were extended only once in the 1940–1950 period. This was done to incorporate a residential area developed for and populated by business and professional leaders of the city representing the conservative groups. City ordinances were passed explicitly forbidding the extension of the corporate city limits to include residential areas developed through industrial expansion. Consequently, almost 90 per cent of the population increase during the 1940–1950 period resided in rural nonfarm areas immediately adjacent to the city. These families generally resented the lack of acceptance evidenced by the more established residents. Rentals and housing expansion to care for the population outside the corporate city limits resulted in a rather clear-cut distinction between the "old" and the "new" in Brashtown.

Brashtown was not an isolated community. It was immediately adjacent to one of the largest cities in the South and to other metropolitan centers. It possessed two radio stations and a daily newspaper. There were the usual civic, social, and fraternal organizations, as well as a city-wide recreation program. Membership and participation in these organizations, however, were rigidly controlled and largely confined to the conservative element of the community residing in the corporate city limits. Generally speaking, newer residents found better "reception" in adjoining cities and consequently turned to these for recreation, or developed and participated in activities largely confined to their own group.

The city-manager and town-council form of government was followed. The town council was elected by majority vote of registered voters in the city and the city manager was appointed by the council. The town council also appointed the board of education and rather generally controlled municipal affairs. Membership in all of these formal organizations was highly stable. The city manager, in 1950, was serving his fifth four-year term in office. Four members of the seven-man council had served 20 consecutive years. All were members of the conservative element in the community.

There was, thus, a distinct "controlling class" of successful merchants, landowners, and established members of the professions in Brashtown. In the main, they were descendants of former "city fathers." They and their families were established residents. Their sons and daughters were destined for positions of leadership and control in the community. As one of the new residents termed it, "Brashtown was a closed corporation." Individuals who attained office usually held the office for a long period of time and generally exercised a great deal of influence in naming their successors. There was also an "interlocking" characteristic in the community power structure in that leaders tended to come from the same conservative element of "old timers." As one of the newly arrived attorneys-at-law in Brashtown summed it up, "There was a definite 'in-group' who controlled business, professional, civic, and social activity in Brashtown. Acceptance from this group was slow and difficult, if not almost impossible, to attain for the newcomer to the community."

Brashtown's School System

The curriculum offerings of Brashtown schools were best described as "academic." Preparation for college was the avowed goal. Although Brashtown took much pride in that "75 per cent of our graduates go to college," less pride was attached to the fact that during the period of 1940–1950 less than 35 per cent of students beginning the first grade completed high school.

Of 16 units required of all students for graduation in 1950, 16 were required constants. Six required units were in the area of Language Arts, including four years of English and two years of either Latin or French; six were in math-science, including algebra I and II, plane geometry, trigonometry, physical science, and either physics or chemistry; four units were in the social studies, including government, ancient history, world history, and United States history. That this was a curriculum strongly emphasizing academic subjects was a matter in which Brashtown took considerable pride. That it was an "inflexible" one was a fact decried by many, including the new superintendent, Mr. John Ash.

In 1950 the Brashtown school system was an independent school system organized on an 8–4 basis. Independent city school systems had been rather common in the state until around 1945, when district reorganization had resulted in a number of independent city systems merging with neighboring county school systems. There were 159 county systems and 196 independent city systems in the state in 1945. By 1950 permissive state legislation encouraging local option on reorganization had helped to reduce the number of independent city system units to 42. Including 159 county administrative units, the state in 1950 had a public school system comprised of 201 separate administrative units, as compared with 355 in 1945.

In 1949 the state board of education had approved, underwritten, and initiated a program guaranteeing each administrative unit comprising the state system of public schools a certain minimum standard of education. State activity in this development was limited to encouragement through financial support and professional consultative service to the local units of administration. Districts were encouraged to use state resources in line with local needs and philosophy. Minimum standards of education for each pupil were to be assured by (1) determining in each administrative unit of the public school system the total cost of providing an adequate program of education; (2) determining the ability of each local administrative unit to provide services, through the use of an economic index of ability-to-pay; and (3) providing state aid to "make up" the difference between the cost of the "essential program" and the ability of the local unit to pay the educational bill. A statewide tax had been levied for this purpose. The tax and the program referred to above had been approved by the people in a statewide referendum.

Ability-to-pay for each county was computed from an index including a number of economic factors relating specifically to that county. The ability-to-pay of an independent school system of an urban center within a given county was determined by economic factors not solely of the urban center itself, but from factors related to both county and city. Thus, gross inequalities of state aid in those counties containing independent and county units of administration were possible. Independent city systems located in urban centers containing most of a county's wealth could thus obtain as much state aid as their poorer rural counterparts where the need was much greater, the per-capita income much smaller, and the tax structure much more narrow. This was true of Brashtown and the county of which it was a part.

In 1948 Brashtown had defeated in local referendum an attempt to merge the independent city system with that of the county. In Brashtown's independent school system and in the county system, state aid amounted to about 65 per cent of the total cost of educational services provided. However, the ability-to-pay within the Brashtown system was in actuality about two or three times that of the remainder of the county, yet they shared equally in state aid. This inequity was furthered in that new industries locating in the county were granted long-range tax exemptions by a county board of commissioners residing in the city but owning property in the county. Thus, the county school system needed money from local sources to provide needed educational services, but the major source of wealth was tax-exempt.

Consequently, Brashtown's city schools were able to attract and retain well-qualified teachers by means of local supplements, while the county schools were experiencing difficulty in obtaining and retaining teachers meeting barest minimum standards of professional preparation and experience. In addition, a local city statute re-

quired pupils residing outside the corporate city limits of Brashtown to pay a monthly tuition fee of $14 and to provide their own
transportation if they attended the Brashtown secondary school.
They were forbidden to attend the Brashtown elementary schools
under any circumstances. For an extended period of time, this ruling
had been a source of constant irritation to county residents.

These factors contributed to "unhealthy" relations between the
city and county school officials, and created a district cleavage between the two separate school systems besides. The influx of new
pupils in the county schools as a result of industrial expansion created
a demand for educational services that could not be provided through
the existing structure of financial support.

The Events

Albert Benson, son of a prosperous banker-merchant, was a native of Brashtown. He had served as superintendent of Brashtown's
schools for 23 years. Prior to this, he had taught in the local high
school for 11 years. After 34 years of service and at the age of 60, he
retired as Brashtown's school superintendent, to assume responsibilities as manager-owner of a local mercantile establishment inherited
from his father's estate.

Former superintendent Benson was interested in the local school
system. He had watched it grow from a small beginning to a place of
significance in the life of the community. He had "helped preserve,"
as he was wont to say, "its academic emphasis in the face of inroads
made by 'progressive' education."

Albert Benson was also interested in who his successor as superintendent would be. He had come to know and had developed respect
and admiration for John Ash, superintendent in the adjoining state,
through association in state and regional professional organizations
over the preceding years. The reputation that John Ash held as an
educational consultant had impressed Benson, although their association had never been "close." Benson felt that there was no one
from the present school staff possessing the personal and professional
characteristics for the position he was vacating. Benson decided that
Ash was "right" for the job.

Upon the recommendation of Benson, John Ash was invited to
visit Brashtown in the spring of 1950 and to meet socially with mem-

bers of the local board of education. After this visit by Ash, there was general concurrence on the part of Benson and the local board that Ash would be suited for the superintendency. Ash later stated that he was asked by Benson if he could be "moved" from his position at that time. He stated that his answer was "yes."

Ash was offered the position within two months after his initial visit to Brashtown. Upon his statement of interest, he was appointed by official board action to a three-year term of office as Brashtown's Superintendent of Schools. In actuality, Ash had very little information about Brashtown's schools, and very little was known by Benson or the board about Ash other than by reputation. The Brashtown Board of Education had followed Benson's recommendation; "after all, Benson is a school man and should be able to recognize one."

Ash later stated that, in accepting the position, he was strongly motivated by a desire to remove himself from an unpleasant set of circumstances that had developed in the district where he was when he was offered the Brashtown superintendency. The circumstances centered around a formal censure by his school board for public remarks he had made relative to the issue of district organization.

He resigned from his old position in June of 1950 and moved to Brashtown in July of 1950. As far as has been determined and by his own admission, Ash made very little effort to ascertain the demands of the new position or the expectations of the board prior to accepting his new position. He soon discovered that the expectations of the local board in this new situation did not go beyond the concept of a superintendent of schools as a municipal fiscal officer concerning himself with the receipt and disbursement of funds for educational purposes within the city school system.

This was a rather limited view of the superintendency, as Ash conceived it. Such activities as his attempts to set up system-wide curriculum committees, his efforts to initiate follow-up studies of graduates and of drop-outs, and his move to provide guidance services were conceived by Ash as significant aspects of a superintendent's responsibilities. However, his efforts met with resistance from a part of the board, some of the teaching staff, and some members of the community.

Ash early hired a local bookkeeper, placed the city system on a fiscally sound centralized accounting plan, and turned his attention and energy to considerations designed to improve the school system.

He did not rely solely upon his own professional judgment. He attempted to interest lay groups, as well as the board and professional school personnel, in these deliberations. A number of sessions were planned and conducted by committees developed by Ash. These were well attended by the lay public. Few of the staff attended at first. Ash began to utilize those staff members who evidenced an interest as consultants or committee chairmen in certain aspects of these activities. As the year progressed, more of the teaching faculty and an unusually large number of patrons became involved in some phase of a study, "What Are the Purposes of Brashtown's School System?" Ash stated that the local secondary school principal somehow never entered into these activities, although an attempt was made to involve him on many occasions.

At this stage, the local board and the local secondary school principal viewed these activities of Ash and his committees as "harmless" and "tolerated them as idiosyncrasies of a new superintendent." However, many parents and teachers began to find some satisfaction in these deliberations in that a medium was provided whereby their "voices could be heard" on affairs concerning the school system and their children. Interest and enthusiasm on the part of many parents and teachers were at a "high pitch." Ash had endeared himself to these persons, and they perceived him as an alert, professionally minded school administrator.

At this time Ash also was "consciously" developing strong identification with certain lay and professional individuals and groups within the school and the community. He was developing an insight into the community power structure and was trying to gain acceptance by key leaders within this power structure. He could detect social unrest and dissatisfaction with the old power structure of the conservative element in the community. He could also detect resistance to changes which purported in any way to disturb the traditional balance of power within the community. Although it was well known that he advocated changes in the local school system, he was at first not identified as an individual advocating radical change.

Subsequent development did not maintain this estimate of Ash's intentions. He soon began to be regarded by some as a threat to established traditions within the school system and, to a lesser degree, within the community. Ash sensed this, but his strong professional and personal convictions that his professional activities were essential to the well-being of the school compelled him to "avoid retreat" from his position that the school system needed critical self-study and evaluation, to serve as a basis for change.

As interested participants in committee deliberations began to reach understandings about desirable educational purposes, attention quite naturally began to shift to a consideration of the kinds of educational experiences and programs best fitted to achieve these purposes. Thus, certain recommendations for program revision, course content, and organization consistent with desired purposes began to be identified and proposed. Some changes in the present system were explicitly discussed and others were strongly implied. Ash consistently contended that the proposed changes were not his own but were the outcome of lay-faculty co-operative study based upon analysis of facts.

When the proposed changes in the school and its program began to gain some popular lay acceptance, Robert Peeples, the secondary school principal, began to complain to Ash that committee actions were beginning to undermine the "present structure of public education in Brashtown." Most of these complaints came near the end of Ash's first year in office, and the termination of the school year temporarily relieved the situation before matters became crucial.

During the ensuing summer, the board came together to re-elect the school staff. Mr. Ash presented them with a recommended staff which did not include Mr. Peeples, who had been high school principal for the past 12 years. Ash stated the following as his reason for not recommending Peeples:

> He does not perform his job in an adequate manner. He has on many occasions demonstrated a lack of confidence in the superintendent and has been most unco-operative in all of our relationships.

The board deferred the matter, but at the next meeting hired Peeples for another year over the protests of Superintendent Ash. Former superintendent Benson attended this meeting at the invitation of one of the local board members. There is no evidence that Benson attempted to "sway" the board's decision, although it was generally known that he supported Peeples.

The second year that Ash spent as superintendent of Brashtown's schools was somewhat more hectic than the first. He continued his committee activities with lay and professional school personnel in deliberations related to school purposes and needs. He also was active in civic and fraternal groups in the city and county and developed considerable status, particularly among patrons of the school. He became more and more identified with the progressive element in the community, yet he managed to maintain social and personal relations with parents, professionally minded school personnel, and conservative leaders of the community.

The Board of Education and the secondary school principal still regarded Ash's legitimate professional activities solely as those related to "custodianship of the educational fund" and regarded his other professional activities as "bothersome." His suggestions for improving the school system were branded by the board as "unrealistic."

However, in December of 1951 Ash received an invitation to present some of his "ideas" on improving Brashtown's schools to the board. At an open meeting in January 1952, chairmen of four separate committees gave reports of the activities of their committees and each raised a question for consideration. These questions were as follows:

1. Do we have a responsibility to extend educational opportunities to children residing outside the corporate city limits of Brashtown? Should we reorganize our school district to include both city and county?
2. Does the present program of studies provide adequate educational experiences for all of Brashtown's children?
3. Are the present instructional methods and materials compatible with what is considered by authorities most appropriate in terms of what we know to be the appropriate nature and conditions of most effective teaching-learning experiences?
4. Are we taking advantage of present opportunities to build and equip adequate school plants to care for present population and anticipated expansion?

At this meeting, Superintendent Ash carefully pointed out that the committee wished only to "raise" these questions, but that they were to him the critical issues facing Brashtown's school system at the present time. "How they are resolved will affect our community for many years to come," Ash said. He also pointed out that they could not be resolved "overnight," and that each deserved careful study and consideration.

A bomb would not have electrified the audience any more. Some members of the board were indignant that these questions and the discussions they evoked should be considered. Others felt that this was a need long neglected. The discussion of these issues by the local board and patrons present was marked by argumentation and heated debate. Before the evening ended, a number of people had committed themselves as "for" or "against" implied changes.

The reports of these four committees soon became common knowledge, and community reaction was similar to that of the board. Some thought Ash to be "dedicated to destroying cherished values in the school." Others perceived Ash as proposing "something our community has long needed." The newcomers to this community, particularly those residing in the county and unable to send their children to the city schools, began to champion Ash. Feeling ran high. People were discussing the issue at every "gate post and street corner." Editorials began to appear in the papers championing Ash and his program as the "panacea for all of our educational ills" on the one hand and damning him as a "zealot engaged in the nefarious business of hoodwinking the public" on the other. Ash stoutly maintained that he had only "given professional leadership to lay-professional committees which identified some critical issues facing the public schools for which he was administratively responsible."

In May of 1952 Mr. Peeples, principal of the secondary school, tendered his resignation. He did so as a "protest" against the actions of Ash in "criticizing and attempting to destroy the system of public schools in Brashtown."

Ash immediately accepted Peeples' resignation and asked the local board to meet and elect a successor. Two members of the board were out of town at this time. Ash invited the remainder of the board to his home for dinner and, while there, they "informally" appointed Jess Wilson, an elementary principal, as principal of the secondary school.

At a formal meeting of the board the following Friday, the board "formally" approved the "informal" appointment of Wilson by a four-to-three majority. The three dissenting board members violently opposed the appointment and openly accused Ash of "manipulating" the board. This charge somehow was called to the attention of the press and was soon public knowledge.

Benson, the former superintendent, made a public statement to the press that he would consider accepting a position in the school system to "restore peace and harmony." Benson did not indicate whether he wished to replace Peeples or Ash.

In June 1952, following the resignation of Peeples, the tenure of office for a member of the local board expired. This board member had been a strong supporter of Ash. He was replaced by a brother-in-law of former superintendent Benson. Two weeks after the appointment of the new board member, Ash received a letter from the Board urging him to resign. He answered the letter with a refusal and a reminder that his contract had one more year to run. The Board did not press the matter.

Benson, the former superintendent, became more and more bitter in his public criticism of Ash. Ash soon discovered that certain city officials and a majority of the local board of education supported the idea of reinstating Benson as superintendent of schools. Benson was most vociferous in his criticism of Ash and verbally based his active bid for reinstatement upon the following three points: (1) that the conservative element in the community was losing control of the schools and that he advocated a return to the "good old days," (2) that his voluntary retirement was not a satisfactory course, as it did not satisfy his "heartfelt desire to serve his home community," (3) that Mr. Ash was not an effective or even an honest school administrator and, consequently, was not the superintendent for Brashtown's schools.

The first reason given by Mr. Benson might be interpreted to suggest that he was seeking to rally the more conservative, traditional elements of the city to his cause. Whether in actuality Benson was aiming to rally political support for personal ends or whether he was the "cat's paw" of the conservative element seeking to retain power over the schools is a speculative question. That he emerged as the champion of the traditional, conservative element in Brashtown in a determined struggle to resist educational change by removing the leadership force which seemed to be the catalyst for change is a matter of record.

Benson was described by a close associate as a sort of "benevolent autocrat" who always knew what was "best for teachers and pupils alike." His tenure of office was not "marred," as he was wont to say, "by people who disagreed with policy." In fact, those who disagreed did so at the risk of their jobs. His stated desire to serve, it was felt by those who knew him well, was based upon an inner drive, a compulsion, to exert control over the school system.

The third stated reason for Mr. Benson's efforts at reinstatement soon became the focal point for heated argumentation and legal activity. Although it originally was initiated as a statement of opinion by Mr. Benson, subsequent events saw it crystallize in the form of specific, formal complaints charging John Ash with "mal-performance of duties in the office of superintendent of city schools of Brashtown."

In September 1952 the local board sent an open letter to John Ash stating that he was officially removed from his responsibilities as superintendent because of mal-performance in office. Ash demanded to know the specific nature of the charges. In October 1952 John Ash received a letter from the local board of education specifying the charges upon which his removal from office was based. This letter is now a matter of public record and reads as follows:

October 9, 1952

Mr. "John Ash"
Superintendent of Schools
"Brashtown," Georgia
Dear Mr. Ash:

This is to inform you that as of now you are relieved of all official duties and responsibilities relative to your responsibilities as Superintendent of Schools as a direct result of mal-performance in office.

Your remuneration will continue through December of 1952 but you will vacate your office immediately.

Specific charges upon which this action is based are:

1. Using for personal use stamps and stationery procured by school funds.
2. Failing to take "stern disciplinary action" against a principal for allowing a pregnant pupil (married) to remain in school during last month of the academic year.
3. Tolerating the actions of a bus driver who allowed boys and girls to sit together with interior lights of bus dimmed on return from a basketball game with county school.
4. Failing to personally check and sign monthly reports of pupils' progress.

It is our sincere desire to avoid all unnecessary adverse publicity for the school system. However, for your information these complaints are based upon information provided by Mr. Benson, Mr. Peeples, and members of the local board. The City Council has advised us that unless you remove yourself from office immediately, we will be forced to turn these matters over to the Grand Jury for their consideration.

Yours truly,

John David Evans
Chairman of Local Board of Education

As John Ash read this letter, he was beset by conflicting emotions. Some of the charges were trivial. Some he considered outright false-hoods. What course should he pursue? He thought of his last position and how he had resigned to avoid certain conflicts with the board. He thought of the cultural conflict in which he had now become enmeshed. Should he accept the board's action? Should he attempt to prove himself innocent of the charges and protect his personal and professional reputation? Had these developments destroyed his effectiveness as a professional educator in this community? What course of action should he pursue?

When Ash had read the letter, he said to himself, "By God, they aren't going to run me out of this situation. I'm going to make a battle out of it and protect my personal and professional integrity. I can reorganize this school system into the vital community institution it should be."

CASE FIFTEEN

Greenfield Builds Its
Third High School

Some of those who were associated with the building of Greenfield's third high school might be inclined to entitle this case study a "Comedy of Errors." However, the problems relating to building the high school were so persistent and serious that, from the standpoint of their effect on community school support, they can hardly be regarded as humorous. Certainly they have not seemed so to the school board members, the superintendent, or the architect.

Greenfield's experience in building its first and second high schools might have suggested that the building of the third high school would not go smoothly. The first high school building, a two-story affair of red brick, was erected in 1903. The principal soon complained that the noise from the horse cars and other traffic disturbed recitations in the school. Its location was not a popular one, even though chosen by an election at which three sites were under consideration. The second high school building was erected in Greenfield in 1915 at a location some ten blocks farther removed from the business district. The location of this building, like that of the first, did not meet with popular approval. Letters to the editor of the *Greenfield Sentinel* at the time the building was being planned objected to the site as "low, swampy ground" which would be subject to flooding during the heavy winter rains. The superintendent answered with a letter contending that in case the proposed site were flooded, water would be eight feet deep at the main business intersection. A recognized authority on school matters stated, when the second school was to be built, that the only reason Greenfield did not build more schools in swamps was that there were no more swamps in which to build them. Editorials and letters to the editor of the *Greenfield Sentinel* as well as the official *Minutes* of the school board for the period from 1900 to 1920 strongly suggest that the first two high schools were not built without trials, tribulations, or criticism.

The Greenfield Community

In 1939, when Greenfield first considered building its third high school, its population was 30,000. The demand at that time came rather from the desire of the faculty than from projections of population. The economy of the community was chiefly agricultural with some lumbering. During the years of World War II, the great demand for lumber made the production of lumber and lumber products Greenfield's major industry. There was an increase of 39 per cent in population in the decade between 1940 and 1950. Also, the Greenfield School District was greatly increased in area and by about one-third in school population by the consolidation of 12 adjacent suburban districts between 1945 and 1950.

The educational and cultural life of Greenfield was strongly in-fluenced by Southern College, which enrolled several thousand stu-dents. Members of the college faculty generally influenced the com-munity to support a good school program. College staff members fre-quently served on school budget committees, and they were invari-ably on the side of greater tax support for the public schools. The education department of the college was very much interested in the Greenfield school program, for it was in the public schools that the college placed student teachers for practical experience in super-vised teaching. The proposed location of the new high school, adja-cent to property owned by the college, was recommended because of its convenience in the placement of student teachers. It was the desire of the college administration to have a modern, comprehensive high school in which to do teacher-training. Since 1926, the teacher-training high school on the college campus had been largely academic although operated jointly by the college and the public schools.

Early Plans for a Third High School

During the depression years, many tracts of land in Greenfield reverted to the city and county through nonpayment of taxes. Some of this land which came into the possession of the City of Greenfield was in turn sold to the Greenfield School District for the amount of the back taxes and street improvements. A major purchase, later forming the nucleus for the new high school site, was acquired by the school district in this manner in 1939. Credit must be given to Superintendent Joe Jones and one or two of the school board mem-bers for this purchase. Files of the *Sentinel* and the Board *Minutes* of 1939 do not reveal any expressed dissatisfaction on the part of the public with the acquisition of the site. According to Gil MacTavish, a long-time member of the school board, criticism of the site was first heard in the late 1940's after public patience had been sorely tried by delay in the preparation of plans for the new building. Those who opposed the site pointed out that its location favored the college section of the community, that it was no longer centrally located, and that the increase in population had made two high schools neces-sary. There was some objection to a large high school of 1,800 or more students.

In March 1940, the district budget committee, which consisted of the five members of the school board and five other taxpaying citizens, was asked by the superintendent, Dr. Jones, to consider the need for a new high school. The Board *Minutes* state:

> Considerable time had been spent in discussing the need of and a possible plan of financing the building of a new high school. The superintendent's idea was that the actual building would be delayed for four or five years. Mr. C——— moved that this Budget Committee go on record as being in favor of the immediate introduction of an educational campaign, looking toward the floating of a bond issue within the coming year sufficient, at least, to build the most important units of the high school plant. The motion was seconded by Mr. D——— and carried.

Pearl Harbor and World War II changed the time schedule but did not alter the purpose of the Greenfield School Board and its superintendent. On April 26, 1943, a subsequent budget committee unanimously recommended a five- to seven-mill tax levy for five years, "the money thus raised to be set aside as a reserve fund for building purposes." A public meeting was held June 8 to discuss the proposed levy. The editor of the *Sentinel*, considered by many as the greatest supporter of public education in the state, was present at the meeting and pledged his full support. It was estimated that the levy would raise $100,000 a year, thus providing a sinking fund of one-half a million dollars for the new building. Public support of the plan was clearly shown by the vote of 333 in favor and only 38 against the levy.

After the action of the original budget committee in 1940, two steps were taken in order that planning might be facilitated. With members of the high school faculty and Ernest Jensen, veteran principal, Dr. Jones began to develop educational specifications for the proposed building. As a second step, the school board voted in July 1941, to employ four local licensed architects to prepare a "Master Plan" for the building for a fee of $2,500. The architects agreed to have the plan ready in 120 days. One of the four employed for this work was Joe Martin, later selected as architect for the new building.

In June 1942, almost a year rather than four months later, the architects submitted three tentative plans. There was no acceptance by the board of any of these plans. One of them, however, was very similar to the scheme which was later used by Martin. In March 1943, two veteran board members reported on a conference which they had held with two of the architects employed to prepare the "Master Plan." These directors proposed paying off the architects with $1,250. At the next meeting, the same month, Superintendent Jones read a proposed letter prepared by the board attorney, Judge Adams. It proposed a settlement on the terms discussed, that is, $1,250. The board approved the letter and directed the superintendent to send it to the four architects. The offer was accepted by the architects.

In February 1944, the school board learned that the City Council of Greenfield was considering opening a street through the site of the proposed high school. This division of the tract by a street which might in future years carry a heavy traffic load would, in the opinion of board members, make the site unsuitable for school purposes. On November 13, the school board received from the Council an agreement providing for the closing of all streets and alleys in the high school site, in exchange for which the school district agreed to deed to the city a street right-of-way through other school property west of the high school site. When this agreement was signed, the Council passed the necessary ordinance to close the streets and alleys as it had agreed to do. This assured the location of Greenfield's third high school.

The teacher-training relationship of the public school with the college, as has been mentioned, had a part in determining the location of the school. This relationship also affected the acquisition of land for the site, since the college owned a considerable tract adjoining the proposed site. Dr. Jones insisted that at least 30 acres were needed for a satisfactory site. The land area acquired by the district from the city comprised about 16 acres. Discussions were started in the early 1940's, with the president of the college and the dean of education, for the acquisition of some land from the college in exchange for teacher-training privileges in the new school. A tentative verbal agreement was reached with the president of the college before he died suddenly in 1943. Dr. Jones, who had carried on most of the negotiations for the district, resigned in 1944 to accept another position. The superintendent who succeeded him, Dr. Harry Edwards, immediately renewed discussions with the acting president and the dean of education. He reported to the board in November 1944, that discussions were proceeding satisfactorily. Shortly thereafter, tentative agreement was rejected by the board for reasons which are not clear. In December, the board voted to ask the college to sell the district approximately 16 acres outright without any relation to teacher-training. Here the matter rested, as far as land negotiations were concerned, until a new college president took office in 1945.

With the arrival of the new president, Superintendent Edwards resumed negotiations for land owned by the college. Although he believed in the advantage of practice teaching in a comprehensive high school, the new president, Dr. Reithel, was not so easy to deal with as his predecessors had been.

Dr. Reithel apparently felt that, in the exchange, it was his responsibility to secure as much for the college as could be had. In discussions with him, the chairman of the school board and the superintendent of schools finally agreed to a 20-year noncancellable contract with a stipulation that if the district terminated the contract in less than 20 years without the consent of the college, it must pay the college three times the value of the land as damages. When the terms of the contract became known in the community, the board justified its acceptance of such terms on the grounds that it had already gone too far to change the high school location. Criticism soon came from individuals who resented the probable influence of the college on the schools of the community. The high school parent-teacher association devoted a meeting to an analysis of the contract by a certified public accountant. He concluded that it was not a bad instrument and that the district received benefits commensurate with those of the college. Criticism of the agreement persisted, however, and added something to a situation which was already disturbed by other matters.

As noted above, Dr. Jones had begun to develop educational specifications for the proposed high school building in 1941. He had prided himself on being a democratic school administrator, one who allowed the staff to make and influence important policy decisions.

Thus, the faculties of the Greenfield High School and the College High School began to develop educational specifications for the new school. Many of the high school faculty members, like Principal Jensen, had been in the old building for a long time—some, as long as 20 years. Many of them had longed for and dreamed of a better building in which to teach. They were well aware of the old building's inadequacies; they knew what they wanted for doing a good job.

However, they had little knowledge and little guidance in building costs. There is certainly no evidence to indicate that there was recognition by the board, Dr. Jones, Mr. Jensen, or the high school teachers that their educational specifications would call for a building with a floor area in excess of 450,000 square feet and at a cost of $6,000,000. As one board member said later when the board learned what the educational specifications called for in the way of facilities, "They wanted a fireplace in every room." While this was certainly an overstatement, the specifications prepared by the faculty committees did call for almost everything that would be required for an ideal school plant. It was only when the architect finally reduced these requests to a tentative floor plan and the area was determined that it became evident that they were unrealistic from the standpoint of cost and space.

Dr. Edwards, who became superintendent in 1944, resumed work on the specifications where Dr. Jones left off. Although the work of the teacher committees had been substantially completed early in 1944, Edwards held several meetings with the faculties of the two high schools during the two years that he was superintendent. No significant changes were made, and the discussions assumed that the building would be built to provide facilities as proposed by the departmental committees. When Dr. Edwards accepted a position in a neighboring state in 1946, his successor, Dr. Golden, received the educational specifications with the understanding that all was in readiness for the architect to begin work on the new high school. It is not surprising that, when it became necessary for Superintendent Golden to inform the high school faculty that the district did not have the necessary bonding capacity to build the school as planned, some of the older members of the staff were incensed and a few considered it a personal affront.

Selection of the Architect

After the favorable vote on the tax levy for the building fund in June 1943, the board discussed procedures for choosing an architect. In September, its *Minutes* record, five architects were invited "to sit with the Board of Education to discuss the ways they would approach the building of the new high school." Four of these were from the state's metropolis and one, Joe Martin, was a long-time resident of Greenfield. During the fall of 1943, special meetings were held with the architects where each presented pictures and drawings of the buildings he had designed. Each architect submitted one or more schemes for the proposed high school, and fees were discussed. After all five architects had met with the board, action on selection was deferred. At the first meeting in May 1944, after Dr. Jones's resignation and Dr. Edwards's election as superintendent and with both men present, the board took final action to select its architect as follows:

> After a long and very careful discussion of the various architects who had been considered by the board for the planning of the proposed new Greenfield High School, it was moved by Mr. ————, seconded by Mr. ————, that the board select Joe Martin of Greenfield as architect for the project on the basis of a 5 per cent commission.

Commenting later on the selection of Martin, the board members who had made the motion to hire Martin said, "Those architects from the big city overawed us with the size of the war projects they had done. We picked Martin because he was a Greenfield man and we would not be subject to criticism from the taxpayers for going outside the community." The hope of avoiding criticism by the selection of Martin was certainly in error, as later events were to demonstrate.

Professionally, Martin had not had extensive experience in planning school buildings. He had designed two high schools, one in the eastern part of the state and one in the southern part. His largest job was the high school in the neighboring community built prior to the war at a cost of $4.00 a square foot. He had established a reputation, at least in Greenfield, for being an economical designer. No one questioned his ability to design a building that would be structurally sound. If there was a question as to his professional competency, it was that he lacked imagination and would design a building which would be a very traditional structure.

His character and reputation were also good. His integrity was not questioned by anyone who knew him; he was a man of good repute, honest and sincere. It was chiefly on the basis of his personality that his selection was open to question by those who knew him best. Those who had worked with him, as contractors, owners, or in other capacities found him a man of firm convictions, often to the point of stubbornness. He was described by one such individual as "the man who is never wrong and who never makes a mistake." When difficulties were encountered with the bearing qualities of the soil, Martin placed the entire blame on the engineer who had made the tests. When there was difficulty with the mechanical system of the building, Martin told the board, "If my engineers have made a mistake, they will pay for it." He lacked skill in working with people—a fact generally recognized by those who knew him well, certainly known to some of the board members who selected him.

Within two weeks of his selection and before a formal contract had been negotiated with him, Martin made his first and last estimate of any costs connected with the building. The school board requested figures on the cost of additional fill necessary on the site if satisfactory drainage was not provided through natural waterways. On May 22, 1944, Martin informed the board that the additional cost would be $150,000 to $165,000. On every occasion thereafter when he was asked for cost estimates on the project or any part of it, he contended that it was not a part of his professional responsibility to estimate costs.

Although selected in May 1944, it was March 1946 before Martin met with the board to discuss contract terms. The board was interested in a commitment from him that he would proceed diligently and not accept other work until the high school plans were completed. The *Minutes* for the March 11 meeting state that "After considering the many delays likely to occur before actual plans are drawn," Martin left copies of a proposed contract for board consideration. From this date to June 1948,[1] the matter of the contract did not come formally before the board. On the latter date, the board directed Superintendent Golden to invite Martin to meet with the board at its next meeting for further discussion. Martin accepted the invitation, met with the board June 28, and presented another contract for board consideration. It was discussed in some detail and the directors made suggestions for changes in it. The *Minutes* state:

> Mr. Martin stated that as soon as the contract is agreed upon he will accept no more architectural work, and will devote himself exclusively to the high school project as soon as current professional obligations are completed; he estimated that these would occupy him for another ninety days, and that as much as a year's time beyond that might be necessary for the completion of the high school plans.

[1] The four-year delay was caused in part by building restrictions during World War II and in part by the imperative necessity to build first the necessary classrooms for the mushrooming elementary enrollment.

Other than two paragraphs on the subject of the architect's services, the contract finally signed followed generally the standard form of the American Institute of Architects. These paragraphs, obviously intended to protect the district from conditions which later developed and which the board anticipated might develop, stated:

> The Architect hereby agrees that he will not accept other work from the date of the signing of this Agreement until the completion and acceptance of the Drawings and Specifications of this building, except as per list of projects attached hereto, without the full consent and approval of the Owner. He further agrees that he will begin work on the preliminary studies of the building within a period of ninety (90) days from the date of the signing of this Agreement and that he will complete the Drawings and Specifications ready for the calling of bids within fifteen (15) calendar months of the date of the signing of this Agreement, provided, however, necessary information is furnished by the Owner at such time or times so as not to delay him in the preparation of the complete Drawings and Specifications. Changes in the Drawings and Specifications, ordered by the Owner after a definite scheme has been approved, shall extend the time limit, as agreed upon by the parties hereto.
>
> In the event the Architect fails to complete the Drawings and Specifications within the agreed time, except as above, or accepts other work in violation of this Agreement, he shall pay the Owner the sum of Ten Thousand Dollars ($10,000.00) as liquidated damages occasioned by his delay in the preparation of the Drawings and Specifications or the acceptance of other work.

Thus, the board felt it necessary to take extreme precautions to guard against procrastination and delay by Martin in the preparation of the plans. Although the contractual agreement stipulated that a list of projects then in progress in Martin's office should be filed with the contract, none was filed. Neither the attorney nor the superintendent is able to say why the list was not filed.

The Final Planning Stage

The third superintendent to work with planning the third Greenfield high school building, Dr. Golden, inherited a set of educational specifications which had been developed democratically and an architect selected by the school board after careful consideration. He assumed the duties of his office in August 1946, after having served two years as assistant superintendent to Dr. Edwards. He was acquainted with the problems of building construction through practical experience in working on school buildings. His experience in the district as assistant to Dr. Edwards gave him further background for the Greenfield superintendency.

After the contract with Architect Martin was signed, the school board decided to call a public meeting to discuss all district building needs, not just the high school project. In August 1948 the board authorized the superintendent to invite the public to a meeting to discuss school needs. A general invitation was given through the *Sentinel* and letters were sent to community organizations asking them to send representatives. The meeting was held in the early fall, with the result that public support was secured for an election to vote $2,500,000 in bonds and a five-year serial tax levy of $250,000 a year to raise $1,250,000 more for school buildings. It was generally understood that about one million dollars of this would be allocated to the high school project. At the election held the latter part of October, the measures received a favorable vote of 924 to 542.

Early in November 1948, a meeting of the board was held in the architect's office, at his request, to "discuss general plans, including such matters as basic design, materials, etc." General agreement was reached on a combined one- and two-story plant of concrete exterior and wood interior. The arrangement of the building and the proposed location of the auditorium, classrooms, library, offices, and the physical education plant were the same as Jones had presented in his original interview. It also bore a remarkable resemblance to one submitted as a part of the "Master Plan" schemes of the four collaborating architects.

Even though the educational specifications prepared by the staff had been furnished to the architect, the *Minutes* state on January 10, 1949:

> Mr. Martin, the architect on the senior high school project, is still accumulating ideas and data on which to base plans for the new building, but . . . . . . apparently none of these have yet been transmitted to the drawing board.

By common consent, but without official action by the board, Principal Littleton, who had succeeded Ernest Jensen in 1944, was working with the architect during this period to develop plans for the building. He was in the best position to interpret the educational specifications which had been prepared by the staff for the architect. Littleton's discussions with Martin were supposedly based on the educational specifications prepared prior to his assuming the principalship of the Greenfield High School. There is nothing to indicate that he ever understood that, when these were reduced to space allocations by the architect, the cost of the building would be prohibitive. He is not likely to have gotten from Martin any idea of the building's probable cost, for the architect on several occasions refused to give estimates to the board.

On April 14, 1949, a special meeting was held "to consider the proposed floor plan for the new Greenfield High School." The president of the college, Dr. Reithel, and the new dean of education were present, since a teacher-training agreement had been worked out between the college and the district. Besides these men and the members of the board, the architect, the superintendent, and the high school principal were present. When it became obvious that the plan prepared by Martin was far in excess of the financial ability of the district and would have to be scaled down or abandoned, the Board was dismayed and several citizens, including the representatives of the college, left the meeting.

The floor plan submitted by Martin, which he said he had developed from the educational specifications and through conferences with Littleton, showed in excess of 450,000 square feet of floor space for a school building to house 1,800 students. Although Martin refused to make any estimate of the probable cost of such a structure, current building costs in the district indicated that it would be in excess of $6,000,000. As this figure was far beyond the bonding capacity of the district, and as the district had present building needs at the elementary and junior high levels as well, it was obvious that the proposed plan was completely unrealistic. The board indicated its desire to have the plan scaled down, through the co-operative efforts of the staff and the architect.

By May 25, 1949, it was possible for the board to set another meeting with the architect for July 27 "for a consideration of the revised floor plan of the new Greenfield High School." The "revised floor plan" contained almost 290,000 square feet, a figure some 40,000 square feet in excess of the maximum number previously considered by the board. Whether the board felt it necessary to set a figure much below that which it was really willing to go in order to exercise some control over the architect and the high school staff, or whether it had become economy-minded with regard to the high school and the total district building program is not known. Whatever the reason, the board directed that the plan be reduced to 210,000 square feet instead of the 250,000 it had previously considered. There may be some significance in the fact that this figure, 210,000 square feet, was about the same amount under the board's previous allowance of 250,000 as the "revised floor plan" was over that figure.

Two architects appeared before the board August 8 with a special request. They stated to the board that Martin had been offered other architectural work, that he found it impossible to accept such work because of the terms of his contract with the Greenfield district, but that he would take the additional work and turn it over to these architects if the board would approve. Apparently, they intended that the new client should think that Martin was actually doing the work instead of the architects who appeared before the board. The *Minutes* state:

> Mr. Martin proposed to them that he would examine the plans on completion and affix his signature as a licensed architect, provided this did not violate his contract with the board. After some discussion, the board denied the request on the grounds that such an arrangement actually constituted the acceptance of new work by Mr. Martin, which his contract with the district specifically forbids.

On October 10 an item appeared in the Greenfield *Sentinel* listing a number of jobs for which plans were being prepared in Martin's office. Most of these were not among those mentioned to the board at the time the contract with Martin was signed. At its meeting on the 10th, the school board discussed the news item, as the members had seen it in the evening paper. The action taken is summarized in the *Minutes* in this manner:

> The board discussed at some length the apparent lack of progress being made on the plans for the new Greenfield High School, and the possibility that the architect had violated his contract by accepting work which was not in his books at the time of the contract. . . . . . The superintendent reported that he had discussed the matter with the district's attorney, and that it was the attorney's advice that the board notify Mr. Martin that it is holding him to the date of November 10, 1949, for the completion of the plans, as set forth in the contract. On motion, the board unanimously agreed to give Mr. Martin such notice.

Matters came to a head with great rapidity when the superintendent sent the notice as directed by the board. A special meeting of the board was held October 19 "to discuss the contract for architectural services between the district and Martin. The board's attorney was present. The chairman of the board, the superintendent, and the attorney reported on a conference held with Martin and his attorney. According to a statement by Martin, made at the conference, the plans were only 35 per cent complete and could not possibly be completed by the November 10 deadline. It was further reported that Martin had stated that "the plans could be completed by April 10" and that there "were no conditions under which he would be willing to withdraw from the agreement."

The attorney for the district analyzed the contract and the difficulties growing out of it for the board. He listed them as follows:

1. It is doubtful that there is evidence to show that Mr. Martin has breached his contract by taking architectural work not listed in the contract as being unfinished.[2]

2. There exists a reasonable doubt whether the board gave Mr. Martin necessary information for completing the plans, as stated in the contract, in view of the obvious impracticality of the prospectus developed over a period of years by the Greenfield High School staff and presented to Mr. Martin as a basis for his preliminary work.

3. As there is no provision for termination of the contract included within it, but instead a ten thousand dollar penalty clause for failure to meet the provisions thereof, it appears likely that Mr. Martin could pay the ten thousand dollars in liquidated damages, with the contract remaining in force indefinitely.

The board was further informed by the attorney that there was no reason why it should not discharge the architect if it wished to do so, but that he would undoubtedly sue for the full amount of the contract fee and that there was a measure of possibility that he might win such a suit. In such event, the attorney said, it would probably cost the district $100,000 and further delay the preparation of the plans. In order to go ahead and make the best of what the board members now knew to be a bad situation, the board took the following action:

[2] At a date several years after the completion and acceptance of the school, evidence indicated that the architect did accept other commissions in violation of his contract with the Board.

In view of these facts, the board unanimously . . . authorized the superintendent of schools to be the sole agent of the board in all subsequent negotiations with Mr. Martin, and asked him to secure, as soon as possible, a definite cost estimate from the architect on the plant now being drawn.

Five days later the board learned at its next regular meeting that the superintendent, Dr. Golden, had had several meetings with Martin and that the latter desired to meet with the board October 31 to discuss the current status of his plans. At the meeting the board approved concrete floor construction for the building. It also reiterated its previous desire "that the architect should plan a building, in conjunction with the superintendent, the floor space of which shall not exceed 210,000 square feet."

A month later, November 30, 1949, another special meeting was held at which Martin "presented a further revision of the plans of the new Greenfield High School which he identified as Scheme No. 4." In response to questions from members of the board, Martin stated that ·he could not say definitely how many square feet it contained under Scheme 4, nor that it was within the limit of 210,000 square feet set by the board." After this meeting, an assistant superintendent scaled off the floor area and found it to be in excess of 260,000 square feet.

It will be recalled that the architect had said in October 1949 that plans could be ready in April 1950. In January, approval was received from the state department of education for classroom sizes. In February, the board met with Martin to approve the lighting system and certain changes requested by Principal Littleton and the head of the science department. In March, it approved the transformer installation and in June completed the agreement with the college for the additional land required for the site. It also paid Martin $10,000 on account for his services. By August, however, the board was back to a discussion of why the plans were not ready and what the architect was doing about them. The superintendent, Dr. Golden, was instructed to "secure immediately from Mr. Martin definite dates on plans for the new building."

At its meeting September 25, 1950, the board discussed a time schedule for the building of the high school. It decided to meet with Martin October 9 to inspect the plans and with the district's budget committee on October 16 to discuss financing. It set October 25 as the date to meet with a citizens' committee widely representative of all community groups, including the various parent-teacher associations, service clubs, chamber of commerce, and labor unions. It agreed to open bids for the new high school November 29 and immediately call a bond election if the low bid was within the bonding limit imposed on the district by law. It would delay awarding a contract for the building until after the bond election was held.

At the meeting with Martin on October 9, the board was confronted with some 50 large pages of detailed drawings but no estimate of the cost of the building. The board members gave careful consideration to the drawings and final approval "realizing that the individual members had not had an opportunity to make a careful study of the highly technical drawings."

Bids, Bonds, and Contracts

Postwar inflation and the Korean War had their effect upon the board's thinking concerning the new school. At a joint meeting with the budget committee in October, Dr. Golden outlined the current financial position of the district. There was extended discussion of the advisability of calling for bids on the new school. The *Minutes* of this meeting state:

> The advisability of proceeding with the building of the high school in view of costs, the international situation, material shortages, etc., was discussed at length. However, it was the unanimous decision of the committee, (as expressed by motion) that a citizens' committee fully representative of the community be called into consultation with the board and budget committee, and that if this group gives its approval, bids be called for the new high school plant.

In its plans for the meeting with representative citizens, the board agreed that the chairman should send letters to community organizations and to prominent individuals urging attendance. It was planned also that the chairman would preside, that Mr. Littleton would explain the need for a new building, and that Dr. Golden would discuss the financial condition of the district and its legal bonding capacity. The members of the board and of the budget committee agreed to answer questions concerning the proposed building. When the meeting was held, as planned, about fifty persons widely representative of the community were present. Following the discussion, those present recommended to the board that it call for bids on the high school building and that,

> If one of the bids received is within the bonding capacity of the district, the people of the district shall be asked to vote such additional bonds as in the judgment of the board are deemed necessary.

With a bid call assured, the board proceeded to qualify contractors for bidding. A special meeting was held to qualify one local contractor, who later refused to submit a bid. Two contractors from the state's largest city were also qualified to bid. On November 13, after an extended discussion of the cost of building and still without any estimate from the architect as to the probable cost of the building, the board voted to set a limit of "two and one-half to two and three-quarters millions" provided this amount was within the financial capacity of the district. The board also voted to call a bond election for December 20 in case the low bid fell within the limits set.

Before the date set for the bid opening arrived, it was necessary for the board to hold a special meeting to learn that plans for the building's electrical system were not ready for prospective bidders. The bid opening was postponed to December 28 and the bond election to January 1951. When the bids were opened, only the two metropolitan contractors submitted bids.

The low bid received, $3,467,468, was almost a million dollars more than the figure set by the board. It exceeded the legal bonding capacity of the Greenfield district by $500,000. After consideration and discussion with local subcontractors present for the bid opening, the board decided to permit the voters to make the final decision through approval or disapproval of two financing measures. The first of these, a bond issue for $2,953,000, would exhaust the bonding capacity of the district. The second, a two-year serial tax levy of $200,-000 a year, would, if approved, build the auditorium. The board thought it wise to make the auditorium a separate issue as it was not absolutely necessary for the school and had been planned to serve the community as well.

There was no organized opposition to either of the two measures in the sense that a group was formed to oppose them. However, several letters to the *Sentinel* criticized the school because it was not a fireproof structure (actually, the plan called for reinforced concrete) and because of high costs. Letter-writers admitted the need for a new high school but expressed opposition to the proposed one. Some opposed the building as a "concrete monstrosity" and others because it was not entirely of wood construction. One wealthy property owner reportedly made statements of what the cost of the building would be to him over the 20-year period of the bond issue. A woman active in an organization of college graduates was responsible for circulating the story that the building would have pink toilet fixtures for girls and blue ones for boys. Traced down, this originated from the fact that pink and blue ceramic tile was used for sanitary purposes in the toilet rooms. Another objection was to the "plush seats" in the auditorium, one lady suggesting that folding chairs would be good enough.

The editor of the *Sentinel*, long a supporter of the public schools, gave the two measures his full support. Through his editorial and news columns he gave the facts and attempted to persuade people to vote for the financial measures. By comparison with a large city high school recently built in the state, he was able to show that Greenfield's proposed school was not exorbitant in cost. By picture and story, he pointed out the inadequacies of the old school. Newspaper support, coupled with the fact that there was no public organized opposition, almost certainly influenced the outcome of the election favorably.

When the returns from the election were in, it was found that the vote favoring the bond issue was 2,619 to 2,037. The serial levy for the auditorium was about the same, 2,478 to 2,179. Greenfield, after almost twelve years of waiting and planning, had voted to build a new high school in an election that turned out the largest total vote in the history of the district. On January 25, 1951, the day following the election, the board held a special meeting and awarded four contracts for the new school. They totaled $3,433,845 and the project was immediately targeted by its critics as "Greenfield's Four Million Dollar High School," the most expensive ever built in the state.

Problems of Construction

Within a month of the signing of the contracts, trouble developed with the electrical contractor. This contractor had been qualified for bidding by the board, as required by law, only after considerable discussion. Pressure from the local bank, with which the firm did its financing, resulted in the firm being qualified to bid even though apparently lacking in the experience necessary to do a large project satisfactorily. Later difficulties with the electrical system bore out the lack of experience. The first difficulty with this contractor developed when the architect refused to approve payment for pipe "dumped on the site" on the grounds that it was not properly stored. This condition was later corrected and payment was authorized.

The real issue with the electrical contractor came when he appeared before the board with his attorney to argue that the make of electrical equipment specified by the architect's electrical engineer was not as good as that of another manufacturer. The attorney contended that the equipment which the contractor proposed to substitute was safer, more readily procurable, and would result in saving the school district money. The city electrical inspector and employees of the local public utility company were presented to support the attorney's contention. The architect and his electrical engineer argued against the proposed change. It became apparent that the electrical contractor had experienced difficulty with the manufacturer of the equipment specified and that this was the real reason for his request. The board refused to approve the change, but the friction that had been established did not aid in good relations either on the job or in the community.

The contract with Architect Joe Martin provided, as is usual in such agreements, that soil tests required by the architect should be at the expense of the district. Common practice is for the architect to secure an engineer to make the tests, supervise the tests as they are made, and have the bill sent to the school district for payment. In the case of the Greenfield High School, a local civil engineer was employed to make the necessary tests and to survey the site to determine the amount of grading necessary.

The work of the engineer was done in 1949. In February of that year, the board paid him $640 for a topographical survey of the site. On October 10 he was paid an additional $288 for "investigating soil conditions." The architect used the results of the survey for his plot plan for the building and to establish his grade levels. The survey later proved to be inaccurate to such a point that several thousand yards of earth had to be moved beyond that shown on the plans. The cost was approximately $5,000. The soil tests were even more inaccurate, and the correction of the error in foundation design even more costly. When excavations were made to the depth shown on the plans, soil conditions were deemed by the contractor to be inadequate for the load to be carried. He reported this to the architect and to Dr. Golden, the superintendent, and the latter brought the matter to the board on April 9, 1951.

The board immediately authorized a study by a firm of consulting engineers from a nearby city. They submitted a report to the board on April 16 indicating two possible courses of action, soil conditions having been found to be less in bearing quality than the design of the building required. The report said that piling could be driven to form a foundation under the footings at an estimated cost of $250,000 or that the footings could be carried deeper by three and one-half feet to a soil of better bearing quality. For the latter, an estimate of $50,000 was made. The board decided to follow the second proposal as the more economical one.

In the eyes of the critics, the building was costing $50,000 more than it should have. They blamed the board, the architect, or the superintendent, according to their personal preference. The fact of the matter was that undue delay had not been experienced because the consulting engineers had done their work and made their recommendations so quickly; also, the footings cost no more than they would have if the first engineer had furnished accurate information. The only actual loss was in the payment for his services, $928. The second set of tests cost the district $725.89, but the board felt that it was money well spent. The final cost of relocating the footings, carrying them to a greater depth, was $48,452 and of the additional grading, due to the error in the survey, $4,991. This error and additional cost came within three weeks of the district's annual budget election and probably contributed to the 17-vote margin by which the budget was defeated. A second election on the same budget a month later resulted in a favorable margin of more than 500 votes.

In the summer of 1951, the contractor indicated that he expected to finish by April 1953. He also said that he could turn over the completed gymnasium wing by January 1, 1953, so that Greenfield High School could play most of its home basketball games there during the 1953 season. At this point, Architect Martin showed his usual "spirit of co-operation." He informed the board that he would oppose acceptance of any part of the building prior to the acceptance of the complete project. Martin was able, by one means or another, to keep the gymnasium from being complete, so the matter never came to an open issue.

Other minor incidents occurred during construction to mar the even tenor of events. One was a rumor that circulated in the community, to the effect that the second floor of the building was so weak that it would shake when a person walked across it. Another occurred when the auditorium seats were installed and Mr. Littleton discovered that the color in the velour upholstery rubbed off on his white shirt. Both occasioned minor crises in the community and caused a recurrence of the ever-present "sniping" criticism. The school board met at the building to examine the floor. It found that there was some spring, but certainly not enough to give any support to the rumor that it was unsafe. As a matter of fact, when furniture was placed in the room, the slight vibration of one walking across the floor could not be noticed. Treatment of the auditorium seats with cornstarch and a vacuum cleaner, by the manufacturer's representative, satisfactorily disposed of that difficulty.

Acceptance, Dedication, Occupancy

The new Greenfield High School building was accepted by the board from the contractors in July 1953. Plans were already under way to begin school in the building in September. Recognizing that there would be considerable public demand for the use of the auditorium, the board had a tentative set of regulations governing its use drawn up and sent to representative community organizations. These organizations were given an opportunity to make suggestions before final adoption of the regulations. The board decided that it would not permit public use of the auditorium until the building had been dedicated the latter part of September. This caused another minor flurry, as reported in the *Sentinel*, when a religious group whose tenets caused its members to refuse to salute the flag requested permission to use the auditorium in August for their state convention. When the board refused this request, based on its former action of no public use until after the dedication ceremonies, the sect went to the local editor, charging that it was denied because of religious discrimination.

The first winter of the building's use found the recurrence of many of the old rumors of dissatisfaction and some new ones. It was reported that the building was settling so rapidly on its foundations that the doors had to be cut off an inch a day to keep them operating. Continued reference to the building as "that concrete monstrosity" by some local businessmen and its obvious resemblance to a modern industrial plant were heard frequently. Heavy rains in November caused water to stand in the street in front of the building, a situation which had occurred every winter since the city had put in storm sewers of inadequate size. The *Sentinel* ran a large picture captioned "Water Standing in Front of the New Greenfield High School," the implication being, as usual, that the building was poorly located. The report was current that there was water over the first floor of the building when it did not even reach the front sidewalk, which was three feet below floor level.

Actual difficulty with water did develop during the second winter of use. The architect had designed the gymnasium floor with wood supports rather than concrete in order to give greater resiliency to the floor. Lack of adequate drainage and poor ventilation under the building caused dry rot in the supporting members and floor joints. After considerable discussion of what could be done, the board employed the same firm of consulting engineers which had made the soil study when difficulty had been encountered with the foundation. The engineers made four recommendations and indicated that they should be carried out in sequence as might be necessary to correct the difficulty. The board demanded that Martin have the work done. After an extended session at a regular board meeting, well reported in the *Sentinel,* Martin agreed to provide the necessary architectural and engineering services to correct the situation and to pay one-half of the cost of the work. The report from the consulting engineers indicated that a part of the water problem under the building was due to the fact that water from the roof drains was carried by pipes to a sump under the building rather than being discharged to the outside as is the customary practice. This was obviously an architectural decision, and if it was a contributing cause of the floor-rot difficulty, it was Martin's responsibility; it was on this basis that Martin agreed to pay one-half of the cost.

Other than this water difficulty, the only major item involving public reaction to the building concerned the acoustics in the auditorium. As the largest meeting place in Greenfield with fixed comfortable seating, the auditorium received extensive public use the first year. Various groups were particularly critical of the acoustics. Martin refused to accept any responsibility for the acoustics, claiming that the board had ruined them when it purchased chairs with upholstered backs and seats instead of chairs with plywood backs as he had planned. After two years of use with more or less constant complaint, the board employed an acoustical engineer from a neighboring state to study the auditorium and make recommendations. His report indicated that the auditorium was "too dead" through use of too much acoustical tile. He recommended replacing some soft wall surfaces with hard plaster and the use of sound filters in the heating and ventilating ducts to reduce noise from that source. His fee was $600 and the estimated cost of the changes was $5,000.

Conclusion

"Experts" in the community estimated that Architect Martin's delay in preparing the plans cost the community from $250,000 to $300,000, largely owing to the inflation of the postwar years and the Korean crisis. The error in the grading survey and the extra cost of the footings added $50,000 to the contract price. Corrections of drainage and ventilation under the building to prevent rot cost another $15,000, and the changes in the auditorium to correct the poor acoustics, another $6,000. The exhaust system for carrying sawdust and other waste from the shops proved inadequate and had to be replaced at a cost of $3,000. A conservative estimate for all of these things would place the additional costs at not less than $300,000. Critics had to place the blame for this somewhere, either with the board, the superintendent, or the architect. Martin got much of the blame, with the board receiving criticism for having employed him or for not discharging him in 1949. As a matter of fact, only one member of the board which employed Martin was still on the board during the planning period. Those who criticized the board ignored this fact. A few felt that if Dr. Golden had known as much about building as he should, he could have prevented the errors that were made and have kept the cost down to a more reasonable figure.

In most respects the third Greenfield High School building is a good educational structure. While certainly not the "dream school" which the high school staff under Dr. Jones and Mr. Jensen envisioned, it does serve well the needs of the youth of Greenfield. Perhaps the fact that Greenfield is now engaged in building its fourth high school building will direct attention away from the third.

The Riverton Dilemma

Dawn broke warmly at 5:16 A.M. on May 3, 1956, in the quiet "bedroom community" of Riverton, a suburban town of 18,000.

By 6:38 P.M., sundown of this day, a fuse had ignited an explosive force which, within hours, rudely shattered the tranquillity of the community. Seated squarely astride the powder keg which erupted with such violence were five men: the Superintendent of Riverton Elementary Schools, Ezra Marsh, and the four members of his Board of Education. (One Board member had resigned shortly before this time.) These were the men charged with the prime responsibility for the welfare of Riverton's 3600 elementary children and the system's 140 administrative, certificated, and classified employees. It was their decision which, with forceful suddenness, precipitated an explosion which prompted a recall action directed against three members of the Board. In addition to the recall action, "mass resignation" of 22 teachers and classified employees at the Morris School resulted, the community divided into warring "pro" and "con" factions, and the State Teachers' Association Ethics Commission, as well as the County Superintendent of Schools and his staff, became deeply involved.

As if this were not trouble enough for embattled Riverton, statewide attention was focused on the public laundering of "dirty school linen." Five minor and four major metropolitan newspapers carried "blow-by-blow" descriptions of the conflict through thousands of column-inches in day-by-day news coverage.

What triggered the immediate and sudden explosion? The Board of Education, on the Superintendent's recommendation, voted to re-assign or "demote" two principals, John Sutton and David Robbins, to the ranks of classroom teachers.

Ironically, the demotion of Principal Sutton never became part of the conflagratory issue. Only the dismissal charges against Principal David Robbins were challenged. The charges became the "igniting spark" when on the afternoon of May 3, 1956, Robbins returned from the district office to advise his staff of his reassignment based upon these shortcomings:

1. A lack of educational leadership in curriculum development.
2. An inability to control his temper in dealing with teachers.
3. Poor parent relations.
4. An unco-operative and unfriendly attitude toward central-office personnel.
5. Favoritism toward certain staff members.
6. Unhappiness because he had not been elected assistant superintendent.

The Central Figures in the Situation

David Robbins, Principal of Morris School. A few hours after David Robbins reported his reassignment to his staff, key patrons "had the word" in the Morris School attendance boundaries. Within days, the controversy had gained powerful momentum. A power struggle materialized as persons and factions aligned themselves for or against the superintendent and his Board majority.

Essentially, it became a contest for survival between Superintendent Marsh and ex-principal Robbins, as well as a question of the survival of the existing Board of Education. At the height of the controversy, the "official line-up" was as follows:

For Superintendent Marsh:	*For ex-Principal Robbins:*
. . . Three members of the Board	. . . One member of the Board
. . . Committee on Sound School Administration	. . . Morris Staff School
	. . . Morris patrons (3 to 1)
. . . Riverton Women Leaders (key community group heads)	. . . Better Education Commission
. . . Ten P.T.A. past presidents	. . . 2,000 valid signatures on a recall petition
. . . Riverton Dads' Club	. . . County School Superintendent
. . . Junior Chamber of Commerce President	. . . Riverton Teachers' Ass'n. Ethics Committee

Ezra Marsh, Superintendent of Schools. When his feet first touched the sod of Riverton in the summer of 1955, Superintendent Ezra Marsh inherited what was to become a "Pandora's box" loaded with trouble for his newly elected administration in a district that for many years had grown and flourished under the dominant personality of its previous superintendent, William Morris. It was after this man that the impending trouble spot, "Morris School," had been named in appreciation for the honoree's guiding hand in the district's growth. During his tenure, the Riverton schools had grown from one school to five and the staff from one of 40 persons to one of 160 persons.

In addition, Ezra Marsh entered a community which had been divided over a unification issue short months before his arrival. The defeat of the proposed unification of Riverton Schools had presented a "slap in the face" both to William Morris and to the Board of Education which had proposed unification with the high school district in which the Riverton elementary district was situated.

The unification plan's failure came after citizens had opposed it in a hearing before the County Committee on School Organization. Having thus succeeded in stopping the unification move, the community subsequently unseated two of the board members who had favored it. Shortly thereafter, Superintendent Morris resigned to accept a position in the northern part of the state.

Marsh also stepped into a district that had had little central-office leadership in improving instruction and curriculum practices. An emphasis on building and physical facilities during a hectic period of growth had led to an almost complete decentralization of curriculum policies. Individual school principals were the "authorities" in instructional improvement.

In the face of these circumstances, Marsh believed that there was a need for the evaluation of curriculum and of staff personnel. In addition, he wanted greater unity of command, more centralization of leadership, and a strengthening of the curriculum. To improve the curriculum, Marsh and the Board initiated a new practice. They assigned curriculum responsibility to assistant principals, and began to co-ordinate the elementary school programs. In turn, curricular responsibility was shifted from principals, and their job became that of "running" the school. (Principal Robbins, for example, had previously devoted much time and study to the reading programs, but this responsibility was assigned to an assistant principal.) At the same time, a plan for adding an hour of "enrichment" classes to the school day was also under study by the assistant principals.

Initially Marsh carried on the program on his own, aided only by occasional consultations with professors in a nearby metropolitan university. All the while he worked on the assumption that the methods and materials in Riverton schools were not up to date and that some teachers took their work too much as a matter of routine.

Six months after Marsh assumed the position of superintendent, the Riverton Board of Education, on their superintendent's recommendation, employed an administrative assistant. Much of the assistant's time at the outset was given over to the evaluation of the program initiated by Superintendent Marsh. This decision was made to permit the superintendent to give more attention to district financial problems.

The assistant superintendent soon began taking an active role in the evaluation of school program and of personnel while stressing the need for greater social experience in classroom procedures. He repeatedly advised that play activities should assume a more important role in the primary grades. Teachers soon became restless and suspicious. Rumors about the promotion of "progressive education" began to spread. The ideas of the new administrators became topics of common conversation to a point where Superintendent Marsh felt called upon to appear before various P.T.A. meetings to explain his objectives and activities. His explanations did not appear to satisfy many school patrons and teachers, and rumors continued. When teachers gave the tag of "progressive" to his program, the superintendent replied, "I don't know what 'progressive' education is, but I know what we are trying to achieve." In spite of the conflicting issues, however, the Riverton School Board continued to support Marsh's program.

In this aura of staff uncertainty, the annual report on the evaluation of administrative personnel was submitted. About the report, Marsh said, "This report to the Board was made, not in the form of 'charges' against two principals, but it consisted of my opinion of all principals and assistants, and the kinds of jobs they were doing.

"I was confronted with a decision. I spent days and nights attempting to reach a proper decision. My final recommendation was made for what I thought was the best for the children of Riverton.

"Could I have left things alone? Could I have saved my wife from emotional strain? Could I have prevented my children from being physically attacked and rejected? Could I not have put my position ahead of the children of Riverton? The answer is 'yes.'

"But why did I place my family life, job security, and twenty-two years of experience in education in jeopardy? I refused to play politics with your children's education. I may not have my position in a few weeks, but I can look every one of your children in the eye and say, 'I didn't let you down.'

"The best is the only thing good enough for the children of Riverton."

The Situation as It Affected the Board Members Who Supported the Superintendent

Much of the animosity directed toward members of the Board evolved from three factors: (1) the personal popularity of the principal around whom the storm raged; (2) the manner in which the reassignment was made; and (3) the refusal to make public the specific charges in support of the generalized grounds for demotion.

Thus the Board found itself faced with a triad of attacks relative to the soundness of its judgment and its action. To every charge, the Board was firm and confident in its rebuttal, with an attorney member usually acting as spokesman. Thus, the Board maintained that "the power and authority to govern and supervise the local school district rests with the members of the school board elected to office by the voters of the district in the traditional American way." They further argued "that such power and authority should not be relinquished to a small group of employee-teachers, a majority of whom do not live in our community."

To the charge of secrecy surrounding the demotion charges, the Board spokesman replied: "In accordance with professional ethical standards and accepted practice, the Board and Superintendent prefer not to make any charges because of the effect on the Principals' ability to secure future employment." He further noted: "Details for the areas of weakness in one case were made available by members of the Principal's own staff."

As evidence that there were "sound and convincing" reasons for the demotions, the Board stated: "The decision to reassign the two principals is supported by numerous specific incidents reported to the Superintendent and to the Board by many citizens. To set forth the details of these reports would be to reveal confidences shared by parents, teachers, and staff." One Board member asserted: "Robbins was reassigned because he did not carry out district policy on reading programs and did not give leadership to his teachers in the administration of this program."

Responding to the charge that criteria for evaluation were lacking, the Board retorted: "Evaluations were made in terms of teaching experience, credentials, rapport with children, and relations with teachers and other staff members."

Standing firm even in the face of "mass resignations" at Morris School, the Board held the door open for their return, but stated clearly: "We consider the mass resignation of twenty-two staff members premature, ill-advised, and contrary to the State Code of Ethics for teachers. They have no real, defensible reasons."

Board member Phillips touched a sore spot by observing: "They (the teachers) perhaps saw the end of preferential treatment, the break-up of certain groups, closer supervision, and a longer day." Expressing no sympathy for the rebellious Morris Staff, the Board further charged: "A small group of teachers chose to by-pass their own ethics committee and directed their anger against the Superintendent and the Board through children and parents. When weakness appeared in both curriculum and personnel, we moved to overcome it. We knew opposition would arise . . . some people always oppose change."

The Situation in the Eyes of the Demoted Principal, David Robbins

Mr. Robbins expressed a belief that an "unjustifiable and unpardonable action had been taken against a man completing ten years of service in Riverton Schools . . . four years as a teacher, one year as a vice-principal, and five years as a principal." He failed to understand how the charges against him could have suddenly occurred or have materialized after five years of apparently satisfactory service as a principal and leader. After submitting his resignation May 6, Robbins did not encourage the staff patrons to champion his cause, but he made no effort to stop them from doing this. Along with his followers, he decried the Board's executive sessions, saying, "I see no need for secrecy . . . I have nothing to hide."

Much of the trouble and blame for the problem, according to Robbins, stemmed from poor communication. He said that there were from the beginning much confusion and concern among the teachers over the curriculum evaluation program. This confusion and concern added to the seriousness of the personnel controversy.

Known as a quiet man by his intimates, Robbins remained relatively silent during the prolonged controversy. But on election eve, with community fever at record peak, he fired this parting shot at the Board which had deposed him: "These men failed to heed the counsel of the Assistant County Superintendent of Schools . . . there is no alternative but a recall vote."

The Situation from the Point of View of the Teachers in the Morris School

The teachers at the Morris School believed that a serious injustice had been done, and it was in this belief that they came to the support of Mr. Robbins, criticizing the Board of Education for a lack of foundation for their charges and for the way in which the two principals had been demoted.

It was in an expression of anger that the Morris teachers said to the Board in the May 20 letter of mass resignation:

> It is our feeling that the issue of moral justice is paramount in this situation. We do not feel that we can stand aside and permit injustice to be done and support it. As a result, we can no longer support the majority of the Board and its administration in the action it has taken.

In further clarification of their feelings and position, the resigning teachers submitted to the Board a document refuting the charges against their principal. To further substantiate their case, the teachers detailed each rebuttal with testimony of teachers, parents, pupils, and prominent persons outside the community having acquaintance with Morris School. In their dramatic conclusion, they proclaimed:

> We believe David Robbins exemplified the highest educational standards, and has always had the best interests of the community in mind. We believe that he has established a school environment in which each pupil receives a good education. We feel his removal would be a distinct loss to our school . . . and to the community. It is our desire to continue to serve under his fine leadership.

The Situation As Seen by the Teachers in the Other Riverton Schools

Aside from the Morris School staff, Riverton's teachers viewed the growing professional flare-up with concern and alarm. As a group, their reaction was to remain apart from the controversy and to refer the problem to the Ethics Committee of the Riverton Teachers' Association. For guidance in this study, they called upon the Ethics Commission and field representatives of the State Teachers' Association.

The official action of the R.T.A. came in the form of publication of a paper entitled: "Report of a Study of a Professional Problem in the Riverton School District," which set forth:

1. An "objective" presentation of the problem and its "background" of development;
2. A presentation of 20 "findings" aimed at clarifying major aspects of the problem; and
3. A presentation of nine "conclusions," which included professionally-arrived-at recommendations for preclusion of future problems of this nature.

Although the major "damage" had been done by the time the R.T.A.'s findings and conclusions were published, the report did serve a valuable purpose: it gave a lucid, unemotional "inside look" and an analysis of the situation. More important, it helped restore a measure of community confidence in the teaching personnel of a strife-torn school system. Repeated attempts by teachers from the Morris School to involve other members of the Teachers' Association in this conflict were not successful. In the words of the President of the Riverton Teachers' Association: "A pressure group is trying to make use of my name and names of my colleagues without our consent. A small group is trying to make the community believe that the teachers who resigned did so because of the action of the school board. That is not the case at all. Some resigned for other reasons."

Nevertheless, the report of the R.T.A. Ethics Committee did make an indictment of all parties concerned. Its recommendations generally paralleled those offered by the State Teachers' Association and the representatives from the County Superintendent of Schools. Yet it tended to be critical and pointed the need for:

1. Better communication from the administration to the staff relative to Board policy and actions;
2. Better personnel administration based upon well-defined criteria, with reasonable time allowed for correction of deficiencies noted;
3. Patience and understanding on the part of patrons, giving the administration and staff an opportunity to work on professional problems;
4. More wisdom on the part of teachers in the use of professional media for arbitration of problems;
5. Examination of district organizational structure with a view toward better definition of authority and central functions;
6. Staff participation and greater democracy in the development of curriculum and educational policies to insure staff co-operation and understanding; and finally,
7. A strengthened and broadened Teachers' Association to better serve the staff and the community.

This report received little attention during the heat of the battle.

The Situation As Seen by Citizens Who Opposed the Board of Education

A major disaster wrought by nature could not have stirred greater reaction from scores of Riverton's citizenry than did the sudden displacement of David Robbins, Principal of the Morris School. Within hours after the announcement of his demotion, groups of citizens met. One thought united them: "What can we do about this?" Those who were angered by the decision of the Board of Education began action to seek the recall of the members. Two of the leaders in the recall movement were Mrs. Robert Boyd and Mrs. Evan Barnes, both solid supporters of the prior school administration and staunch members of the Morris School P.T.A. They promoted the organization of the Better Education Committee of Riverton. Accepting the role of spokesman for the Better Education Committee, Mrs. Boyd attacked the "arbitrary action" of the Board and Superintendent. She questioned their competency to administer Riverton's schools.

Specifically, the Better Education Committee leader charged the Board with repeated violations of the State School Law. "No trace of the evaluation report on the principals was placed in the Board minutes," she claimed. "On this questionable basis, two men were demoted while charges remain hidden." Encouraged by the strength of unity and organization and irked by the Board's continued refusal to compromise or document its charges against Mr. Robbins, the Better Education Committee carried on its proposal to hold a recall election for the three board members who consistently supported the action to "demote" principals Robbins and Sutton.

"Grassroots" organization, which included coffee hours, public meetings, the circulation of printed matter, and actual petitioning, resulted in the collection of 2300 names supporting the recall action. Heartened by the response, the Better Education Committee stated on election eve: "Rising resentment against the three members of the Board has been caused by their insistence on closed-door sessions. The recall petitioners are genuinely alarmed over the threatened breakdown in our educational system. We must elect responsible, competent men who will administer properly and efficiently."

A rising emotional tide caused by the situation brought forth three champions of the fallen Mr. Robbins in opposition to the incumbent board members. Two professional men and a technician, fathers and patrons in the Morris School area, volunteered their names as candidates for what they hoped would be recall-vacated seats on the Board. They were backed by the Better Education Committee. These persons made their position clear by charging that the three members of the Board whose recall was sought had "failed to act in the best interests of the children and community. By their incompetent acts, they would cause teachers to leave the community." Warming to their task, the trio published a steady barrage of charges against the Board of Education, stressing a theme of general incompetence.

The candidates, in a gesture to the anti-Marsh group, observed: "It will be necessary for a new Board to evaluate Superintendent Marsh's administration to determine this administration's responsibility for this chaotic situation. We intend to grant Mr. Marsh the courtesy and rights he did not give to Sutton or Robbins."

One of the candidates charged the Board with using extremely poor judgment in approving a contract for a teacher from the district which Marsh formerly served. In effect, this candidate said, "This was a rejection of the Assistant County Superintendent's suggestions that no more teachers from Mr. Marsh's former district be hired during the dispute." He further charged the Board of being guilty of holding secret meetings and of failure to secure additional revenue for the district by investing cash balances in short-term interest-bearing bonds.

A second candidate contributed additional charges against the incumbents, claiming the "Board has done one thing after another in the past year to prove its incompetence in school affairs." He cited:

1. The alleged hiring of the new superintendent without the recommendation of the County Superintendent's office, which had received $75 for screening services;
2. Demotion of our most experienced principals under recommendation of a superintendent who had not been recommended for our district; and
3. Responsibility for the resignation of many teachers because of the lack of the present superintendent's leadership and organization.

This candidate rounded out the charges by claiming that "the present Board is directly responsible for a breakdown of Riverton's educational system . . . Almost fifty per cent of the staff and administrative personnel have resigned . . . a crippling blow to the future and security of Riverton's children." He concluded by citing the Board for its "failure to establish well-defined, commonly understood personnel policies . . . which has resulted in collapse of teacher and administrative staff morale to the children's detriment."

To promote their unopposed candidacy, the trio published a 12-point statement of intended action upon their election. This platform set forth principles which would remove the evils with which they charged the Board incumbents, as follows:

1. Open public Board meetings, tape-recorded, with a minimum of executive sessions;
2. Fair personnel policies designed to retain qualified employees;
3. Explanation of the curriculum evaluation program;
4. Development of a strong local teachers' organization;
5. Rebuilding of staff morale;
6. Development of a line of clear communication with staff members and schools;
7. Establishment of an evaluation program of personnel;
8. Reassignment of personnel when it would serve the best interests of the children;
9. Acceptance of advice and recommendations of the County Superintendent's office;
10. Acknowledgement of public opinion;
11. Development of an education program which perpetuates the American way of life; and
12. Correction of present Board deficiencies.

The Situation As Seen by Citizens Who Supported the Board

To defend the Board of Education against the charges that had been made, the Committee of Sound School Administration was formed. It was composed largely of present and past community leaders. This Committee criticized as injudicious the use of the recall. It called for a sane and unemotional approach to the problem. The head of this committee charged that the recallists are "a pressure group seeking to replace the existing Board members with 'hand picked' candidates of their own choice." He, along with other citizens, urged the community to avoid the cost of the recall balloting—a cost that he estimated at approximately $700.

Echoing his words was the president of the Dads' Club, who addressed the community through the press, saying: "The use of the recall procedure should be preserved as an instrument of the people to correct charges of misconduct in office by their elected representatives after the general public had had an opportunity to hear both the accusers and the accused." He charged that the recall sponsors "chose to rebuke our mediating efforts and the candidates have avoided public discussion of important issues."

In spite of the efforts of the Committee of Sound School Administration, the citizens of Riverton were not dissuaded from voting on the recall of three members of the Board of Education.

The Epilogue

Election day, July 30, 1956, finally arrived in Riverton. With it came the heaviest vote in a school election in community history, with each separate recall action failing by a margin of 300 votes.

The vote of 2639 ballots cast out of 6970 registered voters represented 37.8 per cent of total Riverton voter registration. The previous high was 33.2 per cent in the 1955 school board election.

Balloting results demonstrated clearly the division of community thinking concerning demotion of two school principals by the Board of Education. In the precinct in which feeling had been most intense—that of the Morris School—the recall action was affirmed by a vote of *two to one*. In the Riverton Elementary School area, from which school principal Sutton was demoted without subsequent fanfare, recall failed by a small margin. It then remained for the school precincts not directly concerned to sustain the Board's action and defeat the recall with decisive *two to one* margins. The so-called neutral precincts turned the tide in favor of the existing Board.

The voting bears out the loyalties and pressures involved in the dispute: a school patronage arising to defend its principal by voting against his accusers; a second school patronage under less emotional pressure in support of its principal; and two remaining school voting areas within the whole "putting down the opposition to sustain a duly-elected Board."

This ended one phase of a school conflict that had attracted wide attention. The embers of this conflict are still smoldering, but there has been an attempt on the part of citizens in this school district to develop a more positive attitude toward the situation. One of the leaders in the recall movement, Mrs. Robert Boyd, wrote in November a letter to the editor of a local newspaper, saying: "I would like to repeat the statement I made to Mr. Marsh, personally, on March 30, as I want everyone to know exactly where I stand. I will be happy to work with you and everyone concerned in this district for the better education of our children.

"It is my wish that all parents should visit the schools and extend their hand to teachers. Only by co-operating can we accomplish what we are all interested in . . . our children's education. It is time for us to forget about choosing sides and be on our children's side and work together."

Changing the Curriculum at Southside

> *In a complex organization, the whole is composed of power structure within power structure, with holders of real authority not always indicated clearly to the eye of the casual observer.*
>
> HAGMAN

If the administrative process is likened to a stream, then the following case may be said to represent various currents, eddies, sandbars, and undercurrents in the stream. The story relates the struggle of a determined principal to produce curriculum change in his school. The flow of information and ideas and the use of communication channels are depicted in this process. The swirl of inharmonious values, representing the new and the old, stability and change, are thrown into relief. How powerful the undercurrent of informal organization can be in its effect upon change is also delineated. Since the desired curriculum change was not successfully consummated, a question is raised of why it was a failure. To answer this question, one is led to a careful assessment of Bell's philosophy and leadership techniques. Such an assessment should lead one to an involvement with issues which are common to many administrative situations.

ʌst beginning his seventh year as principal of the
Soutl   rge in physical stature, Bell was a middle-aged
man ʏ   l most of his life to education. His experience
had b   ʋels in large and small districts and in urban
and rͅ   e he became principal at Southside, he had
been ἰ   rintendent in a large city school. Active in
many o̲ᵣ   ɔth state and local, Bell was regarded by many
colleagues as a̲   anding educational leader. A professor of curriculum in a neig̲ ̲oring university described him as "one of the
best-informed high school principals on curriculum in the metropolitan area."

Southside High School, which Bell headed, was more than 35
years old and housed approximately 2500 students in grades 10, 11,
and 12. It was one of five large high schools in a western city of more
than 300,000 people. Located in one of the more "respectable" areas
of the city, it drew most of its students from the middle socioeconomic
class. For many years its patrons were almost entirely middle-class.
With a recent influx in population, however, a substantial number of
students of lower socioeconomc origin had entered the school. Although they constituted less than a third of the total enrollment, their
influx had created various problems for the administrators and teachers at Southside.

Southside's curriculum was strongly influenced by upper middle-
class values, a situation which resulted in considerable emphasis on
academic achievement. Each year school officials consistently announced that a relatively large proportion of the graduating students
had received scholarships to numerous universities throughout the
country, including some of the oldest, finest, and best established.

More recently, under Bell's leadership, the school was seeking
a more diversified curriculum. Efforts had been made to provide
various kinds of curriculum offerings for students of varying levels
of ability. Shortly after Bell came to Southside, he made changes in
the counseling system, including the adoption of a homeroom organization. When the issue was first raised, teachers were very much
opposed to this change and voted it down. Several months later, after
further discussions, an affirmative vote resulted. Even after the vote,
many of the teachers did not believe that the idea was practicable or
desirable, and they continued to complain. Five years later, however, it was generally accepted that the homeroom organization for

counseling was a marked improvement in Southside's educational system.

The preceding year, one of the teachers had suggested to Principal Bell the idea of forming a special class for gifted students. Bell saw in this another way of diversifying the curriculum and gave his full support to the teacher. Therefore, the teacher had initiated and conducted a class for 30 students who, in the opinion of their counselors, were highly gifted. The content of the course was classical literature and philosophy.

In considering other curriculum alternatives, Principal Bell had recently made a decision to try to initiate a schedule that would allow teachers to have one of their classes for a full half-day each Tuesday afternoon. One purpose of such a schedule was to allow field trips to supplement the more abstract textbook learnings.

He saw in such half-day excursions advantages for educating the students who were not as capable as others. In his own words, he believed "that the traditional academic curriculum could not meet the needs of students with the low levels of ability." He strongly believed that a high school should develop a program that would allow all students to develop their potentialities.

In addition, he believed that a better relationship between teachers and students could be obtained through the plan. By spending an entire half-day with students, he believed the teachers could gain a better understanding of the strengths and needs of students. He was keenly aware of the large size of the Southside High School and was concerned that the teacher-student relationships might be overly impersonal. Bell's decision was also influenced by the successful experience which two other eastern schools had reported.

In Principal Bell's desire to put the half-day schedule into effect, a question that confronted him early was how to initiate the change. With approximately 100 teachers to reach, Bell was sharply aware of communication problems. He knew that the formal and informal systems of interaction would be important elements in instituting the change.

Southside's Formal Organization

Southside High School had a line-and-staff organization. Directly responsible to the principal were two vice-principals. Bell was responsible to an assistant superintendent in charge of curriculum, and the latter reported to the superintendent of schools. When Bell came to Southside, department heads were largely responsible for the supervision and evaluation of teachers. Shortly after Bell's arrival, he assumed the responsibility for evaluating and supervising teachers. Department-head duties then were to pass on information from the administration to teachers, to take care of texts, to be in charge of tests, to have department meetings, and to give information to counselors. When this shift was made, Bell also suggested that department heads might rotate annually and be elected by teachers. This proved to be an unpopular idea and nothing came of it.

When Bell first came, a large proportion of the teachers were middle-aged or older. According to some of the teachers, Bell had in recent years sought to bring in younger teachers with liberal points of view who spoke their mind on educational issues. It was also reported that a part of the difficulty which Bell had incurred in instituting changes in the past was due to the fact that many of the teachers were older and more conservative in outlook.

At Southside High School there were various channels of communication which could be utilized in introducing educational change. The faculty meeting, which convened once monthly, was one means of administrator-teacher communication. Another means involved department heads, the principal, and two vice-principals and was called the *instructional council*. Meeting once weekly, this group discussed procedures and policies pertinent to curriculum.

Still another communication system which most teachers considered important was the suggestion committee. This committee was composed of the principal, two vice-principals, and three elected representatives of the teachers. The representatives were chosen each semester from among the teachers who had free second periods, since this was the time at which weekly meetings were scheduled. All teachers were encouraged to report suggestions, complaints, or questions orally to members of the committee, or to write their ideas anonymously and place them in the boxes of the teacher-representatives. It was generally understood that no names would be mentioned in the meetings of the suggestion committee.

Department meetings were held once every six weeks. At these meetings curriculum matters directly pertinent to departments were discussed and clerical and procedural matters were also handled. Central-office supervisors were available for the various departments in the high school. However, they visited the school infrequently, and most curriculum changes were brought about through committees representing the various city high schools. The assistant superintendent in charge of curriculum, as well as the central-office staff, encouraged local initiative in the different junior and senior high schools.

Southside's Informal Organization

Southside also had its informal communication systems. About 60 per cent of the teachers belonged to clearly defined informal groups whose operations could be easily observed. For various reasons the remaining 40 per cent of the teachers were not attached to any of these defined groups. Several reasons for this were suggested by different representatives of the informal groups.

First, a number of teachers had outside interests, such as family relationships, and they were not interested in developing attachments at school. These persons were interested in coming to school, doing their work, and leaving as soon as possible. Other persons had not become closely attached because they had not been in the school long enough. Often a person taught for as much as a year before he joined a group or before a group accepted him. A third reason why teachers did not establish informal relationships was an innate shyness on their part. As one teacher said, "Some teachers may come to the cafeteria, but they are too timid to associate or form close relations with other teachers." Still another reason was suggested by one teacher, who said, "We cannot get along with some of these teachers, and frankly I don't see how the students can get along with them either." Finally, some teachers did not attach themselves to particular informal groupings even though they were well known and no doubt would have been accepted by different groups. Some of the outstanding leaders in the school would fall into this category, including both teachers and department heads. They interacted informally with a large number of people in the school but were not clearly attached to any one informal group.

There were five informal groups that were clearly defined at the

Southside School. They could be labeled as follows: the small, opposing group, the large social group, the men's group, the cafeteria group, and the women's group.

The small opposing group was composed of older persons, and the chief cohesive element which held them together appeared to be their educational philosophy. This philosophy was described in various ways, but the main theme, as one person put it, was that, "Strict academic pursuit is the function of education."

Most members of the school staff viewed the small, opposing group as generally resisting the policies of the administration when the latter wished to effect change. In general, members were very critical of Principal Bell and his manner of school administration. Jim Newton, one of the leaders in the small, opposing group stated, "The main problem around here is the attitude of Bell. He does not want to listen to what we have to say, and he feels very intense and does not want to take criticism."

Another member of this group called the faculty meeting "a vestigial remain of school administration," and was also critical of the suggestion committee when he stated, "I don't think it is successful so far as the teachers are concerned. The real purpose, I believe, is to give the principal a chance to get his ideas across to us, rather than for us to get our ideas across to him."

Also important in the interpersonal dynamics of the school was the large social group made up of approximately forty teachers. The binding element in this group appeared to be social fellowship, since persons of different ages and somewhat different outlooks were associated with one another. As more than one person stated, "We enjoy being together." Periodically, the members had parties outside of school hours, but they apparently were not all able to meet together at the school. Parts of the group did meet at lunch periods and at free periods during the day. They were generally much more liberal in their outlook than the small, opposing group and were also more friendly toward Principal Bell. There were many persons in this group who supported Principal Bell ardently and spoke words of high praise for him. The following description is typical of how a number of persons in the large social group viewed Principal Bell: "Bell is the greatest of the great. He is a regular fellow who does not throw his weight around. I have worked under several principals and most of them are pretentious and act as if authority gives them special privileges, but you can talk to Bell and tell him a good story the same as you can to anybody. Bell is not a vindictive person, and he is tolerant of other points of view. He operates in a democratic way."

Teachers were more conscious of the large social group and the small, opposing group than they were of other informal bodies in the school. It was also well known that there was considerable organizational rivalry between these two groups. One person in the large social group stated, "We have two groups that are important here. One group we call the senior conservatives, and the other is the liberal element in the school. The senior conservatives say what they want to do, but we defend what we believe is right, too. So the two groups often disagree and oppose one another on school issues."

The third group, the cafeteria group, was composed of eight of the younger teachers in the school. Most of them did not have tenure, as they had been at the school only a year or two. They held common perceptions, among which the following was expressed: "I find Bell very hard to approach and to talk to. I always feel that he leaves me in my place and rapport is not established."

Other persons in the organization had ways of explaining this lack of rapport. For example, a teacher of long tenure stated, "Mr. Bell is basically a shy man. If he meets a person in the hall, he may not give a warm greeting, or on other occasions he may be wrapped up in educational ideas or plans and not notice a person who is passing by. Some people interpret this differently from others. Those who would not ordinarily feel free to visit the office interpret this to mean that Principal Bell would not welcome them."

The men's group was a small aggregation that had lunch daily with one another in the men teachers' room. According to one of the members, the group did not see itself as taking part in developing or opposing policy, except that policies and procedures were often discussed during lunch time and opinions were formed through this process.

The women's group closely followed the lines of the physical education department, but included one other person. This assemblage also met periodically outside school hours away from the school environment. Generally its members were more concerned with policy which dealt directly with affairs in their own department, and they were not often seriously concerned with policies affecting the entire school.

Bell's Relations to the Informal Organization

Principal Bell was aware to some extent of all of the informal groups at the Southside School. Most conscious of the small, opposing group and the large social group, he realized the important part that they played in the school. His closest relationships were established with the large social group. He talked in the smoking room with some of these teachers almost every day. He was consistently invited and attended the social parties which were held outside of school hours. During these parties, which were held about once a month, Principal Bell had opportunities to become better acquainted with some members of his staff. His closer relationship to the large social group created a problem in his own eyes in that he wondered how other persons might view this relationship. Principal Bell expressed concern that members of the small opposing group might view this association as an example of partiality on his part toward the large social group. He was also concerned about how other members in the school would view his association, and at times strongly felt that he should cease attending the monthly parties of the large social group.

According to Fred Olden, a member of the small, opposing group, Bell's participation in the large social group actually was not seen as a problem. "For awhile the older teachers felt that Bell was allying with the younger group, because he would visit with them in the smoking room and go to their parties. But so many of the younger people have kicked over the traces that the idea has now been discarded and the fact that these people happen to be his drinking partners now has little significance."

A variety of perceptions prevailed among members of the large social group about Principal Bell's attendance at parties. A third of the group looked upon this association as highly desirable, and some members thought that it was one of the reasons why they accepted and liked Principal Bell. Although other members in the group had positive attitudes about Bell's attendance, they were not entirely able to forget his position and status. As one person said, "Bell always comes to our parties and we have a little kidding and we get to know one another. I must honestly say, however, that he never loses a certain amount of authority."

Some teachers believed that the social occasions made their group more closely knit. As one teacher stated, "We like to go out and have a couple of drinks, joke, and have fun. We are the closest, best-organized group in the school. We really know one another. We get much better acquainted at the parties. If something comes up and we want something done about it, we can sign petitions after we talk it over."

Principal Bell's relationship to the small, opposing group was not at all close. Although he did sometimes sit with members of this group in the cafeteria, he did not have a close relationship with them. He did successfully interact with a few members on an individual basis. He perceived the group as follows: "Some of these groups in the school bother me, as the downstairs group, for instance. It is made up mostly of older people. They are a rather disgruntled group. In general, they have an academic outlook and are not interested in activity programs."

Jim Newton and Fred Olden, recognized leaders in the opposing group, were the persons with whom he interacted most frequently. Both men had taught at Southside for many years and had been there at least a decade before Principal Bell's arrival. Fred Olden had been a teacher of journalism and in charge of the school paper when Principal Bell first received his appointment. During the second year of his principalship, Bell transferred Olden from the journalism department to a position as social studies teacher. He had viewed Olden's work in journalism as inefficient and incompetent, and he had transferred a younger person into Olden's position. According to Principal Bell, Olden did not like this transfer and had complained about it on different occasions. However, Principal Bell saw the transfer as highly desirable when viewed in terms of its value for students studying journalism. Many other teachers thought the new journalism teacher was an excellent organizer, as well as a person who had a very important influence on the students whom he taught.

Jim Newton, a physics teacher, had the reputation of being very courageous and completely unafraid of voicing his convictions. He fought strongly for high academic standards and opposed anything in the way of activity programs. His point of view was expressed partially as follows: "I am very frustrated with teaching. Since I began, standards have deteriorated. I have to spend half of my time teaching math and reading as a physics teacher. The trouble is all the activity outside of classes. Students are always going or coming to a rally, to music, to drama, or to something like that, so that they are always wild-eyed, and the atmosphere is not one for working. Students do not need to plan what they want to do. Most of them need to learn to work and to learn discipline."

Principal Bell described Newton as a highly intelligent and courageous man. "He is a good man to have in an organization. He makes you think through your operations and be clear about what you plan to do. I would not want to work in an organization where every member was a 'yes' man. Although Newton has a highly critical mind, he serves his purpose here. He is an excellent teacher of physics, and I would not presume to tell him how to teach his classes in physics. He feels free to talk to me, even though we seldom agree."

Thus, Bell's relationship to the small, opposing group was somewhat different from his relationship to the large social group. His own set of values and the set of values held by members in the small, opposing group were so different that they were beyond compromise. The continual struggle which had resulted from this value conflict had, in the words of one teacher, "colored Bell's point of view." The same person, a member of the small, opposing group, gave the following example to illustrate his point. "Some time ago I was concerned about the large number of tardies on the part of students, so I wrote a note to Principal Bell about it. The head of the language department also wrote a similar note about the same time. Bell suggested that we get a committee together to study the problem after he told us that some teachers never did have any problems of tardiness, the indication being that we were at fault. When we came together as a committee, I suggested to Bell that the reason why some teachers might never appear to have tardies was that they never turned in their tardy slips. He immediately set off on a twenty-minute rampage about how the school had improved since he came. It is true that he has brought about improvements since he came, such as, for example, the halls are much quieter now, but that was not related at all to the purpose of our meeting. I had not realized that he was so sensitive until this meeting. We had not at all intended the note as he took it. So next time we will be more hesitant to take things to him."

Initiating the Half-Day Schedule: The First Attempt

In introducing the proposed half-day schedule, Principal Bell had to decide where to initiate the idea. After discussing the matter with his vice-principals, a decision was made to discuss the half-day schedule with the instructional council.

Since the department heads would have some responsibility for carrying out the program, this move seemed desirable to Bell; also, he always found the council a good place to test ideas. With a few exceptions, Principal Bell saw his department-head members as effective leaders. Two of the department heads he saw somewhat differently, since they seldom initiated ideas and, worse, as far as he was concerned, frequently did not comply with ideas that were suggested to them. Generally speaking, the department heads were very loyal to Principal Bell and had closer relationships in general than did the other teachers. One department head, for example, stated: "Bell is quite different from his predecessor. His predecessor would close the door when he was busy and did not want to be bothered, but Bell always asks people in if they come outside his office. He met considerable opposition when he first came to the school seven years ago, but he does not give up easily and continues to try to get his ideas into practice. He is not only a good administrator, but he is also an educator."

Another department head made the following statement: "When Bell came here, the school was actually being run by the dean of girls because the principal in charge at that time was afraid to make decisions. There were also strong cliques in the school, and they were extremely unfriendly to one another. That was not good, and I believe one reason why the situation came about was that we did not have a strong principal. Everybody has his say here now, but you know who is running the school, for Bell is very decisive. I am sure there are people here whose ideas Bell especially respects, but they do not run the school. I believe he judges ideas on whether they are important, whether they can be used for the good of the majority, and whether most of the people want them."

Principal Bell chose one of the regular weekly meetings of the instructional council to present his idea. He explained how the half-day schedule might work. Each Tuesday afternoon would be set aside for the schedule. On the first Tuesday, the regularly scheduled nine o'clock class would have the half-day period. The next week, the ten o'clock class would be scheduled; the following week, the eleven o'clock class; and so on.

The reasons for adopting the schedule were also set forth. First, it would allow the teachers to take excursions to use community resources as learning experiences. For example, the journalism teacher might wish to take his class to see a print shop or a newspaper press. The half-day schedule would also allow teachers who did not take excursions to spend a half-day with one class. The theory behind this proposal was that teachers would have a better opportunity to become acquainted with their students and, as a consequence, could do a better teaching job.

The instructional council was generally favorable to trying the idea, although they raised several problems that had to do with scheduling, with students who might not wish to go on excursions, and with the extra burden that detailed planning might place upon the teachers. Most of the opposition was voiced against the frequency of the schedule, and it was finally agreed that the half-day schedule should be held once every two weeks instead of once weekly.

Bell's next step was to present the half-day schedule to the teachers. This he chose to do with small groups of teachers. His procedure was to ask all of those teachers who had a free first period to meet in the council room. After talking with these teachers, he met those with second periods free, and so on throughout the day. During these sessions the principal presented the idea of the half-day schedule and told the teachers why he believed it would be good to put this into practice at Southside. There was also an opportunity for raising questions and pointing up problems pertinent to the proposed idea. Bell thought the method which he used was a good technique for communicating with teachers because the groups were small, and questions could be raised. He saw this as one of the most effective ways of changing teacher opinion and gaining support for school policy.

Teachers reacted to this experience in different ways. One of the teachers who was a leader in the large social group described the meeting as follows: "I felt the discussions were very superior because all of the teachers could be involved. The group was small enough so all the members could participate, and the atmosphere was conducive to persons' giving their opinions. Of course, there was the problem of the senior conservatives being a part of the group. As it happened, our group was made up mostly of senior conservatives, so we had a hard time getting going."

Olden, one of the leaders of the small opposing group, had a different view: "This meeting did not serve any purpose other than that of the administration. We were indoctrinated into the administration's way of thinking so we would go along willingly, rather than resentfully. Not only were we brain-washed by Bell, but at the same time it was hard on teachers who are already overworked and who do not have the energy or time for such things."

In spite of such opposing views, the use of the small group meetings gave Principal Bell an opportunity to learn about the sentiments of his teachers and to know something about how sentiment was divided on the issue at stake.

In initiating policy changes, he described his usual procedures as follows: "The ideas are sometimes initiated in faculty meetings, but they are almost always taken up in the instructional council so that we can iron out the bugs. Then in important changes we usually discuss the problem with the teachers in small groups. If after such discussions I decide that opinion is closely divided on the issue at hand, I postpone the problem, and a process of education is involved. This may last a year or more. If there seems to be a clear majority of sentiment for an issue or a proposal at stake, then we put the proposal to a vote of the faculty."

Principal Bell was aware that sentiment about the half-day schedule was closely divided. He knew that such a proposal was clearly opposed to the philosophy of persons in the small opposing group and of others in the school. There were others who hesitated because of the problems involved in scheduling and carrying through the program. However, he judged that the sentiment was in favor of the half-day schedule, so he decided to put the issue to a faculty vote. When the votes were counted, a majority of the teachers voted against the half-day proposal. Therefore, Principal Bell did not make further plans immediately to put the schedule into effect. He announced the vote to the faculty, which was only slightly in favor of not adopting the half-day schedule, and he indicated that he hoped that they would reconsider the issue in the future, and that eventually it would be possible to adopt a half-day program at Southside.

Initiating the Half-day Schedule: The Second Attempt

During the following year, Principal Bell did not abandon the idea of instituting a half-day program. His action supported the view that many persons held toward him, namely, that he did not give up easily. Wherever the opportunity presented itself, he attempted to persuade the teachers to his point of view. For example, when someone complained about persons who were taken from their classes to go on excursions, he would point out that the absence would not be necessary with the half-day schedule. Or, when teachers spoke of the individual differences in their classes, Bell pointed out the advantages of field trips in that slower students could have more concrete learning experiences.

After almost a year of this "process of education," Bell decided to put the half-day schedule to a faculty vote for a second time. Even though they were expanding the grade club program at the same time, he judged that there was enough faculty support to get a majority of votes approving the half-day schedule. Therefore, arrangements were made and the votes were cast. When the votes were tallied, there was a clear majority in favor of instituting the half-day program.

The increased favorable opinion for the half-day schedule was attributed to at least two factors. First, according to a number of the teachers, they had come to understand the half-day schedule better and could see its advantages from the standpoint of their own classroom teaching. Second, a number of people voted positively because of their loyalty to Principal Bell. As the following quotation would indicate, some members changed their minds partially out of respect for him and perhaps partially in order to please him.

> At this school the principal tries to get teachers to enter into policy decisions. For instance, if some policy comes up, he will announce it in faculty meetings, and sometimes 90 per cent of the teachers may not like the idea. Then we discuss it later on, and then maybe only 75 per cent of the teachers don't like the idea. He talks to us some more and then maybe 60 per cent are opposed to the idea. At that point you say, "Why not? Let's give him a chance to try out this idea."

Since the vote was taken near the end of the fall semester, the plan was to begin the half-day program at the beginning of the second semester. During the second week of the second semester, the first half-day schedule was instituted.

It did not take many weeks to reveal that all was not going smoothly with the new program. Some of the problems were revealed in informal conversations of teachers. A Latin teacher had this to say, "This program might be all right for some teachers, but it certainly is not appropriate for my class. How can I take a class of students who are studying Latin on a half-day field trip? There is no place in this community that would be suitable for a visit, and I don't like the idea of spending an entire half-day with the same class here at school."

Another teacher found it difficult to hold the same class for an entire half-day and to plan effective learning experiences, as the following statement made during the lunch period shows: "If you are going to have a whole half-day class, you have to have a varied plan. I am not able to introduce enough variety into the teaching situation to make it very successful. Besides, my students are slow learners, and they are hard enough to interest even for one period. I don't think the idea is very practical."

Objections were also raised about how the trips were planned. As one teacher said, "We do not have the time to make pre-visits, and this is important if these excursions are really going to be successful. Also, when we get back to the classroom, we do not have time to follow up on the excursions, because then we must begin thinking about what we are going to do two weeks hence."

Keeping up with the administrative procedures proved to be a burden for some teachers, as the following quotation shows: "There is so much record-keeping in this new schedule. Every student must pay fifty cents for transportation, for instance, and we have to keep a record of this. If we make a mistake, we are responsible for it. This is just another burden in an already long and hard day."

The feature of the program which perhaps caused the most widespread concern among teachers was that some of the teachers came in for extra supervision. Since all of the students in the classes did not always take part in the excursions and could not be compelled to do so, someone had to supervise those who remained behind. Sometimes this fell to teachers who remained at school with their regular classes, but on some occasions, teachers who had the half-day period schedule free lost the period, since they were assigned to supervise students who remained. This aroused negative feelings among teachers, not only because they felt that it was unfair, but also because they were under the impression that the administration had assured them that such a condition was not likely to occur when the half-day schedule went into effect. Although there was considerable clamor about this problem from the inception of the half-day program, it was never satisfactorily solved. A department head almost a year after the program's beginning described its manner of treatment as follows: "We first brought up the problem in the department meeting last fall. The problem was then passed on to the suggestion committee. Nothing happened except that the matter was pushed back to the department heads, who were supposed to solve it. I finally divided the period between two teachers, so they did not lose all of their period. In a way we were left holding the bag. The day that I made this decision, Principal Bell was sick, I believe. At least he was not at school."

Thus, various objections about the half-day program were raised by different groups in the school. Even though the large social group had generally supported the half-day program by their vote, some members began to express reservation about its value. The small opposing group, of course, had objected to the program from the beginning. Olden described the origin of the idea as follows: "What happens around here is that the principal identifies the success of the school with himself. Bell got this idea of the half-day program somewhere in New England. Since there had never been such a thing tried in the West, he wanted to make a success out of it. That is the reason it was started. A problem in education is that administrators go around and get their ideas from administrators, and they should, of course, get more of them from teachers."

Many teachers retained favorable attitudes toward the new program. However, dissatisfaction in general mounted. More and more notes raising objections to the half-day schedule were written to the suggestion committee. Even some of the more loyal followers of Bell began to raise questions. Notes such as the following were received: "I feel that it is too much of a drain on us to carry on this half-day schedule. We are keeping books all the time, and when one excursion stops we have to start getting ready for the next one. It is such a taxing job supervising these students when they are on trips, and I don't think my arteries are going to stand it. There are many other teachers who are also objecting."

As the objections to the half-day program were heaped one upon the other, Principal Bell realized that some action had to be taken. About halfway through the semester, he decided to put the half-day schedule to another vote. Since it was not easy for him to think of giving up the half-day schedule, he decided to propose a vote on two temporizing alternatives. The choice given to faculty members was to vote on whether the half-day program would be continued for the remainder of the semester, or whether it would be dropped and taken up again at the beginning of the next year. Principal Bell made this proposal for two reasons. First, he believed that if the program were postponed until the fall, he and his staff would have an opportunity to iron out some "bugs" in the project. Because he had had to devote a great deal of time to another project that had been going on during the year, he felt that he had not had adequate time for the half-day schedule. He believed that the next year would allow him to give more care and attention to the half-day schedule. A second reason for the postponement was that he disliked the idea of giving up the half-day schedule because, in his own words, "It is very difficult to get such an extensive program started again after you have once given it up."

Having made his decision, Principal Bell announced his proposal at a faculty meeting and promised that the ballots would be available within a few days.

Keeping his promise, Principal Bell had ballots distributed at the beginning of the next week. A large number of teachers participated in the voting, and when the tally was made it was clear that a marked majority of the teachers favored abandoning the half-day schedule for the rest of the semester, with the understanding that it would be continued again the next fall. Although there was some dissatisfaction with the alternatives proposed for the ballot, there was considerable relief among many faculty members in that the half-day program was to be abandoned at least for a few months.

As could be expected, members of the small opposing group were not at all happy with the manner in which the problem was solved. Their attitude was reflected somewhat in the words of Olden as follows: "We don't like to feel that things are being crammed down our throats, but it seems to us that the vote was worded in such a way that you lost whichever way you voted. This is a Russian tactic. I don't know how the ballots got that way, whether they were rigged or not, but they sure seemed that way." That this attitude prevailed among members of the small opposing group was evident to most of the faculty when it became known that Newton had sent an anonymous note to the suggestion committee which set forth in very strong language the feelings which his group harbored. One of the notes attacked the principal in a personal way and spoke rather derisively of the "Russian ballot." Since there was always a written record of the complaints which came to the suggestion committee, and since this written record was distributed among teachers, everyone learned of this note to Principal Bell and it was broadcast rapidly throughout the school. When it became widely known that the note had been written by Newton, considerable sentiment developed both pro and con. Members of the small opposing group generally looked upon this event with considerable glee, while many members in the large social group expressed strong feelings against Newton and argued that Principal Bell did not deserve such harsh words. It was proposed informally that those who wrote letters to the suggestion committee should be divested of their anonymity, and in the future everyone writing notes should sign his name. However, no real action on this issue eventuated.

Faculty members who generally supported Bell looked upon the balloting much more favorably. Many of them appreciated Bell's solution because they felt that their principal had yielded in his own plans and in the process was showing consideration for members of his faculty. Thus, in their own perceptions, Principal Bell was behaving democratically, which, of course, contrasted strongly with the opposite views held by members of the small opposing group.

There were others in the school who perceived Principal Bell's solution as astute administration. In the words of a representative of the cafeteria group, "Bell was very shrewd in the way he handled this problem. We voted on whether to discontinue the program until next fall, or whether not to discontinue it. We did not vote on whether to discontinue it for all time. Bell's excuse was that the program had not been tried sufficiently. In other words, he raised the question of how we could know the real value of the half-day schedule until enough evidence had been collected in order to make a good judgment about it."

Initiating the Half-Day Schedule: The Third Attempt

When school opened in the fall, Principal Bell was determined to make a success of the half-day schedule. He felt that the activity program was well established, and that he could now devote most of his time to the half-day program. He still strongly believed in the value of this program, and he thought that, for the good of the students at Southside, it was worth special efforts to make it successful.

Returning with renewed energy, many teachers also undertook the task with new hope. During the first weeks of the semester, more excursions than ever were taken into the surrounding community. On one day, for example, 357 students went to a local theatre to see the movie "Julius Caesar." On any Tuesday afternoon a number of large yellow buses lined one after the other could be observed in front of the Southside School ready to take the students on field trips.

However, a listener to the school's informal communication system would soon conclude that the old dissatisfaction with the half-day program had not disappeared. Problems of preparing for a half-day's teaching with one class, of finding desirable places to go for learning excursions, of burdensome record-keeping, and of responsibility for supervising students all weighed upon teachers. Finally, the old issue of teachers' losing free periods by having to supervise students who remained behind caused considerable concern among the teachers in Southside. Notes about the problem were written to the suggestion committee, but nothing constructive was done about the problem. As a member of the suggestion committee said, when a fellow teacher inquired about the solution of this problem: "We discussed it in the meeting, this morning, but it was not solved, and I don't think that it can be solved."

Some of the persons who had been most loyal to Principal Bell were no longer able to support the program's continuation. It was with some satisfaction that Olden reported one day to the small opposing group that he had heard that one of the department heads who was one of Bell's loyal supporters had gone to Bell directly and informed him of the widespread sentiment against the recent curriculum innovation. Another loyal supporter of Principal Bell remarked to some teachers, one day in the cafeteria, that she believed the half-day schedule was not feasible. In her own words, "It is like so many things in education. It sounds very good in theory, but it does not work well in practice."

As dissatisfaction mounted for the third time, Principal Bell decided that the faculty should again vote. He proposed that a vote be taken at the end of the semester, as this would give them adequate time to judge its worth, and that at that time the faculty should vote as to whether they wished to drop the half-day schedule or whether they wished to continue it. In the meantime, arrangements were made to study the program's results through an opinionnaire survey of all the faculty members.

A committee was appointed to develop an instrument which could be used for gathering opinions and findings about the half-day program. Having gathered the information, the committee gave a written report to the faculty near the end of the semester.

A few days later, a vote was cast. When the vote was tallied, Principal Bell announced at a faculty meeting that the schedule innovation, which they had tried to make succeed, would be dropped because a substantial majority had voted against it. Once more he stated that he hoped they would be able to try out the half-day program once again sometime in the future.

The next day there was considerable informal talk about the dropping of the half-day schedule. Teachers were generally expressing satisfaction that they did not have to continue with the program. Olden and the members of the small opposing group seemed especially happy that they had finally won out in achieving the objective for which they had worked. Olden thought that the victory was clear-cut: "Principal Bell, you will notice, did not announce the number of votes yesterday at the faculty meeting. There was a good reason for this, because the vote was unanimously in favor of doing away with the half-day schedule."

Other faculty members, on the other hand, expressed the idea that Principal Bell had reported the vote accurately and that only a substantial majority was in favor of abandoning the half-day program. Some teachers expressed regret that the schedule was abandoned because, as one person said, "Even though it was tough for an algebra teacher or a world history teacher, it worked fine for me as a biology teacher."

During the middle of the next semester, Principal Bell reported that more teachers than ever were taking their students into the community. In his own words, "There have been more requests for excursions this semester than ever before, and I perhaps get a devilish pleasure from it. This means, no doubt, that in the future a new plan will have to be derived for meeting this problem. Even though we took a beating in the voting, the half-day program has caused some teachers to change their methods of teaching."

Concepts

CHAPTER FOUR

Viewing Administrative Processes

Thought and theory must precede all salutary action.
WORDSWORTH

Towering high among the Alps is the famous and formidable peak known as the *Matterhorn*. For many years this peak was invincible to the most skillful mountain climber. This invincibility, coupled with its rugged beauty and unusual formations, created a reputation that was spread throughout a great part of the world.

As its fame traveled from nation to nation, more and more sightseers traveled to see this awe-inspiring colossus. Some of these persons viewed the peak from the south, looking up from the Italian side. A very beautiful and frequently photographed view was the one from the picturesque little village of Zermatt on the northeast. Others looked at the mountain from the east and southeast, and still others from the west. In more recent times, travelers have taken a more Olympian view by scanning the peak from rapidly traveling aircraft.

What meaning do these remarks about the Matterhorn have for administrative processes? Analogy, although imperfect, can be used to point up a number of similar relationships between viewing administrative processes and viewing the Matterhorn.

Man and Mountain: Some Analogies

First, there are countless vantage points for observing the Matterhorn. If there were a compass large enough, for example, to draw

367

a circle around the base of this towering peak, 360 different "snap-shots" could be taken if the angles from which the snapshots were taken were all one degree apart. Many are the facets of administrative processes to be encompassed, also. While the Matterhorn is stationary, administrative processes *move* through time. Their goals, their locations, and their expressions change. Because of these changes, the facets of administrative processes are doubtless even more numerous than are the facets of the Matterhorn. In any case, both phenomena offer an almost infinite variety of views.

Another important observation is that none of the views allowed the sighteeers to see the Matterhorn as a *totality*. The various views from the south would leave the northern side obscured, and vice versa. The same condition would hold from the western and eastern sides. Even the more celestial views would not reveal in detail the mountain in its entirety.

Administrative processes, like the Matterhorn, cannot be grasped as a totality from any one view. If a physical object so clearly defined and as objective as the Matterhorn cannot be entirely grasped from a single point of observation, it seems all the more reasonable to believe that intangible and ever-changing administrative processes will not totally yield themselves to any one perspective. If one looks at the leadership processes in a school or a school district, for example, this means that followership processes will tend to be ignored, obscured, or only partially encompassed. Or, if one tries to observe an organization in terms of informal processes, this means that formal processes will be neglected. Thus, anyone who tries to make sense out of the variety of events that make up the "reality" of administrative experience through a single perspective is faced with certain limitations.

Since cases are written records designed to capture a slice of the reality of school administration, the same problem is met when one seeks the total meaning of a case. There is no vantage point from which one can grasp the entire reality of a single case or of a set of cases. Thus, the student of those cases which depict administrative behavior is faced with the problem of selecting the most significant perspective or perspectives for analyzing the experience encompassed in the term, "school administration." Stated differently, what theoretical frameworks can best explain administrative behavior as the latter is described in a case or as it takes place in an administrative situation? Such a question raises some basic problems that must be solved if an adequate conception of administrative processes is to be realized.

Problems in Conceptualizing Administrative Processes

Scholars have used such terms as *role, competency, competency pattern, task, job, function,* and *process* to conceptualize aspects of administration. In the present work, the term *process* is used. It is judged most appropriate because it has a dynamic connotation and, therefore, is more adequate for dealing with movement and change. In addition, it is comprehensive enough to include both the administrator and the situation. The shortcomings of attempts to describe and explain administrative behavior apart from the situation have already been made clear by the research on leadership (4). An adequate conception of the administrative processes calls for a more dynamic and a more inclusive view.

A number of problems arise when process concepts are used. Some of these problems will now be made explicit, particularly as they relate to the concepts that are presented in the following chapters. Figure 4 will serve as a basis for identifying and clarifying some of these problems.

General or specific processes? A number of observations can be made by examining Figure 4. In the first place, the concepts in the inner circles represent processes that are more general in nature. As one proceeds from the center circle to the outside of the figure, the process concepts become more specific. Thus, human behavior is a very general concept for encompassing administrative process. The concept is so broadly abstract that it could apply to the actions of persons in all social settings without, of course, capturing the details or illuminating more specific processes of school administration. In terms of the Matterhorn, it would be like a picture taken from high above its peak with the camera shutter as wide open as possible. Specificity is sacrificed for the broader view.

As one moves from the concept of human behavior outward into the categories of leadership and followership, and beyond these to others, one notes a progressive limitation in view. To continue the analogy, the camera shutter, so to speak, is not so wide open, and the distance from the object to be viewed is perhaps less marked. More specific actions are encompassed at the expense of a general view. There are, of course, many other processes of a still more specific nature not represented in the figure which could be added. For example, staffing could include job analysis and the development of job specifications. Within both of these process concepts are the still more specific ones of interviewing and of keeping records. One problem in conceptualizing processes is already evident and can be stated thus: How many processes should be conceptualized? A second, and related, problem is: How general or how specific should concepts for encompassing the processes be? The greater the specificity, the greater the number of process concepts needed.

Overlapping concepts. Further study of Figure 4 reveals that all the process concepts are to some extent interrelated and overlap-

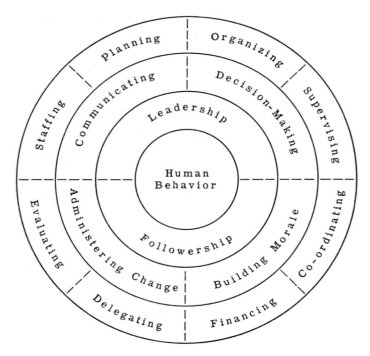

Figure 4. Some Process Concepts.

ping. This overlapping can also be illustrated by referring to the Matterhorn. For example, two persons located ten degrees apart and viewing this peak would have overlapping views. Both would see some of the same formation at the top of the mountain, some of the same snow, some of the same ice, some of the same rocky crags, and so forth.

In a related way, the broken lines of Figure 4 are designed to indicate that there is overlapping not only between and among the process concepts within a given circle, but also between and among those concepts in different circles. For example, communicating is an aspect of decision-making, and vice versa; this illustrates overlapping within a circle. At the same time, communicating is a part of leadership; this illustrates overlapping between circles. A third problem, then, in selecting process concepts is: How shall we deal with overlapping?

Basis of definition. Another observation readily drawn from Figure 4 is that the concepts in the outer circle are those most frequently treated in textbooks on school administration. They are derived basically from an economic view of organization. Such a view looks at the job to be done, divides this job into its component tasks, and seeks ways to perform these tasks as effectively and efficiently as possible. On the other hand, it can be noted that the processes represented by the concepts in the inner circles are more typically the subject matter of the social sciences, particularly sociology and psychology. They are more related to human behavior in general than to the tasks of administration in particular. A fourth problem, then, is: Should we conceptualize processes in terms of the specific tasks of administration, or should we conceptualize them in terms of the behavior of persons doing the jobs?

Some of the problems, then, in conceptualizing administrative processes may be summarized: First, how many administrative processes should be conceptualized? How specific should the processes be? What does one do with the problem of overlapping concepts? Should concepts be chosen on the basis of job division, or more in terms of behavior of the person doing the job? How these problems relate to the concepts chosen for elaboration in this book will be discussed later. The next task is to indicate what administrative processes are judged to offer most conceptual promise.

Process Concepts: Their Purpose and Logic

Whether a given concept is more significant than another must be partially determined by the purpose which it is to serve. One purpose of this book is to present and elaborate some concepts that will be appropriate for illuminating the processes of administrative behavior. On this basis, four concepts are selected: communicating, building morale, administering change, and decision-making. These concepts are judged appropriate for achieving the purpose noted above, and, in addition, it is hoped that they can do the work efficiently. The importance of economy in the achievement of purpose can be illustrated by again referring to the Matterhorn.

For many, many years mountain climbers who were seeking to reach the summit of the Matterhorn thought that the southern perspective held the greatest promise. However, after countless climbers had failed, Whymper, an Englishman, approached the peak from the northeastern side. This approach proved correct; even though the northeastern side appeared more difficult, actually it was much easier to climb. While it would be unrealistic to believe that the concepts elaborated in this book will lead immediately to the summit of a theory of administration, it is hoped that they will be fruitful in economically pushing the frontiers upward.

A definition of what is meant by *conceptualizing a process* is now in order. To arrange sub-concepts in a systematic and interrelated fashion around a more general concept (for example, communication) so that a selected process may be better understood is one way of describing the operation. Such an integration of concepts should enable one to achieve a deeper interpretation of administrative behavior whether such behavior is studied in cases similar to those contained in this book or whether it is viewed in actual administrative situations. Thus, the conceptual frameworks which are presented in the following chapters are designed as aids for understanding action as the latter is represented in administrative processes.

There are a number of reasons why the development and elaboration of the concepts noted above are believed appropriate for describing and explaining administrative processes. Some of these reasons will be noted now.

General in application. The concepts of communicating, building morale, administering change, and decision-making represent processes that can encompass behaviors which occur frequently in administrative situations. Communication and decision-making, for example, are taking place almost constantly in an organization. Morale problems, small or large, are ever present and demanding solution. The administration of change, particularly in times of technological progress and social ferment, also tests the administrator. Thus, if systems of theory could be developed for each of these four chosen processes, a great deal of administrative action could be encompassed.

The processes selected also occur outside of school organizations and often have an important bearing on administration. An explanation of the communication process, for example, would have relevance for understanding the operation of a lay citizens' committee, as well as for understanding the operation of a faculty meeting. It is reasonable to believe that the crucial factors in administering change in a state department of education are basically similar to those encountered in administering change in a school or a school district. There are common elements in a legislature's making decisions on school law and in a school board's making decisions on educational policy. There are common elements in building morale whether such problems relate to parental expectations or the expectations of teachers. Thus, relevant action inside and outside the school organization can be encompassed by the processes selected. The advantage of such inclusiveness should be apparent.

The processes are also general enough to apply to various levels of administration. Any elementary principal must make decisions just as a district superintendent must. A state superintendent administers change, and so does an assistant superintendent in charge of curriculum. Communication is important for the secondary school principal just as it is for a county superintendent. All administrators, of course, are faced by morale problems. It should be clear, then, that the above processes have general significance for all levels of administration.

A problem was raised earlier as to whether more general or more specific processes are most appropriate for describing and explaining the essentials of administrative action. It is evident that the ones noted above are more general than specific. The advantage of general processes over specific processes lies principally in their inclusiveness and wide application. While general in nature, they can apply to very specific behaviors. For example, communication and decision-making are involved in such relatively simple tasks as a principal dictating a letter to a secretary, answering the phone, and conferring with a teacher. These processes can also apply to more complex situations, such as a school board meeting, a lay citizens' meeting, and a meeting of a faculty steering committee. The conceptual frameworks to follow, then, are more general views of administrative processes.

Pertinent to social science research. A second advantage in conceptualizing the processes noted above stems from their relationship to social science research. All the processes have been of great interest to social scientists in various disciplines. Communication, for example, has been investigated through many avenues: semantics, rumor analysis, polling, content analysis, small-group study, sociometry, mass communication, cybernetics, organizational communication, nonverbal communication, individual communication, and advertising psychology, among others. Decision-making has been studied by psychologists, sociologists, and students in the various fields of administration. The dynamics of change has received much attention from students of society and culture as well as from students of the various types of administration. Problems of morale have received wide attention among students of military, business, and public organizations. The fruits of these various research efforts on the different processes offer distinct advantages to persons interested in developing theoretical frameworks. Since not enough research has been done in school administration or related administrative fields to construct a comprehensive theory, it seems reasonable to turn for aid to social science research on behavioral processes related to school administration. An approach to integrating some of the findings from the social science disciplines and from the related fields of administration should thrust forward the quest for the meaning of administrative processes. In addition, such efforts should provide bases for testing the general applicability of social science findings.

In seeking to integrate some of the research findings, one must answer this question: should perspectives be developed for shedding light on how processes *actually* operate, or for formulating ideas on how they *should* operate? In terms of the Matterhorn, should one view its beauty to comprehend and make it verbally explicit, or should one view its beauty with the idea of imagining how it might have been made more beautiful? The perspectives in this book will be oriented chiefly in terms of understanding and explaining administrative processes as they actually happen and not so much in terms of how they should happen. Since the actual and the ideal are interrelated, the treatment cannot completely divorce the two.

The question raised earlier, Should process concepts be defined more in terms of the job or more in terms of the behavior of persons doing the job?, can now be considered. An examination of the chosen processes will reveal a compromise solution. Two of the chosen process concepts—administering change and maintaining morale— are general administrative tasks. That these two process concepts are significant is atttested by the fact that various theories of administration utilize these concepts or variations of them. In describing leader behavior, Hemphill and Coons (6), for example, have used "initiating structure" and "consideration," while Halpin (5) more recently has used the terms "group maintenance" and "group achievement." The definitions given by Barnard (1) to "efficiency" and "effectiveness" are closely related to the two processes, and so are the concepts of "formal goals" and "informal goals" used by various writers. To some extent the same elements are also present in the concepts of "nomothetic" and "idiographic" in Getzels' writings (3), although Getzels' formulation seems more appropriate for dealing with morale maintenance than for explaining change. The close relationship of the present concepts to the "morale" and "innovation" functions described by Dubin (2) is also noteworthy.

Although the two concepts just discussed represent general processes clearly related to the administrative task, the concepts of communicating and decision-making represent processes that are more general in the sense that they apply to other life situations. However, these concepts, to a greater or lesser degree, are implicit or explicit in most theories of administration, and Simon (7), for example, has made decision-making a central concept in his theoretical formulation. Undoubtedly, these two concepts represent processes that fundamentally are intertwined with change and morale in an organization. It seems important, then, that they be developed and elaborated.

Another problem posed earlier was that of overlapping concepts. For this problem there seems to be no easy solution, since it constantly and doggedly pursues any student of human behavior. The psychologist, for example, knows that a certain portion of a population cannot be neatly and precisely classified as extroverts and the remainder as introverts. Most persons will display a combination of introvertive and extrovertive characteristics rather than represent a "pure" type. In the same way, the sociologist knows that observational data cannot be accurately and sharply divided into primary- and secondary-group behaviors. The student of administrative behavior also finds that some of the behaviors associated with maintaining morale are relevant to communicating. Since behavior is expressed as a totality, and often in relation to diverse purposes, the problem under discussion cuts through the various sciences of behavior. Sometimes unrecognized and out of view, and at other times revealing itself openly, the same problem is found in administrative practice, in research on administrative behavior, and in programs for educating administrators.

The most appropriate solution to the problem doubtless lies in theoretical synthesis. Put differently, the more global or molar in character that administrative theories become, the less marked problems of overlapping concepts will be. At present the problem cannot be neatly solved. However, utilizing a small number of concepts should decrease the amount of overlapping. Since only four major concepts are presented in the following chapters, overlapping should be minimized. Such an approach also follows the "parsimony" principle of theory-building.

Relationship to general theory. The 1950's have seen a deeper and more intense quest for a theory of school administration. Researchers investigating administrative behavior have had the need for theory brought home to them. Persons examining or re-examining programs for training administrators have also encountered theoretical problems. It is becoming ever clearer that educational programs for administrators cannot be carefully or soundly designed if they are divorced from administrative theory. Such developments have stimulated thinking and writing on subjects new and relatively unexplored in the literature of educational administration.

While the conceptual perspectives presented in the following chapters are not intended to be complete or final, they certainly have implications for a general theory of administration. They could serve as foundations for theory, in that they are complementary to the cases and thus can be studied and tested in relation to cases and to actual administration. Measured against comprehensive theory, they are skeletal rather than organic wholes—starting points rather than stopping points. They can be conceived as frameworks for theory, or perhaps as partially developed sub-systems in what some day might be a much more fully elaborated system.

Although an over-all unity has been sought, no attempt has been made to draw relationships between and among the various frameworks. Neither has there been a consistent effort to use uniform methods in developing the various frameworks. Thus, some differences in the approaches to the different formulations will be noted. In spite of the limitations of treatment, each of the concepts undoubtedly has implications for general theory. Brief comments about each of the concepts will suggest something of their significance in this respect.

As Barnard has noted, there can be little doubt that an elaboration of the communication process will occupy a central place in any comprehensive theory of administration (1). The process takes place in an organization continuously. It links persons together and allows them to define goals and to devise means of achieving goals. Thus, it is hard to imagine how goals of an organization can be achieved without the use of communication. Stated differently, the quantity and quality of communication in an organization are no doubt a basic determinant of administrative effectiveness. A carefully developed perspective for viewing communication processes, then, will undoubtedly lead to a better understanding of administration.

Another frequently occurring process in an organization is decision-making. In a sense, communication and decision-making complement one another and might be described as different sides of the same coin. Thus, decision-making sometimes may result from a series of communication processes; on other occasions, the making of a decision may set off a series of communicative acts. Even when communication has resulted in clear understanding, problems are not always resolved. Choice between or among ends and means is also required. Therefore, an explanation and description of decision-making would have high priority in a comprehensive theory of school administration.

In order to live and to serve, organizations must change. It follows, then, that adaptability is an important ingredient in effective administrative organizations. In American culture, where nothing is more certain than change, adaptation is especially significant. If

educational organizations do not change, they become outdated, ineffective, and, in extreme cases, dysfunctional. It is also noteworthy
that during change, the dynamics of organization are thrown into relief so that forces affecting human behavior show themselves more
clearly. The appropriateness of a strategy for explaining the administrative change should be evident.

In the achievement of organizational goals, there are always
human factors and potential morale problems. Such problems can be
between or among teachers and teachers, teachers and students, administrators and teachers, teachers and parents, and so on. An organization cannot function well unless human relations problems are
in some way met constructively. In promoting co-operative activity,
the achievement and maintenance of morale become crucial. Administration will be concerned, then, not only about getting a job
done, but also about interpersonal relations and *esprit de corps* of the
persons doing the job. Therefore, a framework for viewing the process
of morale maintenance should be abundantly useful.

Summary

The four concepts of communicating, building morale, administering change, and decision-making are judged to represent basic
processes in administration. Consequently, these concepts serve as
a base for the frameworks presented in the following chapters. There
are three apparent advantages to elaborating frameworks to illuminate the processes to which the concepts refer.

First, the processes are widely applicable in that they cover
many behaviors in many situations. Second, a great deal of social
science research pertinent to these processes is available. Third,
conceptual frameworks to describe and explain these processes
should lay the groundwork for a more comprehensive theory of administration.

A major purpose underlying this book is to illuminate and give
meaning to administrative action. Thus, the cases and the concepts
are designed to develop competencies among prospective administrators in the basic administrative processes. The frameworks are not intended to be complete. Neither is it pretended that they are the only
frameworks for viewing administrative behavior. Rather, they are
offered as examples of conceptual frameworks for interpreting ad-

ministrative action. May they serve some as a stimulus for thought, others as a springboard for research, and still others as a base for further theoretical formulation.

References

1. Barnard, Chester, *Functions of the Executive*. Cambridge: Harvard University Press, 1938.
2. Dubin, Robert, *The World of Work*. Englewood Cliffs, N.J.: Prentice-Hall, Inc., 1958.
3. Getzels, Jacob, "Administration as a Social Process," in Andrew Halpin (ed.), *Administrative Theory in Education*. Midwest Administration Center, University of Chicago, 1958, Chapter VII, pp. 150–165.
4. Gouldner, Alvin (ed.), *Studies in Leadership*. New York: Harper and Brothers, 1950.
5. Halpin, Andrew, "A Paradigm for Research on Administrative Behavior" in Roald Campbell and Russell Gregg (ed.), *Administrative Behavior in Education*. New York: Harper and Brothers, 1957, Chapter V, pp. 155–199.
6. Hemphill, John, and Alvin Coons, *Leader Behavior Description*. Columbus, Ohio: Personnel Research Board, The Ohio State University, 1950.
7. Simon, Herbert, *Administrative Behavior: A Study of Decision-Making Processes in Administrative Organization*. New York: The Macmillan Co., 1957, 2nd ed.

CHAPTER FIVE

Communicating

Communication is a process through which relationships develop or decline, lead to growth or frustration.
RONKEN AND LAWRENCE

The administrator is a key link in the numerous communication systems that make up his verbal environment. His communication with those persons directly responsible to him and with those to whom he is directly responsible is of crucial importance in administration. In addition, he is an important connecting link with those outside the organization. Thus, a major portion of his time is spent communicating; in the broad sense, administrative behavior is communicative behavior. Consequently, concepts for illuminating communication in an administrative organization would necessarily constitute an essential aspect of any comprehensive theory of administration.

Cornerstones of Communication Theory

What are the most appropriate concepts for describing and explaining the communication process? The following are judged to be central: *purpose, communicator, medium, channel, content,* and *communicatee.* These concepts can be illustrated from Case Eleven, "Heartaches and Headaches," where Miss Wright discussed with Miss Simms the problem that was interfering with the latter's teaching. The communication *channel* was the arrangement of human relationships through which the messages were transmitted, that is, between the supervisor, Miss Wright, and the teacher, Miss Simms. The *medium* was an oral, face-to-face one in Miss Simms' classroom. The behavioral and verbal symbols that gave meaning to the interaction were the *content*. Since a *communicator* is defined as the person who transmits content and the *communicatee* as the person who receives content, Miss Simms was at times the *communicator* while Miss Wright was the *communicatee;* on other occasions, the situation was reversed. In other words, the listening and speaking roles shifted during the exchange. The *purpose* mutually shared by Miss Simms and Miss Wright was to solve the personal problem that was interfering with the former's effectiveness. Each of the above concepts needs further elaboration.

Purpose. *Purpose* shapes the communication process and is the benchmark against which effectiveness must be measured. The purposes of communicators have different dimensions and can be classified into various categories. For example, is there a single purpose in the communication, or are there multiple purposes? If there are multiple purposes, which is more and which is less important to the communicator? Is the purpose general or specific? Does it apply to one person or to many persons? Is it primarily personal to the communicator, or does it have a social character? Is the communicator clearly or only vaguely aware of the purpose? Does the purpose concern itself more with thought or more with action? If the purpose is concerned more with thought, is it designed to produce consensus and agreement, or is it designed to stimulate diversity and difference in viewpoint? Is the purpose immediate and short-term, or is it long-term and future-oriented? Such questions suggest some of the dimensions that relate to the concept of purpose.

Communicator. As already implied, the *communicator* is the person who transmits meaning. In most school situations, the communicator's goal—particularly if he is an administrator—is to transmit decision premises to others in the form of facts, unsubstantiated information, and values. In large-audience situations, there is usually one and at most a limited number of communicators. However, in small groups and in informal situations, the communicator role changes frequently and in the course of discussion most of the persons present are usually involved.

How the communicator's listeners perceive him is crucial in determining communication effects. To what extent, for example, do his listeners see him as an expert on the topic about which he communicates? What perceptions do they have of his motives? To what extent do they trust or mistrust him? What perceptions do they have of his previous behavior in the organization? How do they evaluate his present goals? What future intentions do they ascribe to him? These and other questions suggest implications for communication that stem directly from the communicator.

Channel. Communication *channels* follow patterns of formal and/or informal relationships, and through them messages are transmitted. Communication channels can be classified in various ways. Upward channels, for example, are those that link persons in lower organizational levels to persons in higher organizational levels. By contrast, downward channels go in the opposite direction. Then there are horizontal channels that connect persons on the same organizational level. Upward, downward, and horizontal channels can all be classified as relatively open or relatively closed; as relatively short or relatively extended. A distinction can also be made between direct and indirect channels. Thus, in face-to-face communications, the channel is direct. However, when a message is sent to a person through a second person, the channel is indirect.

Organizations can very accurately be described as networks of formal and informal communication channels. With such a definition, various questions can be posed that suggest the relationship of communication channels to the dynamics of an organization. For example, where are the more important informal channels of influence in the organization? To what extent are the informal networks open or closed to various members in the organization, and particularly to the administrator? How stable are the channels, and how frequently are they used? How are formal and informal channels related to speed and accuracy in communication? How is size of organization related to the number, the types, and the interrelationships of formal and informal channels? These and many other questions suggest something of the significance of communication channels in administrative organizations.

Medium. Communication *media* are usually classified as either oral or written. Stated differently, media depend predominantly on either audio or visual senses. Handbooks, manuals, circulars, news letters, daily bulletins, forms for record-keeping, bulletin-board notices, and individual notes are examples of written media. Interviews, conferences, opinion polls, committee meetings, faculty meetings, telephones, radio, and public address systems are examples of oral media. Television is a medium in which both audio and visual senses are involved. Such nonverbal media as buzzers and bells are also an important part of school communication systems.

Various factors have implications for the choice of communication media. For example, how do the effects of written and oral media differ? Will the message need to be referred to again and again? Does it have long- or short-term implications for the organization? Is the communication content such that it would be better "off the record"? Does the content apply to all members of an organization, or to only a limited number? Some of the variables related to communication media are suggested by the above questions.

Communication content. *Content* is defined as the facts, unsubstantiated information, and values that a communicator seeks to transmit to his listeners. Communication content is cloaked in symbols. While words carry the major meanings in communication, there are other important symbols—such as behavior, visual cues, and mechanical sounds. All of the symbols, of course, stand for the things they symbolize, and thus are not the things themselves.

Numerous variables related to content affect communication. Are the sentences short or long? Are the words familiar or unfamiliar? Are they organized in an interesting fashion? Are the central ideas emphasized and made clear? To what extent is the content organized in a novel fashion? Such questions point up some implications of communication content.

The communicatee. The communicatee is the person for whom the content is designed. A great number of persons can be communicatees, as, for example, in such mass-communication media as radio and television. On the other hand, only one person can be involved in a two-person conference. An intermediate number can be involved in large audiences who view and hear the communicator in person.

The meaning that results from a particular communication is highly dependent upon the basic motivations and personality patterns of the communicatee. What are his interests? What does he expect from the communicator and the situation in which he finds himself? How important is authority approval to him? What is his attitude toward his peers? For what is he striving? Is he highly intelligent and keenly critical, or is he less intelligent and less critical? Such queries suggest that the communicatee is a significant element in communication.

Communication Processes

The six concepts just noted can serve as foundation blocks for describing and explaining communication. They represent the structure within which communication flows. However, in order to illuminate communication processes fully, one must go beyond definitions of the above concepts. The interrelationships of the concepts and the interactions of the elements which they represent must be delineated if the dynamics of communication flow are to be adequately explained.

At this stage in communication research, such an undertaking is not an easy task. A key problem is to determine which approach to the use of research findings is presently most strategic for shedding light on the communication process. This chapter proposes to look at research as the latter bears upon and gives meaning to the communication processes which frequently occur and reoccur in administrative situations. On the basis of this criterion, these processes are judged to be relevant: two-person communication, small-group communication, organizational communication, one-way oral communication, and written communication. Although it is true that the above processes have many common features, all of them have certain unique characteristics that have implications for the administrator. For example, the dynamics of a conference between a principal and a teacher should differ in some ways from the dynamics of a speech to a teachers' organization made by the same principal. In other words, a speech may demand quite different leadership skills than a conference which involves two-way communication.

Such an approach to synthesizing research findings is in line with the recent emphasis on situational factors in studying leadership. Although many persons have emphasized the importance of situational factors in leadership, there seems to be considerable difficulty in developing general concepts that have wide application. By getting better conceptualizations of *different* communication situations, perhaps more progress in explaining and predicting leadership behavior could be made. Admittedly, further classification and differentiation within the general classifications of communication situations would be needed. For example, different types of two-person communication may be elaborated and subsumed under the general concept of two-person communication. At the present time, however, developing general theory to explain the five communication situations noted above should be a useful beginning. Such a formulation should enable one to say more about questions of leadership than, "It depends on the situation."

In the treatment to follow, the purpose is not to be exhaustive in delineating the unique characteristics of the different communication situations. However, the data that are included will certainly suggest something of the differences in the five situations. At the same time, some of the features that are common to the five situations will also be apparent.

For example, since two-person communication and small-group communication have many common elements, much of what is said about the former will apply to the latter. However, the section on small-group communication will point up some of the differences between the two. Organization communication, which focuses on informal networks, will be treated independently in a separate section. Since one-way oral communication and written communication demand similar skills in content organization, they will be handled in the final section. Discussion in regard to all of the concepts will focus upon the administrator in order to set forth some implications for *his* behavior. Research from various areas of communication study will be utilized in an effort to illuminate the chosen processes.

Two-person communication. Communication between the administrator and another person may be formally planned or it may arise spontaneously. Thus, a principal can schedule a conference with a teacher, or he can talk to her during a chance meeting in the hall. Formally scheduled conferences usually have clear-cut purposes, but informal interaction is often characterized by less clearly defined purposes. However, since many of the same factors seem to operate in both formal and informal communication, the following discussion is designed to apply to both situations.

The achievement of full and effective communication is not an easy task in that the personal world of colleagues is difficult to fathom accurately. In the words of Albert Schweitzer as quoted by Dooher (4, p. 5): "We wander through life in a semi-darkness in which none of us can distinguish exactly the features of his neighbors; only from time to time through some experience that we have with our companion or through some remark that he passes he stands for a moment close to us as though illuminated by a flash of lightning."

Difficulties in effective communication stem from factors that inhibit and interfere with the full and accurate expression of facts, feelings, and ideas on the part of the communicator as well as those factors relating to the communicatee's lack of awareness, skill, or time in listening to and interpreting what is expressed. With regard to the latter type of difficulties, Nichols and Stevens (21) report that listeners generally operate at a 25 per cent efficiency level. Consideration will now be given to some of the barriers that stand in the way of communication.

Communication barriers. To understand communication disruption, it is necessary to identify the factors in interpersonal interaction that affect meaning. Basically, meaning for the communicatee(s) derives from three sources: perceptions about the personality and position of the communicator, perceptions about the words and other symbols that carry the content, and perceptions influenced by the needs, expectations, and personality patterns of the communicatee(s). The material that follows is organized around these three sources of meaning. Although the discussion focuses upon implications for the administrator, it should be clear that both the administrator and the person to whom he is talking are responsible for effective communication.

Perceptions of the communicator. What are some perceptions of the administrator in the consciousness of personnel that influence communication adversely? A universally recognized factor is that the administrator is seen by personnel as more than a personality: he is a person in a position (10). The position carries legal powers that, in the eyes of many personnel, *can be* used against them. In other words, he has the power to promote or not promote, to transfer or not transfer, to discharge or not discharge. With many personnel, such power is threatening to their careers and their sense of professional security. For example, in Case Seventeen, "Changing the Curriculum at Southside," a number of personnel made statements which suggested that Principal Bell's position created a psychological threat for them. Such threat frequently causes communication to be distorted and misinterpreted. Distortion by personnel may take the turn of withholding information or of relaying only that which the administrator wants to hear. Thus, in Case Four, "The Sword of

Damocles," Teacher White apparently withheld information from the superintendent and the principal. This failure to communicate clearly and fully to the administrators compelled them to make decisions on incomplete and distorted communication. A related problem is seen in Case Eleven, "Heartaches and Headaches," when Miss Simms showed marked concern about keeping her personal problem concealed from both her principal and Superintendent Davis.

In very subtle ways the person talking to the administrator may present himself so that he appears as more intelligent or more talented than he really is. In other cases, emotional blocks may result that markedly diminish the expression of ideas and feelings, and the net result could be communication that shows the person to be less talented or less intelligent than he really is. Personnel, in threatening administrative situations, may become very sensitive to the implications of transmitting to the administrator information that might reflect upon their own work adversely. In such cases, distortion often takes place through diplomatic presentations, delayed communications, highly selective reporting, or avoidance of face-to-face situations with the administrator. Further distortions can result when the administrator (for example, a principal) who first receives what is already a distorted communication transmits it to his superior (for example, an assistant superintendent). The more levels there are in an organization, the greater the likelihood that messages traveling from the "bottom" to the "top" will be distorted. In addition to threat, there are such factors as memory limitations and selectivity arising from individual interests which also make for inaccurate transmission.

Although the legal position that the administrator holds significantly influences the perceptions that personnel have of him in two-person communication, the impact of his personality and his behavior is doubtless even more important. A person's perceptions of the past behavior of an administrator continually influence communication. Thus, certain teachers in Case Seventeen, "Changing the Curriculum at Southside," concluded that Principal Bell was "persistent." This judgment apparently stemmed from perceptions of Bell's past behaviors, and these perceptions influenced the interpretations which personnel made of the communication he issued about the "half-day" program.

Perceptions that personnel have about the motives of the administrator are also extremely important in determining meaning. The perceived motive of the administrator, for example, often causes a person to assess a communication prematurely and incorrectly. This factor, according to Rogers and Roethlisberger (23), is one of the greatest barriers to accurate communication. Thus, if a person thinks that the administrator intends to persuade him to do something that he doesn't want to do, he is immediately on guard, and this strongly affects the interaction. He may communicate on the basis of what he *anticipates* the administrator *will* say rather than on the basis of what he actually says. There is some evidence that persons are on guard less in informal than in formal communication situations and thus are less likely at such times to jump to conclusions.

Much of the meaning in communication stems from nonverbal symbols, in that the latter also determine the perceptions that a person has of the administrator. For example, the physical appearance and voice tone of Superintendent Benson adversely affected the meaning that persons derived from his speeches in Case One, "The Valley City Consolidation Issue." Even the objects on an administrator's desk or the rug on the floor may influence communication. Thus, there are many perceptions that personnel may have about the administrator that are highly influential in shaping the meaning of administrator-staff communication.

Word associations. A second source of meaning is word symbols. Although perceptions of the communicator are very important sources of meaning, it would be a mistake to minimize the role that language plays in communication. Words carry a large part of communication content, and much meaning derives from the perceptions and associations that words stimulate in the listener. Students of semantics have contributed a great deal to clarifying the unique role that words play in communication, and some of their findings will be briefly summarized.

Not only is there a very great quantitative difference in the vocabularies of persons, but there is a great qualitative difference that arises from backgrounds of different experiences. In the words of Ruesch and Kees (24, p. 5), ". . . there is a deepening regard for problems of meaning and concern with the individualistic and idiosyncratic attributes of words as opposed to their dictionary definitions." A great deal of meaning, then, derives from individual experience and social background. Thus, the word *consolidation* in Case One, "The Valley City Consolidation Issue," meant something quite different to persons in the rural districts as contrasted with persons in Valley City itself. This difference existed even though the word was clearly defined legally.

Words through use are often taken for granted in that the listener assumes that the meaning he associates with a word is the same as that held by a communicator. Habitually taking the meanings of words for granted frequently leads to inaccurate meanings and false assumptions. Thus, words are not things, but, rather, they stand for things. A merit salary schedule is not a thing, but it is a word that applies to a procedure which, among other things, affects the financial benefits that teachers receive. However, the word symbol "merit salary schedule" does not derive all its meaning from a defined procedure; the symbol becomes invested by feeling that varies somewhat among teachers but is often related to such things as their concern for status or their relationships to their superiors. Communication, then, is not just exchanging words, but involves an attempted exchange of unique meanings associated with words.

Because of the uniqueness of word meanings, the attempt to achieve perfect understanding meets with formidable barriers. In many cases, the things to which words refer cannot be seen or heard. Thus, there are greater problems in achieving mutual meanings about such intangibles as the learning process, teacher morale, and class atmosphere than about such tangibles as sites, buildings, and desks. Problems of this type can be seen in Case Sixteen, "The Riverton Dilemma," where misunderstandings arose about "progressive education" and "leadership."

Since the same word may have different dictionary meanings, communication is further complicated. The word *set*, for example, has 16 different dictionary definitions. The word *core* has an entirely different meaning when applied to the curriculum from that when applied to fruit. The significance of differing dictionary definitions can be further illustrated by the fact that the 500 most used words in the English language have 14,070 separate meanings (18).

Another factor involved in the meaning of words is that verbal symbols have a history. During their history, word meanings have undergone continual change. King James II of England, for example, described St. Paul's Cathedral as "amusing, awful, and artificial." In our own times, one would say that he thought the cathedral was "pleasing, awe-inspiring, and skillfully achieved" (18, p. 15). Sargent and Belisle (25) have shown the various meanings associated with *administration* during the last hundred years. In Case Fourteen, "The Case of a Tenacious Superintendent," much of the problem which the community faced related to the changing meaning of the word *curriculum*."

As knowledge has expanded and specialization has increased, language has become increasingly complex. As various technologies and specialties have developed, communication in large organizations has been strongly affected. In educational organizations, for example, standardized and intelligence testing is an example of a technology that has created new and complex vocabularies. The development of specialized supervision has brought out many persons with different training, different backgrounds, different interests, and different vocabularies. Thus, the learning problem of one child may involve a psychometrist, a reading specialist, a health specialist, a counselor, a teacher, a principal, a general supervisor, and a psychiatrist, as well as others. The problem of differing backgrounds is further intensified in situations where lay and professional persons communicate about educational problems, as can be noted in Case Eight, "The Gifted Child Committee."

The various factors related to word symbols and the development of language suggest something of the role that words play in determining meaning in communication. A greater awareness of these factors should contribute to more effective communication on the part of the administrator.

Needs, values, and predispositions of the communicatee. Not only is communication influenced by perceptions of the communicator and the meanings derived from the symbols that he uses, but it is also influenced by the concerns, the values, and the motivations of the communicatee himself. Motivation, for example, influences the amount of attention given to a communication. If a teacher has certain home obligations to be met, then individual conferences after school scheduled on short notice may be perceived as a special demand and interfere with attention and understanding. Or a teacher may not be as capable of listening after she has completed a hard day's work as when she arrives at school in the morning. Finally, a teacher may feel that the conference that has been called has little, if any, relationship to the things that she is doing or the things that she would like to do. Thus, she is disinterested, and this affects communication adversely.

The concerns and expectations that teachers have also influence the meaning which results. Thus, if a principal feels that he is not doing his job well and the superintendent asks how he is getting along, the principal may conclude that the superintendent also feels that he is not doing a good job; in fact, of course, the superintendent may not feel this way at all. To take one other example, a teacher who strongly wishes to receive tenure may conclude from a chance encouraging remark by her principal that she will receive tenure; again, her assumption may not be correct at all.

The concern that personnel experience about their positions in an organization has been called "status anxiety." There can be no doubt that this condition causes much misinterpretation of communication among personnel. Doubtless the marked discrepancies in the interpretation of communication by Principal Jones and Teacher Norris in Case Six, "A Coin Has Two Sides," stemmed partly from status considerations. The administrator is also susceptible to status anxiety and, therefore, susceptible to costly misinterpretation. For example, might Principal Jones's concerns about Teacher Norris's role in the informal communication system have stemmed partly from status considerations of his own?

Another factor influencing perception of the communicatee is the values that he holds. It can be hypothesized that the greater the disparity of values that the communicator and the communicatee hold on the issue discussed, the more likely there will be misinterpretation of the communication. Thus, Teacher Norris and Principal Jones in Case Six, "A Coin Has Two Sides," held different values about organizational conformity, and the results for communication are suggested in their separate accounts. Or, members of the "small opposing group" in Case Seventeen, "Changing the Curriculum at Southside," interpreted one example of Bell's behavior as "authoritarian" while some members in the "large social group" interpreted his behavior as "democratic." Doubtless much of this difference in interpretation stemmed from the differences in values that the interpreters held.

Thus, interests, concerns, expectations, and values fundamentally shape frames of reference. These frames of reference filter in, hold out, and even modify communication content and meaning. These various factors make two-person communication very complex and the task of the administrator in some cases rather complicated. It is understandable that Principal Jones was disappointed and even discouraged in his efforts to establish optimum two-person communication with Teacher Norris in Case Six, "A Coin Has Two Sides."

Implications for administrative behavior. If an administrator understands the various factors that affect meaning, he is in a better position to facilitate effective communication. However, comprehending the various factors is not enough. Stated differently, how can the administrator play an effective role in two-person communication in the face of limitations in time, the pressures of the situation in which he works, the imperfections of human personality, and the shortcomings of communication symbols? A basic consideration in meeting his task is his skill as a listener.

Listening skills. Skillful listening calls for good observation and a sensitive ear. Thus, the listener must concentrate not only upon spoken words, but also upon behavior. What is expressed, for example, through the body posture? What are the hands of the communicator saying, if anything? What emotional tone does the voice quality communicate? Are there silent symbols in pauses, eye contact, and hesitations? Do the various behaviors suggest that the person is relaxed, tense, or threatened? What would he say if he sincerely expressed what he is thinking and feeling? Are there clues as to unconscious motivation?

A consideration of the evidence that stems from the above questions will indicate to the administrator whether there are serious influences interfering with the communication process. If the condition of "status anxiety" noted above or other influences interfere with the flow of ideas, then the listener needs to adapt accordingly. In this regard, the suggestions from Rogers (22) are appropriate.

First, a genuine interest in the person communicating with the administrator is essential. If the administrator is busy, gruff, harsh, discourteous, or impatient, this will be communicated and status anxiety will be increased. Second, a permissive atmosphere in which personnel can express their feelings and have them accepted is also important. For example, Miss Wright in Case Eleven, "Heartaches and Headaches," was able to create an atmosphere in which Miss Simms could express her ideas even though she had been blocked in expressing her ideas to other personnel. Stated differently, if the administrator is over-critical or moralistic, the flow of communication is likely to be impeded. Finally, a climate of freedom to express non-conforming ideas is also very important. If the administrator demands marked conformity in an organization, a brake is put upon communication. Naturally, it would not be necessary to apply the methods in precisely the same manner to all people. Lack of time on the part of the administrator may also limit their complete use in some cases.

When emotional interference is at a minimum in two-person communication, then the administrator can concentrate more critically on verbal content. Among other things, this means that he will listen to determine and help define the purpose that his companion is seeking to achieve. If the speaker is setting forth a thesis, then the listener needs to apprehend it and to weigh the evidence in support of it.

Stevens and Nichols (21) suggest six bad habits of listening. Faking attention or pretending to listen is one of these. Listening only for facts without considering the broader meanings is another. Avoiding listening that is considered difficult and over-concentrating on physical appearance and delivery are two other failings. Finally, there are the related habits of easily yielding to distractions and of prematurely dismissing ideas as uninteresting.

Directing communication. In addition to the goal of understanding and minimizing the factors that inhibit communication, the administrator has a second task: namely, to channel the process toward certain ends and within certain time limits. Great skill is required to obtain both purposes. For either purpose, persons need to focus on ideas and problems with a minimum threat to personalities. In achieving such a focus, the administrator will be concerned with the rational and emotional meanings in word symbols. Through questions he will seek to clarify communication content. He will check to see what statements refer to in actuality. He will try to get at the things behind the words and ideas. Although initially this may take time, in the long run it is economical. At every step the administrator will try to avoid communicative behavior that might seem to question the integrity of colleagues; rather, he will focus on ideas, problems, and their solutions. At the end of a conference, a summary of agreements is often useful and can serve as a final check on communication, particularly in those cases where clear understanding is important or in cases where there has been a history of misunderstanding.

As previously noted, administrative communication is very likely to be misinterpreted by personnel with status anxiety and by personnel who have values that differ markedly from those of the administrator. With such communicatees, feedback in the form of checking and rechecking on the meaning and accuracy of communication is essential if clear understanding is desired. For those with status anxiety, special care is needed in dealing with topics or problems that have implications for their future status. Accurate clarification can mean much for such persons, and its achievement usually solves immediate problems. For persons with differing values, the problem is not so simple, however. Even when issues have been clearly defined and communication is clear, problems may still remain because of differing perspectives. Thus, further efforts by the administrator in the way of negotiations may be necessary to arrive at appropriate solutions.

Motivation and communication. Kahn and Cannell (15) have suggested several techniques for increasing the motivation of conferees. For example, it is important that the conferee know the purpose of a conference and see how the purpose relates to his own personal objectives in the organization. The importance of keeping agreements in the use of confidential information is also evident. The implications of this problem can be seen in Case Eleven, "Heartaches and Headaches," in which Miss Simms asked Miss Wright to keep her planned resignation confidential.

Motivation can also be viewed as it relates to the satisfaction or dissatisfaction that persons experience from participating in a conference. Interestingly enough, according to studies reported by Kahn and Cannell (15), conferees remember better the dissatisfaction or satisfaction resulting from the conference relationship than they do the problems or information discussed. This suggests the value of conducting a conference so that the communicatee remembers it with satisfaction. If he is satisfied, he will look forward with pleasure to a similar experience, and the gaining of his co-operation under such circumstances should be easier in the future.

Problems that relate to motivation and frames of reference make for subtleties in communication. To be effective, the administrator needs to be empathic in the sense that he is able to project himself so that he comprehends the feelings, values, and ideas of other persons. In the words of Sullivan, as quoted by Lee (18, p. 52), "in dealing with students, with patients, or with any group or nation, the first step is to see the world through their eyes, to enter into what they are trying to do however strange their behavior seems. Genuine communication is impossible on any other basis."

Group communication. In general, the same generalizations apply to group communication as those noted above under individual conferences. As a matter of fact, some authors have defined a group as two or more persons meeting together for a particular purpose. However, there seem to be some important differences between a group of more than two persons and a situation in which only two persons are interacting. This is all the more true in schools, in which the administrator participates in group and two-person communication.

In groups including administrators, there is three-way instead of two-way communication. If a teacher talks to Principal Jones about Freddy, then the interaction is two ways from superior to subordinate, and vice versa. In a group, however, there is this type of communication plus communication between and among peers. This makes the dynamics of the communication process somewhat different.

For one thing, there is less chance for the administrator to apply feedback techniques to all participants individually because the focus and channels of communication shift. In many ways communication is much less susceptible to administrative control, because of a wider range of values held by group members, as well as because of the individual differences in psychological orientations. Problems of this type and how they relate to group productivity are illustrated in Case Eight, "The Gifted Child Committee." On the other hand, persons susceptible to status anxiety often will be much less threatened by the administrator when they have peer support than when they have individual conferences with him. Thus, in some ways communication may be easier to maximize in a group situation and at the same time be more difficult to direct toward a given objective.

Group communication is also somewhat more complex because more points of view are represented. Unless the group members have almost identical outlooks, conflict between and among peers in the group is to be expected. At the same time, there will be very strong forces in most groups which work toward the development of a uniform opinion. Some of the conditions under which these forces operate have been elaborated by Festinger (6), and a brief summary of his findings follows.

When a group is especially attractive to the majority of its members, the pressure toward uniformity is strong. By contrast, if the group is not cohesive and does not have much tradition, the pressure toward uniformity is generally less marked. Pressure toward uniformity also increases as the topics under discussion take on importance in the eyes of most of the group members. When there are strong pressures toward uniformity, a person holding an extreme view will likely have most of the communication directed to him; the likelihood that he will receive such communication increases as the difference between his opinion and the opinion of other group members increases. The forces to change his opinion or to disagree with him expand in proportion to the degree of his rejection by group members. The likelihood that group members will try to change a nonconformist's point of view is also related to a positive belief that they can change his opinion.

In general, then, the dynamics of group communication are such that strong group pressures influence nonconformists toward group conformity. However, if the persons holding extreme points of view have their attitudes anchored in other groups and see these other groups as highly important to them, they are much more resistant to attitude change. Such circumstances have important implications for administrative behavior both with reference to maximizing communication and also with reference to channeling it in relationship to organizational goals.

Organization communication. Students of cybernetics have frequently spoken of communication networks. They have interested themselves in this concept particularly as it relates to the more advanced electronic machines. However, they also believe that the concept applies equally well to physical-chemical interactions in the brain, as well as to human interaction in social groups. No doubt the concept could be extended to apply to civilizations on the one hand and to atomic particles on the other.

The concept certainly has meaning as it relates to school organization. The vitality of an organization expresses itself through systems of human relationships or communication networks many of which are spontaneous, unscheduled, unplanned, and informal. These various networks in an organization fit together in interrelated systems of communication. Sometimes the communication is such that the aims of the organization are more effectively achieved. In other cases, communication brings subversive influences.

Under optimum conditions, communication networks have certain self-modifying and self-correcting effects, and in a sense display "learning" or "adaptive" behavior (5). Thus, the various communication channels in an organization not only seek information but they receive unsolicited information, transmit information, even subdivide, classify, and store information. On future occasions such information is recalled, selected, recombined, and retransmitted through communication channels (5). In one sense, then, a communication network is to an organization what the central nervous system is to an individual.

The administrator plays a key role in communication systems in schools. In playing the role of an effective communicator, he is faced with many important questions. He can answer such questions more satisfactorily if he understands the communication system in which he finds himself and if he uses his understanding to guide his behavior. The discussion immediately following raises a number of questions that can be useful to the administrator in analyzing the communication networks within which he works. These questions should also be fruitful guides to the researcher in analyzing particular organizations or for designing research for more general purposes.

What are some of the important things that the administrator should look for in the communication system which surrounds him? Of considerable importance is the identification of the *informal* communication systems. Ideally the administrator needs to know more than how the informal groups cluster. For example, what are their core values? For what are they striving? For what reasons are the members of the various groups attracted to one another? To what extent are they attracted?

Informal relationships. Understanding the relationships between and among informal groups in an organization has important implications for the administrator. Which group or groups have values that are opposed to the values held by other groups? To what extent do such groups consciously rival one another? Are there groups that are largely autonomous and relatively independent of other groups in the organization? What proportion of persons in the organization do not belong to clearly defined informal clusters? How do the various groups perceive the administrator, and what in general do they expect from him? Which of the groups are likely to be highly energized positively or negatively on a given issue, and which, if any, are likely to be indifferent?

An understanding of the leadership in the informal groups is another consideration. Studies suggest that leaders in organizations can be characterized in terms of types of communicators (16). In this regard, three types have been suggested: those who *originate* ideas; those who *sanction* ideas; and those who *spread* ideas. There are additional guides to identifying leadership. Who are the leaders of the informal groups? What kind of relationship do they have with the administrator? To what extent do they have contacts with other informal leaders in the organization? What is the nature of their interaction with other informal leaders? Is their communication confined mostly to their own informal group, or do they occupy central roles in the total communication network?

The communication network is affected by the administrator's relationship to the informal groups. To what extent, for example, is he motivated to obtain approval or to develop intimate interpersonal relationships with members of certain groups? Does he tend to favor one group more than another? If so, why does he do this? Has he developed relationships with persons who play liaison roles in the organization and, therefore, are important sources of information? Does he tend to become too personally involved with some members of the organization? Why do some persons have more influence upon him than others? Does he skillfully use the informal communication system to pass on certain kinds of information to staff members? In the process, is he aware of the communication structure, and does he know the persons most appropriate for assisting in such a task? In his various relationships, is he sensitive to the results of uncomfortable probing or indelicate questioning?

Influence structure. The key to the patterns and points of influence in an organization also can be discovered in communication networks. One of the first steps in this process is to determine the persons who are the key influentials. Evidence suggests that one of the best sources to learn about influence patterns is from those who are influentials. They have a special capacity for identifying other influentials and for explaining the influence process.

The familiar saying that so-and-so "carries a lot of weight" suggests still another important question: Among the key influencers, who is more and who is less influential? This question can be answered relative to a single issue, as, for example, the half-day schedule in Case Seventeen, "Changing the Curriculum at Southside." It can also be answered more generally in terms of the range of issues that a person is likely to influence. Thus, the circle of a person's influence, as defined by the number of schools, departments, informal groups, or community organizations, can also be examined. Another dimension of the circle of influence pertains to whether a person affects only those on the inside or whether his influence extends to those outside the organization.[1]

Another less tangible but perhaps more important question is the source of a person's influence. Some leaders achieve influence because of expert knowledge which they transmit. Other types of influence stem from a person's ability to represent accurately the interests of others. Still other influence has its source in official position. Does the influential have a predominantly emotional appeal? Does he tend to be more logical and objective? How aggressive is he? The answers to these and related questions can help the administrator get a better understanding of the influence process and provide clues to guide his own communication.

Rumor in organization. The quantity of research on informal communication networks does not compare with the amount that has been done on small-group and two-person communication. Doubtless there are several reasons for this condition. In the first place, informal communication networks are very complex and are not easily submitted to controlled study. A related reason is that the scope of such systems is very large in that they operate widely in various settings. Informal communication can take place outside the principal's office, in the cafeteria, in the hall, in the smoking room, and even off the school premises. Still another point is that the informal communication is continuous and, therefore, quite different from a faculty meeting, which is held only periodically. Such factors place extreme demands, not only upon the skills of a researcher, but also upon time,

[1] Merton (20), in studying opinion leadership in communities, found that some leaders showed greater interest in communication media that reported national and international affairs while other leaders showed more interest in media that dealt with local matters.

money, and organization. Thus, there is still much to be learned about the dynamics of informal communication systems.

At this stage in the study of informal communication networks, the approach made by students of rumor deserves special consideration. In the last few decades studies of rumor have been made between and among organizations in society and in administrative organizations. Since there is considerable similarity among the various findings, it would be useful to examine them as they relate to informal communication in schools. Before this is done, however, some of the limitations of rumor study as an approach to understanding informal communication networks should be stated.

Rumor is only one kind of informal communication. In extreme cases, rumor can be viewed as a symbol of certain emotional conditions which are closely related to the feelings and motivations of personnel. In a way, rumors serve the same general purposes for an organization that daydreaming does for an individual. Thus, rumors which express hostility toward or fears about persons or work conditions can be viewed as organizational defense mechanisms.

Also notable is the fact that the majority of research, particularly that of Allport and Postman (1) and that of Knapp (17), views rumor negatively. Doubtless one of the reasons why they were attracted to the study of rumor stemmed from the *harmful* effects of this type of communication during World War II. While the works of Festinger and others (7) and the research of Davis (2) are cast within a different framework, research has not sufficiently clarified the dynamics of different types of rumor. Thus, it can be assumed that some rumors are less harmful than others and that some rumors are even beneficial to organizations; further, there is some difference in the forces affecting the flow of these different types of communication. In addition, there is, then, the further question of how rumor transmission relates to various kinds of non-rumor transmission in informal communication networks.

In spite of the limitations of rumor study, the approach, more than any other, has thrown light on informal communication networks. Rumors travel fast, and their vividness makes them easily susceptible to recall. In addition, they are in one sense a kind of tracer which assists researchers in reconstructing the paths of communication networks.

Origin of rumors. Under what conditions are rumors likely to arise? The work of Festinger and others (7) suggests that rumors breed and thrive in situations which are unclear or ambiguous. It can be hypothesized, for example, that the rumor about Teacher White in Case Four, "The Sword of Damocles," would not have persisted if the situation with which the rumor dealt could have been clarified. The point is again illustrated by the fact that in World War II rumors constantly developed in situations where secrecy was the policy and no official information was given.

The "external control" factor also influences the spread of rumor. Thus, when certain conditions are beyond the control of persons, people are more likely to start rumors than if they can exercise influence. In Case Fifteen, "Greenfield Builds Its Third High School," for example, control was in the hands of the school board, but rumors kept emanating from unknown sources in the community. Rumor is also dependent upon how crucial the problems seem to the persons concerned. If the problems are crucial, or if they demand special sacrifices in money or work, then rumors are more likely to flow. Finally, it seems that the presence or absence of rumor is related to the dissatisfactions and satisfactions of personnel. When dissatisfaction accompanies hostile feelings toward those responsible for administering, a seedbed for rumor is present. Thus, one would conclude that personnel satisfaction in Case Four, "The Sword of Damocles," must have been very high, else more hostility would have been expressed toward the administrators in the case.

Kinds of rumor. What types of rumors are likely to get started in an organization? While the studies of Allport and Postman (1) and Knapp (17) relate to the larger community and to negative kinds of rumor, their findings no doubt have implications for rumor in administrative organizations. Allport and Postman (1) in studying 1,000 rumors gathered during World War II, arrived at three types.

About two-thirds of the rumors were described as hostility or "wedge-driving" rumors. The various rumors that were reported in Case Fifteen, "Greenfield Builds Its Third High School," doubtless were expressions of hostility. Rumor that reflects adversely on the personal life of an administrator might well be an expression of hostility. Such rumors might or might not have a factual basis. If there were no objective basis, the administrator would be a scapegoat for the negative feelings of personnel. In some ways he is more strategically located to serve as a scapegoat for a teacher's hostility than are fellow teachers. He is a member of the "out group," and an expression of hostility by teachers toward teachers involves greater risk psychologically than expressing hostility toward a school superintendent to fellow teachers.

About one-fourth of the rumors studied by Allport and Postman were classified as fear or "bogey" rumors. In a school, for example, a rumor that the principal was going to be discharged might stem from fears that he actually would be discharged. This type of rumor is likely to arise in unclear and anxiety-producing situations.

A small percentage of the rumors fell into the wish or "pipe dream" classification. A report that the superintendent of a school system had decided to retire might exemplify this type of rumor. Such a rumor might very well express the wish that the superintendent would retire. Again, this type of rumor is closely related to the emotional tensions and needs of persons in the organization.

While rumors contain an irrational element, they are not entirely emotionally based. Studies show clearly that rumor transmitters strive to make sense out of the stories which they spread. This poses the question of what an effective rumor is like. Thus, the work of Knapp (17) suggests some of the characteristics of an effective rumor. To be successful, a rumor should be short, simple, and capable of carrying a great deal of meaning. It should be coherent and well organized for its purpose. In general, the further removed it is from actual conditions or from the possibility of being easily confirmed or denied, the more likely that it will travel. The more precisely it is adapted to the culture in which it flows and to the immediate feelings of the people involved, the more persistent it will be. Finally, if it is attributed to a person in authority, its creditability is further increased.

Rumor channels. What is known about communication channels and their significance for rumor transmission? The work of Davis (2) suggests four networks in which rumors travel. One of these he calls the "single chain," in which rumor travels from A to B to C to D, and so on. The "gossip chain" is one in which A tells everybody he sees, and he becomes the main factor in the dissemination of the rumor. In the "probability chain," A tells B and both B and A continue to tell the persons whom they contact, and the rumor is further spread by these latter persons. Finally, the "cluster chain" is one in which a rumor spreads within an informal group and stays within this group.

Several studies suggest that a rumor is likely to travel very rapidly between and among the persons in a small cohesive group and then not to be transmitted further.

The channels through which rumor travels are highly dependent upon the personal motivations of those who have an opportunity to spread rumor. Knapp's studies (17) suggest, for example, that some persons in an organization gain a certain status from spreading rumors. In addition, persons who have fears, hostilities, or emotional conflicts related to "grapevine" reports are more likely to listen and to transmit the information.

Rumor transmission depends, of course, upon the extent to which unsubstantiated reports are believed. Allport and Postman (1) suggest that those with adverse attitudes toward the program or person with which rumor deals are more likely to believe the rumor. In addition, rumor believers are more likely to lack faith in their colleagues than are those who reject rumors. Those prone to believing rumors seemingly endure greater hardships and put forth more effort to achieve organization goals than do persons who are more critical of rumors (17).

Festinger (7) found that sociometric choices were very accurate predictors of rumor channels. Thus, rumor was likely to be communicated between and among friends. Isolates in the organization were not as likely to hear rumor as those who had close friendship patterns. Festinger also discovered that the chances were greater that rumor would be carried to those persons who were likely to be affected by the rumor content. In a school organization, for example, a rumor about a physical education program would more likely reach the head of the physical education department than the head of the English department.

Rumor distortion. Many writers have suggested that the "grapevine" is the fastest channel of communication in an organization. An important question, then, is what happens in the process of rumor transmission. The work of Allport and Postman is particularly useful in suggesting what happens to rumors during their travels.

One of the things that happens to rumor, according to the Allport and Postman study (1), is a leveling effect. In other words, the rumor becomes more concise, briefer, and, consequently, more easily transmitted. When a rumor was transmitted through five or six persons, 70 per cent of the details were eliminated. They note, however, that some details always remained, and that these details were judged the more interesting ones. The items remaining were more likely to conform to the expectations of the individuals transmitting the rumor. There was less leveling in the later stages of transmission.

"Sharpening" is another feature of rumor transmission. Allport and Postman (1) found that not only were the details eliminated from rumor, but details were selectively chosen to give a particular character to the rumor. This sharpening took various forms. The quantity of objects, for example, was likely to be increased or decreased depending upon the shape which the rumor took. Time elements were also likely to undergo sharpening. The first items in the transmitted information were more likely to shape the character of the rumor than were the last items.

A related feature of rumor transmission was "assimilation," or the inclination to develop a certain motif or theme in the rumor. Thus, rumor transmitters arranged details to give a certain logical form to the report. Not only did tellers eliminate details, but they also added details to make the story more coherent. In some cases two items were telescoped into one to give the story a particular twist. Knapp (17) also found that rumors were likely to be distorted through such methods as adding striking or esthetic detail, simplifying the plot by putting the story into a familiar form, by giving it a humorous twist, by exaggerating, and by deleting complexities. In all of these cases, the character of the rumor was largely determined by the interests, habits, concerns, and sentiments of the tellers. Since motivations vary from teller to teller, some distortion seems inevitable.

Rumor control. What implications does research on rumor transmission have for administrative behavior? While the administrator cannot completely control rumor in an organization, he can exercise considerable influence upon it. In the first place, the administrator needs to develop skill in analyzing the meaning of rumors. The study of rumors should not only provide insight into the structure of an organization, but should also give some indication of the aspirations, hostilities, and anxieties of persons in an organization. In a deeper sense, rumors may reflect how persons feel about official channels and the organizational climate in general. Thus, rumor is an emotional symbol with an underlying meaning which has importance for administration.

Second, the administrator needs to identify those issues which may be of concern to the members in an organization and to plan formal and informal communication appropriate to the concerns. If persons are concerned about possible changes in salary policy, for example, he can alleviate such concerns and diminish the possibility of harmful rumors by planning and transmitting pertinent communication.

When harmful rumors have started, relevant information should be provided to the persons who are concerned. Naturally, the information should be obtained as quickly as possible, and it should be checked carefully for accuracy. During World War II, "clinics" were developed to combat rumor by providing information to persons concerned. Formal channels can be established at the school or district level for the express purpose of providing information to personnel about "subterranean talk." Thus, the committee of Principal Bell, his two vice-principals, and three teachers in Case Seventeen, "Changing the Curriculum at Southside," served this purpose, among others.

Facts and information cannot completely dispel rumors, because, as already noted, they have strong anchors in emotions. The extent to which facts and information will be effective in curbing rumor is largely dependent upon the trust which personnel have in their administrative leaders. Thus, a third and very important consideration in rumor control is the development in personnel of a belief in the dependability of communication media and a feeling of confidence in their administrators. This can be done only through a consistent, honest, considerate, and sincere record of communication. Inconsistency only increases ambiguity, and dishonesty creates distrust. Belief in a communication is not generated in a moment; its meaning also derives from past events as well as from perceptions about the future.

One-way communication. The communication processes discussed so far have been in a two-way or three-way framework. However, a considerable amount of the communication done by administrators involves one-way communication. Examples of such communication would be a superintendent speaking to a Lions' Club, a Parent-Teachers Association, or a teachers' meeting. The many types of written communication which he disperses to staff and student personnel are additional examples. In one-way communication, immediate feedback is at a minimum, and the administrator has greater control over the content and organization of the communication than in two-way and three-way communication. In addition, the process is formally planned, definitely scheduled, and is generally more explicit in its purpose.

Written communication is inevitably one-way, and the visual senses receive its messages. Oral one-way communication is highly dependent upon the aural senses, although the visual senses also aid in the reception. Thus, the dynamics of these two types of one-way communication undoubtedly differ. The main difference stems from the fact that the communicator is present in oral communication and is absent in written communication. However, since many of the same generalizations apply to the planning and organization of content in both types of communication, the two are treated together.

What are the important characteristics of effective one-way communication? Three steps or phases of the process have been suggested (11). The first of these is getting the attention of the hearers or readers. The second is getting the understanding of the communicatees, and the third is getting the desired action or reaction. Although these steps are not entirely separate, they do form an adequate basis for organizing research findings on one-way communication.

Before presenting some of the findings on one-way communication, it should be emphasized that the research is organized to illuminate the actual effects of communication, and thus does not deal with ethical considerations. There are, of course, difficult ethical questions, especially in regard to the problems of propaganda and emotional appeal. To deal with these questions is beyond the scope of this chapter.

Students of advertising psychology have given much thought to the process of getting the attention of listeners and hearers. Such thought, coupled with related research, has provided some useful findings on the gaining and holding of attention in one-way communication. Many of these findings seem to have relevance for school situations.

Attention-getting. First, it is well to emphasize that the administrator in one-way communication is continually competing against stimuli which demand the attention of his listeners or readers. If a principal is addressing a faculty group at the end of the day, for example, he is competing with fatigue, which works against his attaining the complete attention of teachers. He may also be competing with disinterest among some teachers in that they are not highly involved in the topic about which he is talking. In addition, they may have personal concerns, such as wanting to get home to their families, that interfere with listening. Physical interferences, in the form of noises or auditory difficulties, can also complicate matters. Thus, in planning for one-way communication, the administrator needs to analyze the factors that compete for attention. Such an analysis can provide clues for the timing of communication, for communication content, and for the media and channels to be used.

In order to deal with competing stimuli effectively, Lucas and Britt (19) suggest two goals for the communicator to keep in mind. First, he can select material that relates so closely to the motivation of the listeners that they must necessarily give their attention. Second, the message can be put in such a striking and interesting fashion that the person cannot escape listening. The achievement of the latter goal in one-way oral communication is highly related to the power and quality of the communicator's personality, a variable that is not easily controlled. However, the way material is organized and the ingenuity with which the content is cloaked are important considerations which the administrator can control more easily.

What are some guide lines for getting the visual attention of readers? Advertising psychologists have found several ways to do this. Many of their guide lines seem to relate to pictorial and graphic symbols as well as to word symbols. Thus, Lucas and Britt (19) point to the use of large size, contrast, intensity, isolation, and repetition. For example, the picture that appeared a few years ago showing a stack of elementary school books much higher than a sixth-grade boy used size and contrast gainers of attention. When one presents the percentage of students in the high schools today in relationship to the percentage in 1900, either verbally or graphically, contrast is utilized. When color is used in budget reports to show the proportion of tax funds spent for schools, or highly emotional language is used to describe the role of the school, the concept of intensity is put into effect. A picture of a child alone in a desert would be in line with the concept of isolation. Repetition is exemplified in the technique of making the same point with different but related examples.

Students of speech have also formulated various guides for attention-getting in one-way communication, and Dickens (3), among others, has summarized some of their findings. Some criteria of content designed to gain the attention of communicatees are: significance, humor, uniqueness, familiarity, concreteness, antagonism, conflict, and variation. Highly successful application of the concepts for getting attention in either oral or written communication is dependent upon the creativity of the communicator.

In order to get and hold attention, the administrator also needs to keep in mind the personal desires and motivations of his readers or listeners. To do this he would capitalize more upon intrinsic motivations of communicatees, as contrasted with the use of extrinsic motivation, exemplified in the attention-getting concepts just noted. When the communicator capitalizes on and blends both types of motivation, attention will be achieved most effectively.

Some types of intrinsic motivation seem much more widespread than others. Human-interest situations, for example, catch and hold the attention of most listeners. In a sense, educators are very fortunate in this regard, because their main goal is the welfare of children and adolescents—subjects of widespread human interest. There are many human-interest facets to these subjects, such as unusual personalities, high classroom attainments, and unique athletic feats. Such content is much more likely to get and hold attention than is content that is purely technical and removed from the human situation.

One other example of intrinsic motivation can be noted in the fact that human beings have powerful and similar basic urges. Motivational research has delved rather deeply into some of these considerations, and the implications are not always pleasant nor should the use of such findings necessarily be condoned. However, it is well known that most people have strong desires to belong, to be successful, to achieve recognition, and to improve their skills and abilities. Thus, effective communication will take into consideration these basic urges in personnel.

A discussion of attention-getting in one-way communication should not be concluded without re-emphaszing the fact that there are many symbols other than language that assist in getting attention. There are visual aids, audio aids, audio-visual aids, and innumerable other techniques which an ingenious communicator can use to catch the ear or the eye of communicatees. The importance of gaining the attention of readers or listeners cannot be overemphasized. If there is no attention, there can be no understanding and, therefore, no action or reaction.

Achieving understanding. The second step in one-way communication is getting understanding. While this step is closely related to attention and motivation, there are certain other considerations which the administrator needs to consider.

Recent studies point to the importance of "noise" in communication content. "Noise" is content which gets in the way of understanding. Thus, a prime goal in communication is to devise economical units of language in order to minimize "noise." This principle of economy can be illustrated by the following quote (9, p. 25):

> "Here it is," I said. "It has been observed that the offspring of familial units in the lower economic brackets demonstrate a frequent tendency to sublimate status anxiety by means of organized aggression against societal mores, such aggression taking the form of vandalistic assaults upon institutionalized properties. If I read that correctly, Tom, it means that the children of poor parents often try to smother their sense of inferiority by throwing rocks at the school room windows. Is that right?"

Thus, the briefer and more economical way of organizing content exemplified in the closing sentences is more easily and readily understood than the longer and more wordy initial passage. Several implications for technique stem from this consideration. Vocabulary should be suitable to the audience who listens or reads. In general, shorter and more familiar words are better than the long and less well-known words. In a similar fashion, sentences that are shorter are more effective than those that are long and verbose. Clear illustrations that relate to the experience of the listeners can help in clarifying phrases or words that may not be clear to them. Flesch's "readability yardstick" (8) can be of some use in gauging written communication, particularly for reports that are designed for lay persons. As intimated earlier, because of the unique experiences of different individuals, communication can never be total or complete. However, if the administrator carefully considers such factors as vocabulary, sentence length, and organization, the chances for optimum communication are increased.

Getting results. The ultimate goal in one-way communication is that of action or reaction. The book by Hovland, Janis, and Kelley (11) summarizes a great deal of the research having to do with the effects of one-way communication. The effects, as defined in their framework, are the acceptance of a point of view and, in some cases, a change in attitude on the part of the listener. The findings of some of the more pertinent studies will be briefly summarized.

It is clear that in a one-way communication framework, as in the other frameworks of communication, the personality of the communicator is very important. Research studies suggest that the extent to which the communicator is perceived as a creditable authority is an important factor in determining influence. School administrators, when they bring in well-known speakers to communicate to groups of teachers, are acting in terms of this finding. It is well to point out, however, that even though the immediate acceptance of particular points of view is much greater when the ideas come from experts or well-known authorities, follow-up studies suggest that the effects tend to disappear after several weeks have intervened. Another aspect of personality that affects communication is the degree to which the communicator achieves a trusting attitude in his listeners. If they believe he has an ulterior motive, a strong barrier is immediately erected. If he does not arouse suspicion, his message is more likely to be accepted.

Organization of content has an important effect upon the acceptance gained from the listeners. For example, when only one side of an issue is presented to persons with average or below-average intelligence, they are more likely to be influenced than when both sides are presented (12). On the other hand, the more intelligent person is more likely to accept ideas if both sides are presented. When the conclusion which the communicator wishes to have accepted is made explicit, influence is more likely than when the audience is left to draw its own conclusions.

Various studies show how the personality patterns of listeners affect communication. Janis (13), for example, studied the characteristics of those persons who were very easy and those who were very difficult to persuade. He found that those who were easily persuaded were socially inhibited and had feelings of inadequacy. They rarely criticized others and generally turned their aggression upon themselves. Those who were difficult or impossible to persuade, on the other hand, fell into three categories instead of one. First, there were those who were very hostile in their everyday relations, in that they persistently expressed aggression toward others. Second, there were those who were generally socially withdrawn and seemingly very indifferent to social approval. Finally, there were those with neurotic behavior, which expressed itself in such symptoms as emotional blocks, compulsive thinking, and morbid fears. Such persons present particular problems for the administrator. Undoubtedly, he will often feel it important to change the attitudes or beliefs of these people, and yet he will find it extremely difficult to do so.

Many studies suggest that acceptance and action on the part of listeners depend upon aroused emotions. Research has demonstrated abundantly that facts in and of themselves have a negligible influence on already established attitudes or points of view. There is no precise formula, however, for determining the type or amount of emotion to be aroused. For example, some of the studies of the effect of fear upon the acceptance and implementation of ideas suggest that a minimum amount of fear is more effective than a large amount of fear (14). It seems very clear that effectiveness depends not only upon the arousal of certain emotional needs but also upon making clear how these needs can be met.

Again, it appears evident that for the administrator to devise communication that arouses desires and aspirations on the part of his listeners, he must face not only problems of creating appropriate techniques, but also moral questions. In other words, how can he be both moral and effective? It is also well to note that the administrator is more limited in his capacity for changing attitudes through one-way communication than he is through the informal communication systems or as a leader in small groups. Nevertheless, if his personality and behavior are such that his listeners can identify themselves with him, he can achieve some success.

In brief, then, the formula for successful one-way communication on the part of the administrator involves the achievement of three goals. First, he must gain the interest and attention of his listeners. Second, he must present content in such a way that it is understandable. Third, he must arouse the emotional and psychological needs of his listeners and clearly suggest to them ways whereby they can satisfy these needs. Although the achievement of these goals is not easy, the extent to which the administrator does in fact achieve them is an important measure of his effectiveness in one-way communication situations.

References

1. Allport, Gordon, and Leo Postman, *The Psychology of Rumor*. New York: Henry Holt and Company, 1947.
2. Davis, Keith, "Management Communication and the Grapevine," *Harvard Business Review*, September-October, 1953, p. 44.
3. Dickens, Milton, *Speech: Dynamic Communication*. New York: Harcourt, Brace and Company, 1954.
4. Dooher, Joseph (ed.), *Effective Communication on the Job*. New York: The American Management Association, 1956.
5. Dorsey, John, "A Communication Model for Administration," *Administrative Science Quarterly*, Vol. II, No. 3, December, 1957, pp. 307–324.
6. Festinger, Leon, "Informal Social Communication," *Psychological Review*, Vol. 57, September, 1950, pp. 271–82.
7. Festinger, Leon, and others, "A Study of Rumor: Its Origin and Spread," *Human Relations*, Vol. I, No. 4, 1948, pp. 464–86.
8. Flesch, Rudolph, "A New Readability Yardstick," *Journal of Applied Psychology*, Vol. 32, 1948, (June) pp. 221–33.
9. Gordon, Robert, "A Question of Style," *American Association of University Professors Bulletin*, Vol. 43, No. 1, Spring, 1957, pp. 23–32.
10. Hoslett, Schuyler, "Barriers to Communication," *Personnel*, Vol. 28, No. 2, September, 1951, pp. 108–114.
11. Hovland, Carl, Irving Janis, and Harold Kelley, *Communication and Persuasion*. New Haven: Yale University Press, 1953.
12. Hovland, C. I., A. A. Lumsdaine, and F. D. Sheffield, *Experiments on Mass Communication*. Princeton: Princeton University Press, 1949.
13. Janis, Irving, "Personality Correlates of Susceptibility to Persuasion," *Journal of Personality*, Vol. XXII, No. 4, June, 1954, pp. 504–18.
14. Janis, Irving, and Seymour Feshbach, "Effects of Fear-Arousing Communications," *Journal of Abnormal and Social Psychology*, Vol. 48, 1953, (January) pp. 78–92.
15. Kahn, Robert, and Charles Cannell, *The Dynamics of Interviewing*. New York: John Wiley and Sons, Inc., 1957.
16. Katz, Elihu, and Paul Lazarsfeld, *Personal Influence*. Glencoe, Ill.: The Free Press, 1955.
17. Knapp, Robert, "A Psychology of Rumor," *Public Opinion Quarterly*, Vol. 8, 1944, pp. 22–37.
18. Lee, Irving, *How to Talk with People*. New York: Harper and Brothers, 1952.
19. Lucas, Darrell, and Steuart Britt, *Advertising Psychology and Research*. New York: McGraw-Hill Book Company, 1950.
20. Merton, Robert, "Patterns of Influence: A Study of Inter-Personal Influence and Communications Behavior in a Local Community," in *Communications Research, 1948–49* (Paul Lazarsfeld and Frank Stanton, eds.), New York: Harper and Brothers, 1949.
21. Nichols, Ralph, and Leonard Stevens, *Are You Listening?* New York: McGraw-Hill Book Company, 1957.

22. Rogers, Carl, *Counseling and Psychotherapy*. Boston: Houghton Mifflin Company, 1942.
23. Rogers, Carl, and F. J. Roethlisberger, "Barriers and Gateways to Communication," *Harvard Business Review, XXX*, No. 4, July-August, 1952, pp. 46–52.
24. Ruesch, Jurgen, and Weldon Kees, *Non-verbal Communication*. Berkeley: The University of California Press, 1956.
25. Sargent, Cyril, and Eugene Belisle, "The Concept of Administration," in *Administrative Behavior in Education* (eds., Roald Campbell and Russell Gregg). New York: Harper and Brothers, 1957.

CHAPTER SIX

Building Morale

Everybody has some good in him. My job is to work with the best in everyone.

ANONYMOUS

In this chapter the discussion focuses on administrative behavior, particularly as the latter affects morale. Special consideration is given to those persons in an organization who express unusual or deviant behavior. It is believed that such persons create difficult human-relations problems for the administrator. Throughout the chapter, some relationships between leadership and morale are illustrated from the cases.

Human relations do not exist and morale is not achieved within a vacuum. There are many forces within and outside the school that influence and limit the way in which school personnel behave toward one another. Many of these forces have important implications for morale maintenance, as well as for other administrative processes.

Social Foundations of Morale in Educational Organization

The nature of democratic society and the Hebraic-Christian tradition that undergirds Western civilization is the basic framework in which school administration in the United States operates. For many persons, democracy is a secular version of Christianity. In our political-social setting, the individual is of extreme importance. His development is of paramount concern. In our culture, the state serves the individual.

Hierarchy. The tradition of democracy based on the Hebrew-Christian tradition tends to develop a hierarchy in which one person is responsible to another. This is not peculiar to democracy, but it is a phenomenon of all large-scale organizations. In our political democracy, men elected as top representatives, such as a governor or a senator, are responsible to the will of the masses, and when the people are dissatisfied, they "turn the rascals out."

The market system permits organization and specialization and ties people together. This situation tends to make less readily operable the wishes of the individual and tends to develop the union, the employer's organization, or political beliefs, such as parity for agricultural prices.

Our system, in theory, says that the legislative groups should decide *that* something should be done, and the executive then decides *what* should be done and *how*. It is here that friction develops between the executive office of the president and the Federal Congress, and it is here that the difficulty is likely to develop in relationships between the superintendency and the board of education.

Any large-scale organization must develop a hierarchy in which information has to be sent from one level of the organization to another. Thus, information may pass from a teacher to the principal to the superintendent, or from the foreman in a manufacturing plant to the superintendent to the vice-president. Thus, communication systems, whether by phone, by bulletin, or by radio, have influenced the growth of schools, state bureaucracy, and corporations, and the means of communication have a direct influence on the size of the organization. If Great Britain had known how the Colonists felt in the 1770's, it is inconceivable to many persons that a revolution would have developed. Had the ministers of Great Britain known the facts which did not come to them, some compromise surely would have been found to keep the organization together. Since that date, Great Britain has been much more effective in allowing autonomy to the parts of the Commonwealth than in trying to treat them as the Colonists in America were treated. It is entirely possible to believe that there might have been no Protestant Reformation had the people in the Vatican known how the grass-roots priests felt about certain practices in the mother church. The illustrations indicate the importance of communication in large-scale organizations and the tendency to pass on what information is thought to be most palatable.

The organizational revolution. In the last one hundred years, we have seen a major organizational revolution in the western world.

In the economic field, slightly more than half of the American industry is owned outright by not more than 200 corporations (4). Labor unions have grown to a membership of over 15 million, although a century ago there were almost no labor associations (7). Many large-scale organizations, such as the National Education Association, the American Association of School Administrators, and political parties, have developed in the United States. Thus, an individual is not a member of one organization alone, but rather he is simultaneously a member of a large group of organizations, some of which are not in concordance. Charles Beard said, "The modern society is a great society. It consists of many different groups woven together in a complicated process of production. Every enterprise in the great society rests upon administration. Administration, not the sword, is the keynote of enduring power in the great society." (3, p. 148)

The essence of organization in a democracy is the settlement of problems through discussion. Decisions need to be made as close to the source as possible. For example, a mother comes to a teacher and says, "Johnny doesn't have perfect hearing. Would you give him a seat in the front of the room?" The matter is settled on the spot. Everyone who has dealt with personnel relations knows that this is more satisfactory than the case where so much friction develops between the teacher and the mother that the matter has to be settled by the principal or some other authority in the school system. The necessity for discussion and consent has to be abrogated to a greater or less extent during a severe crisis, such as war. One test of democracy is whether the process of discussion can be resumed after the crisis.

Power factors in a community. Common experience indicates that some persons are more successful than others at getting things done. Sometimes it is assumed that they know the right people, that they have been opportune in their presentations, or that they succeed for some presumably mystical reasons. Generally, administration involves organizing the materials for a purpose and getting people whose influence is felt in the community involved in promoting the matter. Thus, Hunter's study (15) in Atlanta shows clearly that there is a power structure in a large city. The research (10, 12) at the University of Oregon in the study on decision-making indicates clearly that small numbers of persons are involved in community decisions. In addition, the studies (20) in Cheatham County, Tennessee, carried out as part of the Southern States Cooperative Project in Educational Administration, indicated very clearly the power structure in the community and its influence on the making of educational and other decisions.

Social influences. During the last few decades, the social anthropologists and the sociologists have popularized a term known as "class structure." Sometimes this is indicated as lower-, middle-, and upper-class citizens (26); sometimes it is considered as a continuum extending from the lowest-class citizens, who live a little better than animals, to our highest-class citizens, who usually have both wealth and family background.

It is important in human relationships to be cognizant of social-class backgrounds, because most of our teachers are from the middle strain rather than from upper- or lower-class groups and, therefore, are inclined to think differently. It is also necessary to understand the various groups in society that constitute the school population and to understand what the school can do in upgrading education for students of all classes.

Another part of the social foundations that go into an understanding of people is found in Riesman's *The Lonely Crowd* (22), in which he lists three groups: (1) "tradition-directed" persons, who live by fear and superstition; (2) "inner-directed" persons, who have guilt complexes and fear punishment; and (3) "other-directed" persons, who have anxieties and are concerned with the opinions of others. An "inner-directed" person is exemplified in Martin Luther and his famous words, "Here I stand. I cannot do otherwise. God help me." "Other-directed" persons are probably found in large cities more frequently than are "inner-directed" persons. "Tradition-directed" persons seem to inhabit underdeveloped nations. The "inner-directed" persons are most likely to be found in the smaller communities in the older parts of the country and to be more common among the older population group. Other social influences affecting personnel satisfaction are the anonymity of the freedom and the loneliness associated with life in large and rapidly growing cities.

Persons belong to a multitude of groups in our highly organized society. Thus, the industrial foreman, standing as he does between labor and management, may find himself in a difficult position, since he has no comparable group with which to identify. It is not clear whether he belongs to labor or to management. The school principal identifies himself with his teachers and with the office downtown. The family, the labor union, and the political party all exercise powerful and often opposite pressures on an individual.

Few nations exhibit such a variety of ethnic groups and so many economic, social, religious, and recreational organizations as does the United States. We are a nation of joiners, and this is one of our democratic strengths.

There are many social forces that impinge upon and affect morale. An understanding of these forces will help administrators in solving problems in human relations. Beyond these forces, however, there are always present the democratic values of American culture. All human-relations decisions involving the welfare and well-being of individuals are, therefore, ethical decisions.

Leadership

Every organization must have someone in a position of leadership. The sort of leader that is appropriate is dependent in part on the situation. Thus, Winston Churchill led Great Britain with distinction and courage through the bitter days of World War II under a slogan that sometimes was called "Blood, Sweat, and Tears." After Great Britain and her allies had won World War II, the British people promptly dropped Churchill as the Prime Minister because they thought he would not furnish in peacetime, as he had in wartime, the leadership they wanted.

Leadership may be provided for various reasons. In Case One, "The Valley City Consolidation Issue," two superintendents, on the basis of their professional convictions regarding school consolidation, provided leadership that was not in conformity with the wishes of many persons in the community. In Case Twelve, "Dr. Cook Survives," the superintendent became the center of a controversy over professional and legal responsibilities. Dr. Cook won his point over the opposition of the board in a case that has had national repercussions.

Research on leadership. During the past several decades there have been many concerted attempts to study and determine what makes for good leadership. The military forces during World War II were tremendously concerned with finding officers who would provide leadership under combat conditions. Thus, millions of dollars have been spent on this research, which is indicative rather than conclusive. Students of public administration and business administration have analyzed the factors that go to make up leadership. Social psychologists have carried out analytical studies of leadership and have conducted experimental studies of democratic and authoritarian groups, particularly with children. More recently Schools of Education have been carrying on studies of leadership in education, both independently and as a result of the stimulus provided by the Co-operative Study of Educational Administration.

Studies (28) of leadership in small groups indicate that, in our culture, the democratic type of leadership is more effective than the authoritarian. The studies also indicate that the abdication of responsibility that is represented in *laissez faire* leadership results in anarchy or chaos. As a matter of fact, someone in every group will provide leadership, even though it may be very low-level and in no sense professional.

Stogdill reviewed 124 studies on the characteristics of leaders. To those who are looking for clear-cut answers, the review will be disappointing, but there are some indicators.

The factors that have been found to be associated with leadership can be summarized under the following general headings (25):

1. *Capacity* (intelligence, alertness, verbal facility, originality, judgment).
2. *Achievement* (scholarship, knowledge, athletic accomplishments).
3. *Responsibility* (dependability, initiative, persistence, aggressiveness, self-confidence, desire to excel).
4. *Participation* (activity, sociability, co-operation, adaptability, humor).
5. *Status* (socioeconomic position, popularity).
6. *Situation* (mental level, status, skills, needs and interests of followers, objectives to be achieved, and so forth).

These findings are not surprising. It is primarily by virtue of participating in group activities and demonstrating his capacity for expediting the work of the group that a person gains leadership status. A number of investigators have been careful to distinguish between the leader and the figurehead, and to point out that leadership is always associated with the attainment of group objectives. Leadership implies getting work done. The leader is a person who has earned a position of responsibility in co-ordinating the activities of the members of the group in the task of attaining a common goal.

A person does not become a leader by virtue of certain traits *per se*, but the pattern of personal characteristics of the leader must bear some relevant relationship to the characteristics, activities, and goals of the followers. It is appropriate to mention that leaders have opinions on many subjects and are willing to discuss them without attempting to force their opinions on other members of the group. Thus, leadership is an *earned* honor that one is granted because he has demonstrated capacity for co-operative effort.

Leadership and morale. Since leadership is clearly related to the goals and activities of followers, it is fair to ask the question, Leadership for what? In an organization such as the National Education Association, a different type of leader is sought from that for the Longshoremen's Union. In both cases the organization may well have chosen the best sort of person for their organization, but not one who would necessarily serve well in the other organization. In a school, many types of leadership are important. It is frequently and rightly said that the improvement of instruction is the most important function of administrative or supervisory officers in public schools. This chapter is not concerned with leadership in instruction *per se*, but rather with leadership in interpersonal relations, or, as we have called it, morale. Thus, in Case Six, "A Coin Has Two Sides," Jones was concerned with teaching (instruction), but he was also concerned with morale on the staff, and he may have been motivated by personal considerations. In any case, his prayerful solution was the elimination of Mr. Norris.

Principal Nielson provided good leadership in a new school that was threatened with a racial problem. The details are described in Case Two, "The Rock and Roll Ruckus." Principal Bell, in Case Seventeen, "Changing the Curriculum at Southside," provided leadership at Southside High School but failed to carry his faculty along with him. It was his plan, not theirs, and Principal Bell helped to create a morale problem among some of his personnel.

Everyone likes to belong to a successful organization. Thus, if morale is high in an organization, the members may disregard orders from the superior and make the system work. This, of course, makes the administrator "look good." On the other hand, if morale is not high, or if the administrator is not well liked, they may follow the letter of the law and cause failure of the organization that may result in discrediting the administrator so that he is transferred or separated.

Thus, in an extensive statistical study in industry, Baehr and Renck (2) concluded that the employee's attitude toward his immediate supervisor is critically important in the development or maintenance of morale. Pay is relatively unimportant, they conclude, except that it sets a minimum below which employees will not or cannot operate.

In education, morale has been defined as a climate of satisfaction arising from good interpersonal relations and a feeling among employees that they are progressing toward mutually accepted and worthwhile goals (9). Yoder (29), a student of industrial relations, described morale as the positive aspect of a condition of which the negative side is unrest. Everyone agrees that high morale is desirable and that it assists in achieving organizational ends. The problem is to describe and define the conditions that determine morale. The evidence, which is indicative rather than conclusive, suggests there are several factors, one of which is the relationship of an individual to his peers and to his immediate supervisor.

Skills for building morale. It is believed that working with a group is one of the routes to earned leadership. Again and again it has been emphasized that consideration is an outstanding characteristic of real leaders. They tend to make the individuals with whom they deal feel comfortable. Consistently, school administrators have stated that their training in human relationships has been the weakest part of their preparation programs.

The most successful leaders are adept at getting committees and groups to function so that they think through and attack their problems. Not infrequently the wise executive is the one who knows which individuals to include in a particular group. Skill in group work, sometimes called *group dynamics*, is a means to an end, not an end in itself.

Administrators may not expect loyalty and "followership" unless they involve their associates in planning, in co-operative efforts, and thus earn the position of leadership that their status position allows them to seek. Leadership that is achieved is dynamic; that which is prescribed is passive.

Tests of leadership in morale building. Some of the tests of ability to build morale are suggested by the following questions:

1. Is the leader willing to overlook the faults in other persons and to make use of their strengths while helping them with their weaknesses?
2. Is he able to find some good in everyone? A recent cartoon underlines this vividly by saying, "Of all the people in the world, I love Brother Joseph least."
3. Is the leader willing to earn his right to leadership within the group?
4. Is he able to use the informal structure in an organization so that some matters that need correction do not become matters of official record?
5. Is he willing to follow sound principles of organization?
6. Does he write out the issues in dealing with persons before making a decision, or does he rush ahead in authoritarian fashion?
7. Can embarrassment be avoided through private conference for those individuals who made mistakes?
8. With what kind of person are we dealing on this issue? Is the person tradition-directed, inner-directed, or other-directed?
9. Are there power factors in the situation that will influence the decisions?
10. Does the administrator have good skill as a discussion leader?
11. Does he always treat others as he would like to be treated?

Interpersonal relationships. The extensive research (23) at the Western Electric Company has thrown light on morale and interpersonal relationships. Altogether, the studies extended over five years and were divided into twelve periods. Much of the experiment concerned a small group of girls who were isolated in a separate room and asked to co-operate and work as they felt. During each period there was some change in working conditions. Rest periods were instituted, the total day shortened, special lunches prepared, and similar changes introduced. Finally, all the innovations were discontinued and the girls returned to a long work week without rest periods or other special considerations. In every period, including the last, production increased. Thus there was little or no correlation between work output and such things as the intensity of light and length of rest period. The explanation seems to lie in the kind of interpersonal relations which the girls developed among themselves and with their supervisor. They liked to work together in the test room, and the freedom under which they worked relieved them of anxiety.

There is no clear-cut experimental evidence that conclusively indicates the relationship between employee satisfaction and job effectiveness, but it is logical to assume that some such relationship does exist (5). Neither could one prove that a high degree of satisfaction among teachers would result in a good school, but it is unlikely that a highly discontented group of teachers would long operate a successful school.

Policies and work conditions. Chase (8) reported a study that included 1784 teachers and over 200 school systems in 43 states. His findings provide insight into the ways in which administrative policies and practices are related to teacher satisfaction. Three-fourths of the teachers regarded freedom to plan their work as the most important influence on morale. Good salaries and equipment were second in importance, and stimulating professional leadership, which gave recognition to good work and provided opportunities for teachers to participate in making policies on salary-scheduling, working conditions, and curriculum problems, was ranked third. Interestingly enough, some of the factors affecting morale were clearly related to some of the characteristics of personnel. Thus, elementary teachers tended to have better morale than secondary teachers, women better than men, married teachers better than single teachers, those with longer tenure in their school system better than those with shorter tenure, and those rated as the more superior teachers better than those rated as the less superior.

Weber (27), in discussing teacher load, says that, in the eyes of teachers, load is to a large extent a function of the satisfaction one derives from teaching. Where morale is high, responsibilities do not seem onerous. The National Education Association, in a study (18) involving 2,200 teachers, concluded that, if the teaching load is excessive, it appears to be directly related to teaching dissatisfaction. The teachers reported that a friendly, sympathetic principal did much to lighten what might otherwise be a heavy load.

Consistent administrative behavior. In the last few years several studies of the Midwest Administration Center at the University of Chicago have approached teacher satisfaction in another way. They point up the need for consistency of the administrator's behavior, but also indicate that behavior must accord with the teacher's expectations of the principal. This apparently means that when an administrator acts as teachers expect him to act, then there will be satisfaction on the part of teachers. The ability to predict a principal's or superintendent's behavior becomes a measure of individual security. Bidwell (5, 6), whose studies were based on 200 questionnaires and 11 interviews, concluded that teacher satisfaction is largely related to what teachers expect from their administrator and their perception of his behavior.

Moyer's study (17) of teachers and principals in four elementary and three secondary schools also suggests the importance of staff expectations in influencing personnel satisfaction. One goal of the study was to determine whether teachers depended more upon the principal or more upon the faculty group to satisfy their personality needs—in other words, did their attitudes toward authority cause them to be more "leader-centered" or "follower-centered"? Another part of the study collected data about the satisfaction teachers actually received in their professional relationships with their colleagues and their principals. Among other things, Moyer concluded that satisfaction was positively correlated with staff agreement in their attitudes toward leadership. In schools where there was a homogeneous outlook among teachers and the principal, satisfaction was high. A large gap between the principal's attitude and the attitudes of his staff was accompanied by marked dissatisfaction.

Teacher expectation. What kind of behavior do teachers generally expect from administrators? Juilfs (16) came to the conclusion that morale equals personal interest. Morale studies indicate that administrators ought to be competent leaders and that leadership must be earned. If an administrator expects to be a leader, he must have some vision and be able to stimulate those with whom he works and give them support in carrying out new developments. It is imperative, too, that he have honesty and integrity, so that the teachers believe that the administrator will treat them with fairness and honesty and so that they can depend upon his statements completely. Employees want to be recognized as persons of worth and dignity, who are treated as individuals of importance in a democratic society. They want a voice in policy-making that affects their welfare. This means, in school situations, that participating in the development of rating scales, salary schedules, and in-service programs are necessary.

Employees want to feel that they have access to the administrator. Employees who come to their supervisor, be it a school principal or a superintendent, must be assured of a courteous and sympathetic hearing and an explanation made of why the project cannot be undertaken immediately, if it must be postponed. They may expect to help decide whether the matter under consideration should or should not be put into action.

This tends to imply an open-door policy. An open door, of course, is more an attitude of mind than a physical reality. Listening to teachers' grievances is also important in its effects on morale. Both satisfied and dissatisfied teachers have complaints that must be heard sympathetically. If the cause of complaint cannot be removed, the teacher must know why. A lack of interest at this point may cause unfavorable factors to assume large proportions, causing dissatisfaction. Chase (8) concluded that any grievance can become a symbol of injustice, if it is not recognized.

To capitalize on strengths, the administrator should use each member of an organization in the place where he can best serve. Some teachers perform leadership functions in other groups, such as the church, labor unions, and so forth. In these places they can interpret the school organization in which they are working, if they understand their opportunities and plan accordingly. There can be a place where everyone can lead—the captain of the track team, the boy who is not very able intellectually but is the best opener of doors for fire drill, and the teacher who has special knowledge about reading readinesss although she may know little about art. A "critical incident" study of school administrators demonstrated that there is more ineffective behavior in administrator-staff relations than in any other area. According to the same study, administrators are much more effective in the management of fiscal and business affairs than in any other.

Perhaps the factors that affect morale can be summarized as (1) the attitude that administrators show toward employees, (2) relationships that employees enjoy in informal peer groups, (3) the amount of freedom that employees have in planning their work, (4) the opportunity that employees have in planning policies that affect them, and (5) the attitude of employees to their immediate superiors (9). Morale maintenance is also dependent upon the solution of problems at the work level without transferring them to a higher echelon in the organization for solutions.

Since not all problems arise in the work situation, the administrator must expect that he will have to listen to out-of-work problems as well. The interviewers at Western Electric first tried to follow a definite schedule in the interviewing, but soon abandoned it and just let the respondents talk. Often the administrator must do the same. Frequently he must listen to many things and sift from them the points that are important in the organization.

Finally, if an administrator is to be successful, he must be consistent. Admittedly, it is better if he has other qualities and is a democratic administrator; but even an undemocratic administrator, if he is consistent at all times, will be understood and can be respected, if not appreciated. This does not mean, of course, that in a democratic organization the administrator can agree with everyone. He cannot flit from one opinion to the other but must take a position with consistency.

Morale in Large-Scale Organizations

Up to this point we have dealt largely with morale in a work-group setting. There is also the problem of morale in large-scale organization. Here the problems center in delegation of authority. A principal may have good morale in a single school, but it will be shattered if an assistant superintendent interferes in the internal school affairs. Similarly, morale may be high among the central office employees, but if a principal who has participated in the formation of policy fails to interpret the policy correctly, or says, "The central office wants us to do it this way," the possibility of good morale throughout the organization is placed in jeopardy.

The skills and processes in promoting high morale in large-scale organizations are no different from those to be used in work-groups. They involve other persons (sometimes outside the organization), and they are more time-consuming because relationships are less direct. Morale in large-scale organizations always involves the right of appeal. The teacher who is dissatisfied with the principal has the right to talk to the assistant superintendent after he has notified the principal. Thus, formal "channels" must be clearly delineated in large-scale organizations. "Channels" must be used when morale is relatively weak and when human relations are bad. Where relationships are good, administrators confer "all over the place" with employees in informal manner to expedite operations. A principal, for example, may call the stock clerk to ask when supplies temporarily out of stock may be expected. There are, however, organizational routines, such as purchasing, travel, and so forth, where "channels" must always be followed or chaos results. One sign of sophisticated administration is to know when "channels" can or cannot be ignored.

When everyone stays in channels and is unwilling or unable to make decisions in the absence of a directive from a superior or a clear interpretation in "regulations," the road is rutted and everyone stays in his rut—we then have bureaucracy at its worst. Such bureaucracy is found in school systems both large and small. It is common in state governments. The "red tape" encountered in dealing with the Federal Government has caused some universities to question whether or not government contracts should be accepted at all.

In times of crisis, such as the "hundred days" of the Roosevelt administration in 1933, high morale was found in Federal Service. Even though authority was not clearly defined and responsibilities were delegated in haphazard fashion for the new agencies, young men of ability came to Washington to "do something." But when the crisis was over, the young men left to enter private business or to take up other careers that offered greater remuneration or less "red tape."

Certainly no organization as large as a state government or a large city system can operate without clear channels and certain allocation of authority and responsibility. This involves fiscal audit, say, by state auditors, of city expenditures, and the result is almost inevitably friction and at times open warfare. The co-ordination of city-state relationships, or of university-Federal Government relationships, is a special responsibility of the top executive, which is frequently delegated to the business manager. Here again friction can develop between, say, a professor, who wishes to carry out a research contract and who is unconcerned with "overhead funds," and the fiscal officer, who must see that university policy is maintained. In large organizations better morale throughout is promoted when the work group has a feeling of importance and faith in the immediate superior, and when problems are solved, in the main, at the work level. It is not channels which cause the worst in bureaucracy, but the kind of persons who frequently find such administration "by the numbers" pleasant or perhaps exhilarating.

Morale in the cases. The cases in this book illustrate many aspects of morale. Thus, Superintendent Davis in Case Eleven, "Headaches and Heartaches," had instructional problems. How these two situations were dealt with by different subordinates affected the morale of Miss Simms and Mr. Larson. In Case Sixteen, "The Riverton Dilemma," Superintendent Marsh was concerned with curriculum leadership. But he failed to acquaint his colleagues with his desires, and he did not attempt to secure their consent and co-operation. The result was a community shaken to its roots and the morale of personnel keenly disturbed.

Case Four, "The Sword of Damocles," involves a deviant person who was careless about gossip regarding his personal life. How Superintendent Kennedy protected the organization and at the same time maintained morale in handling this personnel problem is described in the case.

Deviants in Organization*

The deviant personality frequently is a "thorn in the flesh" of an administrator. The deviant may, and frequently does, threaten morale within an organization. Everybody enjoys having other persons agree with him on matters that are important or even of little importance, but each has learned by experience that he cannot expect everyone to agree with him. Persons who do not agree with the accepted norm are known as *nonconformists* or *deviants*, and society has dealt with them in many ways. Thus, there are persons who deviate so far from the expected norm with respect to other persons' property that they have been judged guilty of crime and are incarcerated in penitentiaries. We also have unfortunate individuals who deviate so markedly that they have been placed in protective custody in hospitals for the mentally ill or custodial institutions for the care of incompetents. Between these groups that have been taken out of society, we have all sorts of deviations in individuals. As the Quaker

* The author is indebted to colleagues who have participated in the Administrative Behavior Seminar at the University of Oregon, Norman Sundberg and Lucian Marquis, for many ideas in this section of the chapter. The interpretations made are solely the responsibility of the writer.

is reputed to have said to his wife, "Everyone is queer but thee and me, and sometimes I have my doubts about thee."

A nonconformist may deviate from the norms of one group and conform to those of another. Certainly he may belong to many groups, such as labor unions and church organizations, to which he conforms in greater or less degree. The nonconformists with whom this discussion is concerned are of two principal types: (1) the psychological deviant and (2) the person with unorthodox ideas. This is in no sense a catalogue of deviancy. But it classifies a very large number of cases that must be dealt with by a school administrator.

The psychological deviant. Persons suffering from psychological difficulties need help and understanding. The success of Alcoholics Anonymous demonstrates the value of support and understanding for men and women who cannot solve their drinking problems alone. Not many school administrators have had experience with excessive drinkers or drug addicts, for such deviants are uncommon among schoolteachers. However, there are estimated to be 3,500,000 problem drinkers and 40,000 persons affected with drug addiction in the United States. A more common deviant known to all experienced school administrators is one of the estimated 8,000,000 psychoneurotics in the United States, who are hampered in their occupations and their enjoyment of life by their anxieties, hostilities, and fears. A far more difficult deviant and one known to many experienced school administrators is the person with psychopathic disturbances or character disorders, of which there are an estimated 2,000,000 persons in the United States. An occasional administrator will also have had an experience with one of the estimated 1,000,000 psychotics in the United States. Some three-quarter million of these two groups are in one kind of custody or another.

Personalities of psychological deviants. Many deviants are chronic complainers. They have headaches and numerous illnesses (frequently not diagnosable by a physician); they may have chronic fatigue, which hinders their effectiveness as teachers or makes their personal lives less satisfactory than need be. Sometimes they develop ulcers, asthma, or allergies under the stress of living. Still others are worriers. They are tense, over-conscientious persons who are too much concerned with the smaller details of life. Such a person may feel snubbed if someone fails to say, "Good morning." Or perhaps such a person cannot sleep because she gave a student an unsatisfactory grade.

Administrators are likely, too, to meet persons who are self-centered, narcissistic people who manipulate those around them to gain their ends. Frequently they are unable to establish warm and deep relationships among their acquaintances. They quarrel with their families and associates and take to various escapes or unleash various attacks against others, such as excessive, gossipy, malicious tale-bearing or overaggressiveness. The "lone wolf" is another variant, although he does not ordinarily spread dissension or bring unhappiness to anyone but himself.

Such persons sometimes tend to rationalize away their failures or mistakes. "They are all out of step but Jim," said a fond mother of her son on parade. They overcompensate for their errors. This may lead to feelings of failure and frustration. They project their failures onto the actions of others. "I would have made it if Tom hadn't let me down," is not an uncommon statement.

Such reactions become deeper in the case of psychotic persons, and only trained and skilled observers can say when personnel become badly disturbed and need professional psychiatric services.

Many persons in every organization need someone to whom they can unburden themselves. Frequently only the cathartic effect of talking will solve the problem. "I feel better just to have said it," is a common statement. The problem may be a family difficulty, financial worries, or a deep-seated personal problem, to mention only a few. Every organization needs access to psychiatric service for persons who are seriously disturbed and need expert professional help. Sometimes the persons require leaves-of-absence. In extreme cases, rehabilitation in a mental hospital is indicated. An administrator need not be a clinical psychologist; he needs to understand when such services are needed.

Need for referral. The "line of demarcation" between someone who needs a sympathetic and diplomatic listener who can smooth the path of a deviant and one who needs professional help is not always clear. A principal who has good rapport with his staff can frequently find someone on the faculty who can give the necessary friendship. Sometimes listening is enough. For some women, unrestrained tears are helpful, but it is hard on the principal. There are some men who respond to "What do you want me to do? Kick your teeth out?" But such rough treatment is successful probably less than once in one thousand times. To indicate some of the cases that need referral, a few illustrations are furnished.

1. *The depressed person.* This type ranges all the way from the tired teacher who says, "Thank God, it's Friday" to the person so despondent he or she commits suicide. It does little or no good to suggest a vacation or a change of scenery to a seriously depressed person. For the mildly depressed person, a good night's sleep or a trip is frequently sufficient. The trick with depression is to secure professional help in time. The sensitive (and sometimes lucky) administrator does get them to a psychiatrist in time.

2. *The split personality.* All of us exhibit traces of Dr. Jekyll and Mr. Hyde from time to time. Probably no one is always the same serene personality unless it be Pollyanna, and she probably was an uninteresting and not quite human person. It is only when schizophrenia is so marked that the victim cannot return to reality, or lives more in the world of phantasy than in the present, that professional help is necessary. Many such persons have returned from mental hospitals willing and able to lead useful and productive lives in the classroom.

3. *The pathological liar.* Ring Lardner has given us an example in "Alibi Ike" of a baseball player who simply couldn't tell the truth. The hilarious story results in impossible situations, many of which are pathetic rather than humorous. All of us tend to "stretch the truth" from time to time. It is only human to rationalize our mistakes. In dealing with mild deviancy, the administrator need not point out inconsistencies of the "teller." It is sufficient to summarize the facts and to understand, when the inability to tell the truth is very marked, that it is time for professional help.

4. *The persecuted person.* All of us at times feel unappreciated by our superiors, colleagues, or families. Sometimes the "persecution" is real; more often it is fancied. Calm counseling usually is sufficient for most persons. For those with fixed delusions of persecution, it is necessary to get psychiatric help. Otherwise they are most likely to deteriorate and deviate so markedly that they cannot be useful.

How much deviation can be tolerated? The answer depends to some extent on how much of the individual's life is controlled by the group. Less deviation from some standards would be possible in a boarding school than in a day school. More deviation can be tolerated in a large urban school than in a small village school. More deviation will be tolerated among industrial workers than will be allowed among rural teachers. Not only the "work group" but the community determines the allowable deviation. More tolerance can be expected in the graduate school than in an elementary school. In many schools, both the social and professional life are so closely woven that marked deviation results in rejection or elimination. Thus, a teacher with strong fundamentalist religious beliefs usually will be readily acceptable. But if he works zealously to convert others in the faculty, he will probably be rejected. The deviancy may become so unacceptable to all that a transfer is necessary.

What can a deviate do? He can withdraw from the group. More frequently he will fight the group. Principals who consider the superintendent to be reactionary or outmoded frequently play this dangerous and unethical game; sometimes they win. Frequently the deviant abandons or conceals his deviation and follows the way of the group. Probably the best action is to join the group and work toward the changes he considers desirable. The practice of many school administrators in working and broadening the vision of individual members of the Board over a period of years is a case in point.

It is clear that those who deal with psychological deviants, and all administrators must do so, need to know their personnel. Not only must they know them in order to recognize and counsel deviants, but also, if need be, to select others to take their place. If the deviation gets to the point where it is intolerable, the administrator must be prepared to transfer, to dismiss, or to refer for treatment.

In many cases of psychological deviation, an administrator, typically a principal, is among the first to become aware of the problem. While treatment in a school system can be performed better by a consultant who does not have responsibilities in rating, separation, or promotions, fine counseling has been and will continue to be done by principals and superintendents.

The unorthodox thinker. Probably the unorthodox thinker is the most frequent and the most needed nonconformist. In academic life such a person is necessary and may even be priceless. If his unorthodox beliefs are in the economic or political sphere, he may be declared a Communist or possibly a "fellow-traveler." Our history is studded with the names of persons who have been persecuted, disgraced, or even killed for unorthodox beliefs. Billy Mitchell, whose beliefs have been thoroughly vindicated, was dimissed by the military services. Over two thousand years ago Socrates said (21, pp. 113–114):

> And now, Athenians, I am not going to argue for my own sake, as you may think, but for yours, that you may not sin against the God, or lightly reject his boon, by condemning me. For if you kill me you will not easily find another like me who, if I may use such a ludicrous figure of speech, am a sort of gadfly, given to the state by God; and the state is a great and noble steed who is tardy in his motions owing to his very size, and requires to be stirred into life. I am that gadfly which God has attached to the state, and all day long and in all places am always fastening upon you, arousing and persuading and reproaching you. And as you will not easily find another like me, I would advise you to spare me. I dare say that you may feel irritated at being suddenly awakened when you are caught napping, and you think that if you were to strike me dead as Anytus advises, which you easily might, then you would sleep on for the remainder of your lives, unless God in his care of you sent you another gadfly.

The Athenians forced Socrates to drink the hemlock and, without meaning to do so, gave him immortality. Perhaps at this point no more dramatic illustration can be found or, indeed, is needed.

The assumption is made here that, in a democratic society, cultural change is necessary and desirable, and, in a world such as ours, cultural isolation is impossible. Isolation means stagnation and lack of growth. Generally, social scientists agree that societies that have permitted an influx of new ideas have tolerated greater deviation than societies that have not exhibited cultural change.

The importance of nonconformity in ideas is more important in educational institutions than in business or industry. Every university worthy of the name has a number of "indigestibles" who help keep the administration honest and frequently uncomfortable. Almost always they are difficult to live with; always they serve as a reminder that ideas are important and that conformity is not necessarily a virtue. The reasons for encouraging nonconformity are underscored in a dissenting opinion by Justice Oliver Wendell Holmes (1):

> If you have no doubt of your premises or your power and want a certain result with all your heart, you naturally express your wishes in law and sweep away all opposition. To allow opposition by speech seems to indicate that you think the speech impotent, as when a man says that he has squared the circle, or that you do not care

wholeheartedly for the result, or that you doubt either your power or your premises. But when men have realized that time has upset many fighting faiths, they may come to believe even more than they believe the very foundations of their own conduct that the ultimate good desired is better reached by free trade in ideas—that the best test of truth is the power of the thought to get itself accepted in the competition of the market, and that truth is the only ground upon which their wishes safely can be carried out. That at any rate is the theory of our Constitution. It is an experiment, as all life is an experiment. Every year if not very day we have to wager our salvation upon some prophecy based upon imperfect knowledge. While that experiment is part of our system I think that we should be eternally vigilant against attempts to check the expression of opinions that we loathe and believe to be fraught with death, unless they so imminently threaten immediate interference with the lawful and pressing purposes of the law that an immediate check is required to save the country.

Conformity. Educational organizations are at a crossroads of conformity and nonconformity. One of their major functions is to conserve and perpetuate the cultural heritage. But if this be the sole function, then a democratic society will ultimately pass away. The second, and equally important function, is to prepare individuals to become members of a dynamic, complex, and plural society. Preparation for this second function implies the ability to analyze, to criticize, and to create independent acts, which frequently demand nonconforming behavior and unorthodox ideas on the part of both school personnel and lay citizens. Under the American system of education, the school is closely identified with the values of the community, and the policies of the school are set within the community. Since educational policy decisions are made continuously at all levels, no other government organization has such intimate contact with its clientele; even the action of a janitor may be as important as those of the superintendent. This often means that there is less possibility for long-range perspectives, the issues are felt immediately, and the community pressures demand solution. It also means that infringement upon the community norms will be almost instantly challenged, and teachers and administrators are well aware of this and, therefore, are less inclined to promote new ideas. Thus, school employees encounter many significant problems at the crossroads of conformity and nonconformity.

In a military organization, nonconformity cannot be tolerated, since policy-making takes place at a high organizational level and the goals of the organization usually depend on the unquestioned carrying out of decision. The United States Military Forces are much more democratic than those of Nazi Germany or Communist Russia, but they are much less democratic organizations than are desirable in civilian life. In a school, where policy is made at every level, autocratic administration is much more likely to make for inefficiency.

An individual active in public administration needs to have greater safeguards than do individuals in some other organizations. Too often because of loyalty oaths, legislative investigations, or community pressures, the public administrator is likely to become a second-class citizen. Yet public administration is an area in which democratic values are on parade every day, the individual is by necessity under great public scrutiny, and his future career is more closely linked with his present position than in most occupations. Thus, the removal of the nonconformist and the dissenter in public schools ought to be hedged with both legal and procedural standards.

At the same time, it is necessary to distinguish between unorthodoxy and conspiracy. No rational system would willingly or knowingly allow for its own downfall. Conspiracy can never be condoned. Unless the unorthodox ideas involve revolution, the remedy is more discussion.

The unorthodox person must be willing to pay the price for deviancy. If his ideas are proved to be false or without foundation, he may expect at least ridicule, public scorn, or even professional oblivion. The right to choose conformity or deviancy belongs to the individual.

The paradox of education. The school or university has a number of functions, one of which is to pass on the cultural heritage of the race. Thus, in any university one can find in the minds of the faculty or in the books of the library whatever the race has learned in a period of recorded history. This by nature makes the institution the conservator of knowledge and tends to make it a conservative institution.

In the university, and to a lesser extent in the secondary school, there is a second function: to teach the people to make a living, as doctors, nurses, journalists, businessmen, and educators. It also has the responsibility of teaching them to live better by attending concerts, athletic contests, and exhibits of paintings, by making them cognizant of the better aspects of civilized living.

An educational institution has the somewhat paradoxical responsibility of teaching young people to solve the problems which their teachers are not equipped or not bright enough to solve. If political leaders knew how to eliminate war or the fear of war, they would do so immediately. If the doctors had the cure for cancer, they would proceed forthwith in its application. Since there are countless horizons concerning which we do not have the answers, the schools must educate young people to solve the problems which the present generation has not solved. This demands a certain amount of inventiveness. It is no accident that a large number of scientists who worked on the development of nuclear fission were young men, who "didn't know that the problem couldn't be solved," and it is no accident that in the development sections of industrial organizations the researchers are likely to be young men. Thus, in an educational institution the deviant with radical ideas must be protected so long as he does not threaten the establishment of the organization or threaten to tear down the foundationstones of our society. Such action demands courage on the part of our administrators and thoughtfulness on the part of our supporting public.

References

1. *Abrams vs. United States,* 250 U.S. 616 (1919).
2. Baehr, M. E., and Richard Renck, "The Definition and Measurement of Employee Morale," *Administrative Science Quarterly,* Vol. 3, No. 2 (Sept. 1958), pp. 157–184.
3. Beard, Charles, *Public Policy and the General Welfare.* New York: Rinehart & Company, Inc., 1941.
4. Berle, A. A., Jr., *The Twentieth Century Capitalist Revolution.* New York: Harcourt, Brace and Company, 1954.
5. Bidwell, Charles E., "Administration and Teacher Satisfaction," *Phi Delta Kappan,* 37 (April, 1956), pp. 285–288.
6. ————, "The Administrative Role and Satisfaction in Teaching," *Journal of Educational Sociology,* 29 (Sept., 1955), pp. 41–47.
7. Boulding, Kenneth E., *The Organizational Revolution.* New York: Harper and Brothers, 1953.
8. Chase, Francis S., "Factors for Teacher Satisfaction," *Phi Delta Kappan,* 33 (Nov. 1951), pp. 127–132.
9. Culbertson, Jack A. "The Cement of Personnel Relations," *California Journal of Secondary Education,* 31 (Oct., 1956), pp. 353–357.

10. Foskett, J. M., "New Facts about Lay Participation," *Nation's Schools,* 54 (Aug., 1954), pp. 54–63.

11. ——,"Who Discusses School Affairs?" *School Executive,* 74 (Feb., 1955), pp. 63–66.

12. Goldhammer, Keith, "Community Power Structure and School Board Membership," *The American School Board Journal,* 130 (March, 1955), pp. 23–26.

13. ——, "The School Board and Administration in the American Perspective of Government," *The American School Board Journal,* 129 (Nov., 1954), pp. 29–31, and (Dec., 1954), pp. 29–31.

14. Hammons, George C., *The Western Electric Experiments: Human Factors in Management.* Parkville, Mo.: Park College Press, 1946.

15. Hunter, Floyd, *Community Power Structure.* Chapel Hill: University of North Carolina Press, 1953.

16. Juilfs, Erwin, "Research Gives Administration a Formula Morale—Personal Interest," *Oregon Education,* 32 (March, 1958), pp. 6–7 and pp. 41–42.

17. Moyer, Donald C., "Leadership That Teachers Want," *Administrator's Notebook,* 3, March, 1955.

18. National Education Association, *Teaching Load in 1950,* NEA Research Bulletin, 39, February, 1951.

19. OSS Assessment Staff, *Assessment of Men.* New York: Rinehart & Co., Inc., 1941.

20. Pierce, Truman M., and Craig Wilson, "Research in County Educational Administration," *The School Executive,* 72 (Mar., 1953), pp. 96–106.

21. Plato, *Apology of Socrates,* in Miller ed., *The Classics—Greek & Latin.* New York: Vincent Parke & Co., 1909.

22. Riesman, David, *The Lonely Crowd.* New Haven: Yale University Press, 1950.

23. Roethlisberger, F. J., and W. J. Dickson, *Management and the Workers.* Cambridge: Harvard University Press, 1940.

24. Sharma, Chiranji Lal, "Who Should Make Decisions?" *Administrator's Handbook,* 3, No. 8, April, 1955.

25. Stogdill, R. M., "Personal Factors Associated with Leadership: A Survey of the Literature," *Journal of Psychology,* 25 (Jan., 1948), pp. 35–71.

26. Warner, W. L., and Paul S. Lunt, *The Social Life of a Modern Community.* New Haven: Yale University Press, 1941.

27. Weber, C. A., "Teaching Loads," Chap. 7, *Personnel Problems of School Administrators.* New York: McGraw-Hill Book Co., 1954.

28. White, Ralph, and Ronald Lippett, "Leader Behavior and Member Reaction in Three Social Climates," in Darwin Cartwright (ed.), *Group Dynamics Research and Theory.* Evanston, Ill.: Row, Peterson & Co., 1953.

29. Yoder, Dale, *Personnel Management and Industrial Relations.* Englewood Cliffs, N.J.: Prentice-Hall, Inc., 1948.

CHAPTER SEVEN

Administering Change

He that will not apply new remedies must expect new evils.

BACON

The current decades are characterized by a rapidity of change that men have never experienced before. The industrial revolution of the current period is so great in its scope and impact that the industrial revolution of the nineteenth century will probably by comparison look like a slight wave in societal development.

The current industrial revolution is the result of a more direct or conscious effort by men to effect change than were developments heretofore. Man is seeking to improve the lot of man. With this view men everywhere are demanding change. To a remarkable extent the demand is world-wide, reaching areas that only a few decades ago would have been untouched by developments in other parts of the world for many years. Man is giving his most direct attention to scientific change. It is here, through research, that he has learned how to break through barriers and constantly to explore new frontiers. The effects of these scientific advances on man himself, on how he functions as a member of society, and on changes needed in societal functioning are explored much less. In the technical aspects of science, he feels secure and pushes forward. In the area of relations of men to the scientific changes and in the area of relations among men, he is much less secure.

But whether man understands the changes that are occurring and that will occur as a result of the advancements in science, there can be little doubt that the vast changes that are in process will have a marked influence on man and his manner of living. Confronted with these facts, he can either attempt to ride with the tides or he can attempt to study them, understand them, and possibly influence them in desirable directions. It is in this setting that educators today are greatly and properly concerned with change in education.

Looking back a half-century, it is easy to recall conditions that seem to have little relation to today's world. The relatively simple life of the farm or small village was strikingly different from life in one of the vast, sprawling, and feverishly growing conurbations which are increasingly found throughout most of the world. Man's concept of life, its purposes, and his relationship to various forces was then very different. Educational provisions for that period would be of questionable value today. In attitudes, institutions, and practices great changes have occurred. It is probable, however, that men a half-century from now will look back upon the present day as a period considerably more remote than the simple life of fifty years ago appears to us.

With all the technological change which has taken place, one frequently wonders whether social changes are occurring rapidly enough to hold the society together. In addition, are the social changes that are occurring the appropriate ones? Are we not educating and thinking in terms of our relations one to another as might have been defensible in an earlier age of production and communication? Can we expect to be understood in terms that we would like to be understood when we use such a small amount of our productive power to meet the needs of men—in our own and other nations?

And what type of world are we changing toward? Recently, in considering programs that are carried out in economically underdeveloped nations to raise their standards of living, a colleague pointed out that we encourage them to move toward the small, independent farmer, although we ourselves are rapidly moving away from this institution of our past. Is this action defensible? Are we seeking for them an institution regarding which we have a certain nostalgia? If we are not to help them to move in this direction, then in what direction? If agricultural production is to be increasingly handled through vast industrial-agricultural organizations, then what decision-making power remains in the hands of the farmer?

What are the implications of these changes for education? Has the school in our great industrial centers effected the essential changes to make it probable that the individual can play a desired role in the enterprise? Or is he uninformed, frustrated, and unable to deal with the vast organization of which he is a part? What changes are necessary in education as a result of the industrial development of agriculture?

Beyond these questions of socioeconomic relationships within the nation there are many others which may be demanding marked change in education. Among these are: the tremendous world-wide population explosion; the demand of all peoples for respect and opportunity; the reduction or elimination of distance on the earth and the related glimpse into space; the continued growth of ability to produce and the related difficulties of distribution; the concern for the individual in a time when there are vast pressures encouraging conformity.

Assumptions

In turning to an examination of the question of change and the relation of the administrator to it, some assumptions will first be made.[1] The assumptions, based upon past experience, follow. They are not necessarily firmly established and may well be modified in the light of subsequent experience.[2] They do, however, offer a base for thought.

1. Change is inevitable. This assumption would appear established if one accepts the concept that both individuals and institutions seek to maintain an equilibrium. The interrelatedness of people and institutions and the momentum of technological advance in our world make social adaptation and readjustment inevitable. Even the attempt to escape, in itself, produces change. The idea that a society might "freeze" with certain forms for an indefinite period, as ap-

[1] The subject of change is an extremely complex one. Many interrelated and interacting factors are involved in it. This was shown in the important studies on adaptability and related matters carried out by Paul Mort and those associated with him. It is a subject that can be approached from the point of view of organization, finance, public opinion, statute, administrative structure, mores, political theory, or one of a number of other bases. In view of the limited space available, and especially because of the central significance of people in the process of change, it is matters of personnel that have been selected for emphasis in this chapter. This approach is recognized as a limited but also as a most fundamental one. Many problems which, for example, appear to be matters of organization or finance are basically matters of the values, the security, and the competencies of people.

[2] For an excellent analysis and summary of the research on social change from various fields of human endeavor, see the book by Lippitt, Watson, and Westlev (7).

peared to be the case in past societies, appears increasingly unlikely. Certainly in the dynamic American setting, such a condition is not easily imagined.

2. Desirable change is not inevitable. Despite the fact that the change appears certain, it is not inevitable that the change occurring be desirable. It may be change that reflects an attempt to escape facing the real problems of the society. A sharp shift in the direction of science and mathematics in our schools would be change, but change of questionable soundness. In a world marked by inabilities of men to work together, the further emphasis on science as the highest intellectual frontier or challenge could be disastrous. Conceivably, also, our schools could move in the direction of a content-fact emphasis rather than a process-behavior emphasis or a balance between these with great resulting harm.

3. Basic to a consideration of change are the value systems of the individuals and the society concerned. Unless the value systems and commitments are clearly discerned and influence the behavior of those in a position to lead, men are unlikely to grapple in an adequate manner with problems of change. The value system is essential as a base both for considering the desirability of any change and for planning any steps designed to bring about or to facilitate change. The value system is one of the most difficult matters with which to deal, since it is central in the organism and not readily modified. A significant consideration is that the value systems to which persons and groups are committed become a rich source of security (2).

4. Social change can be effected. With an adequate knowledge of men and their institutions, change can be planned and achieved. It should be recognized that in many situations inadequate knowledge is available to enable man to effect it. His efforts may still be marked by much trial-and-error learning.[3]

5. Desirable social (educational) change is difficult to effect. The extreme complexity of individuals, the variation among individuals, and the many group and organizational forces that relate to planned change make it a most complex problem.[4] Many of the cases

[3] For examples of actual change effected through different approaches, see the reports of Corey (5), Sarchet (10), Wormser (12), and Coch and French (3).

[4] The extreme complexity of change processes is shown exceedingly well by Ronken and Lawrence (8) in their analysis of the problem encountered in effecting changes in a factory. Also see the work by Elliott (6).

in this book illustrate the difficulty that confronts the leader in education. Case One, "The Valley City Consolidation Issue," and Case Seventeen, "Changing the Curriculum at Southside," are good examples of the difficulties encountered in achieving desirable change.

The school administrator in a community that has little concern for quality education and for maximum development of its children is confronted with a difficult problem. Such a situation may involve the refurbishing of values by the community or the building of new ones. This attempt to change values may conflict with the wishes of the major power structures. The teaching staff may be quite divided on the issue and on procedures that are judged effective for coping with the problem. As Zander (13) has noted, proposed changes will mean quite different things to different people. Thus, many matters that are or may appear irrelevant to the administrator may markedly affect the course of change. Tensions between the administrator and teachers, or between groups of teachers and parents, will have a bearing on the procedure to be employed. How the feelings of various groups can create tension that influences change can be seen in Case Sixteen, "The Riverton Dilemma."

6. Effective educational change is closely related to planned programs of study and research in schools and school systems. Such research pertains both to the proposed change and to the processes to be employed in achieving it. Much must be learned, not only by those initiating change, but also by those who sanction and those who implement change, if the process is to be well understood and if it is to be effectively planned and completed. The cases in this book offer many illustrations of inadequate study and understanding both of the matter under consideration and of the related individuals and processes.

7. Change in individuals and institutions has some of the same characteristics. Both individuals and institutions seek stability, and, as Coffey and Golden (4) have noted, both have certain "boundary-maintaining" characteristics.[5] Both inevitably change and yet frequently resist change vigorously. Both are complex in their operation,

---

[5] For an excellent treatment of the psychological forces and processes of change within an institution, see the work of Coffey and Golden (4). They give attention to such matters as individual change process, tension and change, characteristics of institutional groups, and group membership and individual change. The dynamics of the processes of change are viewed as they relate to attempts to restore equilibrium.

and they change as a result of a complex of factors that play upon the organism and are in turn played upon by it. Both have "commitments" that significantly affect behavior. Note, for example, the struggle that the informal groups initiated against the introduction of a proposed change in Case Seventeen, "Changing the Curriculum at Southside."

8. Change is facilitated through knowledge and breadth of experience. The mere knowledge that there are other ways of meeting a problem may open the way to change. Wider knowledge and experience may also facilitate change in that the proposed new condition may not appear so forbidding. The administrator who fears a strong teacher organization, for example, might be better able to contemplate a change if he could still envision a satisfactory role for himself and could see the educational service strengthened. The unknown contains threats to roles that create anxiety and even hostility (9). With broader knowledge and experience, the realm of the unknown is reduced. Yet it must be recognized that knowledge may in some cases result in resistance to change because of an awareness of the implications of the change for an individual or group.

9. Strong motivations to perform according to the general norms may undesirably reduce the range of activity and thus interfere with experimentation and *improved* practice. Man has learned much through the variety of approaches that he has made under varying circumstances. In a sense, variations in practice are "controlled" experiments in the vast laboratory of living. As "better" practice comes to be known, there is much pressure to bring the lower performers up to the norms. There is relatively far less emphasis upon the desirability of experimentation and upon the need for individuals and institutions to greatly exceed the norm. There would appear to be an almost inevitable tendency for the norm to be seen as a standard by many individuals and groups. This tendency, unless countered, may result in change itself losing a most important stimulant. Are our high schools, for example, becoming more like one another rather than clarifying goals and moving forward to higher levels of educational achievement? Does each school and each school system have a unique quality related to its purposes and the situation?

10. Much change is effected through modification of related situations rather than through a direct approach. Possibly Mr. Bell in Case Seventeen, "Changing the Curriculum at Southside," could

have led in more rapid curriculum change through first centering attention upon a study of needs of students or concerns of teachers rather than "offering" a plan.

Relatively simple changes may, of course, be effected through direct action. Even in a complicated change, a direct approach may also be taken, but generally it would not stand alone but rather would be a part of a complex set of actions. The educational service is especially complicated, pertaining as it does to children and youth and being participated in by parents and community as well as by those with a legally prescribed responsibility. Frequently, therefore, the administrator may look to himself and to others involved in the situation when questioning the desirability of a given practice. Considerable exploration may well precede action, and direct action may come late and only as one element of a totality.

To decide the specific approach needed, a consideration of the organization or institution as a totality rather than as a series of relatively separate elements is required. Elements both inside the organization and outside of it must be recognized. There must be an awareness of the fact that even a matter which appears to have little relationship to the contemplated change or a matter that may appear to be rather unimportant may prove to be otherwise. A grasp of the social setting as a whole can give the administrator a reasonable security based upon knowledge and understanding—a security that cannot be achieved in any other manner and that is a basic element in effective leadership.

Blocks to Desirable Change

While some of the blocks to change have been suggested in the assumptions made above, it is desirable to identify them directly. Although they will be listed separately, it should not be assumed that they operate alone. Actually, a configuration of the blocks frequently influences a situation when needed change is not forthcoming.

1. *Lack of knowledge of varied practices, plans, and courses of action.* Lack of knowledge remains a major deterrent to change. This fact needs to be kept in mind in such periods as the present, when much attention is given to other factors. The individual who knows no other way of doing something, who has experienced no other so-

ciety and its approaches to a problem, may be limited in his vision. The undesirable features of parochialism, which have long been recognized, remain.

Knowledge may be lacking not only in the case of individuals. Status leaders also may be lacking in knowledge, and the teacher group or the community may be in the same condition.

Knowledge is important both with reference to the particular service or area that is under consideration and also with reference to approaches that may be made to a problem in attempting to effect a solution. Knowledge of oneself and of others and their perceptions is necessary, if desirable change is to be effected. For the administrator interested in change, knowledge is imperative.

2. *Lack of ability to work together.* It must be recognized that knowledge of a subject or even of the elements in change is not enough. It is possible to have extended knowledge and yet have little of the ability that is essential if a group is going to effect change in its procedures. The people of France may have as excellent a knowledge of politics and economics as those of England. They may quite possibly be better informed. But they do not have as highly developed an ability to function for the common good. Somehow they lack necessary common commitments and the related skills that provide an essential cement for a smooth-functioning society. The English may speak of "muddling" through, but what they have reference to may be an important ingredient in social functioning.

The ability of a school staff or of a community and school to work together in a highly effective manner is not easily achieved nor readily retained. It has about it some of the elements of a *gestalt*, in that it is something beyond the sum of the parts. It is easier to recognize as being present or absent than to explain. It represents a certain balancing or interrelating of many individuals who themselves continue at the same time to be in the process of change. It, therefore, must be constantly sought, though it be recognized that it is not to be attained in any fixed form. Much is known regarding many of its elements and more knowledge must be sought, but the likelihood that it cannot be precisely prescribed must be recognized.

The public schools of our society have contributed greatly toward the development of individuals who can work together. Our diversity as a people emphasizes the need for education with this purpose. Yet association with status leaders, groups of teachers, and citizen committees constantly reveals shocking illustrations of people who have little competence in this regard. A major responsibility of the administrator is assisting staff and citizens to develop competence in working together to achieve desirable change.

3. *Lack of adequately defined common purposes or commitments.* This lack was notable in Case Sixteen, "The Riverton Dilemma." Here the superintendent and teachers appeared to lack common purposes, and teachers engaged in rumor-spreading regarding "progressive education."

Much that is done in any society and by any people reflects a past need or purpose rather than a present one. The almost inevitable tendency of institutions to formalize suggests that the forms continue past the point of usefulness. While this must be recognized, it is also important to note that institutionalization is essential if significant change is to be effected. The clarification of goals and the development of commitments by the various parties involved appear to be an essential base for change. Unless these occur, individuals move in diverse ways, and change, which is sought, cannot be effected. Since institutions often do not have the commitment of people who were not involved in their initial establishment and development, procedures must be followed to refurbish commitments. This is one of the most difficult tasks of the leader. It involves the energizing of people, because value systems are forces of energy and emotion. It pertains to the central rather than the peripheral aspect of the man. Thus, the process is more than knowledge; it is the force that gives the knowledge and ability to work together a social significance. This is not quickly achieved.

It is to be noted that a lack of commitments may characterize an individual. But it may also characterize a school staff, a community, or a nation. Many of our communities do not pursue vigorously the commitments that they profess. It can only be concluded that they have not developed or re-established their commitments so that they may be something more than verbalisms. Probably their professions are not their true commitments. It is encouraging to note that many recent criticisms of the schools reveal a concern about purposes. The criticisms, therefore, constitute a base for a re-examination of purposes and the clarification of commitments.

4. *Inadequate norms.* Norms that are developed and accepted generally tend to reflect past practice. This is inevitable because of

the very meaning of "norm." When the significance of norms in behavior is realized, the powerful block to change that they constitute can be readily appreciated. Norms regarding both a practice with which one is concerned and regarding the manner in which attempts at change are made are important. The significance of inadequate norms is further emphasized when attention is given to the fact that frequently norms become standards. In the case of many individuals and groups, norms may be more powerful than the commitments referred to in "3" immediately above. In fact, maintaining the status quo as reflected in the norm may become the commitment. While norms properly influence commitments and purposes, the administrator and others interested in change must go back to social values for a base for critically evaluating existing norms and for conceiving more adequate norms.

5. *Matters related to security.* The problems of security are many in reference to change. There is both the security of the individual and the security that may or may not characterize a group. Furthermore, security problems may be directly related to the change in prospect or may have only a most indirect or tangential relationship. Then, too, "too great" security or unthinking and apathetic satisfaction with what is may be as large a block to change as is insecurity.

Generally, an individual and a group will resist change unless they have adequate feelings of security to embolden them to try the untried. Thus, a background of security in the situation is essential. Security also must be able to be perceived in the anticipated situation. In a group in which there is little group support, tension among members, and lack of confidence in the administration, desirable change is not likely. Insecurity may result from various types of changes. In Case Thirteen, "The Rotating Librarian," the librarian with the new assignment was a threat to many. In Case Sixteen, "The Riverton Dilemma," the evaluation of the curriculum resulted in much feeling of insecurity.

The difficulties related to insecurity when a "new" development is faced are found in many communities where the superintendent of schools and the organized teaching group are in the process of making changes. The group may be emotionalized against the superintendent because of past manipulation or domination, real or imagined. The superintendent may be thoroughly in agreement with the idea that the profession should play a stronger part in educational matters. At the same time, he may be rather insecure in the face of a proposed change, for he cannot help wondering how his own position will be affected, and he may not be sure that the new developments will improve the educational service. Therefore, he is likely to assume that the past relationships, which he knows, are more conducive to a strong educational service.

Security is thus much more than security in the specific matter under consideration. It relates sharply to the past experiences of the individual and the profession, both in the school and in the larger society. It is a matter of "feeling" perhaps more than of actual status. What is felt is real, however, and can be a powerful influence on behavior.

6. *Role concepts.* Frequently change involves a change in role expectations on the part of a number of people or groups, and concepts of role are not modified easily. Consider, for example, a superintendent and teachers' group where the question at issue is a procedure for salary-schedule development. Should the superintendent, the teaching group, a citizens' group appointed by the board of education, or a committee of representative teachers, administrators, board members, or citizens of special competence and interest take the initiative in doing the essential studies? If a committee is chosen, does this procedure challenge the role of the superintendent as the executive officer of the board of education? If the superintendent takes the initiative, does this not challenge the role of a mature professional group? In Case Fourteen, "The Case of a Tenacious Superintendent," there were sharp differences between the role of the superintendent as seen by the old and as seen by the new groups in the community. The superintendent was not sure of the role expectations of the board of education, and he thought a great deal about the role he should fill.

The conflicts in role produce tension, fear, and misunderstanding and thus may block desirable changes. On the other hand, conflicts in role may stimulate much change over a period of time. Probably rigidly established roles about which there is little or no disagreement, as well as sharp conflict in role expectations, both tend to work against change because of the deadening power of status quo in the one instance and because of the resultant insecurities in the other.

7. *Lack of leadership competency.* The complexity of the leadership task is apparent when the administration of change in the

school and community is considered. Even when full recognition is given the various other forces and factors that relate to the process of change, the significance of the leader remains. For it is the leader or those sharing leadership with him who must have: essential knowledge concerning the matter considered for change and concerning processes by which change may be effected; ability to help a group overcome its failures and achieve mature group status; understanding of the perceptions of various individuals and groups in the school and in the community; ability to help groups and individuals examine and strengthen their commitments; understanding of status, feelings, and competence in achieving that measure of security that facilitates change; awareness of the impact of norms on behavior and skill in analyzing and improving norms or in helping a group do this; understanding of himself (motives) and of his role and of that of others in the process of change. All of these matters involve high competence in the co-ordination of energies based upon perception, communication, and motivation that produces a climate conducive to growth. So significant and difficult is the task of administration that it is understandable that Adams (1, pp. 207–8) has said that administration is "not only the faculty upon which social stability rests, but is, possibly, the highest faculty of the human mind."

It would be unrealistic to suppose that this "highest faculty" is highly developed in large numbers of people or that the status leaders of educational systems have generally achieved it in abundant measure. The widespread concern regarding the pre- and in-service preparation of administrators is testimony regarding the work that remains to be done in the area of selecting and preparing men to meet this challenge more effectively. Many of the cases in this book reveal lack of certain leadership competencies. None perhaps contain more striking illustrations than the tortuous trail revealed in Case Fifteen, "Greenfield Builds Its Third High School."

8. *The size of organizations.* The large organization, which increasingly characterizes society, hampers change for a number of reasons. Chief among these are the fact that change, if effected, is so widespread and affects so many people, and that the larger organization increases the distance between the point of action and the point of decision-making, with the resultant increase in problems of understanding and communication.

To make a change in the educational program of a single small school district is relatively simple compared to making a change in the program of a large centralized unit. In the small district it may be possible to develop common purposes and even to regard the whole procedure as an experiment. If it doesn't work out at the end of a period, a return is relatively easy. In the large district, however, there will be groups and communities that almost certainly will not accept the desirability of the proposed change, and they will be much less readily assured that the whole matter may be regarded as an experiment. Thus, before any change is made, vastly greater effort must be devoted to the development of understanding, and even after the change is agreed upon, considerably greater resistance may be expected.

The problems of administration related to the large-scale organizations are coming to be more widely recognized. There are problems resulting from the tendency for power to be located increasingly at the center, problems associated with the stereotyped bureaucrat, and problems of how and in what manner the people shall participate in decision-making. Related to these issues are matters such as communication, authority, delegation, deconcentration of power, and decentralization. The metropolitan areas offer an excellent laboratory for work in regard to questions such as these. Is it inevitable that personnel in large-scale organizations must feel far removed from decision-making and unable to do much about it? Are teachers and parents to be expected to feel frustrated and resentful when they speak of the "downtown" office?

The Activation of Change

Since certain assumptions regarding the process of change have been made and some of the forces militating against it have been briefly examined, attention will now be turned to its activation. Obviously, the problem of activating change is one that relates to the specific circumstances found in varying situations. However, there are some conditions that appear to facilitate it or at least to accompany it. A few of these will be offered. The list is not offered as an inclusive one, but rather as a suggestive one. An administrator concerned with change should get from it suggestions regarding approaches that might well be considered.

1. An organization must have personnel and resources for the specific purposes of studying its various institutions and of making plans for change. This may have the form of a research and development department in a large organization. In a smaller organization, it may be an individual or committee. In many instances, some assistance from outside the institution may be desirable as the study is carried forward and the plans are developed.

Too frequently, in the present normative world, institutions may be drifting in accord with norms rather than consciously and openly studying their standards and achievements and planning desirable modifications in them. Too few school systems have a plan for essential continuous study of the functioning of the institution. Responsibility for this should probably be fixed upon a committee with some rotation of membership. The committee's membership should be widely representative of staff and people of the community. Its function should be the stimulation of study, evaluation, and planning. It should not attempt to carry on such study and planning itself, but rather it should see to it that organization and resources are available to carry them forward. The committee would engage in an overall or broad type of evaluation and planning based upon the results of various studies carried forward.

The committee should have opportunity to probe or stimulate probing in various directions, including those that may frequently be regarded as sensitive ones. Studies of the functioning of formal and informal organization, of social values of staff and parents, of climate and security, for example, would be essential, as well as studies of matters that are more peripheral to the values of the individuals involved.

The fixing of responsibility upon some agent for the planning of change is significant in that it gives formal recognition to the need for planned change. The conscious and open acceptance of this need is itself an important step for an institution or individual. The agent with this responsibility should be clearly seen as one with staff responsibility. It should have no line responsibilities other than the stimulation of change through study and planning. It should not be responsible to any one group or power in the institution or community. Rather, it should be so established that it would enjoy a large measure of independence from administration, professional organizations, board of education, and various community groups. In a large organization it would probably need a small staff directly responsible to it.

2. Knowledge regarding many phases of the organization and its functioning would need to be developed. Many administrators are unaware of the manner in which decisions are actually made in the school and community in which they are status leaders. Teachers and citizens are also uninformed. Until knowledge regarding these matters is widespread or at least readily available, sound action is not likely to occur. Knowledge, of course, is not enough. It may be secured and yet change may not follow.

Knowledge and wisdom regarding the hopes and achievements of man are also essential. This calls for deep probing of the past and present, for the formulation of hypotheses regarding life and its purposes, and the development of plans for experimentation in the future. How this wisdom is to be developed is too large and difficult a task for this chapter. However, its significance must be recognized. For change in any institution may be in undesirable directions as well as desirable ones, and judgments will need to be made regarding the positive or negative effects of various proposals and developments.

3. The leader must become "primarily an expert in the promotion and protection of values." To institutionalize effectively is "to *infuse with value* beyond the technical requirements of the task at hand" (11, p. 17). "As an organizatoin acquires a self, a distinctive identity, it becomes an institution" and there results a *"concern for self-maintenance"* (11, p. 21).

With this general concept in mind, Selznick elaborates some of the reasons why leaders fail. He sees failure largely in terms of: (a) failure to set goals sharply; (b) superficial acceptance of goals that do not "genuinely influence the total structure of the enterprise"; (c) the confounding of *"organizational* achievement or survival . . . with *institutional* success"; and (d) the concept that the role of the institutional leader is little or nothing more than the "interpersonal" leader.

These matters are emphasized here because they are regarded as central if desirable change is to be effected. The leader must be more than the "human relations" expert. He must do more than assure smooth drifting. This, of course, is not to say that he is free to mold the organization as he personally may wish. There are basic social values to which the society, the institution, and the leader must be committed.

4. Administration must be carried on in such a way that the energies of the people will be released through commitment to the commonly derived and held purposes. To do this requires a co-operative approach to problems and issues. Co-operation must be achieved between the various groups directly responsible for carrying the institution forward and also between these groups and the community. No other approach assures the energizing of so many people toward the goals.

5. A climate must be achieved in which communication is facilitated. Such a climate is likely to be found only where all parties regard the institution as theirs, because they have become involved in it and the achievement of the goals. A climate is needed where all are free to evaluate frankly and to seek improvement. Under optimum conditions, the sensitive individual "protectors" of the status quo who regard the institution as their own, without reference to others, are not found. The inadequacies and potentialities of all individuals are regarded in a mature manner.

6. A high quality of security both for the institution and for the individuals in it is present. There is recognition that each is involved and consequently has not only a right but a responsibility to further the attainment of the ends. Various parties recognize their obligation to provide desirable security conditions for others. The administrator, no less than the teacher, may need proper security, if he is to furnish outstanding leadership. Under optimum conditions, the citizens and the teachers give him strong support. Mutual respect and confidence are high among the various parties. This is not a listless, smug security, but one that is based upon vigorous, co-operative endeavor devoted to basic values and cognizant that fairness will prevail while the goal is pursued. Much of the security is to be gained through experience in carrying an institution forward, although some of it may pertain to the more directly developed provisions and organizational practices that give security.

The attainment of a climate of high-quality security must be recognized as the responsibility of the various people involved. It cannot be achieved by the administrator alone, although he has a large role to play in connection with it.

7. The norm of experimentation and change must be estab-

lished. In many schools and school systems, security is found in tradition. As long as one does what has been done for many years, he is not subject to criticism. This is true even though what is done may not further the basic ends of the institution. Change must come to be expected and, provided it is carefully planned and carried forward, it must be regarded as of worth. Change will be less threatening when it is seen as action research rather than as a program that sharply breaks with the past. Individuals and groups need thus to be freed from the hand of the past *per se* and also from the hand of the present norm, if they are to seek desirable change. In a society that looks to the future, the development of this point of view should be less difficult. Yet the very extent to which it looks to the future may give some people feelings of greater need to tie to what is known—the past and present. However, if the educability of man is accepted, the golden age would appear most certainly to be found in the future.

8. Individuals must be selected, appointed, and promoted in accord with the promise that they have for administering change. The large-scale organization too frequently becomes concerned with the organization *per se* rather than with the institutional objectives. As a result, appointments and promotions go to individuals seen as safe for the organization. To be "safe" is to constitute no threat to changing the organization in the direction of professed values. Thus, a shift toward promoting those who are expert in promoting and protecting values will give security to the change leaders and signify that the expectation of change has been accepted as a desirable norm.

9. In the large-scale organization, effective decentralization must be achieved. This must be genuine decentralization rather than mere deconcentration. This means that genuine opportunity for decision-making must be established at the local level. Parties at the local level must have the power to act in their own right as well as for the larger institution. They must be delegated significant responsibility and their actions in these delegated matters should not be subject to review and approval by the central body. Unless they have significant power, decentralization has not been achieved. Rather, power remains at the center but has only been deconcentrated.

Such a development is essential if citizens, staff, and even administrators are to become involved in the building of an institution of integrity; if they are to be able to strive to achieve values. Without the opportunity to build an institution with a vitality, a life of its own, they become mere functionaries preserving an organization rather than constructing an institution.

The revitalization of the parts of an organization along these lines offers much promise for the essential experimentation that is basic to sound change. It offers also opportunity for the development of men who can serve as change leaders, whether they be administrators, staff, or lay citizens.

In Conclusion

The various factors that have been mentioned relative to the activation of change must be recognized as suggestive only. They constitute no blueprint. In fact, a blueprint should not be sought. What is much more promising is the development of a mature staff and administrator who, in co-operation with a community, seek values. In this pursuit, as Selznick has stated, it is necessary to avoid utopianism, with its over-generalized purposes and the naïve belief that when technical problems are solved, institutional ones will be solved also. In addition, opportunism, with its short-sightedness, must also be avoided. In the place of utopianism and opportunism, responsible leadership and action are needed.

Selznick has further stated (11, p. 152–53):

> The art of the creative leader is the art of institution-building, the reworking of human and technological materials to fashion an organism that embodies new and enduring values. The opportunity to do this depends on a considerable sensitivity to the politics of internal change. This is more than a struggle for power among contending groups and leaders. It is equally a matter of avoiding recalcitrance and releasing energies. Thus, winning consent to new directions depends on how secure the participants feel. When many routine problems of technical and human organization remain to be solved, when the minimum conditions for holding the organization together are only precariously met, it is difficult to expend energy on long-range planning and even harder to risk experimental programs. When the organization is in good shape, from an engineering standpoint, it is easier to put ideals into practice.

Finally, Selznick emphasizes the need for a strategy that envisions the future (11, p. 154):

If one of the great functions of administration is the exertion of cohesive force in the direction of institutional security, another great function is the creation of conditions that will make possible in the future what is excluded in the present. This requires a strategy of change that looks to the attainment of new capabilities more nearly fulfilling the truly felt needs and aspirations of the institution. . . .

Might it not well be to note that the problem of change in the sense indicated is not the responsibility of the creative leader only? It is also the responsibility of the creative staff and the creative community. The above paragraphs can be rewritten inserting "creative staff" and "creative community" after "creative leader" and "administration." When this is done, perhaps we have a firm base for planning desirable change in educational practice. Then the paralysis of the status quo and the destructiveness of the drift of opportunism will give way to the realization of instructional integrity and the attainment of noble goals.

Of course, the creative leader has a distinct responsibility in this matter that somewhat separates him from staff and community (11, p. 154): "The executive becomes a statesman as he makes the transition from administrative management to institutional leadership."

The administrator examining his own behavior with reference to change may raise many questions. Among them should be: Are my social values in accord with the fundamental principles of a democratic society? Do I recognize that I am likely to be helpful only when perceived as a source of help? How adequate are my understandings of the perceptions of others? Do the procedures I employ give others the fundamental security which results from having helped refurbish the commitments of an institution? Am I "practicebound"? Have I adequately assisted the staff and citizens to re-examine and clarify the purposes of the school? Do I perceive change as a totality? Can I differentiate my role as an executive in an organization from that of my role as an institutional statesman?

References

1. Adams, Brooks, *The Theory of Social Revolutions*. (New York: Macmillan Company, 1914), pp. 207–208, as quoted by Daniel E. Griffiths, in *Human Relations in School Administration* (New York: Appleton-Century-Crofts, Inc., 1956), p. 3.

2. Bavelas, Alex, "Some Problems of Organization Change," *Journal of Social Issues*, Vol. 4, 1948, pp. 48–52.

3. Coch, Lester, and John R. P. French, Jr., "Overcoming Resistance to Change," *Human Relations*, Vol. I, 1948, pp. 512–32.

4. Coffey, Hubert S., and William J. Golden, Jr., "Psychology of Change Within an Institution," Chapter IV (pp. 67–102), *National Society for the Study of Education, 56th Yearbook*, Part I, 1957. University of Chicago Press.

5. Corey, Stephen, *Action Research to Improve School Practices*. New York: Bureau of Publications, Teachers College, Columbia University, 1953.

6. Elliott, Jacques, *The Changing Culture of a Factory*. New York: Dryden Press, 1952.

7. Lippitt, Ronald, Jeanne Watson, and Bruce Westley, *The Dynamics of Planned Change*. New York: Harcourt, Brace and Co., 1958.

8. Ronken, Harriet, and Paul Lawrence, *Administering Change: A Case Study of Human Relations in a Factory*. Boston: Harvard University, Graduate School of Business Administration, 1957.

9. Safer, Cyril, "Reactions to Administrative Change," *Human Relations*, Vol. 8, No. 3, 1955, pp. 291–316.

10. Sarchet, Bettie B., *Block Groups and Community Change*. Human Dynamics Laboratory, University of Chicago, 1955.

11. Selznick, Philip, *Leadership in Administration*. Evanston, Ill.: Row, Peterson and Co., 1957. Reprinted by permission.

12. Wormser, Margaret, "The Northtown Self-Survey: A Case Study," *Journal of Social Issues*, Vol. 5, No. 2, pp. 5–20.

13. Zander, Alvin, "Resistance to Change—Its Analysis and Prevention," *Advanced Management*, January, 1950, pp. 9–11.

CHAPTER EIGHT

Decision-Making

The distresses of choice are our chance to be blessed.
W. H. AUDEN

Lying close to the nerve center of administration is the decision-making process. It is to administration what a switch-throwing mechanism is to an express train; it controls direction by selecting between and among alternative tracks or courses of action. When a particular course of action has been entered upon, there is seldom, if ever, a complete turning back. When the school-board members officially decided that Architect Martin should design the high school in Case Fifteen, "Greenfield Builds Its Third High School," for example, they were at a "point of no return." The choice crucially affected the cost and quality of the school building that finally resulted.

Decision-making, then, is a primary source of control and a definer of action, and it is understandable that various scholars have viewed the process as the key to administration. It frequently involves intense wrestling with relevant facts against a background of value conflicts. Its stringent demands on decision-makers no doubt contribute to the feeling of many top executives, from the President of the United States down to local school superintendents, that administration is a lonely profession. Obviously, an adequate conception of administration must deal with decision-making.

The fact that there are various foci for viewing choice processes is reflected in such labels as individual decision-making, group decision-making, and organizational decision-making. The locus of individual decision-making is the person, and the process may take place physically isolated from other members of an organization. The locus of group decision is a collection of people small enough to interact and resolve a choice situation; the process takes place in face-to-face relationship. Organizational decisions have been defined as a "process of people acting upon one another toward a conclusion" (17, p. 41). Thus, organizational decisions may not directly and continually involve a large proportion of the membership. Also, the locus of operations may shift, and much of the effective influence may be informal.

This chapter recognizes the advantage of viewing decision-making as an organizational process. However, even as the currents affect the power and flow of a stream, so do the processes of individual decision-making and group decision-making affect organizational choice. By the same token, the administrator's role in decision-making is not limited to choices arrived at in isolated privacy; in addition, he influences and, in turn, is influenced by the decisions of groups, organizations, and other individuals. Unity of treatment is sought by focusing upon the individual decision-making of the administrator in relationship to the various types or units of decision. Thus, material on group and organizational decision-making is included to point up the implications for individual administrators. In this sense, the discussion is oriented toward *individual* decision-making.

Various reasons support an individual decision-making perspective. For example, the capacity and willingness to make decisions are, no doubt, two of the most important characteristics of the administrative leader. Certainly not everyone wishes the responsibility for deciding issues related to group or organizational welfare, even if he has the capacity for such action. Therefore, focusing on individual decision-making undoubtedly offers advantages for gaining a better understanding of administrative leadership.

The literature of school administration has as yet incorporated little material on individual administrative decision-making. By contrast there is a great body of writing on group decision-making. The latter type of writing has been strongly influenced by students of "group process" and is patterned on the model of "democratic administration." Such a model provides an excellent *ideal*. However, it is not always appropriate for describing and explaining many of the *realities* of administrative decision-making. Such a model largely ignores or oversimplifies the individual aspects of choice. Thus, a close look at the latter would seem advantageous.

The individual choices of administrators may be classified into three types. First, there are those decisions that are relatively lacking in self-awareness, in the sense that they are repetitive and habitual. Answering a telephone, coming to the office daily, and greeting a teacher in the hall are examples of acts stemming from such decisions. Second, there are executive choices that are made within the framework of clearly established policy. Deciding to prepare a budget, to call a special board meeting, and to employ a new teacher are examples of these decisions. Finally, there are those decisions that are deliberate and are made in the absence of neatly prescribed policy. Such decisions most typically occur during changes or reorientation in policies or in the face of serious morale problems. Superintendent Marsh was confronted with both of these conditions in Case Sixteen, "The Riverton Dilemma." Such decisions severely test the leadership competencies of administrators. The following concepts are specifically designed to illuminate choices related to the initiation of change and to the solution of morale problems.

Ingredients of Decisions

The personality pattern of the administrator significantly determines how he receives, filters, evaluates, and reacts to communication related to choice situations. Although various studies in recent years have dealt with decision processes, only a few have focused directly upon the individual personalities and specific behaviors of decision-makers.[1] As Block and Peterson (5, p. 34) have noted, "It is curious that the variables involved in the decision behavior of individuals have received the attention of so few psychologists." In spite of the paucity of specific studies, the more general investigations of social scientists suggest something of how personality bears upon choice processes.

Personality and decision process. Of the various psychological concepts for explaining human behavior and personality, three have had frequent use: *cognition, feeling,* and *volition.* All of these are clearly related to decision-making. Cognition bears upon such intellectual aspects of decision as perceiving choice situations, con-

[1] For a survey of the studies on decision-making in the community setting, see the review by Rossi (20). For a more general survey, see the recent UNESCO study (25).

ceptualizing issues, gathering facts, interpreting facts, and weighing values. Superintendent Kennedy, for example, in deciding whether or not to retain Teacher White in Case Four, "The Sword of Damocles," had to study, to interpret, and to assess the various factors related to the choice; these activities involved cognitive functions. Feeling has to do with the emotional components of choice, such as fear of consequences or feelings arising from previous or anticipated criticism. Thus, Superintendent Kennedy on different occasions expressed feelings of anger and concern when he could not get full information on the rumor that was circulating among the school personnel and members of the community. Volition is the control factor that shapes decision-making. Thus, volition propelled Superintendent Kennedy to investigate the choice situation that confronted him. It enabled him to arrive at voluntary acts when faced with various choice points in the total decision process.

Decision premises. Decision premises are continually provided the administrator by the communication networks that surround him. These premises may be classified into three types: *facts, values,* and *unsubstantiated information.*[2] As these premises impinge upon the administrator, they activate cognitive equipment, arouse emotions, and put volition to work. Each of these premises deserves further discussion.

Values. The purposes and anticipated outcomes of a decision reflect underlying values. These values may be of various types—personal, educational, economic, or moral. Thus, equal educational opportunity for all children is an educational value, honesty is a moral value, and the advancement of one's career is a personal value. Most decisions that relate to change and morale problems involve a whole complex of such interrelated values.

Values are not always dressed in the same clothing. Sometimes they are found under the cloak of law. Compulsory school laws, for example, reflect the underlying value of universal public education. Or, laws requiring the bonding of school officials doubtless stem from such values as honesty and efficiency. Some of the most stable and

[2] Simon (22) has suggested two types of decision premises: facts and values. The third type of decision premise is added here because the administrator must weigh and assess much unsubstantiated information that he is not in a position to prove or disprove. Case Four, "The Sword of Damocles," graphically illustrates this point.

treasured of society's values are incorporated in and insured by laws.

Values are also cloaked in school policies. Thus, policy guide lines for the conduct of school board meetings inevitably reflect certain values. For example, a policy of open meetings may suggest that the dissemination of public information is esteemed. In many cases unwritten policies are important elements in decisions in that they reflect what are considered to be tested values among the persons involved. Although policies are less general in application and less stable in character, they are similar to laws in that they highlight what are considered to be significant guides to decision-making.

If all of society's values were incorporated into a consistent set of laws and policies, decision-making in social institutions in some ways might be greatly simplified. However, a myriad of less explicit and more private values repose outside of legal statements, yet they continually have implications for decisions. Such personal values as social status and economic security, which the administrator may strive to achieve, are not insured by law, although they may influence decisions. The same is true for many social, economic, and educational values. Thus, in Case One, "The Valley City Consolidation Issue," a whole myriad of interrelated and conflicting values were demanding the attention of Superintendent Benson. The intertwined and sometimes contradictory values were crucial elements with which he had to grapple. Whether such values are hidden or overt, professional or nonprofessional, related to formal or informal organizational aims, they are important ingredients of administrative decisions.

Facts. Another element in decisions is facts. A *fact* may be defined as a statement about a condition, object, or event that would be accepted as accurate by two or more observers. Facts have to do primarily with conditions relating to the means and strategies for achieving educational ends. Thus, the actual cost of the school building in Case Fifteen, "Greenfield Builds Its Third High School," was a factual premise that was related to such value premises as educational opportunity and financial economy. Other facts that were psychological in nature also influenced various choices related to Greenfield's third high school. For example, how citizens *felt* about paying taxes to build the buildings was an important fact influencing the final decision. Thus, feelings are facts and can be viewed by the decision-maker as objective data, although they may in fact have very subjective bases. In Case Seventeen, "Changing the Curriculum at Southside," for example, it was a fact that some teachers felt that Bell was authoritarian and some felt that he was democratic. Whether Bell in fact was authoritarian is not clear because of conflicting reactions.

Facts are basic to clarifying alternative courses of action. Thus, many school districts have research departments whose main function is to provide facts to serve as one basis for decisions. Others call upon experts to develop facts. Careful planning always implies the gathering of empirical evidence, and the latter is associated with the scientific aspects of administration.

Unsubstantiated information. Another type of information that the administrator must assess in making decisions is, accurately speaking, neither fact nor value; this ingredient that infiltrates many choice processes might be called *unsubstantiated information.* It is most at home in the informal communication systems of an organization. Rumor, gossip, hearsay, and unchecked reports about persons, places, or events are examples of this decision ingredient. Thus, this type of decision premise in Case Seven, "Alice Smith, Transfer," put Jane Adams in an unenviable choice situation. She was forced to decide what to do about reports that she could not substantiate. Similar information markedly influenced a decision about a major personnel problem in Case Four, "The Sword of Damocles."

Thus, facts, values, and unsubstantiated information are important ingredients of the choice process. A basic problem is posed when one asks how facts, values, and unsubstantiated information fit together, play upon, and in turn are shaped by the personality of the decision-maker. The question raises the complex problem of decision-making dynamics.

Decision Dynamics

Theories usually have emphasized the effects of cognitive influences on decision-making and have neglected the effects of feeling as an influencer of individual choice. However, such theories have distinct limitations, a few of which will be noted now.

Cognition and choice. How do theories that emphasize the influence of cognitive factors explain decision-making? A commonly held one assumes that administrative choice examines relevant facts and selects from alternative means the one most appropriate for achieving a clear-cut objective; thus, the essential relationship is a means-end one. Such a model, as related to Principal Jones's decision to discharge Teacher Norris in Case Six, "A Coin Has Two Sides," might be diagrammed as follows:

Some Alternative Means		*Single End*
Discharging Norris		
Transferring Norris	→	Educational Welfare of Students
Retaining Norris with closer supervision		
Persuading Norris to give up teaching		

Figure 5

The model suggests that Principal Jones clearly identified the end that he desired to attain. Second, he formulated alternative means for handling Norris as they related to the chosen end. Finally, the facts indicated that he could best achieve his goal by discharging Norris.

Inadequacy of a means-end model. Does such a decision-making model accurately apply to the administrator? When Principal Jones made his choice, was he led by the facts to select a particular means (that is, discharging teacher Norris) from among alternative means, all of which related to the single end of student welfare? The answer in this case is clearly negative, since a number of values or ends were involved in the choice. In addition to the educational welfare of students, there were such additional values as the individual welfare of Teacher Norris, Principal Jones's status, the general morale of teachers, and community relations. Thus, the choice really involved resolving conflict between and among multiple ends. It is evident from the case that Jones's *feelings* about the welfare of Teacher Norris were highly important in influencing the decision process and that these feelings heightened the conflict involved. As the conflict increased, feelings were doubtless intensified. A means-end model of decision-making does not adequately explain Jones's process of decision-making. Analyses of other choice situations related to change and morale problems will also reveal the limitations of a means-end model to explain decision-making. Even in highly technical choices, where human considerations are minimum, there is conflict between such ends as economy and benefits. Any decision that involves organizational change and/or serious morale problems will call for the resolution of conflict between and among multiple ends.

Limits in fact-gathering. Some have contended that decision-making involves getting all the facts pertinent to the issue being decided. However, this demands highly systematic and comprehensive procedures on the part of the administrator. Justice Holmes was more accurately realistic when he said that the art of living "consists in making correct guesses on insufficient information." In other words, the administrator even in the most desirable situations cannot have access to *all* the facts. In many cases he is limited in time and resources. In addition, the pressures of the existing situation further complicate matters. Thus, an analysis of the bases of Principal Jones's decision to discharge Teacher Norris, which are contained in the reports to the central office, suggest that feelings and values were much more influential than objective facts in the decision. The case also shows some of the pressures that interfered with fact-gathering on the part of Principal Jones.

The above argument is not intended to deny or to minimize the importance of the ideal of complete and relevant data for decision-making; rather it seeks to make the point that in actual administrative situations procedures for comprehensive and exhaustive data-gathering are neither typical nor always feasible. Thus, means-ends models of theory, which assume that all relevant facts are used in choice situations, are not accurately descriptive. An acknowledgment of this point is the first step in moving to more ideal methods of decision-making.

Perhaps it would be instructive to raise the question of why rational models of decision have assumed such importance in administrative literature. No doubt their importance stems from at least two fountainheads. First, the model reflects a cultural ideal toward which decision-makers aspire in spite of the pressures, emotions, and conflicts that confront them. Although psychoanalytic literature has made some inroads on the concept of "rational man" through documenting some of man's irrational tendencies, reasoned action is still a central value in a democracy. Undoubtedly it is not easy for the practitioner to accept a difference between his performance and this cultural ideal. In addition, students of administration who have dealt with problem-solving and decision-making also have highlighted the rational aspects of choice. It can be hypothesized that the scholar is likely to project his own commitment to scientific values and rational procedures into explanations of the decision-making behavior of administrators.

Second, in the more objective and technical aspects of our culture, great progress has been made in achieving highly rational procedures. Data-processing machines, for example, embody rational models that have provided the basis for the new field of "operations research" (7). Operations researchers have tackled and solved complex management problems in business and military organizations. They have made decisions involving extremely complex data in a highly rational manner. For example, the marketing potential of a company's products has been decided by this method. Problems in the control of traffic in and out of airports have been resolved through operations research. The number and types of parts needed during the life of a given machine have also been decided through mechanical processes.

Such decisions, it will be noted, are very technical ones and involve technical data. They are not fraught with the swirling value conflicts and attendant feelings that typically impinge upon and enter into many of the decisions of school administrators. If there is a kinship between operations research problems and administrative decisions related to organizational change and/or morale problems, it is not a close one. It is reasonable to conclude, then, that a model of choice involving a clear-cut and single end, and that maintains that facts play the major roles in choice, has distinct limitations for comprehensively and accurately depicting individual decision-making in the administrative setting.

More comprehensive model needed. What framework, then, is appropriate to portray a more adequate picture of decision-making? One is needed that can show that choice situations consist of multiple goals or ends. Figure 6 includes this and other elements in the choice process. Although the illustrations to follow are again drawn from Case Six, "A Coin Has Two Sides," is it not true that the model would accurately apply to all the cases included in this book that represent decisions involving morale problems or organizational change?[3]

The inner circle in Figure 6 represents aspects of personality

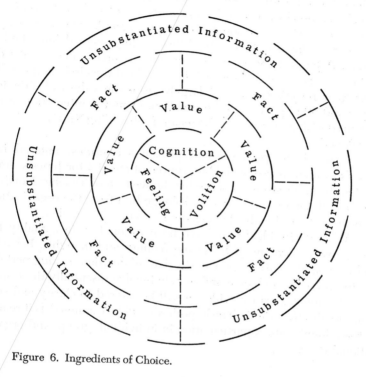

Figure 6. Ingredients of Choice.

that affected the decision. In the next circle are represented multiple ends. Such values or ends as community relations, educational welfare of students, teacher morale, individual welfare of Teacher Norris, and Principal Jones's own status influenced the decision. Various facts influenced the choice, such as Norris's assignment to teach a mixed health class, the questionnaire returns from parents, Jones's

[3] Aspects of the model are illustrated from Case Six, "A Coin Has Two Sides," for the sake of clarity in communication. It is recognized that the illustrations are in no sense proof of the appropriateness of the model. Such proof would be dependent upon various other factors, such as the validity and completeness of the case report, the representativeness of the case, and the correctness of the inferences made about the case.

visits to Norris's classroom, and Norris's responses to Jones during their interviews.

The lines are broken to suggest that there was an interplay of values, facts, unsubstantiated reports, and aspects of personality in the choice process. Also, values or ends are placed in the center of the circle next to the personality concepts to emphasize their core position and influence. Since all of these values seemed important to Principal Jones, they were very significant forces affecting his decisions. Facts are placed toward the outside of the circle in the belief that their meaning stemmed largely from the values of Principal Jones and other persons in the situation. From the interaction of the various decision ingredients, the means for handling Norris was finally developed.

Some of the premises and pressures doubtless entered into Jones's awareness. An overriding source of conflict for Jones seemed to stem from his strong concern for the welfare of Teacher Norris in the face of counter pressures to dislodge him from the organization. Choice for Jones involved somehow resolving this conflict.

Although its ideal may have been rationality, in actuality the process was more one of balancing feelings and thoughts, behavior and rationality. This chapter posits that all decision-making pertaining to problems of change and morale involve essentially the *resolution of conflict*. Further evidence will be offered to clarify and substantiate this hypothesis. The hypothesis will be examined as it relates to the administrator's participation in individual, group, and organizational decisions.

Decision-Making as Conflict Resolution

American school superintendents have been characterized as members of an anxious profession (24). Their anxiety is, without doubt, partially a product of the conflict that attends decision-making. Conflict is especially prevalent in decisions related to controversial issues, to proposed change, to personnel satisfaction, and to threat from changes within or outside the organization. In the United States, where change and progress, local controversy and debate, are often prevalent, conflict is a frequent companion of the administrator. Problems of choice are further intensified in the United States, whose culture is typified by pluralistic values, many of which are paradoxical and some of which are even contradictory. For example, such values as co-operation and competition, stability and change, initiative and compliance, central planning and local autonomy, and dominance and submission illustrate opposing factors that at times lead to cultural contradictions.[4]

Conflict and individual decision-making. From the administrator's perspective, conflict can stem from any one or a combination of two general sources: differences between his own values and those of another individual or group, and differences in values as reflected in what different individuals or groups expect from him. These categories, it will be apparent, are not mutually exclusive. To clarify them further, some illustrations will now be noted.

Value conflicts with others. Conflict arising from differences in the values of administrators and other persons can be illustrated from Gross's study (12). Specifically, he showed that New England superintendents frequently held values about administrative procedures that diverged quite markedly from those of school board members. He found, for example, that 70 per cent of the school superintendents believed that they should nominate teachers and the board should approve them; however, only 20 per cent of the board members held this view. He also revealed that 90 per cent of the superintendents felt that they should recommend texts and that the school board should approve them, although less than half the board members agreed. Finally, 90 per cent of the superintendents thought that teachers should bring their complaints to them first, although 50 per cent of the board members believed that they should receive teacher complaints first.

Such differences in values or expectations inevitably lead to some type of conflict for administrators. Conflict is heightened no doubt by the fact that school board members have legal powers that make superintendents subordinate to them. Conflict, of course, can arise with many other individuals or groups. Differences in values might arise, for example, inside the school organization, between a superintendent and his assistant superintendent, or between a superintendent and a chapter of the American Federation of Teachers.

---

[4] For additional contradictions that confront the administrator in a democratic culture, see the chapter by Barnard (2) entitled "Dilemmas of Leadership in the Democratic Process."

Conflict can also arise with persons and groups outside the school.

Conflicting expectations from others. A second source of conflict stems from contrasting expectations of different individuals or groups whom the administrator serves. Again the findings of Gross's study are relevant. He found, for example, that a substantial number of people pressured both the school board and the superintendent to place *less* emphasis on athletics while a substantial number generated pressures to put *more* emphasis on athletics. Slightly more than half of the superintendents had received pressures to give more attention to the three R's while most of the superintendents and about half of the school board members received pressures from patrons to add more courses to the curriculum. Finally, there were examples of pressure from personnel to raise salaries and, at the same time, there were counter-pressures from other groups or individuals to keep taxes down. Under such conditions, the administrator is between conflicting interests that in some way must be resolved. Again, such conflicts can stem from inside the school, from outside the school, or from a combination of school personnel and lay members.

Conflict arising from diverse expectations is often intensified by uncertainty as to precisely what the relevant individual and group expectations are as well as uncertainty about the extent to which expectations are being achieved. For example, basic dilemmas for the superintendent can arise because he is expected to play the dual role of leader and follower. In other words, he is expected to play an important role in the development of policy and at the same time to execute school board policy. Studies suggest that expectations on this matter vary to some extent from community to community, from board member to board member, and even from one specific situation to another within a given community. Thus, uncertainty about leadership and followership roles may arise, particularly where the administrator is relatively new on a job. Ash, in Case Fourteen, "The Case of a Tenacious Superintendent," experienced this dilemma as superintendent of Brashtown.

Another problem for the administrator is that, although he is responsible for getting the job done, he is dependent upon others to see that it is done. On the other hand, the administrator cannot completely control the selection of all the personnel with whom he must work. Even if he did, he could never predict precisely the quantity or direction of the energy output of personnel. Thus, the unpredictability and uncertainty about personnel performance, especially among deviants or incompetents, further complicates the task of meeting differing expectations.

Problems of evidence. Conflict can also be intensified because the administrator is unable to demonstrate clearly the extent to which he and his staff are meeting the expectations of others. This situation arises from the administrator's inability to obtain precise, definitive, and comprehensive measures of the results of the educational system that he administers. He is able to count accurately the numbers of students who enter and graduate from the system, but he is not able to show a clear, objective, and detailed picture of the qualitative effects that the system has upon the students. The educational administrator is at more of a disadvantage than the business executive in this regard; for the latter, the number and kind of products manufactured is a sufficient measure to demonstrate how performance relates to goals and expectations. Owing to the complex and intangible nature of the educational process, clear-cut evidence cannot be easily and summarily communicated. Thus, the administrator has difficulty offering ultimate and unquestionable evidence to counter the claims of his critics.

Spalding (24), in characterizing the school superintendency as an anxious profession, argues that a central reason for administrator anxiety is the inability to define and measure effectiveness. He notes at least four criteria that can be used for judging the effectiveness of a school system: teaching methods, desired changes in the knowledge, values, and behavior of pupils, scientific management of an organization, and desirable interpersonal relations within the school system. He further notes that not only is there a lack of agreement as to which of these criteria is most important, but, in addition, there is a difference of opinion as to how these concepts are operationally defined and, therefore, a difference of opinion as to data that are relevant for making judgments. This disagreement resides not only among lay persons but also among members of the educational profession. Since the problem of measuring administrative effectiveness is a beclouded one, the end result for the administrator can be the intensification of conflict.

It would seem, then, that the administrative scene is a welter of differing values and numerous conflicts when morale problems are faced and/or change is initiated. When the administrator becomes emotionally involved, or when he feels strongly about the values in question, then the conflict is more *personal* in nature. Such conditions are more likely to prevail when the administrator has values that are different from those of the other persons who are involved in the decision. The conflict is more *social* in nature, from the administrator's point of view, when conflicting values are esteemed highly and are defended by persons other than himself. Under these circumstances the administrator can be much more emotionally detached, although strong feelings can exist among others.

In a culture so diverse in values as the American one, the demands on the administrator in handling conflict are very exacting. In writing about the pressures on the administrator, Coleman states: (6, p. 15) ". . . . . This makes the school administrator's job a tremendously difficult one; he must keep the community on his side, resist pressures from powerful subgroups, and administer the schools, all at the same time."

Thus the following quotation, attributed by Gross (12, p. 46) to a New England school superintendent, is understandable: "I am going to retire eight years before I have to. I am tired of all this nonsense, all the phone calls about the bus being too early, or too late. I am tired of the political interference with teacher appointments. I am sick and tired of the stupid policy of the school board that we must always hire local girls regardless of their qualifications, that we must shell out contracts to their friends, that we must make special concessions to their 'constituents.' A man who tries to be an educator has a hard time of it when his school board does not really want him to be one."

Conflict and group decision-making. The administrator typically spends considerable time participating in group decisions. Conflict in decision-making can also be illustrated within this context, in that the process is a compound of thought and feeling, so that conflict is generated between behavior that is emotionally based and behavior that is cognitively based.

Self-oriented needs and group goals. Conflict is illustrated in the concepts of "open agenda" and "hidden agenda." The former refers to consciously planned and explicitly formulated items or objectives of a decision-making group, while the latter refers to unconsciously pursued and unapparent individual objectives. How behavior is expressed in relation to these two "agenda" is well illustrated in the work of Marquis, Guetzkow, and Heynes (18). Their findings are based upon studies of 72 different decision-making bodies in government and industry. Decision-making groups were chosen to meet certain criteria. In size they could be no smaller than five or larger than 17 including the leader. No more than two groups could come from any one organization, and there could be no overlapping of membership. All conferees had to have worked with one another previously. Finally, the groups' main function had to be decision-making, and the decisions made had to be directly related to the operational processes of the conferees' organizations.

By thorough preliminary investigation, reliable methods for observing and classifying behavior were developed (8). The data that were later obtained reflected conflicts between the achievement of rational goals and the satisfaction of emotionally based individual needs. Thus, considerable behavior was directed toward satisfying "self-oriented" emotional needs. For instance, some participants showed strong personal needs to dominate. Others expressed strong aggression toward the status leader or toward their colleagues. Still others obtained opportunities for personal catharsis. Such behavior was in conflict with efforts toward group decision-making. It interfered with such functions as information-seeking, information-giving, problem-proposing, and solution-proposing, as well as with other behaviors directly related to the achievement of explicitly defined goals. Such data reflect, then, the conflict in groups that stems from the contrasting demands of emotion on the one hand and the attainment of reasonably defined goals on the other.

Individuals and group conformity. The work of Asch (1) again illustrates in a different way how cognition and feeling generate conflict in judgments. Although the persons in his experiments were not administrative personnel, the study does have implications for group decision-making and administration.

The subjects, who were college students, made individual choices in group situations when the expressed opinion of the remainder of the group was unanimously opposed to the subjects' own perceptions. For example, group members were asked to match a given line with one of equal length among three unequal lines. Unknown to the subject, all of the other group members were primed to give the *same* incorrect answers. Their errors ranged from one-half to three-fourths of an inch. After all members had expressed the same *incorrect* judgment, the subject was asked to make his choice.

Approximately one-third of the subjects consistently sided with the majority even though this view was clearly contrary to their own perceptions. Interestingly enough, a majority in groups of 4 induced as much conformity in subjects as a majority in groups of 8 or 16. Also, if only one other person expressed an opinion contrary to the majority, subjects were much more likely to state their true perceptions than if the erroneous opinion was unanimously expressed.

Thus, decision-making groups *can* be tyrannical, in the sense that the minority may conform to the majority even though the latter's position is irrational and unsound. The subjects, for apparently emotional reasons, made a choice that was contrary to the "evidence" provided through their sense organs. This is a dramatic example of how feelings can be more forceful than knowledge in individual choice, and how individual choice, in turn, may affect group decisions. Is is not reasonable to believe that in choices involving more intangible administrative problems, where the evidence is less clear-cut than in the examples above, emotional forces will play an even greater role? Thus, there is danger that unsound group pressures can crush creativity and that the unique ideas and insights of individuals can be stifled.

Open conflict. Another type of conflict sometimes arises in groups which is more easily recognized than that which stems from the clash of feeling and fact. This more easily recognized conflict stems from an honestly expressed difference of viewpoint among group members pertinent to a formally defined issue. In other words, energy is directed predominantly toward attaining constructive decisions, but conflict arises because of different values, different definitions, or different interpretations of the problems. To be sure, such differences do not stem entirely from cognitive considerations. Values themselves become invested with sentiment and feeling, thereby adding an emotional element to decision-making.

Conflict may arise between the administrator and group members because the former represents a different organizational hierarchy than other group members and, therefore, brings particular interests and values to the decision-making situation. The resulting conflict may be more or less emotionally based, depending upon the intensity with which the values in question are held, the nature of previous administrator-staff interactions, and other variables as well.

Conflict and organizational decision-making. As already implied, the setting for administrative decisions cannot be confined to the administrator's office or to a particular group where he is presiding. Wherever he is, he cannot ignore the fact that he is responsible to an organization that is a composite of formal and informal decision-making units. It can be demonstrated that in this broader setting, decision-making involves the resolution of conflicts. Organizations, just like individuals and small groups, have both rational and emotional expressions in that some organizational behavior is directed predominantly toward clear-cut organizational goals; other behavior, based principally upon feeling and sentiment, may be largely unrelated and sometimes even opposed to the achievement of organizational goals.

Organizational design. The rational design of an organization is expressed in charts and in the stated rules and regulations for governing the behavior of persons in official positions. Such expressions reflect carefully thought-out plans designed to achieve organizational goals as effectively and efficiently as possible. Thus, in this sense, organizations are rationally abstract inventions or engineered tools that can be changed easily or even be abolished.

When one views the concrete behavior of organizational members, however, another picture is obtained. Although much behavior is clearly related to chart positions and stated rules and regulations of the organization, many actions and activities cannot be classified as clearly official. In addition to behaving as superintendents, vice-principals, or teachers, members of organizations behave as *whole* persons with definite psychological and social needs. Motivations to meet these needs are frequently overpowering and take precedence over official rules and regulations. Thus, certain motivations of the "Sorority Gals" in Case Seven, "Alice Smith, Transfer," had much more effect upon the behavior which they expressed toward Alice Smith than did the official rules of the organization.

Institutional aspects of organizational life. In organizational life, there inevitably develop certain customs that become invested with sentiment. Some of these may be related more to the formal aspects of organization, such as having class periods 50 minutes in length, as can be noted in Case Seventeen, "Changing the Curriculum at Southside." Others may be related more to the informal life of organizations, such as periodic smoking-room sessions, where teachers chat, relax, and smoke, again evidenced in "Changing the Curriculum at Southside." Whatever their origins, customs have values for persons and so are highly esteemed. For this reason, institutions develop that, in contrast to the paper expressions of organization, are difficult to change. Thus, a procedure that seems to an outsider to be an unimportant means can become an important end in itself to the persons who use it.

Conflict, then, between rationally projected plans and existing institutions frequently enters into and influences decisions, particularly under conditions of change. Various cases in this book show how conflict arises when "new" plans are proposed that interfere with "old" ways of behaving. The problem is heightened in older organizations that have had more time to develop formalized procedures, and in which the latter have become invested with values and feelings. Thus, the stable and older culture of Brashtown in Case Fourteen, "The Case of a Tenacious Superintendent," posed difficult decision problems. In a rapidly changing society, organizational conflict seems inevitable.

Although it is conceivable that a proposed decision could interfere with institutions so widely that universal resistance would be aroused, such is not the usual circumstance. More commonly, certain segments of an organization are more basically affected than others. The "small opposing group" in Case Seventeen, "Changing the Curriculum at Southside," for example, was more resistant to the half-day schedule, not only because it interfered with certain institutions, but also because it reflected educational values counter to the ones to which they were strongly committed. Thus, a great deal of energy was summoned to prevent the organization from making a decision favorable to the plan. This energy was expressed through already established relationships and channels. Organizational rivalry between the "small opposing group" and the "large social group" emerged as the issue of the "half-day" program came into focus. Conflict was the inevitable result.

Types of Conflict

Conflicts can be classified into two general types: those involving content of which the administrator is clearly aware and those involving content of which he is largely unaware. The latter type of content will be called *latent*, while the former will be called *manifest*. What characteristics distinguish these two types?

Manifest content in conflict. The content of conflict that is manifest to the administrator can be placed in one of three classifications: those containing two or more predominantly negative values, those containing two or more predominantly positive values, and those containing positive and negative values (16). Each of these classifications needs illustration.

If an administrator has to decide whether to resign or to follow instructions that are completely counter to his beliefs, the resulting conflict would involve two negative values. In other words, he ordinarily would prefer *not* to resign, and to betray his own values would be distasteful. Many conflict situations of this type face the administrator, and they are popularly labeled as the "choice between two evils." Superintendent Ash in Case Fourteen, "The Case of a Tenacious Superintendent," faced such a choice.

Since the administrator has limited resources at his disposal, he is often confronted with decisions that involve conflict between two or more positive values. If he has to decide whether to employ a school psychologist or a curriculum consultant, when both personnel are needed, conflict involving two positive values would result. This type of decision is more easily solved than conflict situations involving two negative values although the process may not be totally pleasant.

Many choice situations are popularly described by the statement, "It is not a black or white matter." In such cases, conflict involves both positive and negative elements. The decision of Principal Jones to discharge Norris, as described in Case Six, "A Coin Has Two Sides," was of that type. Or, a principal might see positive value in suspending a problem student; on the other hand, he might see some negative learning results for the student. Since there are multiple consequences to most decisions, many actions bring both positive and negative results. Thus, this type of conflict is doubtless the most frequent one for the administrator. Many of the cases in this book contain conflict situations of this type.

In the illustrations above, the content of conflicts was limited to two contrasting or two similar values. This is doubtless a simplification in that more than two competing values make up the content of many decisions. However, it can be hypothesized that, although choice content initially may involve more than two values, elimination of less significant values will occur, so that conflict in the final stages will be between the two major values.

Conflict resulting from manifest content may be intensified under two conditions. First, intensification results when the negative consequences of projected courses of action related to conflicting values are judged to be closely equal. For example, if a superintendent considers resigning his job as distasteful as bowing to the will of a school board, conflict is likely to be intense. Intensity decreases as the unpleasant consequences of projected courses of action are perceived as unequal. Second, the more important the projected consequences are to the administrator and to others affected by the decision, the greater will be the ensuing conflict. Decisions assume importance when large numbers are strongly concerned and they are divided in their expectations. Although a minimum of conflict stems from the manifest content of many administrative decisions, those relating to organizational change and personnel satisfaction may involve intense conflict.

  Latent content in conflict. As already noted, the manifest content of conflict is that part that is perceived by the administrator. He recognizes the contradictory elements in a given choice and he can describe them. This applies to himself as an individual making a choice, to a group making a choice, or to an organization making a choice. To be sure, he can never discern all of the content elements in decisions, but the distinction is one of emphasis; such a distinction maintains that the essentials of many decisions will be readily manifest to the administrator.

On the other hand, important content in many conflicts remains latent. For example, the administrator may have strong motivations that are unconscious and that conflict with the demands of the situation. Thus, he may have strong needs not to displease others or to arouse negative feelings in others, and he may find himself in a situation that demands action that will likely displease some personnel. Or he may have unconscious needs to be dependent while he is confronted with decisions that call for independence. Conflict then arises. Under such circumstances, the content of the conflict is characterized as "latent."

The content of conflict may also remain latent in group decision-making situations. Thus, the administrator may be focusing on getting a formal decision made and not be aware of some of the "hidden agenda" interfering with the process. For example, was the administrator clearly aware of the sources of conflict that were interfering with decision-making during the long board meeting in Case Five, "Democracy: Riverbank, U.S.A."? From the viewpoint of organizational decision-making, the same question could be asked about Principal Bell in Case Seventeen, "Changing the Curriculum at Southside."

How well the administrator perceives and handles the latent and manifest content in choice situations undoubtedly helps to determine the length of his own tenure. In addition, the execution of such decisions relates closely to effective change and high morale in an educational system. Therefore, competency in conflict resolution is very essential to the administrator.

Volition and Conflict Resolution

So far, the roles played by the feeling and cognizing aspects of personality in the decision-making process have been emphasized. What role does volition, the third angle in the triangle of personality, play? How does it affect the contradictory forces of thought and feeling? Generally speaking, its role is to obtain a harmonious and balanced relation between these forces. It does this through influencing voluntary acts at selected key points in the total choice process. The popular descriptions "iron-willed" and "weak-willed" applied to a leader suggest something of the significance of volition in the choice process. Thus, when Superintendent Benson voluntarily committed himself and remained committed to consolidation as the solution to Valley City's conflicts on school reorganization in Case One, "The Valley City Consolidation Issue," the total decision process was considerably affected. Volition also affects decisions by shaping and controlling thought and feeling, and some of these effects will now be considered.

Cognition. Smith's study (23), which focused upon "philosophic-mindedness," suggests something of the direction that thought processes may take in the investigation of choice situations. He postulated three qualities of thought and established some empirical relationship between the presence of these qualities in principals and their effectiveness as administrators. Undoubtedly additional research is needed to demonstrate clearly how extensive the influence of these qualities actually is in guiding administrative decisions.

Comprehensiveness. A *comprehensive view* implies that the administrator looks at decision situations in a broad as well as a specific context. In handling complex problems, for example, there are many types of information to assess. Some of this information may be highly technical and may come from specialists with views prescribed by narrow contexts. For example, Miss Carpenter, the trained librarian, in Case Thirteen, "The Rotating Librarian," brought very specialized information to Principal Evans in her efforts to influence decision processes. Laski (14, p. 102) has set forth some limitations of the expert:

> For special knowledge and the highly trained mind produce their own limitations which, in the realm of statesmanship, are of decisive importance. *Expertise,* it may be argued, sacrifices the insight of common sense to intensity of experience. It breeds an inability to accept new views from the very depth of its preoccupation with its own conclusions. It too often fails to see round its subject. It sees its results out of perspective by making them the center of relevance to which all other results must be related. . . . It has, also, a certain caste-spirit about it, so that experts tend to neglect all evidence which does not come from those who belong to its ranks. Above all, perhaps, and this most urgently, where human problems are concerned, the expert fails to see that every judgment he makes not purely factual in nature brings with it a scheme of values which has no special validity about it.

As social, technological, and other data pertinent to choice situations become more and more complex, the expert will likely assume an even greater role in decision-making processes. An administrator with a comprehensive view will be one that seeks relationships among diverse data and diverse values. To harmonize the views of the citizen and the expert, who are sometimes impatient with one another's values, becomes an increasing challenge to all public administrators, and certainly the school administrator is no exception. To do this implies the outlook of a generalist.

Another aspect of comprehensiveness, according to Smith, is the time context of a decision. Volition that orients cognitive processes only toward the immediately practical or expedient interferes with theoretical or long-term considerations. Thus, a key question in understanding conflict situations is to determine what time period or periods are significant. This refers not only to the time period of the decision, but also to the time period affected by the decision. Thus, the citizenry chose unionization in Case One, "The Valley City Consolidation Issue," and this decision is still affecting Valley City's schools more than ten years later. No doubt decision-makers who focus widely on the time context of choice situations are in a better position to see the various facts and values involved. Such a focus also relates to the spatial context of a decision. The decision process in Case Twelve, "Dr. Cook Survives," for example, would have been markedly different if it had not moved out of the community to encompass persons at the state level and, finally, at the national level.

Penetration. Another thought process that bears upon decision-making is penetration. This quality helps to free the administrator from what Smith calls the "tyranny of the obvious" by questioning what seems self-evident and what is usually taken for granted. Such investigation enables the administrator to examine such things as stereotypes or obsolete practices and to clarify the value traditions that surround choice situations.

Penetration, according to Smith, also assists one in formulating the key questions about the value assumptions in decisions. Such questions can in turn assist in the analysis and evaluation of value conflicts. The importance of raising key questions and of analyzing basic values is evident in such cases as "Greenfield Builds Its Third High School," in which Greenfield's citizens, according to the author, had to pay unnecessarily an additional $300,000 for their school. Penetration in thought is sensitive to implications and is skillful in separating the relevant from the irrelevant. Thus, the administrator who thinks penetratingly will not only get a better picture of the value premises in decision situations, but will also understand something of why the premises have come to be valued.

Flexibility. The third aspect of behavior elaborated by Smith is flexibility. Although this characteristic is related closely to the feeling aspects of personality, it will be treated at this point. In order for the administrator to achieve flexibility, it is necessary that he be relatively free from psychological rigidity. Rigidity is largely emotionally based and can show itself in various settings. Stress situations, for example, frequently test the administrator's tendency toward rigidity. If he can assess stress situations about as accurately as non-stress situations, he is displaying flexibility.

Rigidity, according to Smith, may also occur where the administrator's response is not adapted to the uniqueness of the choice situation. Thus, there may be a tendency to react in a non-adaptive way to situations that on the surface are similar to previous situations but in actuality are markedly different. In such cases, psychological sets or predispositions interfere with correct interpretations and, in turn, with appropriate responses. Did not Principal Bell in Case Seventeen, "Changing the Curriculum at Southside," for example, react in a similar manner to three basically different situations when he arranged for the various faculty votes?

Another aspect of rigidity relates to the tendency to react to the person proposing the idea rather than to the idea itself. Thus, a school superintendent may get a more favorable hearing for his idea from one of his principals than a teacher would receive from the same principal even though she proposed the same idea. Actually, the value of an idea is largely independent of its transmitter, although the latter may be able to influence strongly its implementation. Rigid psychological sets can lead either to the rejection of useful ideas or to the acceptance of erroneous ones.

Rigidity is also present in the tendency to see only one or two sides of a decision situation when in actuality there may be many sides and various alternative solutions. Thus, the administrator may consistently see "either-or" solutions when there are many other alternatives. The capacity to suspend judgment is also dependent upon relative freedom from rigidity. Suspended judgment or deciding not to decide immediately is often the basis for administrative actions.

Suspended judgment should not be equated with indecisiveness or with an inability to exercise volition. An overintellectual approach may lead to inaction in the sense that so many sides are explored that decision processes are paralyzed. Barnard (2) has noted the limitations of decision-makers who have such "ultra-judicial" minds that they cannot decide.

In summary, then, volition can direct cognition in a comprehensive, penetrating, and flexible fashion. When volition plays such a role, the decision-maker is in a better position to understand self and situation and to comprehend the contradictory forces that make for conflict in the decision process. By so doing, the decision-maker can bring to light some of the elements of conflict that would ordinarily remain latent. When latent elements are made manifest, the administrator obtains a deeper understanding of the choice situation that should provide an advantage to him at crucial choice points in the total process.

Volition and feeling. That leaders need to control their feelings is a widely accepted proposition. In this regard, volition plays the role of curbing and channeling feelings. Before discussing this role, some of the sources of feeling in decision processes will be made clear.

Origins of feeling. Feelings originate in values to which an individual group or organization is committed. Thus, Superintendent Garnett in Case Five, "Democracy: Riverbank, U.S.A.," chose the "Conyers Site" and developed strong feelings about its values. Intensity of feeling about values is no doubt positively related to the strength of one's commitment to the values.

Feelings are most likely to become intense when the values to which one is committed are destructively threatened or seemingly can be maintained only through sacrifice or frustration. Since Bell's values and those of the "small opposing group" in Case Seventeen, "Changing the Curriculum at Southside," were in some ways mutually contradictory, the presence of one was a threat to the other. Consequently, both parties experienced strong feelings. Some of these feelings were characteristically hostile and others were colored by fear. Under such circumstances, clash between these feelings and the plan for change was unavoidable in the organization in question.

To be sure, the capacity that an individual has for tolerating conflict will affect the intensity of his feeling. This generalization can be illustrated from the work of Getzels and Guba (10), who studied the decision-making behavior of officer personnel at Maxwell Air Force Base. When a group of officers were asked to resolve the same choice situation, some officers experienced considerably more conflict than did others. All personnel involved were administered the Guilford-Martin Inventory to determine how their personality characteristics were related to the intensity of conflict they experienced. Persons who were high on *felt* conflict were found to have greater "feelings of inferiority," to be more "introvertive" and "nervous," than those who were low on *felt* conflict. Much more research is needed to show clearly how personality patterns are related to feeling in decision processes.

Significance of feelings in choice. The task of volition in controlling feelings is somewhat paradoxical. Strong feelings interfere with objectivity and, yet, the administrator typically feels strongly that certain goals or values are desirable. If he becomes highly involved personally in the projected results of choice outcomes, he is likely to be strongly motivated to preserve or achieve the values that seem important to him; however, high involvement leads to strong concern for certain specific consequences—a condition that limits possibilities and increases the likelihood of failure and frustrating feelings on his part. A posture of detachment, on the other hand, helps the administrator to be more objective and less the victim of intense feeling; however, at the same time, marked detachment may mean a lack of commitment that will minimize energy and motivation. Thus, the problem is one of balance. More specifically, how can the administrator maintain a relatively detached view when values that he esteems highly are threatened? Can he learn, for example, to deploy strategies skillfully and to take risks and still remain relatively detached? To what extent can volition assist him to play the administrative role with the same detachment that he would display in a game of chance? Certainly, the problem is a central one for the administrator, and science has only skirted its fringes.

Value framework. As already noted, volition plays a crucial role in decision-making through its capacity or incapacity to create independent acts at key points in the process. In this regard, a fundamental consideration would seem to be a commitment on the part of the decision-maker to a value framework. An administrator is at a distinct disadvantage if his total basis for decision is what others expect from him. Since decision-making involves the resolution of conflict, extreme tendencies to please or to depend on others may result in the administrator's being victimized by contradictory pressures with little in the way of a personal buttress. In addition, he may remove himself from conflicts that involve crucial organizational or educational values. Goodlad (11, p. 378) has stated this problem with reference to the school principal: "Like some members of his faculty he comes to have no sense of direction other than a driving desire to please everyone, and, since pleasing everyone is impossible, his administrative activity becomes inefficient to the point of personal collapse." In other words, there are other bases of decisions besides what is judged to be pleasing to others, and not the least important is a sound and well-defined value framework to which the administrator is committed.

Can the characteristics of an adequate value system for decision-making be precisely delineated? Can value systems be arranged in hierarchies in which, for example, certain moral and certain educational values take precedence and selected personal values rank lower in the hierarchy? If such hierarchies can be developed, can they be consistently applied to the solution of problems in all situations?

The answers to all these questions are apparently negative. Few, if any, values seem to take complete and absolute precedence in all decision situations. There are several reasons for this. First, values vary from one section of the country to the other. Thus, the value of racial tolerance varies in its meaning and its application in different parts of the country. Second, a limited number of values is present in any one choice situation. Consequently, the number and relationships of values vary from one choice situation to another, and their effects must often be weighed in terms of their consequences for the given situation. Ibsen's play *The Wild Duck* points up in a dramatic way the limitations in the uncritical application of values. Young Werle in this play committed himself to tell the truth absolutely and completely. In so doing, not only did he destroy the happiness of a family, but he also caused one of the members to take her life. Thus, although honesty is essential in human relationships, it may sometimes conflict with other values.

Is the administrator morally bound to tell the whole truth, if long-lasting evil is the result? When is he justified in withholding information? Such questions suggest the conflict that he must sometimes resolve.

An administrator must somehow exercise choice so that he achieves organizational ends with moral means. As Frankel (9, p. 16) has stated: "The problem of Might *versus* Right, of efficiency *versus* moral ideals . . . is in many ways the germinal problem of political philosophy." However, as Frankel (9, p. 17) goes on to say, the choice is not a simple one between efficient power and inefficient virtue: "There is only an undiscriminating and a discriminating use of power, an unimaginative and an imaginative use, a use for ends that are imposed on us and a use for ends we choose for ourselves freely and responsibly."

Courage. Related to the creation of independent acts is the quality of courage. Courage is expressed when decisions are made that entail clear risks for the administrator. Loss of social status, threat of economic reprisal, or loss of professional position are examples of such risks. Courage enters when the decision-maker's chances for personal loss are increased because of a commitment to a cause beyond himself. For example, there is the striking case of Daniel Webster deciding an issue in favor of preserving the Union and at the expense of what many historians believe was a chance for the presidency of the United States. Thus, on a January night in 1850 when Clay asked Webster to speak out in favor of preserving the Union, Webster, after examining the issue, did so at considerable risk to his career. Webster's own statement, as quoted by Kennedy (13, p. 68), revealed something of the basis of his decision: "I shall stand by the Union . . . with absolute disregard of personal consequences. What are personal consequences . . . in comparison with the good or evil which may befall a great country in a crisis like this? . . . Let the consequences be what they will, I am careless. No man can suffer too much, and no man can fall too soon, if he suffer or if he fall in defense of the liberties and Constitution of his country." Although the decisions of school administrators are generally much less striking than the above example, nevertheless they are frequently invested with more or less courage. Did not the superintendent in Case Twelve, "Dr. Cook Survives," show courage in his forthright stand on the issue of personnel appointments? The uneasy tenure of administrators suggests that they must frequently make choices at some risk to their status. This capacity to show courage is fundamentally dependent upon emotional conditions. Not only are fears that stem from risk to status overcome, but powerful feelings that arise from a commitment to a value or cause beyond one's self also have their effects.

Avenues for Resolving Conflict

If decision-making is basically the resolution of conflict, how can the administrator achieve this objective? This question can be answered only in relation to the various units of choice: individual, group, and organization. Without seeking to be exhaustive, some of the constructive avenues to conflict resolution will be noted.

Resolving individual conflict. The resolution of conflict may occasion be handled near its source by delegating the task to the persons directly involved. Barnard (3, p. 194) suggests this approach, among others, in his succinct statement on decision-making: "The fine art of executive decision consists in not deciding questions that are not now pertinent, in not deciding prematurely, in not making decisions that cannot be made effective, and in not making decisions that others should make." However, routine and executive decisions rather than those involving change and morale problems are more typically delegated. In addition, decisions involving organizational conflict are often referred to the administrator for resolution. Thus, delegation of decision-making has some limitations in resolving personal conflict for the administrator. Even when he can delegate, he must still carry the responsibility for the final outcomes of decisions.

Personal conflict can sometimes be resolved by a reassessment and new ranking of the values in the choice situation. For example, Principal Bell, in the earlier episodes of Case Seventeen, "Changing the Curriculum at Southside" seemed to place great value on getting the "half-day program" into effect. Later in the decision process, however, he seemed to reassess the situation and to behave as if the morale and expectations of teachers were more important than the half-day schedule. New rankings in values may result either because of a change in the situation or because of the development of new insights or understandings on the part of the administrator.

Another approach is to devise a solution or strategy that is sufficiently creative to reduce the conflict resulting from contrasting personal values. This point can be illustrated from Case Twelve, "Dr. Cook Survives." Undoubtedly Dr. Cook experienced some personal conflict when he was faced with the probable loss of his position for not giving in to what seemed to him to be unreasonable demands from the school board. By devising the strategy of gaining support for his positions from citizens in the community and from professional organizations outside the community, he undoubtedly was able to face the situation with less conflict. The strategy that he created helped him to retain his position and to deny the demands of the board members. Such an approach to conflict resolution requires both courage and creativity on the part of the administrator.

Still another way to deal with conflict is that of compromise. Instead of continuing to struggle toward a goal or value that is difficult or impossible to attain, the decision-maker may accede to the demands of the situation and accept some other value that he esteems less highly. Thus, some of Valley City's citizens in Case One, "The Valley City Consolidation Issue," undoubtedly accepted unionization rather than consolidation, although they originally preferred the latter.

In the American culture, compromise has been looked upon by some observers with much disdain. A realistic view of administration would indicate, however, that compromise is often essential to the attainment of co-operation. In the words of John Randal, as quoted by Lee (15, pp. 90–91):

> Now anybody who is at all capable of learning anything from experience knows that the only way to get along with people, the only way to do anything together with anybody else, is through compromise. You don't need exceptional brains to realize that; you need only to be married or to have a friend. Co-operation between human beings is possible only if they are willing to compromise; and politics, the art of co-operation, of group action, is at bottom nothing but the practical application of the methods of compromise.

Although compromise is frequently a wise choice, it does have its limitations. There is, for example, danger of compromising one's self rather than the issues, or of avoiding conflict when crucial values are at stake.

The opposite side of compromise is non-compromise. This means that one value is esteemed so highly by the decision-maker that he holds to it at all costs. History has recorded the lives of many persons whose names are now famous because even in the face of death they remained true to a cause or value. Apparently such persons died with less personal conflict than they would have had if they had lived and betrayed the value in question.

The administrator is limited in his capacity to be completely non-compromising. Stated differently, the forces beyond him are so many and so compelling that a continually non-compromising stand can be maintained only at great costs such as the loss of position or the lack of co-operation. On the other hand, it is no doubt true that administrators have some core values that cannot be compromised. When such values are involved, the administrator must abide by them. To do otherwise would increase rather than decrease the personal conflict experienced.

So far, in dealing with the resolution of individual conflict, the discussion has focused on conflict in which the content is manifest. What about conflict where the content is latent and, therefore, unrecognized by the administrator? Although little can be said on this matter at present, it seems that a major goal of the administrator is to make the latent content of conflict manifest, because it is easier to deal effectively with the manifest type of content. Since individual conflict involving latent content usually stems from unrecognized needs or goals of the administrator, the ancient admonition to "know thyself" seems appropriate.

Resolving group conflict. Compromise, delegation of decisions, reassessment of values, and creative solutions, discussed in relation to resolving individual conflict, also apply to the resolution of group conflict. Since all of these pertain to approaches to the handling of manifest content in conflict, the remarks pertinent to resolving group conflict will be limited to the resolution of conflict involving latent content.

A central source of conflicts in groups, as noted earlier, is found in the contrasting goals or values signified in the terms "hidden agenda" and "open agenda." "Hidden agenda," it will be recalled, refers to individual goals, such as the need to express hostility toward authority figures, or the need to dominate others in group decision situations. Behavior that is expressed to realize these values or needs is described as "self-oriented." Since it is not necessarily related to and is often in conflict with behavior that is directed toward achieving the formally defined purposes (that is, "open agenda") of a group, it is a latent type of content in group conflict. It is usually not talked about, is frequently not recognized, but always shapes the course of group decisions.

The work of Marquis, Guetzkow, and Heynes (18) suggests some clues pertinent to resolving group conflict. In their study of 72 decision-making conferences, they found that the most productive decision conferences, as measured by the number of items completed, were those with a minimum of behavior classified as "self-oriented." Productivity, in other words, was negatively correlated with the amount of "self-oriented" behavior among conferees.

A related finding was that the degree of satisfaction with decisions among conferees was negatively correlated with the amount of "self-oriented" behavior which was evidenced during the decision process. Finally, the study revealed that conferees were much more likely to be satisfied when the leader played an active role in getting the discussion focused on the decisions to be made. Leaders who gave little or no direction to the decision-making process created dissatisfaction among conferees.

A number of implications can be derived from the study of Marquis, Guetzkow, and Heynes. The first and most significant is that the administrator needs to be able to recognize "self-oriented" behavior and to understand something of its basis. This is particularly true in cases where the behavior directly and consistently conflicts with the formal purposes of the group. Only when the administrator is able to recognize the effects of such behavior is he in a position to react constructively.

For example, are there not implications for the appointment or selection of members to serve on decision-making groups? Perhaps selection procedures can be used that will minimize the amount of over-destructive "self-oriented" behavior likely to be expressed in decision conferences. This is particularly true in cases where the administrator has had ample opportunity to become acquainted with his personnel and in cases where he is responsible for appointing decision-making groups.

Since "hidden agenda" to a greater or less extent exist in all groups, careful selection of decision-makers cannot solve the problem of conflict completely. Thus, the administrator as a leader of groups needs to employ other techniques. For example, if he can skillfully keep conferees aware of the problem at hand and can channel the discussion so that it relates to the decision to be made, less conflict may result. In the process, of course, it is important that feelings be expressed in an atmosphere that is not overly-critical.

Can the administrator devise techniques or organizational arrangements that can be utilized with conferees outside of decision-making conferences? For some personnel there are undoubtedly constructive roles in the organization through which they can alleviate "self-oriented" needs while contributing to the organization. The person seeking recognition, for example, may be able to realize this goal in a variety of ways. If the administrator can assist such a person to find constructive ways to get recognition outside the decision-making conference, then the "self-oriented" behavior during decision conferences is likely to be reduced. Thus, the problem could be solved both ethically and effectively.

Resolving organizational conflict. In all types of decision, timing is a significant factor, and this is particularly true in terms of organizational decisions in the sense that a larger number of personnel are involved.

In this regard, the resolution of conflict before it reaches the crisis stage is highly desirable. Coleman (6), by analyzing various cases of community conflict, has defined six stages in community conflict and crisis. Although Coleman's generalizations apply to the community, they also have implications for internal school organization. The first stage of conflict is one in which the administrator becomes a defendant. Second, a period ensues in which a small opposition continually opposes the administration. In the third stage, a large majority of the people are neutral, neither actively supporting nor opposing the administration. A fourth stage finds an active group—generally, a minority actively supporting the administration. In the fifth phase, because of effects resulting from mass communication media or blunders on the part of the administrator, the large neutral group become active opposers. In the final phase, those opposing the administration gain their ends. The fifth stage, in which a large acquiescent majority readies itself for action against the administration, can be decisive in determining the administrator's survival. From a strategic standpoint, it seems desirable to handle conflict satifactorily earlier than the fifth stage—for example, in the second stage.

The importance of recognizing and of constructively handling crisis decisions can be further illustrated from Coleman's study. In the late 1940's and early 1950's, community controversy over the schools arose in Pasadena and Denver. The Denver superintendent, among other things, conducted a citizens' survey and conferred at length with a critical citizens' committee. He acted in the early stages of the conflict, and the controversy in Denver never reached a crisis. In Pasadena, on the other hand, the superintendent apparently refused to heed the critics either in meeting with them or in explaining the school's position clearly; a crisis developed there that reached the final crisis stages. The results undermined the superintendent and apparently led to his dismissal.

Various arrangements have been developed to handle conflict in decision processes constructively. For example, Selznick (21) has pointed to the techniques of formal and informal co-optation for dealing with crises that threaten an organization. Formal co-optation involves the opposing parties in a publicly recognized discussion or decision-making group, such as a citizens' committee. During the process of discussion, understandings are achieved and agreements are made. The agreements do not necessarily bring crucial changes in policy so far as the organization in question is concerned. The tremendous growth in the number of citizens' committees studying school problems during the decade 1948–1958 was perhaps partially a result of the administrators' efforts to cope with the widespread criticism of the schools. Many of these committees have undoubtedly helped to resolve conflict constructively.

In informal co-optation, behind-the-scenes negotiations are made with the opposing groups or persons, and these are unaccompanied by public pronouncements. Commitments may be made to the opposing parties that have a crucial effect upon future policy development and the program of a school. Since schools apparently enjoy greater political independence than other organizations devoted to public administration, undoubtedly leaders in educational organizations have used informal co-optation less than have administrators who have worked in other settings. However, the technique undoubtedly has been used in such areas as school board decisions and school-community relationships. In informal co-optation, unanticipated consequences may arise as a result of commitments that in the long run prove costly to the organization. This is particularly true when the persons to whom commitments are made are key influentials.

Conflict can often be constructively resolved through informal discussion and negotiation with the persons involved. Mediation and arbitration arrangements are formally recognized ways of settling conflict in industrial organizations, although they have not received systematic use in educational administration.

Specific action clues, depicting how the administrator interacts with others in the resolution of conflict situations, are not easily indicated. Martin and Simms (19), by studying the biographies of such persons as Franklin Roosevelt and Henry Ford and by interviewing a number of contemporary business executives, have generalized about the tactics that individual administrators use in order to influence decisions. Skillfully taking counsel from subordinates, establishing loyal relationships and alliances, being flexible on positions and programs, and maintaining smooth-flowing communication channels were some of the successfully used techniques. In addition, such techniques as compromise, stalling, expression of dramatic behavior, display of contagious confidence, and maintainence of a detached relationship with subordinates so that the emotional attachment of close friendship does not interfere with the administrator's ability to make organizational decisions are typically used. These techniques for dealing with power and for achieving influence come from business and public administration. It is not clear to what extent they apply to other areas of administration.

The use of these techniques may on some occasions raise ethical questions. Thus, in influencing the events around him, the administrator is faced with choosing effective as well as ethical means. Conflicting values and energies, as well as other constraints, will prevent his achieving perfect solutions. In the words of Belisle and Sargent (4): "For it is the task of the administrator in pursuit of his obvious historical and social function as a member of this profession (school administration) to induce ever-changing creative harmonies out of the conflicts within the reach of his influence, while never fully satisfying the competing demands within himself as person, professional, and situationally responsive actor." Although the demands on the educational administrator are stringent, the challenge of his task is great. Effective resolution of ever-emerging individual, group, and organizational conflicts cannot help but increase his personal wisdom and contribute to the common good.

References

1. Asch, S. E., "Effects of Group Pressure Upon the Modification and Distortion of Judgments," in *Groups, Leadership and Men* (Harold Guetzkow, ed). Pittsburgh: Carnegie Press, 1951, pp. 177–190.
2. Barnard, Chester, "Dilemmas of Leadership in the Democratic Process," in *Organization and Management*. Cambridge: The Harvard University Press, 1948, Chapter II, pp. 24–50.
3. ———, *The Functions of the Executive*. Cambridge: The Harvard University Press, 1938.
4. Belisle, Eugene, and Cyril Sargent, "The Concept of Administration," in *Administrative Behavior in Education* (ed. by Roald Campbell and Russell Gregg). New York: Harper and Brothers, 1957.

5. Block, Jack, and Paul Peterson, "Some Personality Correlates of Confidence, Caution and Speed in a Decision Situation," *Journal of Abnormal and Social Psychology*, Vol. 51: 34–41, July, 1955.

6. Coleman, James, *Community Conflict*. Glencoe, Ill.: The Free Press, 1957.

7. Elrod, J. T., "Operations Research; A Tool for Management," *Houston Business Review*, Vol. 3, No. 7, September, 1956, pp. 3–6.

8. Fouriezos, Nicholas T., and others, "Measurement of Self-Oriented Needs in Discussion Groups," *Journal of Abnormal and Social Psychology*, Vol. 45; 682–690, 1950.

9. Frankel, Charles, "Efficient Power and Inefficient Virtue," in *Great Moral Dilemmas*, (R. N. MacIver, ed.). New York: Harper and Brothers, 1956.

10. Getzels, Jacob, and Egon Guba, "Role, Conflict and Effectiveness: An Empirical Study," *American Sociological Review*, Vol. XIX, April, 1954, pp. 164–175.

11. Goodlad, John, "The School Scene in Review," *School Review*, Vol. LXV, Winter, 1957, pp. 371–387. Copyright, 1957, by the University of Chicago.

12. Gross, Neal, "Easing Strains and Tensions Between Superintendents and Board Members," *Nation's Schools*, Vol. 56, 43–47, (October) 1955.

13. Kennedy, John, *Profiles in Courage*. New York: Pocket Books, Inc., 1957. By permission of Harper and Brothers.

14. Laski, Harold, "Limitations of the Expert," *Harper's Monthly*, Vol. 162, Dec. 1930–May 1931, pp. 101–110.

15. Lee, Irving, *How To Talk With People*. New York: Harper and Brothers, 1952.

16. Lewin, Kurt, *Dynamic Theory of Personality*. New York: McGraw-Hill Book Company, Inc., 1935.

17. McCamy, J. L., "Analysis of the Process of Decision Making," *Public Administration Review*, Vol. 7, pp. 41–48, 1947.

18. Marquis, D. G., Harold Guetzkow, and R. W. Heynes, "A Social Psychological Study of the Decision-Making Conference," in *Groups, Leadership and Men* (Harold Guetzkow, ed.). Pittsburgh: Carnegie Press, 1951, pp. 55–67.

19. Martin, Norman H., and John Howard Simms, "Thinking Ahead: Power Tactics," *Harvard Business Review*, Vol. 34, No. 6, Nov.–Dec., 1956, pp. 26–36; 140.

20. Rossi, Peter, "Community Decision-Making," *Administrative Science Quarterly*, Vol. 1, No. 4, March 1957, pp. 415–443.

21. Selznick, Philip, "Foundations of the Theory of Organization," *American Sociological Review*, Vol. 13 (Feb. 1948), pp. 25–35.

22. Simon, Herbert, *Administrative Behavior*. New York: the Macmillan Company, 1957 (2nd ed.).

23. Smith, Philip, *Philosophic-Mindedness in Educational Administration*. Columbus: The Ohio State University Press, 1956.

24. Spalding, Willard, *The Superintendency of Public Schools—An Anxious Profession*. Cambridge: Harvard University Press, 1954.

25. The International Sociological Association, *The Nature of Conflict*. Paris: UNESCO, 1957.

Administrative Behavior and Its Milieu: an Annotated Bibliography

Since studies related to administrative behavior are found in many disciplines, one must to some extent play the role of the packrat. The references which follow are drawn from various fields of study and are judged to be among the more unique attempts to illuminate administrative behavior. Burrowing into the various references should enable the reader to ferret out considerable information and numerous ideas which he can carry away, evaluate, and put to worthwhile use.

I. ADMINISTRATION

Campbell, Roald, John Corbally, and John Ramseyer, *Introduction to Educational Administration*. Boston: Allyn and Bacon, 1958, 434 pp. A textbook on administration that departs from the traditional text. It includes material on administrative behavior and the social setting in which administrators function.

Campbell, Roald, and Russell Gregg (eds.), *Administrative Behavior in Education*. New York: Harper and Brothers, 1957, 547 pp. This book, which contains writings by various authors, is a comprehensive approach to summarizing social science literature as it applies to educational administration.

Davis, Keith, *Human Relations in Business*. New York: McGraw-Hill Book Co., Inc., 1957, 557 pp. Deals with such problems as organizational structure, role playing, group dynamics, communication analysis, and human relations training. Many findings from the disciplines of sociology, psychology, economics, and industrial management are included in the book.

Educational Leadership, "What Are We Finding Out in Related Fields?" May, 1956. This issue contains statements from scholars in various social science disciplines. The authors seek to show what their respective disciplines can contribute to education and administration.

Gross, Neal, Ward Mason, and Alexander McEachern, *Explorations in Role Analysis*. New York: John Wiley and Sons, 1958, 379 pp. This book is based upon data gathered from extensive interviews with superintendents and board members in New England. The research is cast within role theory, and the data are carefully analyzed. The book represents a sophisticated approach to the study of the superintendent-school board relationships.

Guetzkow, Harold (ed.), *Groups, Leadership and Men.* Pittsburgh: Carnegie Press, 1951, 293 pp. This book, edited by Guetzkow, summarizes the results of five years of social science research on problems of groups and organizations, both in industry and in the Navy. It is one of the most significant books of research on administration.

Hagman, Harlan, and Alfred Schwartz, *Administration in Profile for School Executives.* New York: Harper and Brothers, 1955, 315 pp. A book which draws on studies from fields other than school administration. Such "factors" as leadership and organization are treated, as well as such "functions" as evaluation and co-ordination.

Hall, Calvin, and Gardner Lindsey, *Theories of Personality.* New York: John Wiley and Sons, Inc., 1957, 572 pp. A critical survey of the major theories of personality.

Halpin, Andrew (ed.), *Administrative Theory in Education.* Chicago: Midwest Administration Center (University of Chicago), 1958, 188 pp. A discussion of issues in theory building is included, along with some examples of theory.

Koontz, Harold, and Cyril O'Donnell, *Principles of Management.* New York: McGraw-Hill Book Company, Inc., 1955, 664 pp. The authors seek to summarize the "principles" of management as related to the business world. Principles are organized under the categories of staffing, organization, direction, and planning.

Morphet, Edgar, R. L. Johns, and Theodore L. Reller, *Educational Administration: Concepts, Practices and Issues.* Englewood Cliffs, N.J.: Prentice-Hall, Inc., 1959, 556 pp. A balanced and comprehensive book on school administration. Research from various disciplines are carefully related to problems and issues related to educational administration.

National Society for the Study of Education, *In-service Education,* Fifty-sixth Yearbook. Chicago: The University of Chicago Press, 1957, 376 pp. See especially Chapter IV, "Psychology of Change Within an Institution."

Phi Delta Kappan, "Research in Educational Administration," Vol. 37, No. 7, April, 1956. The entire issue is devoted to a report of investigations carried out by the various CPEA centers throughout the country. Such problems as the selection of administrators, school-community problems, consulting services, and the role of research in advancing administration are discussed.

Pigors, Paul, and Charles Myers, *Personnel Administration.* New York: McGraw-Hill Book Company, Inc., 1947, 614 pp. This book, which focuses on problems in business organizations, emphasizes the human elements in personnel administration.

————, and ———— (eds.), *Readings in Personnel Administration.* New York: McGraw-Hill Book Company, Inc., 1952, 483 pp. The book contains selected readings from various authors, selections which complement the editors' text, *Personnel Administration.*

Simon, Herbert, Donald Smithburg, and Victor Thompson, *Public Administration.* New York: Alfred A. Knopf, Inc., 1950, 582 pp. This book departs from the more traditional public administration texts. It focuses on administrative behavior, and assumes that there can be a science of administration, "not a science in the sense that physicists have achieved, but a science in a sense of an objective understanding of the phenomena without confusion between facts and values." The authors have drawn findings from the social sciences to bolster their theories.

Waldo, Dwight, "Administrative Theory in the United States: A Survey in Prospect," *Political Studies,* Vol. 2, No. 1, February, 1954, pp. 70–86. An interesting discussion of trends and possible future developments in administrative theory.

————, *Perspectives on Administration.* University of Alabama, University of Alabama Press, 1956, 143 pp. A theoretical and philosophical approach to the *study* of administration.

————, *The Study of Public Administration.* New York: Doubleday and Company, Inc., 1955, 72 pp. An excellent overview of some of the problems in public administration. Discussion includes such topics as administrative study and the social sciences, the value problem in administrative study, and trends in the study of public administration.

II. COMMUNICATION

Babcock, C. Merton, "A Dynamic Theory of Communication," *Journal of Communication,* Vol. 2, No. 1, May, 1952, pp. 64–68. Various elements in communication are set forth and their respective roles in the process are described.

Bavelas, Alex, and Dermot Berrett, "An Experimental Approach to Organizational Communication," *Personnel,* Vol. 27, March, 1951, pp. 366–371. The purpose of the experiment was to test the problem-solving ability of three different groups with varying communication patterns. A major finding was that the pattern that was most accurate and most rapid had the poorest morale among its membership.

Cook, P. H., "An Examination of the Notion of Communication," *Occupational Psychology,* Vol. 25, No. 1, January, 1951, pp. 1–14. A major assumption of this work is that good communication does not make for good relationships as much as good communication takes place because of good relationships. The author discusses the vital part that attitude plays in the process.

Corson, John, "Weak Links in the Chain of Command," *Public Opinion Quarterly,* Vol. 9, Fall, 1945, pp. 346–349. A study of the effectiveness of downward communication in one branch of the Bureau of Old Age and Survivors Insurance.

Culbertson, Jack, "Here Is One That Did!" *The School Executive,* Vol. LXXVI, April, 1957, pp. 68–69. A description and evaluation of a technique for improving upward communication in a large high school.

Dahle, Thomas, "Transmitting Information to Employees," *Personnel,* Vol. XXXI, No. 3, November, 1954, pp. 243–246. A summary of findings from a doctoral thesis which tested five different means of communicating to employees.

Davis, Keith, "A Method of Studying Communication Patterns in an Organization," *Personnel Psychology,* Vol. VI, Autumn, 1953, pp. 301–312. Various findings are included about the nature of informal communication in an organization.

Dooher, M. Joseph, ed., *Effective Communication on the Job.* New York: American Management Association, 1956, 294 pp. An excellent series of writings which seek to bridge the gap between understanding research findings and relating them to administrative situations.

Festinger, Leon, "Informal Social Communications," *Psychological Review,* Vol. 57, September, 1950, pp. 271–282. This work, based upon a large number of experiments, is one of the most concise statements available about communication as a process. Hypotheses about the effects of group pressures on communication, the direction of communication in a group, and the determinants of change in group relationships are set forth.

Hayakawa, S. I., *Language in Thought and Action.* New York: Harcourt, Brace and Company, 1939, 307 pp. A study which focuses on the role of words in the communication process. The relationships of words to things and of words to behavior are analyzed.

Hovland, Carl, Irving Janis, and Harold Kelly, *Communication and Persuasion.* New Haven: Yale University Press, 1953, 315 pp. This book summarizes a great deal of research and is appropriate for those who are interested in a better understanding of the problem of downward or one-way communication in an organization.

Kahn, Robert, and Charles Connell, *The Dynamics of Interviewing.* New York: John Wiley and Sons, Inc., 368 pp. Interviewing is conceived and analyzed as a communication process. A bibliography is included.

Pigors, Paul, *Effective Communication in Industry.* New York: National Association of Manufacturers, 1949, 87 pp. Pigors seems to throw some light on communication processes by analyzing each of the following elements: facts, feelings, and the intent of the communicator. These elements are discussed in terms of how they can be understood for the improvement of meaning in communication. A number of criteria of effective communication, as well as a bibliography of approximately 100 titles, are included in this work.

Redfield, Charles, *Communication in Management*. Chicago: The University of Chicago Press, 1953, 290 pp. A comprehensive treatment of the problem of communication in industry. The first part of the book discusses various techniques of communication, both written and oral, while the second part deals with concepts for explaining communication in an organization.

Roethlisberger, F. J., *Management and Morale*. Cambridge: Harvard University, 1941, 194 pp. A general argument for management to take steps to facilitate upward communication. The problems of achieving such a goal are set forth and described.

Wiener, Norbert, *The Human Use of Human Beings*. Garden City, N.Y.: Doubleday Anchor Books, 1956, 2nd ed., 199 pp. The thesis of the book, as stated by Wiener, is that "society can only be understood through a study of the messages and the communication facilities which belong to it; and that in the future development of these messages and communication facilities, messages between man and machines, between machines and man and between machine and machine are destined to play an ever-increasing part."

III. COMMUNITY ORGANIZATION

Barnett, H. G., *Innovation: The Basis for Cultural Change*. New York: McGraw-Hill Book Company, Inc., 1953, 462 pp. An attempt to synthesize what is known about innovation, which is defined as the "appearance of novel ideas." The nature, conditions, and consequences of innovation are discussed. Examples are drawn from primitive as well as from the more technologically advanced societies.

Bendix, Reinhard, and Seymour Lipset, eds., *Class, Status and Power*. Glencoe, Ill.: The Free Press, 1953, 725 pp. One of the more comprehensive collections of studies dealing with aspects of the political, social, and economic life of communities.

Boulding, Kenneth, *The Organizational Revolution*. New York: Harper and Brothers, 1953, 286 pp. The author shows how organizations in the American setting have grown in size and number and speculates on some of the causes and effects of this growth. Case studies are included.

Cook, L. A., and E. F. Cook, *A Sociological Approach to Education*. New York: McGraw-Hill Book Company, Inc., 1950, 514 pp. Part II, entitled "The Community Frame of Life," gives a number of cases which seek to describe and explain the nature of small towns, the small city, the large city, and a great metropolis.

Greer, Scott, *Social Organization*. New York: Doubleday and Company, Inc. 1955, 68 pp. A brief and simply written discussion centering around such concepts as group structure, human groups, and changes in organizations. Concrete illustrative material is included.

Hollingshead, A. B., *Elmtown's Youth*. New York: John Wiley and Co., 1949, 480 pp. One of the few studies which has tried to study the effect of social class on the actual behaviors of students in the institution of the school.

Merton, Robert, *Social Theory and Social Structure*. Glencoe, Ill.: The Free Press, 1957, 645 pp. A collection of essays on sociological theory, social and cultural structure, the sociology of science, and the sociology of knowledge. The orientation is theoretical and the approach is that of functional analysis.

Riesman, David, *The Lonely Crowd*. New Haven: Yale University Press, 1950, 386 pp. A sociological analysis of the motivation and values of persons in present-day society.

Seeley, John R., Alexander Sim, and Elizabeth W. Loosley, *Crestwood Heights*. New York: Basic Books, 1956, 505 pp. A report on a study of the culture of a suburban town. The report is based upon a five-year period of study, during which time clubs, homes, schools, churches, and other aspects of community life were investigated through observation and interview.

Warner, William Lloyd, and Paul S. Lunt, *The Social Life of a Modern Community*. New Haven: Yale University Press, 1941, 460 pp. A pioneer study of the nature and functions of socioeconomic class.

Whyte, William F., *Street Corner Society*. Chicago: The University of Chicago Press, 1943, 366 pp. A report of the life, leadership, and organization in an Italian slum.

IV. DECISION-MAKING

Coch, Lester, and John French, "Overcoming Resistance to Change," in *Readings in Social Psychology*, ed. by Guy Swanson, *et al.* New York: Henry Holt and Company, 1952. Groups which participated in making their own decisions about how changes were to be instituted enjoyed higher production and morale and better labor-management relations than groups which did not participate in the decisions.

Cronbach, Lee J., and Goldine C. Gleser, *Psychological Tests and Personnel Decisions*. Urbana, Ill.: University of Illinois Press, 1957, 165 pp. An application of decision-theory to applied personnel problems. A sophisticated and systematic analysis, but very technical in the middle sections.

Guetzkow, Harold, "An Exploratory Empirical Study of the Role of Conflict in Decision-Making Conferences," *International Social Science Bulletin*, Vol. 5, 1953, pp. 286–300. Seventy-two meetings involving 700 people were studied. Conditions which led to conflict in decision-making and conditions which led to consensus are delineated.

Hunter, Floyd, *Community Power Structure; A Study of Decision-Makers*. Chapel Hill, N. C.: University of North Carolina Press, 1953, 297 pp. The study is an investigation of power as it relates to community decisions. It assumes that the community is a "primary power center," and that "power relations can be observed most easily in a community." The size of the city studied was 500,000. The author concluded that decisive power concerning civic issues in the city was wielded by 40 men. How these men were distributed among the various economic, political, civic, and educational organizations is described. The study should be enlightening to any student of administration.

Lewin, Kurt, "Group Decision and Social Change," in *Readings in Social Psychology*, ed. by G. E. Swanson, *et al.* New York: Henry Holt and Company, 1952, pp. 459–473. Various studies dealing with decision-making are summarized. The general conclusion was that change is brought about more effectively if those who are directly affected have an opportunity to participate in decisions pertinent to the change.

Luce, Duncan, and Howard Raiffa, *Games and Decisions*. New York: John Wiley and Sons, Inc., 1957, 509 pp. A description of how mathematicians attempt to apply their concepts to such elements in decision-making as conflict of interest, subjective probability, and values. Both individual and group decision-making are treated.

Marquis, E. G., *et al.*, "A Social Psychological Study of the Decision-Making Conference," in *Groups, Leadership and Men*, ed. by Harold Guetzkow. Pittsburgh: The Carnegie Press, 1951, pp. 55–67. This study took place over a period of several years and involved 72 decision-making bodies in actual organizations. Attempts were made to develop criteria to judge the effectiveness of a decision-making conference.

McCamy, James, "An Analysis of the Process of Decision-Making," *Public Administration Review*, Vol. 7, No. 1, 1947, pp. 41–48. Decision-making is set forth as the core of administration and is defined as the "process of people acting upon one another toward a conclusion." Various elements in the process are elaborated.

Pierce, Truman, *et al.*, *Community Leadership for Public Education*. Englewood Cliffs, N.J.: Prentice-Hall, Inc., 1955, 312 pp. Ways of making community decisions, such as balloting, defaulting, and delegating, are described in this book. The importance of values in the development of social policy is emphasized.

Simon, Herbert, *Administrative Behavior: A Study of Decision-Making Processes in Administrative Organization*. New York: The Macmillan Company, 1947, 259 pp. A comprehensive and general description of organization, the nature of decisions, the place of value and fact in decisions, and the psychology of decisions is given. The author seeks to show why individual behavior in an organization perforce must fall short of rationality. The reference is generally regarded as a very important contribution toward the general understanding of administrative behavior.

Thrall, R. M., *et al.*, *Decision Processes*. New York: John Wiley and Sons, 1954, 332 pp. The collection of articles in this book is an outgrowth of an eight-weeks seminar on designing experiments in decision-making.

V. LARGE-SCALE ORGANIZATION

Argyris, Chris, *Personality and Organization.* New York: Harper and Brothers, 1957, 291 pp. A framework for describing personal behavior in organizations. The author emphasizes the conflict which arises from the clash of individual needs and organizational demands.

Barnard, Chester, *Functions of the Executive.* Cambridge, Mass.: Harvard University Press, 1938, 334 pp. A book which has markedly influenced students of organization. Theoretical in nature, it attempts to shed light on the dynamics of administration. It points up the importance of informal organization.

Blau, Peter, *Bureaucracy in Modern Society.* New York: Random House, Inc., 1956, 127 pp. An analysis of the concept of bureaucracy. Such factors as specialization, division of labor, and rationality are discussed.

————, *The Dynamics of Bureaucracy.* Chicago: University of Chicago Press, 1955, 269 pp. A report of carefully conducted studies dealing with human interaction in a large organization.

Christie, Richard, ed., *Continuities in Social Research.* Glencoe, Ill.: The Free Press, 1954, 279 pp. One of the most useful statements that has appeared on behavior in the military organizations. It summarizes and interprets many of the findings in the first two volumes of *The American Soldier* by Samuel Stouffer, *et al.,* (Glencoe, Ill.: The Free Press, 1948).

Dubin, Robert, *The World of Work.* Englewood Cliffs, N.J.: Prentice-Hall, Inc., 1958, 448 pp. An analysis of the nature of work organizations and the relationships of individual members to them. Contains extensive bibliography.

Merton, Robert, ed., *A Reader in Bureaucracy.* Glencoe, Ill.: The Free Press, 1952, 464 pp. An anthology of thoughtful articles dealing with various aspects of large-scale organizations.

Parkinson, C. Northcote, *Parkinson's Law and Other Studies in Administration.* Boston: Houghton Mifflin Company, 1957, 112 pp. A satirical "analysis" of bureaucrats and bureaucratic methods.

Roethlisberger, F. J., and W. J. Dickson, *Management and the Worker.* Cambridge: Harvard University Press, 1940, 615 pp. A pioneer study that is worth the attention of any student of administration. It has influenced students of organization to give more attention to the social motives of personnel and to place less emphasis on economic motives.

Safer, Cyril, "Reactions to Administrative Change," *Human Relations,* Vol. 8, No. 3, 1955, pp. 291–316. An empirical study of organizational change in three British hospitals five years after nationalization.

Selznick, Philip, "Foundations of the Theory of Organization," *American Sociological Review*, Vol. 13, February, 1948, pp. 25–35. A short and succinct statement on the dynamics of organization. Some basic postulates are set forth to describe and explain the operation of an organization.

Weber, Max, *From Max Weber: Essays in Sociology*. New York: Oxford University Press, 1946, 490 pp. A classic statement on the nature and functions of bureaucratic organization.

Whyte, William H., *The Organization Man*. New York: Simon and Schuster, 1956, 429 pp. Critical analysis of some assumptions underlying modern organizations and "group" techniques.

VI. LEADERSHIP

Adorno, T. W., and others, *The Authoritarian Personality*. New York: Harper and Brothers, 1950, 990 pp. Research findings designed to provide a better understanding of a particular type of "authoritarian" personality are the substance of this report.

American Association of School Administrators, *The American School Superintendency* (Thirtieth Yearbook). Washington 6, D.C., The Association, 1952, 663 pp. See especially Chapter IV, "The Organization of the Superintendency," which sets forth the leadership functions of the school superintendent.

Baltzell, E. Digby, "Bell Telephone's Experiment in Education," *Harper's Magazine*, Vol. 210. March, 1955, pp. 73–77. A description of a unique approach to training leaders.

Browne, C. G., and Thomas Cohn, *The Study of Leadership*. Danville, Ill.: The Interstate Printers and Publishers, 1958, 487 pp. An anthology of readings on leadership. Selections relate to the analysis of leadership, the dynamics of leadership, and the identification and training of leaders.

Davies, Daniel, *A Developing Concept of the Superintendency*. New York: Columbia University, CPEA Series, 1953, 40 pp. A very concise theoretical statement about administrative processes specifically related to education. Processes are derived from certain assumptions concerning the school administrator, the job, and the social setting.

————, and Robert Livingston, *You and Management*. New York: Harper and Brothers, 1958, 272 pp. A practical and simple guide to administration. The book is written within a group process framework.

Fleishman, Edwin, Edwin Harris, and Harold Burtt, *Leadership and Supervision in Industry*. Bureau of Education Research Monograph #33. Ohio State, 1955, 110 pp. A measurement study of factors in human relations attitudes and a follow-up of the effects of a human relations course. Effectiveness of the training depended on the situation to which the foreman returned.

Fortune Magazine, "The New Management," January, February, and

March, 1955. A statement on some trends in business leadership.

Gibb, C.,"Leadership," in *Handbook of Social Psychology.* Cambridge, Mass.: Addison Wesley Publishing Co., 1954, ed. by Gardner Lindzey, Chapter 24, pp. 877–920. A comprehensive review of the literature and research on leadership.

Gordon, Thomas, *Group-Centered Leadership.* Boston: Houghton Mifflin Company, 1955, 366 pp. Leadership is viewed as shared responsibility, and various facets of this view are elaborated.

Gouldner, Alvin, *Studies in Leadership.* New York: Harper and Brothers, 1950, 736 pp. A significant collection of articles by 34 authors in various social science fields. The introduction is an especially cogent discussion of problems in defining and studying leadership.

Henry, William, "The Business Executive—A Study of the Psycho-Dynamics of the Social Role," *The American Journal of Sociology,* 54:286–291, January, 1949. A study of business executives in relation to the demands of the setting in which they operate.

Lippitt, Ronald, Jeanne Watson, and Bruce Westley, *The Dynamics of Planned Change.* New York: Harcourt, Brace and Company, 1958, 312 pp. Such problems as motivation, initiation of change, phases of change, and the change agent's role are discussed in this book. Problems of internal and external relationships as they relate to change are also treated.

Miller, Van, ed., *Providing and Improving Administrative Leadership for American Schools.* New York: Columbia University, 1951, 74 pp. (Report of 4th Annual Meeting of the National Conference of Professors of Educational Administration, Ithaca, New York, August 27–September 2, 1950.) A description of the competencies needed for educational leadership. Some of the implications for training leaders are also set forth.

Review of Educational Research, "Research on Human Relations and Programs of Action," 1953, Vol. 23, No. 4. A collection of numerous theoretical and concrete studies of leadership.

Ross, Murray, and Charles Hendry, *New Understandings of Leadership.* New York: Association Press, 1957, 158 pp. Summary of "small group" research on leadership.

Seligman, Lester, "The Study of Political Leadership," *American Political Science Review,* Vol. 44, No. 4, December 1950, pp. 904–915. Various approaches to the study of leadership are described and analyzed: trait, small-group, large organization, typologies, and biographies. Weaknesses and strengths of these various approaches are made clear. A critical and concise statement on the problem of conceptualizing leadership.

Selznick, Philip, *Leadership in Administration.* Evanston, Ill.: Row, Peterson and Company, 1957, 154 pp. A sociological interpretation of kinds and qualities of leadership in Public Administration.

Shartle, Carroll, *Executive Performance and Leadership.* Englewood Cliffs, N.J.: Prentice-Hall, Inc., 1956, 302 pp. The book is partially based upon a ten-year inter-disciplinary study of leadership at the Ohio State University. The chapter on "Administrative Motivation" throws light on administrative behavior.

Tead, Ordway, *The Art of Administration*. New York: McGraw-Hill Book Company, Inc., 1951, 223 pp. A general statement on the nature of leadership. The point of view emphasizes the importance of group-centered direction.

VII. MORALE AND HUMAN RELATIONS

Allport, Floyd, *Theories of Perception and the Concept of Structure*. New York: John Wiley and Sons, Inc., 1955, 709 pp. The book carefully reviews the current major theories of perception. More important, the author critically analyzes and evaluates the theories from the standpoint of these criteria: agreement with facts, generality, parsimony, immediate experimental utility, logical consistency, and exploratory value.

Benne, K. D., and B. Muntyan, *Human Relations in Curriculum Change*. New York: Dryden Press, 1951, 363 pp. A collection of writings on human relations and group methods in producing change.

Bidwell, Charles E., "Administration and Teacher Satisfaction," *Phi Delta Kappan*, Vol. 37, April 1956, pp. 285–288. An excellent summary of numerous researches on morale conducted by the Midwest Administration Center, University of Chicago.

Cabot, Hugh, and Joseph Kahl, *Human Relations*. Cambridge: Harvard University Press, 1953, 333 pp. Part I brings together a number of social science concepts related to human relationships; Part II contains 33 cases which have been used in a human relations course.

Chase, Francis S., "Factors for Satisfaction in Teaching," *Phi Delta Kappan*, Vol. 33, November, 1951, pp. 127–132. A study which seeks not only to identify factors which are associated with morale but also to establish the relative importance of these factors.

Combs, Arthur, and Robert Fisk, "Summary and Critique of Problems and Research Needs in Administration," *Journal of Social Issues*, Vol. 10, No. 2, 1954, pp. 49–58. The article contains useful theory for explaining behavior on the basis of personal perceptions. It makes specific application of perceptual theory to school administration.

Devereux, George, *Therapeutic Education*. New York: Harper and Brothers, 1956, 435 pp. A very stimulating but somewhat sketchy attempt to answer the question of the effect of the school on mental health. An exploration of the psychopathogenic effects of the school system is included.

Dubin, Robert, *Human Relations in Administration*. Englewood Cliffs, N.J.: Prentice-Hall, Inc., 1951, 573 pp. The book contains a carefully selected series of readings which are organized under such topics as informal organization, authority, motivation, bureaucracy, and power. Case materials are also included.

Griffiths, Daniel, *Human Relations in School Administration*. New York: Appleton-Century-Crofts, 1956, 458 pp. Discusses a number of social science concepts which relate to human relations, among which are perception, power, authority, morale, and communication. Substantive problems are also discussed, such as faculty meetings, working with school boards, and working with specialists. Thirty short case studies are included in the book.

Hughes, James, *Human Relations in Educational Organization*. New York: Harper and Brothers, 1957, 425 pp. Deals with such concepts as role, sentiments, attitudes, and adjustment as they relate to organization. The book contains an extensive bibliography.

Kluckhohn, Clyde, and Henry Murray (ed.), *Personality in Nature, Society, and Culture*. New York: Alfred A. Knopf, Inc., 1948, 561 pp. A collection of readings which seek to illuminate the relationship between personality development and the various social, biological, and cultural factors which influence the process.

Maier, N.R.F., *Principles of Human Relations*. New York: John Wiley and Sons, 1952, 474 pp. This book is written from the standpoint of industrial relations and contains a great deal of illustrative case material.

Mueller-Deham, Albert, *Human Relations and Power*. New York: Philosophical Library, 1957, 410 pp. The author believes that human relations are determined by the attitudes of the participants and the various external forces (that is, power) which impinge upon them. Relationships are classified into various types, and the concept of power is carefully analyzed. Implications for politics and ethics are also set forth.

Pfiffner, John, *The Supervision of Personnel: Human Relations and the Management of Men*. Englewood Cliffs, N.J.: Prentice-Hall, Inc., 1951, 454 pp. A very readable book which concentrates on the human elements in administration.

Tagiuri, Renato, and Luigi Petrullo (eds.), *Person Perception and Interpersonal Behavior*. Stanford: Stanford University Press, 1958, 390 pp. The book brings together much of what is known about interpersonal perception. Two aspects of the problem are given special attention: the process of perceiving and the relationship of perception to behavior.

Viteles, Morris, *Motivation and Morale in Industry*. New York: W. W. Norton and Company, 1953, 520 pp. A comprehensive treatment of the problem of industrial morale. Theory is included, and the findings of a large number of experimental studies are summarized.

Worthy, James, "Factors Influencing Employee Morale," *Harvard Business Review*, 28: 61–73, January, 1950. One of the most extensive studies on morale that has as yet been conducted. It involved 100,000 employees of Sears Roebuck and Company.

VIII. SMALL-GROUP STUDIES

Cartwright, Dorwin, and Alvin Zander (eds.), *Group Dynamics—Research and Theory.* Evanston, Ill.: Row, Peterson and Company, 1953, 642 pp. Recent thought and research on such aspects of small-group life as cohesiveness, pressures, standards, goals, structural properties and leadership.

Festinger, Leon, *et al., Social Pressures in Informal Groups.* New York: Harper and Brothers, 1950, 240 pp. A study of the nature of informal groups as these actually operated to influence life in a housing project.

Hare, A. Paul, Edgar Borgatta, and Robert Bales (eds.), *Small Groups.* New York: Alfred A. Knopf, Inc., 1955, 666 pp. The book contains references on current as well as early small-group theory. Research is included on such topics as communications, leadership, role differentiation, and perception. An annotated bibliography of 584 references is also included.

Hoslett, Schuyler (ed.), *Human Factors in Management.* New York: Harper and Brothers, 1951, 327 pp. The book includes 13 articles dealing with human relations, some of which are based upon research. They deal with such problems as morale, productivity, supervision, training leaders, and leadership.

Strodtbeck, Fred, and Paul Hare, "Bibliography of Small Group Research," *Sociometry,* Vol. 17, No. 2, May, 1954, pp. 107–178. This bibliography, containing more than 1400 references, is one of the most complete collections of references on small-group research.

Swanson, Guy, *et al.* (eds.), *Readings in Social Psychology.* New York: Henry Holt and Company, 1952, 680 pp. An excellent collection of studies by social psychologists, relating to problems in human relations and human interaction.

SELECTED PERIODICALS

Administrative Science Quarterly
Advanced Management
American Sociological Review
Harvard Business Review
Human Organization
Human Relations
Journal of Abnormal and Social Psychology
Journal of Applied Psychology
Journal of Communication
Journal of Conflict Resolution
Journal of Personality
Journal of Social Issues
Personnel

Personnel Administration
Personnel Psychology
Public Administration Review
Public Opinion Quarterly
Sociometry

Index

A

Adaptability, 377–78
Adjustment mechanisms, 40
Administration:
  of change (*see* Change)
  consistency in, 423–24, 426
  expanding concept of, 77
  of large-scale organizations, problems in, 450
  levels of, process concepts and, 373
  other than school, process concepts and, 373
  theory of, process concepts of, 376–78
Administrative behavior, 368, 369, 372, 376
  as communicative behavior, 380
  consistency in, morale and, 423–24
  in controlling rumors, 404–5
  new views on importance of, 77
  teacher expectations of, morale and, 424–25
  with understanding of communication barriers, 392–95
Administrative processes, 367–79
  administering change (*see* Change)
  cannot be fully grasped from any one perspective, 368
  changing nature of, 368
  communicating (*see* Communication)
  concepts of:
    advantages of general over specific, 373–74
    deemed significant, reasons for choosing, 372–78
    general, 369, 370
    overlapping of, 370–71, 375–76
    problem of choosing, 371, 375
    purposes of, as basis for choosing, 372
    specific, 369–370

Administrative processes (*Cont.*)
  conceptualizing:
    defined, 372
    problems in, 369, 370, 371
  decision-making (*see* Decision-making)
  morale-building (*see* Morale, building)
  persons in, understanding, 38–39
Administrator:
  communication and, 380, 393–94
    (*see also* Communication)
  developing understanding of, 26
  as listener, 392–93
  motives of, as perceived, 387–88
  organizational communication and, 397, 398, 404, 405
  perception of, by personnel, 386–88
  professional concepts of, conflicting with role expectations, 45–47
  teacher placement by, 425
  training of:
    case-method (*see* Teaching, case-method)
    changing goals in, 74–75
  use of personification concept by, 47–49
Analysis, case, 26–50
  from educational viewpoint, 27–32
  methods of, and range of perspectives, 26
  from political science perspective, 33–38
  from psychological viewpoint (*see* Psychology)
  selection of perspectives for, 65, 368
  sociological approach to, 44–50
  unsatisfactory, characteristics of, 101–2
Anxiety:
  administrative, 468, 471
  effect on communication, 391, 392, 394
Attitudinal changes, as goal of case-method teaching, 84–85